"In this readable and informative book, Jean Truax paints an unforgettable picture of Aelred of Rievaulx as an important player in the tumultuous public affairs of his day, a counsellor to kings and bishops, and a moderator in legal disputes. This context shows Aelred's historical writings—his *Report of the Battle of the Standard, Lament for David I of Scotland, Genealogy of the Kings of England*—to be integrally related to his public sermons, hagiographies, and correspondence. Drawing out the implications of passing comments and puzzling omissions in Walter Daniel's *Life of Aelred of Rievaulx*, Truax builds a persuasive case that Aelred's reputation among his fellow monks fell under a shadow due to his political activities outside the monastery's walls and, most especially, to his support of Henry II in his quarrel with Thomas Becket who, four years after Aelred's death, became England's most famous saint and martyr."

> —Ann W. Astell
> University of Notre Dame

"Aelred is eminent for his monastic teaching and spiritual doctrine on friendship. Presenting Aelred as politician and peacemaker, this book offers a brilliant perspective into a previously neglected feature in the life of the most distinguished abbot of Rievaulx. Jean Truax has accomplished a mammoth service by organizing an incredible amount of resources so as to create and evaluate the influential public life of this Cistercian abbot. Aelred is presented in his contemporary setting moving among friends and rivals as spiritual *abba*, abbatial administrator, historian, builder, mediator, and counselor to kings and to St. Thomas Becket."

> —Abbot Thomas X. Davis, OCSO
> Abbey of New Clairvaux

"This meticulously researched, thoroughly documented study describes fully for the first time Aelred of Rievaulx's political career. Most scholars focus on Aelred's spirituality, friendships, or monasticism. Truax reconstructs his patronage networks that financially supported his abbey and ensured its survival during the anarchy of Stephen's reign, his influence on neighboring Celtic rulers, and his advisory roles to two kings, Scotland's David I and England's Henry II. Uniquely, she uncovers his friendships for and support of cloistered women, which he saw as equal to monks, and his opposition to Archbishop Thomas Becket, which shaped Aelred's posthumous reputation. This important new perspective enriches the massive scholarship on Aelred."

> —Sally N. Vaughn, PhD
> Professor, Department of History
> University of Houston

"With an abundance of well-documented detail, Jean Truax portrays Aelred as a man of exceptional energy, who remained actively engaged in monastic and public affairs up to the end of his life. By sticking to the historical record and avoiding sterile discussions of Aelred's personality or motivations, she brings out the rich texture of the abbot's life within the context of Rievaulx, the wider church, and the Anglo-Norman world. This book offers the fullest portrayal to date of his role as a mediator in all of these areas. Although Jean Truax does not claim to have unraveled all the complexities of Aelred's biography, her study gently loosens some of its most resistant knots."

> —Elias Dietz, OCSO
> Abbey of Gethsemani

CISTERCIAN STUDIES SERIES: NUMBER TWO HUNDRED FIFTY-ONE

Aelred
the Peacemaker

The Public Life of a Cistercian Abbot

Jean Truax

α

Cistercian Publications
www.cistercianpublications.org

LITURGICAL PRESS
Collegeville, Minnesota
www.litpress.org

A Cistercian Publications title published by Liturgical Press

BX
4700
.E7
T78
2017

Cistercian Publications
Editorial Offices
161 Grosvenor Street
Athens, Ohio 54701
www.cistercianpublications.org

Scriptural translations are those of the author of the volume and the translators of the appendices.

1	2	3	4	5	6	7	8	9

Library of Congress Cataloging-in-Publication Data

Names: Truax, Jean, 1947– author.
Title: Aelred the peacemaker : the public life of a Cistercian abbot / Jean Truax.
Description: Collegeville, Minnesota : Cistercian Publications, 2017. | Series: Cistercian studies series ; number two hundred fifty-one | Includes bibliographical references and index.
Identifiers: LCCN 2016036691 (print) | LCCN 2016039604 (ebook) | ISBN 9780879072513 | ISBN 9780879070533 (ebook)
Subjects: LCSH: Aelred, of Rievaulx, Saint, 1110–1167. | Christian saints—England—Biography.
Classification: LCC BX4700.E7 T78 2017 (print) | LCC BX4700.E7 (ebook) | DDC 271/.1202 [B] —dc23
LC record available at https://lccn.loc.gov/2016036691

For the Cistercians at Kalamazoo, with thanks

Contents

Abbreviations

CAR   *Cartularium Abbathiae de Rievalle ordinis Cisterciensis fundatae anno MCXXXII.* Edited by J. C. Atkinson. Surtees Society 83. Durham: Andrews and Co., 1889.

CCCM   Corpus Christianorum, Continuatio Mediaevalis

CF   Cistercian Fathers Series

CS   Cistercian Studies Series

CSQ   *Cistercian Studies Quarterly*

CTB   Becket, Thomas. *The Correspondence of Thomas Becket, Archbishop of Canterbury 1162–1170.* Edited and translated by Anne J. Duggan. 2 vols. Oxford: Clarendon Press, 2000.

DNB   *Oxford Dictionary of National Biography.* Oxford: Oxford University Press, 2004. http://www.oxforddnb.com.

EEA   *English Episcopal Acta*

EHR   *English Historical Review*

Ep(p)   Epistle(s)

Historical Works   Aelred of Rievaulx. *The Historical Works.* Translated by Jane Patricia Freeland. Edited by Marsha L. Dutton. CF 56. Kalamazoo, MI: Cistercian Publications, 2005.

J   *The Letters of Saint Bernard of Clairvaux.* Translated by Bruno Scott James. London: Burns and Oates, 1953.

MGH   *Monumenta Germaniae Historica*

MTB   *Materials for the History of Thomas Becket, Archbishop of Canterbury.* Edited by James Craigie Robertson. 7 vols. RS 67. London: Longmans, 1875–1885.

Northern Saints	Aelred of Rievaulx. *The Lives of the Northern Saints.* Translated by Jane Patricia Freeland. Edited by Marsha L. Dutton. CF 71. Kalamazoo, MI: Cistercian Publications, 2006.
PG	Patrologiae cursus completus, series Graeca
PL	Patrologiae cursus completus, series Latina
RB	The Rule of Saint Benedict: *RB 1980: The Rule of St. Benedict in English.* Edited by Timothy Fry. Collegeville, MN: Liturgical Press, 1982.
RS	Rolls Series
SBOp	*Sancti Bernardi Opera.* Edited by Jean Leclercq, Charles H. Talbot, and H. M. Rochais. 8 vols. Rome: Editiones Cistercienses, 1957–1977.
S(S)	Sermon, Sermons
Vita A	Walter Daniel. *The Life of Ailred of Rievaulx by Walter Daniel.* Edited and translated by Frederick M. Powicke. Oxford: Oxford University Press, 1978.
Vita Bern	William of Saint–Thierry, Arnold of Bonneval, and Geoffrey of Auxerre. *Vita Prima Claraevallis Abbatis:* PL 185:221–466. Edited by Paul Verdeyen, CCCM 89B.

Aelred's Works

Editions and translations of Aelred's works are listed in the Bibliography, 282–84 below.

Latin Abbreviations

Anima	*De anima*
Gen Angl	*Genealogia regum Anglorum*
Iesu	*De Iesu puero duodenni*
Inst incl	*De institutione inclusarum*
Lam D	*Lamentatio Davidis Regis Scotorum*
Mira	*De quodam miraculum mirabile; De sanctimoniali de Watton*
Oner	*Homiliae de Oneribus Propheticis Isaiae*

Spec car	*Speculum caritatis*
Spir amic	*De spirituali amicitia*
SS Hag	*De sanctis ecclesiae Hagulstadensis*
Stand	*Relatio de Bello Standardii*
Vita E	*Vita Sancti Edwardi*
Vita N	*Vita Sancti Niniani*

English Abbreviations

Battle	*Report on the Battle of the Standard* (=Stand)
Dialogue	*Dialogue on the Soul* (=Anima)
Formation	*On the Formation of Anchoresses* (=Inst incl)
Friendship	*Spiritual Friendship* (=Spir amic)
Genealogy	*Genealogy of the Kings of the English* (=Gen Angl)
Hexham	*The Saints of the Church of Hexham and Their Miracles* (=SS Hag)
Lament	*Lament for King David I of Scotland* (=Lam D)
Life of Edward	*Life of Saint Edward, King and Confessor* (=Vita E)
Life of Ninian	*Life of Saint Ninian* (=Vita N)
Miracle	*A Certain Wonderful Miracle; The Nun of Watton* (=Mira)
Mirror	*Mirror of Charity* (=Spec car)

Bernard's Works

Editions and translations of Bernard's works are listed in the Bibliography, 284–85 below.

Csi	*De consideratione*
Ep(p)	*Epistola(e)*
SC	*Sermones super Cantica canticorum*
Tpl	*Liber ad milites templi (De laude novae militia)*
V Mal	*Vita sancti Malachiae*

Titles, abbreviations, and textual divisions for the historical works follow those used in Cistercian Publications books because the

Pezzini critical edition (CCCM 3) was not available when this book was written. Thanks to the generosity of Brepols Publishers and Bart Janssens, page references to the forthcoming critical edition have been added.

Acknowledgments

When I first stumbled into a Cistercian session at the International Congress on Medieval Studies at the University of Western Michigan in Kalamazoo, I was an older, part-time graduate student. After the session I asked a question of the presenter, who took me by the hand and led me to the Cistercian Publications table in the exhibit hall, where she showed me where to find a translation of the text about which she had spoken, along with everything else I ever wanted to know about Saint Bernard of Clairvaux. Over the years I continued to attend the group's sessions, but I never found a topic to present until I started working on a study of Count Theobald IV of Blois-Chartres. Before long, in what I am now convinced was an act of divine intervention, I found myself writing instead about Saint Bernard and his life-changing influence on the count. The welcome that I received, the thoughtful comments on my presentation, and the other opportunities that soon came my way ultimately convinced me to write this book. Of all the people who welcomed me to the joys of Cistercian scholarship, I would especially like to thank Marsha Dutton and Father Mark Scott, OCSO.

Today all of us stand on the shoulders of the devoted editors and translators who have made so many of the works of the early Cistercians accessible under the imprint of Cistercian Publications. I owe a special debt to the scholars who have allowed me to publish their translations of some of Aelred's writings as appendices to this book. R. Jacob McDonie contributed a letter written by Aelred of Rievaulx to Bishop Gilbert Foliot of London, and Peter Jackson and Tom Licence provided Aelred's sermon for the translation of the relics of Edward the Confessor in 1163. Both of these originally appeared in *Cistercian Studies Quarterly*. Marie Anne

Mayeski has graciously allowed me to include her previously unpublished translation of a sermon by Aelred for the feast of Saint Katherine of Alexandria. I also owe a great deal to the army of unknown readers who commented so thoughtfully not only on this book but also on my original proposal and on my articles that have appeared in *Cistercian Studies Quarterly*.

I also want to thank Patricia Torpis, Patricia Orr, and Sandra Worth for reading and commenting on early drafts of this work. Marie Anne Mayeski, Martha Krieg, and Sandra Worth helped me refine my tortured translation of the letter from Rievaulx to Archbishop Thomas Becket that appears as appendix 5, and I hope it now somewhat resembles modern English. I am also grateful to the Rev. Elias L. Rafaj for his original icon of Aelred, which appears as the frontispiece of this book.

I am especially grateful to the editor of this book, Marsha Dutton, who has suggested new approaches, refined my thinking, and turned me into a devotee of the Oxford comma.

As always, I must especially thank Professor Sally Vaughn of the University of Houston, who supervised my graduate work and has remained a friend and mentor ever since. Her continued attention to the work of a former student is much appreciated.

And finally, special thanks are due to my husband Greg, who not only tolerates but encourages my obsession with the Middle Ages.

Jean Truax

Chapter 1

Introduction

The Three Lives of Aelred of Rievaulx

Most historians consider Aelred of Rievaulx the greatest of the early English Cistercians, second only to Saint Bernard of Clairvaux himself as the foremost of the twelfth-century Cistercian fathers. Information about his life and works can be easily found in the excellent biographies by Aelred Squire, Brian Patrick McGuire, and Pierre-Andre Burton and in Marsha Dutton's introductions to the English translations of his works in the Cistercian Fathers series.[1] So why produce yet another book, particularly one like this, which will focus on only certain aspects of Aelred's life? There are several reasons for this effort, the first of which is simply better to appreciate the true volume and scope of this early Cistercian's accomplishments. Throughout his tenure as abbot of Rievaulx, Aelred played three roles: as author, monastic administrator, and political operative. As an author, he produced spiritual treatises,

---

[1] Aelred Squire, *Aelred of Rievaulx: A Study*, CS 50 (Kalamazoo, MI: Cistercian Publications, 1981); Brian Patrick McGuire, *Brother and Lover: Aelred of Rievaulx* (New York: Crossroad, 1994); Pierre-André Burton, *Aelred de Rievaulx 1110–1167: De l'homme éclaté a l'être unifié, Essai de biographie existentielle et spirituelle* (Paris: Les Éditions du Cerf, 2010); Marsha L. Dutton, Introduction to *The Life of Aelred of Rievaulx and the Letter to Maurice*, ed. and trans. Frederick M. Powicke, CF 57 (Kalamazoo, MI: Cistercian Publications, 1994), 19–40; Introduction to *Aelred of Rievaulx: The Historical Works*, trans. Jane Patricia Freeland, ed. Marsha L. Dutton, CF 56 (Kalamazoo, MI: Cistercian Publications, 2005), 1–35; Introduction to *The Lives of the Northern Saints*, trans. Jane Patricia Freeland, ed. Marsha L. Dutton, CF 71 (Kalamazoo, MI: Cistercian Publications, 2006), 1–31.

works of history, and numerous sermons delivered both inside and outside the abbey, most of which are available in English translation and have been extensively analyzed. As an administrator, he was responsible not only for Rievaulx itself but also for five daughter houses: Warden, Melrose, Dundrennan, Revesby, and Rufford. Calculating the net worth of this monastic empire is probably impossible given the availability and quality of the records, but masterful studies of Rievaulx by Janet Burton and Emilia Jamroziak make it possible to understand the complexity of assembling the abbey's sizable holdings piecemeal from the donations of its neighbors and protecting those lands and rights in times of political uncertainty.[2]

Aelred's role in the public affairs of his day, however, is the area that has received the least attention from modern historians. As several of them have ruefully observed, Aelred's close friend and biographer Walter Daniel was simply not interested in his subject's public life. He wrote as a hagiographer and emphasized his subject's role as abbot of Rievaulx, his sanctity and good example, and his concern for the monks committed to his care.[3] History's view of Aelred might be more balanced if his personal letters had survived, but without these we know him largely from his own writings, which contain little autobiographical information, and from Walter

---

[2] Janet Burton, "The Estates and Economy of Rievaulx Abbey in Yorkshire," *Cîteaux: Commentarii Cistercienses* 49 (1998): 29–93; Emilia Jamroziak, *Rievaulx Abbey and its Social Context, 1132–1300*, Medieval Church Studies 8 (Turnhout: Brepols, 2005).

[3] Maurice Powicke, Introduction to Vita A, li–liii; Maurice Powicke, *Aelred of Rievaulx and His Biographer Walter Daniel* (Manchester: Manchester University Press, 1922), 32, 42; Dom Alberic Stacpoole, "The Public Face of Aelred," *Downside Review* 85 (1967): 196–97; Marsha L. Dutton, "The Conversion and Vocation of Aelred of Rievaulx: A Historical Hypothesis," in *England in the Twelfth Century: Proceedings of the 1988 Harlaxton Symposium*, ed. Daniel Williams (Woodbridge: Boydell Press, 1990), 31; Dutton, Introduction to *Life of Aelred*, 49–66; Pierre-André Burton, "Aelred face à l'histoire et à ses historiens: Autour de l'actualité Aelrédienne," *Collectanea Cisterciensia* 58 (1996): 161–63; Marjory E. Lange, "Walter Daniel: The Eyes through Which We First See Aelred," unpublished paper presented at the Cistercian Studies Conference held within the 45th International Congress on Medieval Studies, May 2010.

Daniel's incomplete biography. An attempt to recover what can be known about Aelred's public life will help to redress the balance and show the true scope of the abbot's accomplishments.

A second reason for focusing on Aelred's life outside Rievaulx is to place his historical writings in context. It is evident that he wrote on multiple levels, and it is possible, for example, to read *The Report on the Battle of the Standard* as at the same time a tribute to Rievaulx's founder, Walter Espec, an allegory on the struggles of the monastic life, and an admonition to Henry II to learn from history how to build a civil society based on law and justice.[4] Any battle would have sufficed as a symbol of struggle, monastic or otherwise, but this battle was especially significant to Aelred since it took place only a few miles from Rievaulx and involved the founder and patrons of the abbey and other personal friends.[5] It is also interesting and valuable to understand that this work, and two others, were written at a critical stage during the peace negotiations that finally ended the Anglo-Norman civil war between King Stephen and the Empress Matilda in 1154. In the same way, his *Life of Edward the Confessor* and the companion sermon probably preached at the translation of the Confessor's relics in 1163 were composed just as the deadly quarrel between Archbishop Thomas Becket and King Henry II reached a critical stage.

As the years have gone by, it is natural that Aelred's historical writings have come to be valued for their spiritual lessons and

---

[4] Mariann Garrity, " 'Hidden Honey': The Many Meanings of Saint Aelred of Rievaulx's *De bello standardii*," CSQ 44, no. 1 (2009): 57–64; Elizabeth A. Freeman, "Aelred of Rievaulx's *De Bello Standardii*: Cistercian Hagiography and the Creation of Community Memories," *Cîteaux: Commentarii Cistercienses* 49 (1998): 9, 27; Pierre-André Burton, "Le récit de la *Bataille de l'Étendard* par Aelred de Rievaulx: Présentation et traduction," *Cîteaux: Commentarii Cistercienses* 58 (2007): 7–41; Marsha L. Dutton, "This Ministry of Letters: Aelred of Rievaulx's Attempt to Anglicize England's King Henry II," in *Monasticism Between Culture and Cultures: Acts of the Third International Symposium, Rome, June 8–11, 2011*, ed. Philippe Nouzille and Michaela Pfeifer, *Analecta Monastica* 14 (2013): 190–91; Elias Dietz, "Ambivalence Well Considered: An Interpretive Key to the Whole of Aelred's Works," CSQ 47, no. 1 (2012): 71–79; Pierre-André Burton, *Aelred de Rievaulx*, 421–25.

[5] See below, chap. 6:132–34.

historical insights and for the sheer power of his prose more than for the political value they had at one time. But an understanding of that political value is essential for us to fully appreciate Aelred's genius. I make little attempt here to analyze the multiple levels on which Aelred wrote, and I ignore spiritual and allegorical interpretations of his works in favor of their practical application to events of the day. Indeed there is nothing that I can add to the insights of people like Pierre-André Burton, who live the monastic life as Aelred himself did. What a secular historian can do is to place Aelred in context and perhaps in so doing deepen the understanding of his work and cast additional light on his underappreciated third role as politician, mediator, and negotiator outside his abbey's walls.

A third reason for focusing on Aelred's public life is that it may clarify what might be termed the mystery of Aelred's reputation. It is clear from the preface to Walter Daniel's biography, addressed to the unknown Abbot H, that Aelred was somewhat under a cloud at the time of his death and that Walter Daniel wrote at least in part to ward off criticism and polish his subject's tarnished reputation. Evidently there were detractors ready and waiting, for Walter hoped that the prayers of Abbot H and his monks would "make truth prevail over the opinion of many."[6] Aelred's enemies occasionally appear in the *Vita*. When Aelred was elected the third abbot of Rievaulx in 1147, Walter reported that some said that ambition had brought him to the position, exclaiming, "how many jealous busybodies this man of peace had to endure," and bemoaning the "malignant and misguided men who rose up against him."[7]

Walter also recorded the story of the unnamed abbot of a daughter house who visited Rievaulx and violently attacked Aelred with

[6] Walter Daniel, *The Life of Ailred of Rievaulx* [Vita A], ed. and trans. Maurice Powicke (Oxford: Oxford University Press, 1978), 1; Walter Daniel, *The Life of Aelred of Rievaulx*, trans. F. M. Powicke, CF 57 (Kalamazoo, MI: Cistercian Publications, 1994), 89 (hereafter CF 57). Abbot H was probably either Hugh of Revesby or Henry of Waverly (Powicke, Introduction to Vita A, xxix–xxx).

[7] Vita A 26, pp. 33–34; CF 57:115; Dutton, Introduction to *Life of Aelred*, CF 57:30–31.

curses and blasphemies. In response Aelred prayed, "Lord King of everlasting glory, may this man, I beseech thee, speedily suffer an end to his malice, for you know false are the things which, in his angry folly, he ascribes to me." The visiting abbot left without being reconciled to Aelred, and seven days later he was dead.[8] The hint of enemies' troubling Aelred's career resurfaces at the end of the *Vita*, in Aelred's last speech to his monks: "My soul calls God to witness that, since I received this habit of religion, the malice, detraction or quarrel of no man has ever kindled any feeling in me against him which has been strong enough to last the day in the domicile of my heart."[9]

Occasionally the tone of the *Vita* seems defensive, as when Walter Daniel described the gifts heaped upon the new monastery at Revesby, where Aelred became the first abbot in 1143. Walter hastened, almost too quickly, to explain that Aelred accepted the donations only because of the chaotic conditions of the civil war, saying that the donations to Revesby "helped the possessors of goods to their salvation, and that if they did not give, they might well lose both life and goods without any payment in return."[10]

At times Walter implies that Rievaulx may have suffered a reputation for laxity. A long passage describes how prospective monks whom no other house would accept came from all over Europe to find a compassionate home with Aelred and his brethren. The abbot often left the decision to admit an applicant to the brothers themselves, with the result that many were received whom he did not even know. In discussing Aelred's reason for his policy, Walter provides a unique insight into Aelred's character: "He was very diffident and indulgent to the feebleness of everyone, and would never disappoint anyone who appealed to him in the cause of charity."[11] In return, Walter shows, Aelred's monks adored their abbot, clustering around him in the quarters constructed for him when his physical infirmities required special consideration: "He

[8] Vita A 37, pp. 44–45; CF 57:123–24.

[9] Vita A 50, pp. 57–58; CF 57:134–35.

[10] Vita A 20, p. 28; CF 57:111; Dutton, Introduction to *Life of Aelred*, CF 57:28–29.

[11] Vita A 30, p. 39; CF 57:119.

did not treat them with the pedantic imbecility habitual in some silly abbots who, if a monk takes a brother's hand in his own, or says anything that they do not like, demand his cowl, strip and expel him."[12] Walter portrays Rievaulx during Aelred's abbacy as a loving, supportive community that welcomed all who approached its gates. But it is possible that some of those "silly abbots" considered those conditions too permissive for a proper monastic life.

Walter was right to suspect that critics lay in wait, for he was soon forced to compose a letter directed to a Lord Maurice, probably the prior of the Augustinian house of Kirkham, answering criticisms of the *Vita* made by two unnamed prelates.[13] Abbot Maurice had suggested that Walter respond to what was apparently the main complaint by revising the *Vita* to include the names of the eyewitnesses to Aelred's miracles. Walter replied with a separate letter listing the names of the witnesses to the miracles and adding several new ones. He suggested that it be placed at the front of the *Vita*, to serve as a table of contents.[14]

He also responded to two other charges. The prelates had criticized him for saying that Aelred had lived as a monk at the court of David I of Scotland before he entered Rievaulx. Walter could scarcely maintain that his subject had been a virgin, since Aelred himself had admitted in his *On the Formation of Anchoresses* that he had failed to preserve his own virginity in the praiseworthy manner of his sister. Walter, however, brushed aside the criticism, saying that in speaking thus he had been referring to Aelred's charity, not to his chastity.[15] The unknown critics had also objected to Walter's description of Aelred's body prepared for burial as

---

[12] Vita A 31, p. 40; CF 57:120.

[13] "Walter Daniel's *Letter to Maurice*," in Vita A, p. 66; CF 57:147. For the identification of Lord Maurice as the prior of Kirkham see Dutton, Introduction to *Life of Aelred*, CF 57:66–67; Powicke, Introduction to *Life of Ailred*, xxx–xxxi. On the letter in general, see Thomas J. Heffernan, *Sacred Biography: Saints and Their Biographers in the Middle Ages* (Oxford: Oxford University Press, 1988), 103–13.

[14] *Letter to Maurice* 4, p. 81; CF 57:158.

[15] *Letter to Maurice* 4, pp. 75–76; CF 57:154–55; Aelred, Inst incl 3.32; CCCM 1:674–77; CF 2:93–96; Dutton, Introduction to *Life of Aelred*, CF 57:25–26. See Vita A 2, p. 4; CF 57:91 for the original passage.

"glowing like a carbuncle and smelling like incense," maintaining that Walter had written without proper caution. But he explained that he had been indulging in the permissible rhetorical device of hyperbole and mocked his detractors for being ignorant of such techniques.[16] The *Letter to Maurice* makes explicit what Walter had hinted at throughout the *Vita*: that Aelred had made enemies during his career who did not scruple to attack his reputation even after death.

Modern historians have not been blind to this question, and two suggestions as to the cause of this animosity have been advanced. John Boswell stated categorically in 1980, "There can be little question that Aelred was gay and that his erotic attraction to men was a dominant force in his life."[17] He did not specifically address the issue of Aelred's reputation, but Brian Patrick McGuire, who generally agreed with Boswell's analysis, has argued that Aelred developed a circle of intimate friends who enjoyed greater access to him than did the larger community at Rievaulx and that this access was resented by those who did not enjoy the privilege, leading to criticism after the abbot's death.[18] A second, and more likely explanation, advanced by Marsha L. Dutton and others, is that Aelred was simply too talented, too well liked, and too ambitious for his own good. He spent too much time away from the monastery, resolving quarrels, giving advice, preaching, and generally mingling with the great and near-great of society, which perhaps contributed to dissatisfaction among his monks, laxity within the monastery, and jealousy among those less in demand.

---

[16] *Letter to Maurice* 4, pp. 76–77; CF 57:155–56; Dutton, Introduction to *Life of Aelred*, CF 57:14. See Vita A 58, p. 62; CF 57:138 for the original passage.

[17] John Boswell, *Christianity, Social Tolerance and Homosexuality: Gay People in Western Europe from the Beginning of the Christian Era to the Fourteenth Century* (Chicago: University of Chicago Press, 1980), 222.

[18] Brian Patrick McGuire, "The Cistercians and Friendship: An Opening to Women," in *Hidden Springs: Cistercian Monastic Women*, ed. John A Nichols and Lillian Thomas Shank, Medieval Religious Women, 3 vols. CS 113 (Kalamazoo, MI: Cistercian Publications, 1995), vol. 3, bk.1, 174–75; McGuire, *Brother and Lover*, 93–94; McGuire, "Sexual Awareness and Identity in Aelred of Rievaulx (1111–1167)," *The American Benedictine Review* 45 (1994): 190, 222.

Furthermore, this theory would also explain the bias in the *Vita* toward Aelred's sanctity and miracles and the neglect of his public career.[19] This study will return to the question of Aelred's reputation later. Although Walter's *Vita* has numerous shortcomings, it does offer some insights into Aelred's public life.

Walter Daniel's View

Despite a general lack of enthusiasm for life outside Rievaulx, Walter Daniel's few references to Aelred's public life make it plain that the abbot corresponded with a wide circle of acquaintances, that he was much in demand as a guest speaker, and that he often traveled away from Rievaulx on the business of his abbey, his order, and the church in general. Walter wrote that Aelred "was sending letters to the lord Pope, to the King of France, the King of England, the King of Scotland, the Archbishops of Canterbury and York and nearly every bishop in England, also the most distinguished men in the Kingdom of England and especially to the Earl of Leicester."[20] Supporting this statement is only the testimony of surviving library catalogues from Glamorgan, Cirencester, Norwich, Coggeshall, and Rievaulx itself, which at least prove that Aelred's correspondence was esteemed enough to be collected and circulated after his death.[21]

Aelred was also in demand as a public speaker while he was still abbot of Revesby, for Walter Daniel recorded that the local bishop invited him to preach to the clergy in synod. He later wrote that, in total, Aelred preached some two hundred sermons to the monks of Rievaulx, the English clergy, and the laypeople.[22] Today,

---

[19] Dutton, Introduction to *Life of Aelred*, CF 57:8, 72–79; Powicke, Introduction to *Life of Ailred*, lxiv–lxvi; P.-A. Burton, "Aelred face à l'histoire," 162–63.

[20] Vita A 32, p. 42; CF 57:121.

[21] Anselm Hoste, *Bibliotheca Aelrediana, A Survey of the Manuscripts, Old Catalogues, Editions and Studies Concerning St. Aelred of Rievaulx*, Instrumenta Patristica 2 (Steenbrugis: Abbey of St. Peter, 1962), 137–38. For the listing in the Rievaulx catalogue see 154.

[22] Vita A 20, 32; pp. 28, 42; CF 57:111, 121–22.

however, it is possible to identify only a handful of Aelred's sermons preached outside the abbey. Two would have been delivered at major public occasions: the translation of the relics of the saints of Hexham on March 3, 1155, and the translation of the relics of Saint Edward the Confessor to the new shrine in Westminster Abbey on October 13, 1163.[23] In addition, one sermon indicates that it was preached at an episcopal synod at Troyes,[24] while two others are labeled *in Synodo* without any indication of the location or occasion.[25] Two sermons were directed to abbots and one to nuns, but again they do not identify the particular monasteries addressed and the events that occasioned Aelred's visit.[26] Marie Anne Mayeski has further suggested that Aelred preached his homily on Saint Katherine of Alexandria at the consecration ceremony of a religious woman, perhaps an anchoress.[27]

Walter had only slightly more to say about his abbot's travels away from Rievaulx. He recorded a statement that Aelred made to his monks as he lay on his deathbed: "Often I have begged your permission when I had to cross the sea, or it was my duty to haste to some distant region, or I had occasion to seek the King's court; and now by your leave and with the help of your prayers I

[23] Dutton, Introduction to Northern Saints, CF 71, 14–20; Peter Jackson, "*In translacione sancti Edwardi confessoris*: The Lost Sermon by Aelred of Rievaulx Found," CSQ 40, no. 1 (2005): 45–64; App. 4:260–73.

[24] Aelred, S 28; CCCM 2A:229–38; Aelred of Rievaulx, *The Liturgical Sermons: The First Clairvaux Collection, Advent-All Saints*, trans. Theodore Berkeley and Basil Pennington, CF 58 (Kalamazoo, MI: Cistercian Publications, 2001), 380–94; Aelred Squire, "Two Unpublished Sermons of Aelred of Rievaulx," *Cîteaux: Commentarii Cistercienses* 11 (1960): 104–16. Ralf Lützelschwab has suggested that Troyes was a scribal error for the Council of Tours in 1163: "*Vox de coelis originem ducitis*: Aelred of Rievaulx as Preacher at Synods," unpublished paper presented at the Cistercian Studies Conference, held within the 49th International Congress on Medieval Studies at the University of Western Michigan, Kalamazoo, MI, May 8–11, 2014. See below, chap. 9:200–201.

[25] Aelred, SS 63–64; CCCM 2B:152–69; CF 80; Hoste, *Bibliotheca*, 87.

[26] Aelred, SS 143–44, to abbots; CCCM 2C:376–89; S 179, to nuns; CCCM 2C:608–15.

[27] Marie Anne Mayeski, "'The Right Occasion for the Words': Situating Aelred's Homily on St. Katherine," CSQ 33, no. 1 (1998): 45–60. For a discussion of this sermon see below, chap. 5:110–13.

go hence, from exile to the fatherland."[28] Aside from this general statement, Walter reported only two specific trips that Aelred made outside the monastery, both to Rievaulx's daughter house at Dundrennan in Galloway.[29] While Walter gives unfortunately few details about Aelred's correspondence and his activities away from Rievaulx, the few hints that he drops indicate that the abbot had a large circle of acquaintances and that he traveled widely outside the monastery.

Similarly Aelred himself dropped only a few hints about his travels. In his *Dialogue on the Soul*, written toward the end of his life, he and his partner in the *Dialogue*, a monk named John, reminisced about visiting London. Aelred asked, "Do you remember London and how vast it is? Do you call to mind how the river Thames flows past it, how Westminster Abbey beautifies its western side, how the enormous Tower stands guard over the east and how Saint Paul's Cathedral rises majestically in the middle?"[30] But there is no information given about the number of visits, the timing, or the reasons for them. In the *Lament for David I*, Aelred described a visit to the Scottish court in which he observed the king living as a monk, keeping the monastic hours, and performing manual labor in the gardens. He noted that the visit took place during the last Lent of the king's life, which would place it in the spring of 1153, but gave no details of his mission, stating only that it concerned "some urgent need of our house."[31]

Since Walter Daniel and Aelred himself were so maddeningly reticent about the abbot's activities outside the monastery, one might hope that the documentary record would help to fill in the blanks and allow construction of a more complete picture of Aelred's travels. Anyone who works with Anglo-Norman charters soon realizes that it is possible to construct itineraries for major figures by listing the dates and locations of the charters that they

[28] Vita A 50, p. 57; CF 57:134.
[29] Vita A 38–39, *Letter to Maurice*, 4, pp. 45–46, 74–75; CF 57:124–26, 153–54.
[30] Aelred, Anima 2.1; CCCM 1:708; CF 22:73.
[31] Aelred, Lam D VI; CCCM 3:10; CF 56:58–59.

witnessed. Most often these documents record property transactions, and the attesters frequently have no obvious ties to any of the parties to the transaction or to the property itself; they apparently witnessed the charters simply because they happened to be present for the occasion. Some twelfth-century English churchmen witnessed royal charters so frequently that the historian wonders how they ever had time to fulfill their ecclesiastical responsibilities at home. This, however, is not the case with Aelred; charters bearing his attestation are relatively rare. One interesting fact does emerge from this collection of documents, however. When Aelred did witness a charter, it often recorded the resolution of a dispute rather than a property exchange. This pattern suggests that while Aelred may not have been a frequent visitor to any royal, noble, or ecclesiastical household, a talent for mediation and conflict resolution caused people to call on him to help in times of trouble.

Conflict Resolution in the Middle Ages

Disputes were often settled in the Middle Ages in a way quite different from today. Cases that today would usually be definitively resolved in a court of law, with one party winning and the other losing, were often settled during the medieval period by mediation and compromise, with solutions favored in which both parties came away with some positive gain.[32] Thus in a property dispute between a monastery and a layman, the layman might

[32] Frederic Cheyette, "Suum cuique tribuere," *French Historical Studies* 6 (1970): 287–99; Stephen D. White, *"Pactum . . . Legem Vincit et Amor Iudicium*: The Settlement of Disputes by Compromise in Eleventh-century Western France," *American Journal of Legal History* 22 (1978): 281–301; Wendy Davies and Paul Fouracre, *The Settlement of Disputes in Early Medieval Europe* (Cambridge: Cambridge University Press, 1986), 233–36; Patrick Geary, "Living with Conflicts in Stateless France: A Typology of Conflict Management Mechanisms 1050–1200," in *Living with the Dead in the Middle Ages* (Ithaca: Cornell University Press, 1994), 125–60; Geary, "Moral Obligations and Peer Pressure: Conflict Resolution in the Medieval Aristocracy," in *Georges Duby: L'écriture de l'histoire*, ed. Claudie Duhamel-Amado and Guy Lobrichon (Brussels: DeBoeck Université, 1996), 217–22; Emily Zack Tabuteau, "Punishments in Eleventh-century Normandy," in *Conflict in Medieval Europe*, ed. Warren C. Brown and Piotr Górecki (Aldershot: Ashgate, 2001), 131–49; Geoffrey

receive the land in question only to turn it over to the religious institution in return for spiritual benefits. Alternatively the monastery might receive the property, with the layman who had contested its ownership agreeing to hold it in fief. Disputes between two lay parties might end in a marriage alliance between the contending families. Naturally, in some cases lack of documentary evidence, inadequate or conflicting rules, or the inability of the court to enforce its decisions, caused the parties to a dispute to seek a mediated compromise.

In addition, ties of kinship and friendship were complex and interlocking, and a dispute between two individuals might easily spiral out of control, drawing an entire community into the conflict. A resolution that publicly humiliated one party might lead to more trouble later on. On the other hand, a compromise in which everyone came away with something might prevent claims from being reopened, especially if benefits continued into the future, as would be the case in which a monastery granted ongoing spiritual benefits to a former opponent and his family. The emphasis in medieval conflict resolution was first of all on restoring peace between the contending parties and their wider kinship groups rather than imposing a preordained solution to be enforced by the court. Perhaps the *Leges Henrici Primi*, itself a document concerned with the rules and niceties of court procedure, said it best: "For an agreement supersedes the law and amicable settlement a court judgment."[33]

It is clear that the services of a mediator would be crucial in this type of dispute resolution, and who would be a better candidate to help in these circumstances than a respected monk or other churchman who had no obvious interest in the outcome of a case and whose asceticism made him the ultimate disinterested outsider? Not only did his detachment from the world fit him to

---

Koziol, "Baldwin VII of Flanders and the Toll of Saint-Vast (1111): Judgment as Ritual," in Brown and Gorecki, *Conflict*, 151–61.

[33] *Leges Henrici Primi*, ed. and trans. L. J. Downer (Oxford: Clarendon Press, 1972), C. 49, 5a, 164–65.

act as an unbiased mediator, but also his holiness might seem to give him special access to God and allow him to determine the divine will in each case. A respected cleric was often the one person who could be trusted to offer impartial advice and settle disputes according to justice and God's will.[34]

As one of the oldest, strictest, and most successful of the new religious orders, the Cistercians earned their fair share of the public's veneration. They were besieged at various times with requests from other religious communities for advice on the conduct of their affairs and even for incorporation into the Cistercian Order itself. And given the high level of respect that they enjoyed, what could be more natural than for the believing public to turn to them for advice, comfort, and mediation in times of trouble and confusion? Under these circumstances, it would have been strange indeed if Aelred, as abbot of the foremost Cistercian abbey in England, had not had a role to play on the public stage.

[34] Henry Mayr-Harting, "Functions of a Twelfth-Century Recluse," *History* 60, no. 200 (1975): 337–52; Susan J. Ridyard, "Functions of a Twelfth-Century Recluse Revisited: The Case of Godric of Finchale," in *Belief and Culture in the Middle Ages: Studies Presented to Henry Mayr-Harting*, ed. Richard Gameson and Henrietta Leyser (Oxford: Oxford University Press, 2001), 236–50; Christopher Holdsworth, "Hermits and the Power of the Frontier," *Reading Medieval Studies* 16 (1990): 59–62, 70–71; Tom Licence, *Hermits and Recluses in English Society, 950–1200* (Oxford: Oxford University Press, 2011), 3–6, 49–52, 150–72; Patricia J. F. Rosof, "The Anchoress in the Twelfth and Thirteenth Centuries," in *Peace Weavers*, ed. John A Nichols and Lillian Thomas Shank, Medieval Religious Women, 3 vols., CS 72 (Kalamazoo, MI: Cistercian Publications, 1987), 2:135–36; Jean Leclercq, "Solitude and Solidarity: Medieval Women Recluses," in *Peace Weavers*, 2:77–79.

Chapter 2

Precedents

In the Footsteps of Saint Bernard

If Aelred had been seeking a model for his public career, he
would have had to look no further than the example set by members of his own order, especially the most famous of them all,
Bernard of Clairvaux. A complete discussion of Bernard's public
career would fill several books the size of this one, so a single
chapter can only highlight a few of his more noteworthy exploits.
Furthermore, Bernard was by no means unique; a number of other
Cistercians left their monasteries to become bishops, archbishops,
and even popes or undertook special projects in the public arena
without permanently leaving the monastery.

It is evident from Bernard's correspondence that he was first
and foremost an intercessor and mediator. His letters poured forth
from Clairvaux, and no cause was so small that it escaped his
notice. He wrote to Queen Adelaide of France to intercede for a
man named Wicard, whom the queen had caused to be deprived
of all his goods and driven into exile.[1] Another letter begged the
duchess of Burgundy to approve the marriage of the son of Hugh
de Bese, who had asked Bernard to approach her on behalf of his
family.[2] A letter to Bishop Geoffrey of Chartres asked for consideration for a recluse who had left his cell without permission
and subsequently desired to return. Since the letter stated that it

---

[1] Bruno Scott James, *The Letters of Saint Bernard of Clairvaux* (London: Burns &
Oates, 1953), Ep 122 (hereafter J). Not in SBOp.

[2] Bernard, Ep 121 (SBOp 7:301–2; J125).

concerned the bearer, it seems that the man had come to Bernard for help on his own.[3] A laywoman experiencing marital difficulties went to Bernard for counseling and returned home to the bishop of Verdun with a letter in which Bernard exhorted him to welcome her home as a penitent.[4] Several letters record Bernard's efforts to obtain justice for one Humbert, who had been disinherited by Count Theobald of Blois, Chartres, and Champagne, the feudal overlord of Clairvaux.[5] Bernard involved the count in many of his projects and wrote to him frequently, on one occasion remarking, "I am afraid of bothering you with my constant scribbling."[6] It is evident from even these few examples that Bernard did not restrict himself to matters close to home or those involving only the Cistercian Order. The patterns of his correspondence indicate that he involved himself with most of the major issues and events of his time.

Bernard and Other Religious Orders

For example, it is well known that Bernard frequently offered his advice and his influence to other communities.[7] He wrote to remonstrate when Pope Eugenius III was deceived into ordering the reinstatement of certain renegade monks who had defied reforms instituted by the prior of the Grande Chartreuse.[8] The abbot of the Benedictine monastery at Vézelay sought his help when Countess Ida of Nevers prevented merchants from coming to do business in the town.[9]

[3] Bernard, Ep 55 (SBOp 7:147; J58). Possibly also Ep 57 (SBOp 7:149; J60).

[4] Bernard, Ep 62 (SBOp 7:155; J65).

[5] Bernard, Epp 35–38 (SBOp 7:92–97; J36–37, 39–40, 59).

[6] Bernard, Ep 41 (SBOp 7:99–100; J43). Also J44, not in SBOp. For other letters to Count Theobald see Epp 37–40 (SBOp 7:94–99; J39–43). Also J46, not in SBOp. For the relationship between the two men, see Jean Truax, "*Miles Christi:* Count Theobald IV of Blois and Saint Bernard of Clairvaux," CSQ 44, no. 3 (2009): 299–320.

[7] Julian Haseldine, "Friendship and Rivalry: The Role of *amicitia* in Twelfth-century Monastic Relations," *Journal of Ecclesiastical History* 44 (1993): 390–414.

[8] Bernard, Ep 270 (SBOp 8:178–80; J340).

[9] Bernard, Ep 375 (SBOp 8:338; J418).

Bernard promoted the reform of houses of secular canons by persuading them to adopt the rule of Saint Augustine, which required the secular authority to give up the right to appoint the abbot. He persuaded Count Theobald to agree to this change in the cases of Saint-Martin de Épernay and Saint-Loup, and Theobald then took the initiative in bringing a group of canons from Saint-Jean de Sens to effect the same reforms at Saint Quiriace in Provins.[10] As a close friend of Norbert of Xanten and the Premonstratensian canons, Bernard was instrumental in their acquisition of the land on which the abbey of Prémontré itself stood. He also arranged for lands in Jerusalem given to him by King Baldwin to be transferred to the canons, as well as the church of Saint Paul at Verdun and lands at France-Vale.[11]

The Knights Templar also benefited from Bernard's sponsorship. When founders Hugh de Payens and Andrew de Montbard returned to France from the Holy Land in 1126, they visited Bernard to enlist his support with the clerical establishment. In addition, Bernard persuaded Count Theobald to offer his financial support by donating land near Provins to the new order and allowing his vassals to make contributions from their own lands.[12] In 1129 at Troyes, Bernard chaired a church council that developed the formal rule of the Templars. The abbots of Cîteaux, Pontigny, and Tre Fontane were also present.[13] To further promote the new

---

[10] Michel Veissière, *Un communauté canoniale au Moyen Age: Saint-Quiriace de Provins (XIe–XIIIe siècles)* (Provins: CNRS Editions, 1961), 38–41; Auguste Nicaise, *Épernay et l'Abbaye Saint-Martin de cette ville*, 2 vols. (Châlons-sur-Marne: J. L. Le Roy, 1869). For the foundation, see 17; no. 4, p. 119; and no. 6, p. 123. For donations by Theobald, see no. 5, p. 121, and no. 9, p. 128.

[11] Bernard, Ep 253 (SBOp 8:149–55; J328).

[12] *Cartulaire général de l'ordre du Temple 1119?–1150*, in *Recueil des chartes et des bulles relatives à l'ordre du Temple*, ed. the Marquis d'Albon (Paris: Librairie Ancienne, 1913), no. 9, p. 6; Malcolm C. Barber, *The New Knighthood: A History of the Order of the Temple* (Cambridge: Cambridge University Press, 2003), 13.

[13] "The Latin Rule of 1129," in *The Templars: Select Sources Translated and Annotated*, trans. Malcolm Barber and Keith Bate (Manchester: Manchester University Press, 2002), 31–33; "Gesta in Concilio Trecensi Anni MCXXVIII," in *Recueil des Historiens des Gaules et de la France*, ed. Léopold Delisle, 24 vols. (Paris: Victor Palmé, 1869–1967), 14:231–33; Pierre Ponsoye, "Saint Bernard et la Règle du Temple,"

order, Bernard wrote a treatise, *In Praise of the New Knighthood*, extolling the virtues of the Templars.[14]

Saint Bernard frequently offered advice and spiritual counseling to members of other religious orders, sometimes unsolicited, but often when troubled monks or their superiors came asking for his help. For example, the abbot of St. Pierremont, an Augustinian house in the diocese of Toul, sent a wayward member of his house to Bernard for counseling after the man had left the order and married unlawfully.[15] Similarly, Bernard wrote to Abbot Luke of the Premonstratensian house at Cuissy regarding another monk who had disgraced himself with a woman, and again it is clear that the abbot had first contacted Bernard to solicit his advice.[16] Sometime around 1130, when the Benedictine abbots in the province of Rheims held a preliminary meeting aimed at establishing an annual general chapter according to the Cistercian model, they invited Bernard to attend. Although he was unable to do so, he responded with a letter of advice and encouragement.[17]

Bernard also gave frequent assistance to women's monasteries and to individual religious living within them. He rejoiced with the virgin Sophia because she had "cast away the false glory of the world,"[18] and he encouraged a wayward nun who was now

---

Études Traditionelles 364 (1961): 84–85; Martha G. Newman, *The Boundaries of Charity: Cistercian Culture and Ecclesiastical Reform, 1098–1180* (Stanford, CA: Stanford University Press, 1996), 147; Marie Luise Bulst-Thiele, "The Influence of St. Bernard of Clairvaux on the Formation of the Order of the Knights Templar," in *The Second Crusade and the Cistercians*, ed. Michael Gervers (New York: St. Martin's Press, 1992), 57–65.

[14] Tpl (SBOp 3:213–39; Bernard of Clairvaux, *In Praise of the New Knighthood: A Treatise on the Knights Templar and the Holy Places of Jerusalem*, trans. M. Conrad Greenia, CF 19B [Kalamazoo, MI: Cistercian Publications, 2000]); Newman, *Boundaries*, 184–87; Janet Burton and Julia Kerr, *The Cistercians in the Middle Ages* (Woodbridge: Boydell, 2011), 199–200.

[15] Bernard, Ep 76 (SBOp 7:183; J79). For another letter to an Augustinian house see Ep 82 (SBOp 7:214–16; J84).

[16] Bernard, Ep 79 (SBOp 7:210–12; J81).

[17] Bernard, Ep 91 (SBOp 7:239–41; J94).

[18] Bernard, Ep 113 (SBOp 7:287–91; J116). See Ep 115 (SBOp 7:294–95; J118) for a nun thinking of becoming a recluse.

determined to live a better life, noting, "From now the integrity of your life will not be undermined by the corruption of your heart."[19] A letter from Peter Abelard to Bernard mentioned Bernard's visit to Heloise's abbey of the Paraclete and said that the nuns, who had been looking forward to his visit for a long time, had found his eloquence that of an angel rather than a mortal man.[20] On the basis of a comparison of early liturgical books from the Paraclete with those in use by the Cistercians of the same period, Father Chrysogonus Waddell suggested that Bernard might have had other contacts with the convent and assisted Heloise with the organization of the Paraclete liturgy.[21] Bernard also helped write the original rule for the convent of Jully, where his sister Humbelina became the second prioress. He visited the convent in 1128 when his aunt Aanolz, the widow of Walter de la Roche, became a nun there and witnessed a charter in which she transferred an annuity of ten pounds to the convent.[22] As will be discussed in detail in chapter 5, even though the Cistercians eventually refused to undertake formal supervision of the Gilbertine monasteries, they provided help to the English order in other ways. Here it can be noted that Gilbert of Sempringham consulted Saint Bernard about the formulation of his order's rule, and Abbot William of Rievaulx suggested the addition of lay sisters to the order.[23]

---

[19] Bernard, Ep 114 (SBOp 7:291–93; J117).

[20] Peter Abelard, Ep 10 (*Epistolae*, PL 178:335–40).

[21] Chrysogonus Waddell, "St. Bernard and the Cistercian Office at the Abbey of the Paraclete," in *The Chimaera of His Age: Studies on Bernard of Clairvaux*, ed. E. Rozanne Elder and John R. Sommerfeldt, Studies in Medieval Cistercian History 5, CS 63 (Kalamazoo, MI: Cistercian Publications, 1980), 76–121; Jean Leclercq, *Women and St. Bernard of Clairvaux*, CS 104 (Kalamazoo, MI: Cistercian Publications, 1989), 56–57.

[22] Jean-Baptiste Jobin, *Histoire du prieuré de Jully-les-nonnains avec pièces justificatives* (Paris: Bray et Retaux, 1881), 208–10, no. 3; Constance H. Berman, *Women and Monasticism in Medieval Europe: Sisters and Patrons of the Cistercian Reform* (Kalamazoo, MI: Medieval Institute Publications, 2002), 92–93, no. 55; Berman, "Were There Twelfth-Century Cistercian Nuns?" *Church History* 68 (1999): 825–27; Leclercq, *Women and St. Bernard*, 55.

[23] *The Book of St Gilbert*, ed. and trans. Raymonde Foreville and Gillian Keir (Oxford: Clarendon Press, 1987), 44–45; William of Newburgh, *Historia Rerum*

Saint Bernard and Episcopal Elections

Saint Bernard intervened regularly in French episcopal elections, sometimes with unexpected results. When Archbishop Raynald of Rheims died in January 1138, the citizens of Rheims seized the opportunity to throw off archiepiscopal governance and establish a commune administered by a mayor, making a substantial payment to King Louis VII for the privilege. A state of open feud developed between the commune and the cathedral chapter, despite the king's demand that the citizens respect the rights of the churches of the city, and violence ensued. Saint Bernard traveled to Rheims to mediate the quarrel, and his stirring address to the crowd in the marketplace had an unexpected result—his own election as archbishop. A letter from King Louis urged him to accept, but Saint Bernard refused, and Samson de Mauvoisin was elected in his place.[24]

At about this time, the same thing happened at Langres. Upon the death of the bishop, the archbishop of Lyon and two members of the Langres chapter approached Saint Bernard for help in selecting a candidate and obtaining permission from Pope Innocent II to proceed with an election. Two possible nominees were agreed on, and papal permission was granted on the express condition that the agreement be honored, but once the archbishop had returned home, he chose a different candidate. Saint Bernard appealed to Rome, and the pope responded by quashing the election. Then, to his utter amazement, Saint Bernard found himself chosen as bishop, an honor that he speedily declined. The prior

---

Anglicarum, in *Chronicles of the Reigns of Stephen, Henry II., and Richard I.,* ed. Richard Howlett, 4 vols., RS 82 (London: Longmans, 1884–1890), 1:54; *Institutes of the Gilbertine Order*, in William Dugdale, *Monasticon Anglicanum,* ed. John Caley, Henry Eales, and Bulkeley Bandinel (London, 1846), vol. 6, pt. 2, insert after p. 945; xix, xxxvi; Marsha L. Dutton, "Were Aelred of Rievaulx and Gilbert of Sempringham Friends? Evidence from Aelred's *A Certain Wonderful Miracle* and the Gilbertine Lay Brothers' Revolt," forthcoming in *American Benedictine Review*, 2017. See below, chap. 5:115–20.

[24] Bernard, Epp 318, 449 (SBOp 8:251, 426–27; J209–10).

of Clairvaux, Godfrey de la Roche, was then selected in his place and was consecrated in October 1138.[25]

In 1142 the episcopal election to the see of Bourges was contested between Pierre de la Châtre and Cadurc, the royal chancellor. Pierre de la Châtre was the choice of the cathedral chapter, but King Louis VII refused to accept him, even after he had been consecrated by Pope Innocent II. The king excluded Pierre from the city, so he took refuge with Count Theobald in Champagne while Bernard stepped in to mediate the quarrel. Despite his best efforts, though, the quarrel lasted for almost two years before Pierre was finally allowed to take possession of his see.[26]

In 1151 Pope Eugenius III appointed a commission of three, including Saint Bernard, to investigate the disputed election of a new bishop of Auxerre. Considering the candidate proposed by Count William of Nevers to be totally unsuitable, Bernard suggested his fellow Cistercian, Alan of Regny, abbot of L'Arrivour, instead, but the rest of the commission refused to go along with his recommendation. The pope upheld Bernard's choice, but Bernard also had to make his case with Louis VII before Alan could receive his consecration.[27]

Bernard also intervened in one English episcopal election, and this controversy not only kept Aelred's home in the north of England in turmoil for many years but also involved Aelred personally at the beginning of his monastic career. After the death

---

[25] Bernard, Epp 164–70 (SBOp 7:372–85; J179–86); Giles Constable, "The Disputed Election at Langres in 1138," *Traditio* 13 (1957): 119–52; Newman, *Boundaries*, 199–200.

[26] Bernard, Ep 219 (SBOp 8:80–82; J293); Herman of Tournai, *Narratio restaurationis Abbatiae Sancti Martini Tornacensis*, PL 180:125–26; Sigebert of Gembloux, *Chronica, Auctarium Corbeiense, Continuatio Praemonstratensis, MGH Scriptores, Scriptores (in folio)* 6:452; T. Boutiot, *Histoire de la ville de Troyes et de la Champagne méridionale*, 2 vols. (Troyes: Duffey-Robert, 1870), 1:199–200; Annie DuFour-Malbezin, *Actes des Évêques de Laon des origines à 1151* (Paris: CNRS Editions, 2001), 20; Guy DeVailly, *Le Diocèse de Bourges* (Paris: Letourzey et Ané, 1973), 38–40; Deira Hugenholz and Henk Teunis, "Suger's Advice," *Journal of Medieval History* 12, no. 3 (1986): 202; Marcel Pacaut, *Louis VII et les Élections Épiscopales dans le Royaume de France* (Paris: J. Vrin, 1957), 94–100.

[27] Bernard, Epp 275–76, 280, 282 (SBOp 8:186–88, 192–94, 196–97; J345–48).

of Archbishop Thurstan of York in 1140, the cathedral chapter chose Abbot Henry de Sully of Fécamp to succeed him, but Pope Innocent II refused to approve the election because Henry would not resign his abbacy. King Stephen rejected the chapter's next choice, Waldef of Kirkham, undoubtedly because he was the stepson of King David of Scotland. Finally, the chapter elected the archdeacon of East Riding and treasurer of York Minster, William fitz Herbert, but King Stephen's capture at the battle of Lincoln in February 1141 delayed William's consecration.[28] By the end of the year, significant opposition to William fitz Herbert had surfaced, centered around the Cistercians in the north of England, Abbot William of Rievaulx and Abbot Richard II of Fountains, as well as Priors Cuthbert and Waldef of the Augustinian houses of Guisborough and Kirkham and Master Robert of the Hospital of Saint Peter in York.[29] The papal legate, Henry of Winchester, referred the matter to Pope Innocent II, and Aelred himself was part of the legation that carried the Cistercians' case to Rome.[30] At the same time Bernard launched a vigorous letter-writing campaign against William, appealing to Pope Innocent II to quash the election.[31]

[28] John of Hexham, *Historia*, in *Symeonis Monachi opera omnia*, ed. Thomas Arnold, 2 vols., RS 75 (London: Longmans, 1882–1885), 2:306–7; Gervase of Canterbury, *Chronica*, in *Chronicles of the Reigns of Stephen, Henry II., and Richard I.*, ed. William Stubbs, 2 vols., RS 73 (London: Longmans, 1879–1880), 1:123; R. L. Poole, "The Appointment and Deprivation of St. William, Archbishop of York," EHR 45, no. 178 (1930): 276–77; Christopher Norton, *St. William of York* (York: York Medieval Press, 2006), 80–81; Derek Baker, "*Viri Religiosi* and the York Election Dispute," in *Councils and Assemblies*, ed. G. J. Cuming and Derek Baker (Cambridge: Cambridge University Press, 1971), 87–100.

[29] John of Hexham, *Historia*, 2:311; David Knowles, "The Case of Saint William of York," *Cambridge Historical Journal* 5, no. 2 (1936): 162–65; Norton, *St. William*, 82; Poole, "Appointment," 277–78.

[30] Walter Daniel, *The Life of Ailred of Rievaulx* [Vita A] 14, ed. and trans. Maurice Powicke (Oxford: Oxford University Press, 1978), 23; Walter Daniel, *The Life of Aelred of Rievaulx*, trans. F. M. Powicke, CF 57 (Kalamazoo, MI: Cistercian Publications, 1994), 107.

[31] Bernard, Ep 346 (SBOp 8:288–89; J187); C. H. Talbot, "New Documents in the Case of St. William of York," *Cambridge Historical Journal* 10, no. 1 (1950): 1–5; Christopher Holdsworth, "St. Bernard and England," *Anglo-Norman Studies* 8 (1986): 149–51; Norton, *St. William*, 82–83.

After Innocent died in 1143, Bernard continued to appeal furiously against William fitz Herbert throughout the brief pontificates of Celestine II and Lucius II,[32] until finally Eugenius III ordered a new election.[33] The involvement in the affair of three prominent Cistercian abbots—Bernard of Clairvaux, Richard II of Fountains, and William of Rievaulx—is especially significant, for it illustrates the growing tendency of the Order to involve itself in matters of high ecclesiastical politics.

Bernard and Court Politics

Bernard did not restrict himself to ecclesiastical affairs but at the same time intervened forcefully in political matters touching the royal court itself. An incident involving Stephen of Senlis, the reforming bishop of Paris, is particularly revealing. Around 1127–1129, just as Bernard was actively involved with support for the Knights Templar, a quarrel broke out between Stephen and his chapter over reforms that the bishop was attempting to institute in the diocese, including the introduction of the Canons Regular of Saint Victor. When the chapter appealed to King Louis VI for protection, he took their side and forbade the bishop to make any changes. When Stephen went ahead with his project, the king confiscated the episcopal regalia, whereupon the bishop placed the diocese under an interdict. Violence broke out in the city, causing the bishop to flee for his life.

At this point, probably in 1129, the Cistercian abbots as a group, led by Stephen Harding, the abbot of Cîteaux, addressed a cautionary letter to the king.[34] Subsequently Louis VI met with certain representatives of the church, including Archbishop Henry of Sens and two Cistercian abbots, Bernard and Hugh of Mâcon, abbot of Pontigny. Nothing came of the meeting, and the king subsequently appealed to Pope Honorius II, who lifted the inter-

---

[32] Bernard, Epp 235–36 (SBOp 8:108–12; J202–3) and J204; not in SBOp.
[33] Bernard, Epp 238–40, 252 (SBOp 8:115–24, 148–49; J205–8).
[34] PL 182:149–52; Newman, *Boundaries*, 146–47.

dict. This act called forth a letter of protest from Saint Bernard, cosigned by Hugh of Pontigny.[35] The proceedings also turned the king's anger against Archbishop Henry of Sens, and again Bernard, together with Stephen of Cîteaux and Hugh of Pontigny, protested to the pope.[36] At length the quarrel was temporarily patched up, although the exact terms of any agreement between the king and the archbishop are unknown. The important point is that this incident shows the involvement of other Cistercian abbots besides Bernard in public affairs. Stephen Harding and Hugh of Pontigny may have elected Bernard as their spokesperson, but all of them were concerned to support the reforming bishop of Paris in his difficulties with the king.

Bishop Stephen's troubles were not at an end, for some four years later a tragic incident occurred while he was traveling near Gournay-sur-Marne. His companion, Prior Thomas of Saint Victor, was a key agent of the bishop's reform policies and had introduced far-reaching administrative reforms aimed at curbing the rapacity of the archdeacon of Paris, Theobald Notier, who forced litigants in his courts to pay heavy bribes in order to have their cases judged. Notier's nephew, also named Theobald, attacked the party and murdered Prior Thomas, who died in the bishop's arms. The bishop took refuge at Clairvaux with Bernard, who immediately wrote to the pope on his behalf. Bishop Geoffrey of Chartres, as papal legate, convoked a council at the royal abbey of Jouarre to investigate the situation and punish the guilty. Count Theobald and Count William of Nevers attended, along with Bernard, Abbot Peter the Venerable of Cluny, and an assortment of other clergymen.[37] Once again Bernard had involved himself

---

[35] Bernard, Ep 46 (SBOp 7:135; J49). See also Ep 47 (SBOp 7:136–37; J50), in the name of Bishop Geoffrey of Chartres, and Ep 48 (SBOp 7:137–40; J51), from Saint Bernard to Cardinal Haimeric, the papal chancellor.

[36] Bernard, Ep 49 (SBOp 7:140–41; J52). See also Epp 50–51 (SBOp 7:142–43; J53–54).

[37] Jean Quéguiner, "Jouarre au XIIe et au XIIIe siècles," in Yves Chaussy et al., *L'abbaye royale Notre-Dame de Jouarre*, 2 vols., Bibliothèque d'histoire et d'archéologie chrétiennes (Paris: G. Victor, 1961), 1:91–92; *Recueil des Historiens des Gaules et de la*

in a matter of high ecclesiastical politics that reached all the way to the royal court of France.

Saint Bernard also became involved in a vicious quarrel between Count Theobald and King Louis VII in 1142, when Count Ralph of Vermandois, the king's second cousin, seneschal, and close friend, decided to repudiate his wife Eleanor, Count Theobald's niece, in favor of the king's sister-in-law Petronilla. After the second marriage was deemed valid by the bishops of Tournai, Senlis, and Laon, Bernard wrote to the pope, asking him to uphold the count's first marriage to Eleanor.[38] The pope referred the matter to a council to be held at Lagny, which agreed with Bernard and also pronounced the first marriage valid.

Relations between Count Theobald and King Louis VII had never run smoothly, and at this latest insult the king became so angry that he invaded and laid waste Count Theobald's lands, burning the town of Vitré.[39] Outraged, Bernard sent off an impressive series of letters to the pope, the king, Abbot Suger, and various other important ecclesiastics.[40] He demanded to know what Theobald had done wrong, writing, "If it be a sin to love righteousness and hate iniquity, he would be without excuse."[41] With the situation still unresolved when Celestine II succeeded Innocent II in 1143, Bernard wrote to Rome again for help, stating, "Count Theobald is a son of peace, and what he asks for, I

France, ed. Léopold Delisle, 24 vols. (Paris: Victor Palmé, 1869–1967), 15:334–34, nos. 9–10; Bernard, Ep 158 (SBOp 7:365–67; J164).

[38] Bernard, Ep 216 (SBOp 8:76–77; J294).

[39] Sigebert of Gembloux, *Continuatio Praemonstratensis*, 6:452; *Annales Sanctae Colombae Senonensis, MGH Scriptores, Scriptores (in folio)*, 1:107; Marcel Pacaut, *Louis VII et son Royaume* (Paris: S.E.V.P.E.N., 1964), 42–45; Karl Ferdinand Werner, "Kingdom and Principality in Twelfth-Century France," in *The Medieval Nobility: Studies on the Ruling Classes of France and Germany from the Sixth to the Twelfth Century*, ed. and trans. Timothy Reuter (Amsterdam: North Holland Publishing Co., 1978), 269–70.

[40] Bernard, Epp 216–17, 220–22, 224, 226, 358 (SBOp 8:76–78, 82–89, 91–93, 95–96, 303; J294–98, 300, 302, 304).

[41] Bernard, Ep 216 (SBOp 8:76; J294).

ask for too."[42] In April 1144, Bernard traveled to Paris with the count's seneschal, André de Baudemont, on a peacemaking mission, which bore no fruit.[43] Finally, Pope Eugenius III reversed the decisions of his predecessors and granted Count Ralph his divorce.[44] In this case although the situation was not resolved as Bernard would have wished, these events show him vigorously involved in upholding the interests of the family of Count Theobald, his feudal overlord and the protector of his abbey.

Bernard and the Papal Schism of 1130

Perhaps Bernard's most significant activities in the realm of ecclesiastical politics began in 1130, when the papal election again split between two claimants. Under the leadership of the papal chancellor Haimeric, the death of Pope Honorius II was kept secret long enough for a small group of cardinals to meet and elect Gregory of San Angelo as Pope Innocent II. Disagreeing with this move, the rest of the cardinals elected a rival, Peter Pierleoni, who took the name Anacletus II.[45] Scholars have long agreed that both individuals were worthy successors of Saint Peter and have proposed a number of reasons for the disagreement between the two parties. Stanley Chodorow saw a split among the cardinals dating from about 1119 regarding the solution to the investiture controversy, with the hard-line Pierleoni faction maintaining that the spiritual

[42] Bernard, Ep 358 (SBOp 8:303; J304).

[43] *Cartulaire du Temple*, 217, no. 332.

[44] John of Salisbury, *Historia Pontificalis*, ed. and trans. Marjorie Chibnall (Oxford: Clarendon Press, 1986), 12–13.

[45] Suger, *Vie de Louis VI Le Gros*, ed. and trans. Henri Waquet (Paris: Société d'Édition Les Belles Lettres, 1964), 256–59; Robert of Torigny, *Chronica*, in *Chronicles of the Reigns of Stephen, Henry II., and Richard I.*, ed. Richard Howlett, 4 vols., RS 82 (London: Longmans, 1884–1890), 4:117; William of Malmesbury, *Historia Novella*, ed. Edmund King, trans. K. R. Potter (Oxford: Clarendon Press, 1998), 6–9; Henry of Huntingdon, *Historia Anglorum: The History of the English People*, ed. and trans. Diana Greenway (Oxford: Clarendon Press, 1996), 486–87; John of Worcester, *The Chronicle of John of Worcester*, ed. R. R. Darlington and P. McGurk, trans. P. McGurk and Jennifer Bray, 3 vols. (Oxford: Clarendon Press, 1995–1998), 3:188–89, 232–33.

and temporal aspects of a bishopric could not be split apart.[46] David Berger and Mary Stroll have suggested that anti-Semitism may have played a part in the disagreement, since Peter Pierleoni's great-grandfather had been a convert from Judaism.[47]

There is agreement, however, on the fact that Chancellor Haimeric's influence with the key leaders of the Gregorian reform in northern Europe resulted in Innocent II's acceptance by the kings of France and England and the Holy Roman Emperor. Among Innocent's crucial supporters were Bernard of Clairvaux, Norbert of Xanten, Abbot Peter the Venerable of Cluny, and Bishop Geoffrey of Chartres.[48] Bernard wrote numerous letters supporting Innocent II's claim, to the archbishop of Tours, Master Geoffrey of Loreto, the bishops of Aquitaine, the citizens of Genoa, Pisa, and Milan, and the Emperor Lothar III.[49] In the second book of the *Vita Prima Sancti Bernardi*, Arnold of Bonneval shows that Bernard's influence was instrumental in securing the recognition of Innocent II by Louis VI of France at the Council of Étampes in 1130.[50]

[46] Stanley A. Chodorow, "Ecclesiastical Politics and the Ending of the Investiture Contest: The Papal Election of 1119 and the Negotiations of Mouzon," *Speculum* 46, no. 4 (1971): 613–40.

[47] David Berger, "The Attitude of St. Bernard of Clairvaux Toward the Jews," *Proceedings of the American Academy for Jewish Research* 40 (1973): 105–6; Mary Stroll, *The Jewish Pope: Ideology and Politics in the Papal Schism of 1130* (Leiden: Brill, 1987), 160–64.

[48] *Councils and Synods with Other Documents Relating to the English Church*, ed. D. Whitelock, M. Brett, and C. N. L. Brooke, 2 vols. (Oxford: Clarendon Press, 1981), vol. 1, part 2, 755–57; PL 179:96–97; Mary Stroll, *Jewish Pope*, 164; Hugenholz and Teunis, "Suger's Advice," 204; Jean Leclercq "Les Lettres de Guillaume de Saint-Thierry à Saint Bernard," *Revue Bénédictine* 79 (1969): 375–82.

[49] Bernard, Epp 124–26, 129–33, 137 (SBOp 7:305–19, 322–29, 333; J127–29, 31–32, 134, 138–40); Stroll, *Jewish Pope*, 96–99; Bruno Scott James, *St. Bernard of Clairvaux: An Essay in Biography* (London: Hodder and Stoughton, 1957), 99–114; Hayden V. White, "The Gregorian Ideal and St. Bernard," *Journal of the History of Ideas* 21, no. 3 (1960): 335–41; Helene Wieruszowski, "Roger II of Sicily, Rex-Tyrannus, in Twelfth-Century Political Thought," *Speculum* 38, no. 1 (1963): 58–59.

[50] William of Saint-Thierry, Arnold of Bonneval, and Geoffrey of Auxerre, *Vita Prima Sancti Bernardi Claraevallis Abbatis* [Vita Bern] 2:3; William of Saint-Thierry, et al., *Vita Prima Sancti Bernardi Claraevallis Abbatis, Liber Primus*, ed. Paul Verdeyen, CCCM 89B (Turnhout: Brepols Publishers, 2011), 92–93; William of Saint-Thierry et al., *The First Life of Bernard of Clairvaux*, trans. Hilary Costello, CF 76 (College-

On January 13, 1131, at Chartres, Bernard arranged a meeting between Innocent II and King Henry I of England, a meeting that led to Henry's recognition of Innocent as the rightful pope in the disputed election.[51] Scholars agree that Bernard's influence was crucial in persuading Henry I to accept Innocent as pope.[52] Later, in 1135, Bernard wrote to Louis, asking him to allow the French bishops to attend Innocent II's council at Pisa.[53] He also wrote to Henry I of England requesting financial aid for the pope[54] and to the Emperor Lothar, suggesting that he travel to Rome to place Innocent on the throne.[55] Bernard himself traveled twice to Italy, in 1133 and again in 1137–1138, working hard to persuade the people of Milan and Pisa to support Innocent.[56] He also made two visits to Aquitaine to convince Duke William X to abandon his

---

ville, MN: Cistercian Publications, 2015), 81–82; Suger, *Vie de Louis VI*, 258–61; François Petit, *Norbert et l'origine des Prémontrés* (Paris: Éditions du Cerf, 1981), 276; Franz-Josef Schmale, *Studien Zum Schisma des Jahres 1130* (Cologne: Böhlau, 1961), 221–32; Elphège Vacandard, "Saint Bernard et le schisme d'Anaclet II en France," *Revue des questions historiques* 43 (1888): 85–95; Aryeh Grabois, "Le schisme de 1130 et la France," *Revue d'histoire écclésiastique* 76 (1981): 593–612; Timothy Reuter, "Zur Anerkennung Papst Innocenz II: Eine neue Quelle," *Deutsches Archiv für Erforschung des Mittelalters* 39 (1983): 395–416; E. Amélineau, "Saint Bernard et le schisme d'Anaclet II (1130–1138)," *Revue des questions historiques* 30 (1881): 63–64.

[51] Vita Bern 2:4; CCCM 89B:93; CF 76:82–84; Bernard, Ep 138 (SBOp 7:334; J141); Orderic Vitalis, *The Ecclesiastical History*, ed. and trans. Marjorie Chibnall, 6 vols. (Oxford: Clarendon Press, 1969–1980), 6:420–21; Robert of Torigny, *Chronica*, 119; Suger, *Vie de Louis VI*, 260–61; William of Malmesbury, *Historia Novella*, 9–10; Henry of Huntingdon, *Historia*, 486–87; *La Chronique de Morigny (1095–1152)*, ed. Léon Mirot (Paris: Picard, 1912), 53; Schmale, *Schisma*, 233–36; Vacandard, "Saint Bernard," 95–96; Amélineau, "Saint Bernard," 64–65.

[52] Holdsworth, "St. Bernard and England," 147–48; Denis Bethel, "English Black Monks and Episcopal Elections in the 1120s," EHR 84, no. 333 (1969): 691–92; Herbert Bloch, "The Schism of Anacletus II and the Glanfeuil Forgeries of Peter the Deacon of Monte Casino," *Traditio* 8 (1958): 168; Newman, *Boundaries*, 193–99.

[53] Bernard, Ep 255 (SBOp 8:161–62; J133).

[54] Bernard, Ep 138 (SBOp 7:334; J141).

[55] Bernard, Ep 139 (SBOp 7:335–36; J142).

[56] Vita Bern 2.8–12; CCCM 89B:95–99; CF 76:87–92; Bernard, Epp 130–33, 137 (SBOp 7:325–29, 333; J132, 134, 138–40); Amélineau, "Saint Bernard," 72–82.

support of Anacletus II.[57] With the backing of Bernard and other powerful reformers, Innocent gradually consolidated his hold on the papacy, achieving victory with the death of Anacletus in 1138 and the condemnation of Anacletus's remaining followers at the Second Lateran Council the following year.[58]

Throughout his pontificate, Innocent relied heavily on Bernard's judgment. For example, in 1133, while the struggle was still going on, an episcopal election in the see of Tours was contested between a certain Hugh and a monk of Fontaines-les-Blanches named Philip. Innocent appointed Bernard to investigate the matter, and he annulled Philip's election. Philip appealed to Innocent, who upheld Bernard's decision, with the result that the disappointed Philip took refuge with the antipope Anacletus. Remarkably, Philip later repented and became a monk and then prior at Clairvaux.[59]

A special relationship existed between Bernard and Innocent, and the latter never forgot that he owed his possession of the papal throne to Bernard's active intervention. In return, Bernard unstintingly offered his advice to Innocent and the Roman Curia. Difficulties in the church of Orleans that culminated in the murder of the sub-dean Archibald called forth a spate of letters from Bernard to the pope, the papal chancellor Haimeric, and Cardinal John of Crema.[60] He wrote to the pope on behalf of the bishops of Troyes and Trier when they had difficulties with the clergy in their dioceses.[61] He and Peter the Venerable of Cluny, another fervent supporter of Innocent's papacy, both wrote to Innocent to enlist his support for Arnulf, the bishop-elect of Lisieux, who was being kept out of his see by Count Geoffrey of Anjou.[62]

---

[57] Vita Bern 2.32–40; CCCM 89B:111–18; CF 76:86–92; Vacandard, "Saint Bernard," 107–21; Amélineau, "Saint Bernard," 82–92.

[58] *La Chronique de Morigny*, 71–75; Orderic Vitalis, *Ecclesiastical History*, 6:508–9, 528–31.

[59] Epp 150–51, 431 (SBOp 7:354–58, 8:411–13; J155–57).

[60] Bernard, Epp 156–57 (SBOp 7:363–64, 370–71; J162–63, 165–67).

[61] Bernard, Epp 152, 178–80, 230, 323, 432–34, 437–39 (SBOp 7:397–402, 8:100–101, 258–60, 413–14, 416–17; J158, 218–22, 264–69).

[62] Bernard, Ep 348 (SBOp 8:291–93; J252); Peter the Venerable, *The Letters of Peter the Venerable*, ed. Giles Constable, 2 vols. (Cambridge, MA: Harvard University Press, 1967), Ep 101; 1:261–62.

Many of Bernard's letters are letters of introduction for highly placed churchmen who evidently turned aside to visit Bernard at Clairvaux and enlist his support in whatever project had caused them to set out on the road to Rome.[63] Eventually the flood of letters became so great that Innocent must have expressed his annoyance, for Saint Bernard was forced to apologize: "I was urged on by the love of my friends for, if I remember aright, I wrote very little on my own behalf. But there can be too much of a good thing."[64]

Bernard and Pope Eugenius III

Bernard also later occupied the same position of advisor to his fellow Cistercian, Bernard Paganelli, abbot of S. Anastasio alle Tre Fontane near Rome, who was elected pope in 1145 and took the name Eugenius III. Bernard wrote immediately to congratulate this former monk of Clairvaux on his election and followed up with a long letter of advice now known as *De Consideratione*.[65] He also sent a letter to the entire Roman Curia begging them to "help and comfort with your fervent support what is clearly the work of your hands."[66] Bernard's correspondence gives the impression that once again he had become a veritable gatekeeper for the papacy, and no cleric dared to approach the Holy See without a letter of introduction from him.[67] He wrote letters of introduction on behalf of such highly placed clerics as Cardinal Robert Pullen, Abbot Peter the Venerable of Cluny, and Abbot Suger of St. Denis, all of whom should have been well known in Vatican circles. Occasionally Bernard himself seems to have felt the situation

---

[63] Bernard, Epp 171, 173–74, 210–15, 339, 349–51, 435–36 (SBOp 7:385–87, 8:69–75, 279–80, 293–94, 415; J211–12, 215, 280–91). Also J213, not in SBOp.

[64] Ep 218 (SBOp 8:78–79; J292). Similarly, Ep 351 (SBOp 8:294–95; J289).

[65] Bernard, Ep J314, not in SBOp; Bernard, Csi (SBOp 3:379–494; Bernard of Clairvaux, *Five Books on Consideration: Advice to a Pope*, trans. John D. Anderson and Elizabeth T. Kennan, CF 37 [Kalamazoo, MI: Cistercian Publications, 1976]).

[66] Bernard, Ep 237 (SBOp 8:113–15; J315).

[67] Bernard, Epp 246–47, 249, 251, 262, 270, 277–78, 284–86, 291, 294, 305, 309 (SBOp 8:137–39, 140–41, 144, 147–48, 171, 178–80, 189–90, 198–202, 208, 211–12, 222, 229; J322–23, 325, 327, 335, 337, 340, 349–50, 354, 356, 359, 371, 412–13).

somewhat absurd, as when he wrote to assure Robert Pullen that he had no need of letters of introduction from him,[68] or when he began a letter to the pope on behalf of Peter the Venerable by saying, "It would be silly for me to write to you on behalf of the Lord Abbot of Cluny, to act as if I wanted to befriend a man whom all the world befriends."[69] It is only a slight exaggeration to say that a black market existed in Bernardine letters. On one occasion he complained to the pope that someone had obtained false letters of recommendation from him through the bishop of Beauvais.[70] In another letter he explained to the pope that he had to have a new seal made because the old one had been forged and many false letters had been sent out using it.[71]

The Cistercians and the Second Crusade

For his part, Pope Eugenius III entrusted Bernard with arguably the most important undertaking of his pontificate, the Second Crusade. As Otto of Freising, himself a Cistercian, told the story, interest in an expedition to the Holy Land developed at the court of King Louis VII of France following the fall of Edessa to the Muslims in 1144. The king consulted Bernard about the desirability of the enterprise, and Bernard deferred the decision to the pope.[72] Before the papal bull *Quantum Praedecessores* had even reached France, another Cistercian, Bishop Godfrey of Langres, preached a sermon calling for an expedition to the Holy Land at the king's Christmas court at Bourges.[73] The pope himself was

---

[68] Bernard, Ep 362 (SBOp 8:309–10; J316).

[69] Bernard, Ep 277 (SBOp 8:189; J349).

[70] Bernard, Ep 269 (SBOp 8:178; J339).

[71] Bernard, Ep 284 (SBOp 8:199; J354).

[72] Otto of Freising, *Gesta Friderici I Imperatoris*, in MGH *Scriptores, Scriptores rerum Germanicarum in usum scholarum separatim editi* (Hannover: Hahnsche Buchhandlung, 1978), 46:54; Otto of Freising, *The Deeds of Frederick Barbarossa*, trans. Charles Christopher Mierow and Richard Emery (New York: Columbia University Press, 1953), 70.

[73] Odo of Deuil, *De profectione Ludovici VII in Orientem*, trans. V. G. Berry (New York: Columbia University Press, 1948), 6–7; Jonathan Phillips, *The Second Cru-*

unable to leave Rome for the launch of the crusade at Vézelay on Palm Sunday 1145, so he sent Bernard a formal commission to preach the crusade.[74] Bernard's preaching on that occasion was so stirring that the organizers ran short of the white cloth crosses being given to those who committed themselves to the expedition, so the abbot had to tear up his own garments to fill the demand.[75] Bernard immediately drafted a series of letters to be sent out along with the papal bull to local recruiters in areas that he would not visit himself.[76] As these letters are presented in modern printed editions they appear to be personal letters addressed to one ruler, but as Jean Leclercq has demonstrated, these texts exist in multiple recensions, and the surviving manuscripts are scattered throughout Europe.[77] Bernard also organized a network of other preachers to help in the task, including the Cistercian abbots Reynald of Morimond, Adam of Ebrach, and Gerlach of Rein.[78] Bernard himself then undertook a yearlong preaching tour in Flanders and Germany, culminating with a visit to the king's Christmas court at Speyer, where Conrad III himself took the cross.[79] In general the response was so great that, as Bernard himself wrote, "towns and castles are emptied, one may scarcely find one man among

sade: Extending the Frontiers of Christendom (New Haven: Yale University Press, 2007), 62–65.

[74] Odo of Deuil, *De profectione*, 8–9; Otto of Freising, *Gesta Friderici*, 55; Otto of Freising, *Deeds*, 71–73; Phillips, *Second Crusade*, 66.

[75] Odo of Deuil, *De profectione*, 8–9; Otto of Freising, *Gesta Friderici*, 58; Otto of Freising, *Deeds*, 73–74; Suger, "L'Histoire du roi Louis VII," in *Vie de Louis le Gros par Suger suivie de l'histoire du roi Louis VII publiées d'après les manuscrits*, ed. Auguste Molinier (Paris: Picard, 1887), 157–60; Phillips, *Second Crusade*, 66–68.

[76] Bernard, Ep 308 (SBOp 8:328; J397); Phillips, *Second Crusade*, 69–76. Also J391; not in SBOp.

[77] Jean Leclercq, "L'Encyclique de Saint Bernard en faveur de la croisade," *Revue Bénédictine* 81 (1971): 282–308.

[78] Otto of Freising, *Gesta Friderici*, 60; Otto of Freising, *Deeds*, 75; Phillips, *Second Crusade*, 76–77.

[79] Odo of Deuil, *De profectione*, 10–11; Otto of Freising, *Gesta Friderici*, 58–59; Otto of Freising, *Deeds*, 74–76; Phillips, *Second Crusade*, 68–97; Burton and Kerr, *Cistercians in the Middle Ages*, 194–96; Philip of Clairvaux, *Vita Prima* 6 (=*Vita Secunda*); PL 185:373–94. This fragment is included in Migne as part of the *Vita Prima*, but not in CCCM 89B.

seven women, so many women are there widows while their husbands are still alive."[80]

It is clear from the examples given here that Bernard not only played a leading role in most of the important ecclesiastical events of his time but also gave unstintingly of his time, effort, and influence on behalf of the throngs of individuals who beat a path to the gates of Clairvaux seeking his help. This chapter has focused on Bernard as the Cistercian with the most notable public career, but even this brief overview has revealed a number of other Cistercians who interested themselves in matters of ecclesiastical and secular politics and who went on to hold high offices in the church. The prior of Clairvaux, Godfrey de la Roche, became bishop of Langres; Alan de Regny, the abbot of L'Arrivour, became bishop of Auxerre; Henry Murdac of Fountains Abbey became archbishop of York, and of course Bernard Paganelli of Tre Fontane became Pope Eugenius III. Abbots William of Rievaulx and Richard II of Fountains spearheaded the protests against Archbishop-elect William fitz Herbert that led to the promotion of Henry Murdac to the see of York, and, on the other side of the channel, Stephen Harding of Cîteaux and Hugh of Pontigny added their voices to Bernard's in vociferously protesting the king's ill-treatment of Stephen of Senlis, the bishop of Paris. Together with the abbot of Tre Fontane, they assisted at the council of Troyes, where the rule for the Templars was created. Bishop Godfrey of Langres and the abbots of Morimond, Ebrach, and Rein joined Bernard in preaching the Second Crusade. Furthermore, a number of Cistercians involved themselves in the papal schism of 1159 and the quarrel between King Henry II and Archbishop Thomas Becket of Canterbury. These are only a small sample of the Cistercians who became involved in the world outside their own order. Martha Newman has compiled a list of over sixty Cistercians who became bishops and cardinals between 1126 and 1180.[81]

---

[80] Ep 247 (SBOp 8:140–41; J323).

[81] Newman, *Boundaries*, 148, 247–51. For more on the Cistercian tradition of advising rulers see *Boundaries*, 171–90; Elizabeth A. Freeman, *Narratives of a New*

Bernard himself explained the apparent contradiction in the lives of these contemplatives who nevertheless involved themselves in worldly affairs. In Sermon 50 on the Song of Songs, he noted that although the first great commandment enjoins love of God and only the second speaks of loving one's neighbor, practicality often requires us to pay more attention to worldly affairs:

> Who will doubt that in prayer a man is speaking with God? But how often, at the call of charity, we are drawn away, torn away, for the sake of those who need to speak to us or be helped! How often does dutiful repose yield dutifully to the uproar of business! How often is a book laid aside in good conscience that we may sweat at manual work! How often for the sake of administering worldly affairs we very rightly omit even the solemn celebration of Masses! A preposterous order; but necessity knows no law. Love in action devises its own order.[82]

For Bernard, the requirement of charity pushes the monk out into the world and requires him to minister to the needs of his neighbor, whether that need takes the form of a poor man at the monastery gate or a matter of high secular politics. It is clear that if Aelred of Rievaulx had been seeking guidance in his pursuit of a public career, he had numerous role models within his own order from whom to choose.

Order: Cistercian Historical Writing in England, 1150–1220, Medieval Church Studies 2 (Turnhout: Brepols, 2002), 62–70.

[82] Bernard, SC 50.2.5 (SBOp 2:81; Bernard of Clairvaux, *On the Song of Songs* III, trans. Kilian Walsh and Irene M. Edmonds, CF 31 [Kalamazoo, MI: Cistercian Publications, 1979], 34); Henry Mayr–Harting, "Two Abbots in Politics: Wala of Corbei and Bernard of Clairvaux," *Transactions of the Royal Historical Society*, 5th ser. 40 (1980): 234.

Chapter 3

Son of the North
Aelred in Context

Aelred and his fellow monks undoubtedly came to the Rye valley seeking the peace and solitude of the monastic cloister, but that was hard to attain given the unsettled times in which they lived. Thanks to his historical writing, Aelred himself is most closely associated with the reigns of King Stephen of England and King David I of Scotland, the Anglo-Norman civil war, and the Scottish invasions, but in later life he became a supporter of Henry II and witnessed the beginning of that king's long quarrel with Archbishop Thomas Becket. Furthermore, disputed episcopal elections at York and Durham and the ambiguous relationship between the Scottish church and the archbishop of York kept the northern church in turmoil throughout much of his lifetime.

In Aelred's case, references in the sources that can be securely dated are scarce, too few to allow the construction of a timeline or chronological biography. For example, as abbot of Rievaulx, Aelred would have attended the general chapters of the Order at Cîteaux and would have visited the daughter houses of his abbey annually. Works by Walter Daniel, Jocelin of Furness, and Reginald of Durham sometimes mention incidents that took place during these visits, but most often without giving the date of the event. Further hints of Aelred's travels and activities outside the cloister are found in the occasional charter bearing his attestation, but these too are often undated. Thus Aelred cannot be placed among the advisers of Duke Henry of Normandy as the provisions of the Treaty of Winchester were being hammered out or at the side of Henry Murdac as the latter sought to take possession of his see of York, but it was inevitable that these and other pivotal events would impinge on the solitude of the monastic cloister. Furthermore, Aelred's historical writings show that he was keenly interested in events beyond the walls of Rievaulx. This chapter will describe some of these crucial events and the circumstances leading up to them and will place Aelred's early life in its context. Appendix 1 provides a convenient summary of the key dates and events in Aelred's lifetime.

Early Life

Aelred was born in 1110 at Hexham in Northumberland, the son of a family whose roots were sunk deep in northern soil, perhaps descended from the small group of families that had carried Saint Cuthbert's bones from the Holy Isle of Lindisfarne first to Chester-le-Street and then to Durham. Aelred himself gave some information about his ancestors in *The Saints of the Church of Hexham and Their Miracles*, which he composed for the Augustinian canons at Hexham and probably presented as a sermon on the occasion of the translation of the relics of the five holy bishops of Hexham in 1155.[1] His great-grandfather, Alfred son of Westou, had been sacristan of Durham cathedral and custodian of the shrine of Saint Cuthbert.[2] It is likely that Alfred held the church of Hexham

---

[1] Aelred Squire, *Aelred of Rievaulx: A Study* (London: SPCK, 1981), 40; Pierre-André Burton, *Aelred de Rievaulx 1110–1167: De l'homme éclaté a l'être unifié, Essai de biographie existentielle et spirituelle* (Paris: Les Éditions du Cerf, 2010), 494. For a review of the evidence, see Marsha L. Dutton, Introduction to Aelred of Rievaulx, *The Lives of the Northern Saints*, trans. Jane Patricia Freeland, ed. Marsha L. Dutton, CF 71 (Kalamazoo, MI: Cistercian Publications, 2006), 14–16. James Raine suggested that Aelred was a spectator at the translation and wrote his account afterward for the canons' use (James Raine, ed., *The Priory of Hexham: Its Chroniclers, Endowments, and Annals*, 2 vols., Surtees Society 44 and 46 [Durham: Andrews and Co., 1864], 1:lxxv).

[2] Aelred, SS Hag XIV; Raine, *Priory*, 1:190; CCCM 3:94; CF 71:87–88; Squire, *Aelred*, 5–6.

as a benefice and maintained curates there. Aelred related that his great-grandfather was responsible for the discovery of Bishop Alchmund's relics in the church at Hexham, after the saint directed the parish priest in a vision to inform Alfred of the location. Elated with his discovery, Alfred attempted to carry one of the saint's fingers back to Durham with him, but the casket miraculously became so heavy that it could not be moved to its final resting place until the missing member was replaced.[3] Alfred's son Eilaf followed in his father's footsteps as a member of the chapter at Durham until William of St.-Calais, bishop of Durham, replaced the secular clerks in the cathedral with monks.[4] Eilaf therefore received permission from the archbishop of York to occupy and restore the ancient church at Hexham, which was in a sad state of disrepair; in time this work was carried on by his son, another Eilaf.[5]

The effects of the Gregorian reform, however, were beginning to be felt in northern England, and this Eilaf, Aelred's father, would be the last married priest at Hexham. Archbishop Thomas II of York gave the church of Hexham to Augustinian canons in 1112/1113, leaving the properties of the church to Eilaf for his lifetime. In *The Saints of Hexham*, Aelred portrayed the change as having actually been initiated by his zealous father, who "feared that after his death the church would be given to others who, even if not less worthy, would certainly be less careful than he." Eilaf therefore approached the archbishop and begged that the church be committed to the care of Augustinian canons.[6]

Richard of Hexham told the story a bit differently in his *History of the Church of Hexham*. He wrote that Archbishop Thomas initiated the change and that the canons initially lived in great

[3] Aelred, SS Hag XV; Raine, *Priory*, 1:194–98; CCCM 3:101–3; CF 71:95–99.

[4] Simeon of Durham, *Libellus de Exordio atque Procursu istius hoc est Dunhelmensis Ecclesie: Tract on the Origins and Progress of this the Church of Durham*, ed. and trans. David Rollason (Oxford: Clarendon Press, 2000), 194–97, 226–31.

[5] Aelred, SS Hag XV; Raine, *Priory*, 1:191–92; CCCM 3:95; CF 71:89–91. The temporalities of Hexham had fallen under the jurisdiction of York when the see of Durham was vacant because in 1069 Archbishop Aethelwine had fled William the Conqueror's devastation of the North (Raine, *Priory*, 1:lvi–lvii).

[6] Aelred, SS Hag XIV; Raine, *Priory*, 1:192; CCCM 3:96; CF 71:91.

poverty because Eilaf retained the church's temporalities, so in 1138 Aelred's father finally agreed to donate the property to the canons and became a monk at Durham.[7] Walter Daniel related an incident that has been interpreted as evidence of Eilaf's lingering resentment at the loss of his benefice.[8] In the *Letter to Maurice* he related that when Aelred was only four or five years old, he announced to his family that Archbishop Thomas had died, before the news had had time to travel to Hexham by normal means. His father responded, "True, my son, he is dead who lives an evil life." News of Thomas's death arrived three days later.[9] If Eilaf's statement is interpreted as a sign of bitterness, it contrasts with both Aelred's account and that of Richard of Hexham, since in both of those narratives Eilaf clearly donated the church and its property voluntarily.

These works, however, were written for different purposes. Aelred wrote *The Saints of Hexham* as a sermon to celebrate the translation to a new shrine of the relics of the five holy bishops of Hexham: Eata, Acca, Frethbert, Alchmund, and Tilbert. As Marsha Dutton has pointed out, Aelred's work established a chain of custody for the relics, proving by their resistance to being moved and the miracles they worked that the relics were authentic.[10] This purpose was best served by making the transition from Aelred's

[7] Richard of Hexham, "History of the Church of Hexham," in Raine, *Priory*, 1:55–56; Frederick M. Powicke, Introduction to Walter Daniel, Vita A, xxxv–xxxvi; Marsha L. Dutton, "A Historian's Historian: The Place of Bede in Aelred's Contributions to the New History of His Age," in *Truth As Gift: Studies in Honor of John R. Sommerfeldt*, ed. Marsha L. Dutton, Daniel M. La Corte, and Paul Lockey, CS 204 (Kalamazoo, MI: Cistercian Publications, 2004), 427; Marsha L. Dutton, Introduction to *The Life of Aelred of Rievaulx and the Letter to Maurice*, trans. Maurice Powicke, CF 57 (Kalamazoo, MI: Cistercian Publications, 1994), 20–22; Aelred Squire, *Aelred*, 10; Brian Patrick McGuire, *Brother and Lover: Aelred of Rievaulx* (London: The Crossroad Publishing Co., 1994), 22–25; Ann Lawrence Mathers, *Manuscripts in Northumbria in the Eleventh and Twelfth Centuries* (Cambridge: D. S. Brewer, 2003), 239.

[8] Powicke, Introduction to Vita A, xxxv.

[9] "Walter Daniel's Letter to Maurice" 2, in Vita A, p. 72; CF 57:151–52.

[10] Marsha L. Dutton, "Saints Refusing to Leave: Aelred of Rievaulx's *The Saints of Hexham* as an Inverted *translatio*," *The Medieval Translator*, vol. 15, *In principio fuit interpres*, ed. Alessandra Petrina (Turnhout: Brepols, 2013), 187–200.

family to the canons voluntary. This was a purpose that Richard of Hexham probably shared, since it served no purpose to sow seeds of conflict between the parties at this stage.

Walter's motivation, however, was completely different. He wrote the *Letter to Maurice* in response to critics of his *Life of Aelred* who refused to believe in Aelred's miracles.[11] The purpose of this particular story was to show that Aelred had had the gift of prophecy as a child, a common hagiographical device, and the statement regarding Thomas's character attributed to Eilaf was probably a secondary consideration. It is made more striking by the fact that Thomas does not seem to have lived a particularly wicked life. At the beginning of his pontificate, he refused to make a profession of obedience to Archbishop Anselm of Canterbury, but the conflict was eventually resolved.[12] Aelred himself remarked that Thomas "had a wonderfully kind disposition."[13] Walter stated that when the news of Thomas's death arrived at Hexham, the people began to weep and lament because their father had died.[14] The worst thing anyone could accuse him of was gluttony.[15] Aelred died in 1167, and Walter wrote the *Letter to Maurice* well after that date, after the *Life of Aelred* had been completed and circulated. Archbishop Thomas II of York had died in 1114, more than fifty years before, so it is probable that Walter had little knowledge of or interest in his character.

There was, however, another bishop on the scene at that time who definitely lived an evil life, Bishop Ranulf Flambard of Durham, the rapacious tax gatherer for King William Rufus and a womanizer who at one point attempted to seduce the saintly recluse Christina of Markyate.[16] Perhaps Walter mixed up his

---

[11] "Walter Daniel's *Letter to Maurice*," pp. 66–67; CF 57:147–48.

[12] Sally N. Vaughn, *Anselm of Bec and Robert of Meulan: The Innocence of the Dove and the Wisdom of the Serpent* (Berkeley, CA: University of California Press, 1987), 337–39.

[13] Aelred, SS Hag XVIII; Raine, *Priory*, 1:202; CCCM 3:108; CF 71:106.

[14] "Walter Daniel's *Letter to Maurice*" 2, p. 72; CF 57:152.

[15] Hugh the Chanter, *The History of the Church of York 1066–1127*, ed. and trans. Charles Johnson (Oxford: Clarendon Press, 1990), 49; Frank Barlow, *The English Church: 1066–1154* (London: Longmans, 1979), 82.

[16] J. F. A. Mason, "Ranulf Flambard (c. 1060–1128)," DNB 9667, accessed February 23, 2016; *The Life of Christina of Markyate, A Twelfth Century Recluse*, ed. and trans. C. H. Talbot (Oxford: Clarendon Press, 1959), 40–45.

bishops and meant to have Eilaf comment on the character of Ranulf of Durham, not Thomas of York. But there is a simpler explanation that reconciles the evident hostility in Walter Daniel's tale with the generosity noted by Aelred and Richard of Hexham. Eilaf's comment may express a resentment commonly felt when family property and revenue fell into the hands of the church as a result of the twelfth-century reforms. Some donors to religious institutions may have simply seen the handwriting on the wall and concluded that since they were about to lose their property anyway, they might as well have the spiritual benefits of making an outwardly willing gift.[17]

Aelred's two brothers, Samuel and Aethelwold, apparently lived out their lives as laymen.[18] It is likely, given his family's long-standing ties with Durham, that Aelred himself was educated in the cathedral school there.[19] Aelred maintained close ties with the clergy of Durham throughout his life.

When Aelred was about fourteen years old, he joined the court of King David I, who had just succeeded his brother Alexander as king of Scotland. There he had as his companions the king's son Henry and stepson Waldef, and it is likely that he received further education with them. Later Aelred wrote of Prince Henry, "I lived with him from the very cradle, and we grew up as children together." He referred to the king himself as the one "whom I loved beyond all mortals."[20] When he grew older he attained the position of steward of the king's household.[21]

---

[17] Raine, *Priory*, 1:lxvii.

[18] Richard of Hexham, *Church of Hexham*, 55; Dutton, Introduction to *Life of Aelred*, 20.

[19] Dutton, "Historian's Historian," 423; Dutton, Introduction to *Life of Aelred*, 23; Mathers, *Manuscripts*, 239; P.-A. Burton, *Aelred de Rievaulx*, 98. For the view that Aelred was educated at Roxborough see Aelred Squire, "Aelred and King David," *Collectanea* 22 (1960): 357.

[20] Aelred, Gen Angl XIII; PL 195:737; CCCM 3:56; CF 56:121; Dutton, Introduction to *Life of Aelred*, 25.

[21] Vita A 2–4, pp. 2–9; CF 57:91–96; Powicke, Introduction to Vita A, xxxix–xli; Squire, *Aelred*, 14; Dom Alberic Stacpoole, "The Public Face of Aelred," *The Downside Review* 85 (1967): 189–90; R. L. Graeme Ritchie, *The Normans in Scotland* (Edinburgh: Edinburgh University Press, 1954), 249–55; Frederick M. Powicke, "The Dispensator of King David I," *The Scottish Historical Review* 23, no. 89 (1925): 34–40.

Opinions are divided as to exactly how much influence Aelred had in the royal household. For example, G. W. S. Barrow believes that Aelred did not enjoy the degree of responsibility that later stewards are known to have exercised and says that his work may have been solely to do with food service.[22] Others have been more willing to grant Aelred the steward's traditional position as the lord's representative and custodian of the household finances.[23] In the letter that now forms the introduction to Aelred's *Mirror of Charity*, Bernard of Clairvaux wrote that Aelred had sought to decline the assignment to write the work because he had insufficient literary skill, having "come to the desert not from the schools, but from the kitchens."[24] Aelred's warm remembrance of Prince Henry, however, and his lifelong friendship with David's stepson Waldef argue otherwise.

Typically Walter Daniel is of little help in resolving the question, for the sole incident from Aelred's years at court that he recorded concerned a knight who became jealous of Aelred's position and launched a public attack on him for his influence and his access to the king's treasure. The story, as Walter told it, was of course designed to show Aelred's patience and humility, which eventually won the man over and made him a lifelong friend.[25] It seems unlikely, however, that a knight in King David's service would notice, let alone become jealous of, a member of the household staff. Furthermore Aelred did represent David I on at least one diplomatic mission, the journey that took him to Walter Espec's castle and then to Rievaulx in 1134.[26]

Regardless of Aelred's exact degree of responsibility in the Scottish royal household, his years there may have allowed him to

[22] G. W. S. Barrow, Introduction to *Regesta Regum Scottorum*, vol. 1, *The Acts of Malcolm IV King of Scots 1153–1165 together with Scottish Royal Acts prior to 1153 not included in Sir Archibald Lawrie's Early Scottish Charters*, ed. G. W. S. Barrow (Edinburgh: Edinburgh University Press, 1960), 32–33.

[23] Dutton, Introduction to *Life of Aelred*, 24; Squire, "Aelred and King David," 357–58; P.-A. Burton, *Aelred*, 121–22.

[24] Aelred, Spec car, Prol. 2; CCCM 1:3; CF 17:70.

[25] Vita A 2–3, pp. 5–7; CF 57:92–95.

[26] Vita A 5, p. 10; CF 57:96.

become acquainted with the great magnates of the north. Robert de Bruce, William Peverel, Walter de Gant, Walter Espec, Alan de Percy, Eustace fitz John, and Malise of Strathearn are all known to have witnessed or received charters of David I between the time of Aelred's arrival in 1124 and his departure for Rievaulx in 1134.[27] These were some of the magnates who would not only shape the turbulent politics of the north throughout Aelred's lifetime but would also become the guardians and benefactors of Rievaulx Abbey.

Scotland under David I

The Scotland where Aelred arrived in his fourteenth year was very far from being the unified and independent country that it later became, either politically or ecclesiastically. David's father, King Malcolm III, had done homage to William the Conqueror in 1072.[28] After Malcolm's death in 1093, his three sons, Edgar, Alexander, and David, succeeded him in turn. The first of these, Edgar, was able to attain the throne only with the support of the Conqueror's son, William Rufus.[29] Ties between the two kingdoms were further strengthened by the marriage of King Henry I of England to Malcolm's daughter, Edith (Matilda), in 1100.[30]

[27] *The Charters of King David I: The Written Acts of David I King of Scots, 1124–53, and of His Son Henry Earl of Northumberland, 1139–52*, ed. G. W. S. Barrow (Woodbridge: Boydell, 1999), Robert de Bruce, nos. 16, 23–25, 27–28, 30–31, 34, 41, 45–46, 49. William Peverel, no. 28. Walter de Gant, no. 29. Walter Espec, no. 46. Alan de Percy, no. 16. Eustace fitz John, nos. 16, 29. Malise of Strathearn, nos. 33, 44.

[28] *The Anglo-Saxon Chronicle*, ed. and trans. Michael Swanton (New York: Routledge, 1998), AD 1072; Richard D. Oram, *David I: The King Who Made Scotland* (Stroud, Gloucestershire: Tempus Publishing Ltd., 2004), 30–31.

[29] *Anglo-Saxon Chronicle*, AD 1093; William of Malmesbury, *Gesta Regum Anglorum: The History of the English Kings*, ed. and trans. R. A. B. Mynors, R. M. Thomson, and M. Winterbottom, 2 vols. (Oxford: Clarendon Press, 1998), 1:724–27; Orderic Vitalis, *The Ecclesiastical History*, ed. and trans. Marjorie Chibnall, 6 vols. (Oxford: Clarendon Press, 1969–1980), 4:274–75; Oram, *David I*, 39–48.

[30] Eadmer, *Historia Novorum in Anglia*, ed. Martin Rule, RS 81 (London: Longmans, 1884), 121–25; Saint Anselm, *Epistolae*, in *Sancti Anselmi Cantuariensis Archiepiscopi Opera Omnia*, 6 vols. (Stuttgart-Bad Canstatt: Friedrich Frommann Verlag, 1963–1968), nos. 177, 242–43; *Councils and Synods with Other Documents Relating to*

Edith's younger brother, David, spent his young adulthood at the English court.[31] He got his first taste of political power when he received the territory of Cumbria in southern Scotland, apparently a deathbed bequest from his brother Edgar, who died in 1107.[32] In late 1113 David made an advantageous English marriage with the widowed Matilda de Senlis, countess of Huntingdon and Northamptonshire.[33] His second brother, King Alexander, performed military service with Henry I in 1114 on the English king's campaign in Wales against Gruffudd ap Cynan, and it is possible that his marriage to Henry's illegitimate daughter Sibylla took place at this time.[34]

The close ties between the two kingdoms had several implications. On the positive side, harmonious relations between the two royal families contributed to peace on the border. But the same close ties called into question the status of the ruler of the Scots. Were Edgar, Alexander, and David really independent monarchs, or were they merely vassals of the English king, eternally bound by ties of fealty to do his bidding? The question was most acute for the third brother, David, who was indisputably the man of Henry I of England for the counties of Huntingdon and Northampton-

---

the English Church, ed. D. Whitelock, M. Brett, and C. N. L. Brooke, 2 vols. (Oxford: Clarendon Press, 1981), vol. 1, pt. 2, no. 111, pp. 661–67; John of Worcester, *The Chronicle of John of Worcester*, ed. R. R. Darlington and P. McGurk, trans. P. McGurk and Jennifer Bray, 3 vols. (Oxford: Clarendon Press, 1995–98), 3:96–97; Vaughn, *Anselm of Bec and Robert of Meulan* (Berkeley, CA: University of California Press, 1987), 223–24; Oram, *David I*, 50–57.

[31] Orderic Vitalis, *Ecclesiastical History*, 4:274–75; *Regesta Regum Anglo-Normannorum 1066–1154*, vol. 2, *Regesta Henrici Primi 1100–1135*, ed. Charles Johnson and H. A. Cronne (Oxford: Clarendon Press, 1956), no. 818a; Aelred, Gen Angl XIII; PL 195:736; CCCM 3:55; CF 56:119–20; Lois L. Huneycutt, *Matilda of Scotland: A Study in Medieval Queenship* (Woodbridge: Boydell Press, 2003), 94–95; Oram, *David I*, 57–58.

[32] Oram, *David I*, 60.

[33] Orderic Vitalis, *Ecclesiastical History*, 4:274–75; Jocelin of Furness, *Vita S. Waltheni Abbatis, Acta Sanctorum*, August 3, 248; Huneycutt, *Matilda*, 89; Oram, *David I*, 64–65.

[34] Oram, *David I*, 65; *Brut y Tywysogion or The Chronicle of the Princes, Red Book of Hergest Version*, ed. and trans. Thomas Jones (Cardiff: University of Wales Press, 1955), 79.

shire. As the king's brother-in-law, raised at the English court, married to an English wife, and possessed of vast lands in England and on the border, David's outlook was more English than Scottish, and his closest associations were with his Anglo-Norman neighbors and friends, rather than with the native Gaelic lords over whom he ruled. David's mother, Saint Margaret, was known for introducing the barbaric Scots to modern European customs, and David himself is often credited with "feudalizing" Scotland.[35] While modern historians have tended to praise these innovations, the native magnates sometimes failed to agree and often looked on David as an outsider, viewing his new ideas with suspicion. The details of David's struggle to enforce his will on the mighty lords of Scotland[36] do not form a major part of Aelred's story, although he clearly had a close relationship with one of these men, Fergus of Galloway.

The Scottish Church

The challenge to Scottish unity and independence was exacerbated by the peculiar status of the Scottish church. The situation dated from at least 1070 when Archbishop Lanfranc of Canterbury refused to consecrate Thomas of Bayeux to the archbishopric of York because he had refused to make a written profession of obedience, similar to the ones that were routinely given by Canterbury's suffragan bishops.[37] At the same time, Thomas also claimed the allegiance of the bishoprics of Worcester, Dorchester, and Lichfield, which had always been subject to Canterbury. This was a crucial point for Thomas, because if those bishoprics did

---

[35] Oram, *David I*, 7–8; Squire, "Aelred and King David," 362–65.

[36] Oram, *David I*, 89–119.

[37] Hugh the Chanter, *History of the Church of York*, 6–9; William of Malmesbury, *Gesta Pontificum Anglorum: The History of the English Bishops*, ed. and trans. M. Winterbottom and R. M. Thomson, 2 vols. (Oxford: Clarendon Press, 2007), 1:50–53; H. E. J. Cowdrey, "Lanfranc, the Papacy, and the See of Canterbury," in *Lanfranco di Pavia e l'Europa del secolo XI: nel IX centenario della morte (1089–1989): atti del convegno internazionale di studi (Pavia, Almo Collegio Borromeo, 21–24 settembre 1989)*, ed. G. D'Onofrio (Rome: Herder Editrice e Libreria, 1993), 460–62.

not belong to York, he would have only the bishop of Durham subject to him, and thus he would not have enough suffragans to perform his own consecrations without the loan of someone whose allegiance was to Canterbury.

William the Conqueror was at first inclined to support Thomas, since there was no precedent for Lanfranc's demand, but Lanfranc prevailed upon him to refer the matter to Rome. In the meantime, Thomas consented to make a profession of obedience to Lanfranc personally, so the latter was willing to consecrate him as archbishop. The two men journeyed together to Rome in the fall of 1071, where Pope Alexander II granted them their palliums. Because the question of the allegiance of the three bishoprics touched upon the king's interests, Alexander referred both matters back to England for settlement, sending his own representative, the legate Hubert, along with the returning archbishops.[38] The matter was decided generally in Lanfranc's favor at meetings held at Easter 1072, with all three of the disputed bishoprics being granted to Canterbury. By way of compensation, Thomas and his successors received jurisdiction over Scotland.[39]

The Scottish bishops were therefore subject to an archbishop whose loyalties lay not in Scotland but in England, a situation no independent ruler could be expected to tolerate. This issue was to bedevil David even before his ascent to the throne in 1124, from the time of his revival of the see of Glasgow in 1113 with the appointment of his personal chaplain John as bishop.[40] In 1122, Archbishop Thurstan of York suspended John from office for refusing to accept his authority, and when John's appeal to Rome

[38] William of Malmesbury, *Gesta Pontificum*, 52–55; Cowdrey, "Lanfranc, the Papacy, and the See of Canterbury," 463–64.

[39] *Regesta Regum Anglo-Normannorum: The Acta of William I (1066–1087)*, ed. David Bates (Oxford: Clarendon Press, 1998), nos. 67–68, 177; Lanfranc, *The Letters of Lanfranc Archbishop of Canterbury*, ed. and trans. Helen Clover and Margaret Gibson (Oxford: Clarendon Press, 1979), no. 3; Cowdrey, "Lanfranc, the Papacy, and the See of Canterbury," 464–71; Martin Brett, *The English Church Under Henry I* (Oxford: Oxford University Press, 1975), 14–19.

[40] Oram, *David I*, 68; Brett, *English Church*, 19–25; J. C. Dickinson, *The Origins of the Austin Canons and Their Introduction into England* (London: SPCK, 1950), 245–50.

was rejected, John left on an extended pilgrimage to the Holy Land. Pope Calixtus II recalled him early in 1123 and ordered to him to return to his diocese.[41]

In 1125 John and a Scottish delegation traveled to Rome in company with Archbishops William of Corbeil of Canterbury and Thurstan of York. The two English archbishops were going to obtain the newly elected William's pallium from the pope. The Scottish delegation also sought a pallium for Bishop Robert of St. Andrews. Not only did the Scots fail in this attempt, but Thurstan of York took the opportunity to raise the issue of John's refusal to make his profession of obedience. John neatly sidestepped the issue by maintaining that he was part of a delegation on a different matter and could not be expected to answer on another subject. A date in 1127 was set to reconsider the matter, but by then Henry I of England and David of Scotland had reached their own compromise. King Henry convinced Thurstan to drop his insistence on John's profession of obedience and to consecrate Robert of St. Andrews without a profession of obedience. Richard Oram suggests that this agreement was in return for David's agreeing to accept Henry's daughter Matilda as heir to the English throne after the death of Henry's only son in 1120.[42] This temporary compromise solved the immediate problems, but the dispute was renewed after Henry I's death,[43] and the larger issue of the subjugation of the Scottish church to York continued to fester.

David I is often given credit for founding most of the bishoprics in Scotland, but information about the organization of the church in Scotland is scanty before his reign. Gordon Donaldson has shown that most of the episcopal sees were in existence before the twelfth century, although some may have been without a

[41] Oram, *David I*, 149; Simeon of Durham, *Opera Omnia*, ed. Thomas Arnold, 2 vols., RS 75 (London: Longmans, 1882–1885), 2:264; *Historians of the Church of York and Its Archbishops*, ed. James Raine, 3 vols., RS 71 (London: Longmans, 1879–1894), 3:28–47. For other letters on this subject see Raine, *Historians*, no. 22, pp. 40–41, nos. 24–27, pp. 44–47.

[42] Oram, *David I*, 79–81, 149–50.

[43] Oram, *David I*, 125–26; *Historians of the Church of York*, 3:49, 66–67.

bishop or otherwise in decline.[44] Under the leadership of David, a number of Scottish sees were either established or revitalized, and in general these bishops held themselves aloof from both Canterbury and York. Bishops Cormac of Dunkeld, Gregory of Moray, and Macbeth of Ross are first mentioned as witnesses to a charter of David in favor of Dunfermline Abbey in 1128.[45] The see of Brechin was in existence as early as 1124, when David granted a market to the bishop, but the recipient's name was not recorded.[46] Gregory of Dunkeld, Edward of Aberdeen, Andrew of Caithness, William of Moray, Samson of Brechin, and Symeon of Ross all appear in royal charters; we have no information about their consecrations.[47]

In 1155 Pope Adrian IV issued a bull ordering the Scottish bishops to obey the archbishop of York; this is the first mention of Bishop Lawrence of Dunblane.[48] As late as 1159, Bishop William of Moray and Nicholas, chamberlain to David's grandson, King Malcolm IV, went to Rome bearing a petition asking that the bishop of St. Andrews be made the metropolitan for Scotland. The tide was beginning to turn, for although Pope Alexander III turned down their request, he did appoint William of Moray as his legate for Scottish affairs.[49] Aelred must have been keenly interested in

[44] Gordon Donaldson, "Scottish Bishops' Sees Before the Reign of David I," *Proceedings of the Society of Antiquaries of Scotland* 87 (1952–1953): 106–17; Oram, *David I*, 156–58.

[45] *Charters of King David I*, no. 33; D. E. R. Watt, *Series Episcoporum Ecclesiae Catholicae Occidentalis ab Initio usque ad Annum MCXCVIII, Series VI, Britannia, Scotia et Hibernia, Scandinavia*, Tomus I, *Ecclesia Scoticana* (Stuttgart: Anton Hiersemann, 1991), 43, 66, 72.

[46] *Charters of King David I*, no. 243.

[47] *Charters of King David I*, Gregory of Dunkeld, nos. 86–87, Edward of Aberdeen, nos. 171, 173, Andrew of Caithness, nos. 132, 136, 156–57, William of Moray, nos. 214–15, Samson of Brechin, no. 136, Symeon of Ross, no. 171; Watt, *Ecclesia Scoticana*, 6–7, 16, 31–32, 43–44, 66–67, 73. In general, see Raymonde Foreville, *L'Église et la Royauté en Angleterre sous Henri II Plantagenet (1154–1189)* (Paris: Bloud and Gay, 1943), 64–69.

[48] *Regesta Pontificum Romanorum ad Annum Post Christum Natum 1198*, ed. P. Jaffé, rev. W. Wattenbach, S. Loewenfeld, F. Kaltenbrunner, and P. Ewald, 2 vols. (Leipzig: Veit, 1885–1888), no. 10000; *Councils and Ecclesiastical Documents Relating to Great Britain and Ireland*, ed. Arthur West Haddan and William Stubbs, 3 vols. (Oxford: Clarendon Press, 1869–1878), 2:231; Watt, *Ecclesia Scoticana*, 37.

[49] Barrow, Introduction to *Acts of Malcolm IV*, 14; Watt, *Ecclesia Scoticana*, 66–67.

these events from his days at the Scottish court, and his travels to visit Dundrennan and Melrose, the Scottish daughter houses of Rievaulx, would have afforded him the opportunity to keep abreast of further developments.

Aelred Comes to Rievaulx

Perhaps Aelred even had a small role to play in the ecclesiastical politics of the day, for it was a mission from King David to Archbishop Thurstan of York that brought him to the gates of the new abbey of Rievaulx in 1134. Walter Daniel was vague about the details of the trip, stating only that while Aelred was visiting the archbishop on some unspecified business, an unnamed close friend told him about the monastery, which had been founded only two years earlier. Wanting to learn more, Aelred set out for Helmsley, where the abbey's founder, Walter Espec, offered him hospitality for the night and took him to visit Rievaulx the next day. Aelred spent the day with the monks, returning to Walter Espec's castle that evening. The next morning Aelred started for home, but when he reached the road leading to the abbey gates, he was seized by an irresistible urge to turn aside and become a part of the new community.[50] Walter Daniel's emphasis was on the working of the Holy Spirit in Aelred's soul to bring about his sudden conversion. He remarked that as the young man turned down the road toward the abbey he was "aflame with the heat of the Holy Spirit,"[51] inviting comparison with the conversions of Saint Paul and Saint Martin of Tours. Marsha L. Dutton has suggested, however, that the business that brought Aelred to Rievaulx in fact concerned his own future, part of a plan engineered by King David, Archbishop Thurstan, and Walter Espec with the goal of bringing the talented young man to the new community at Rievaulx.[52]

[50] Vita A 5–7, pp. 10–16; CF 57:96–100.
[51] Vita A 7, p. 15; CF 57:99.
[52] Marsha L. Dutton, "The Conversion and Vocation of Aelred of Rievaulx: A Historical Hypothesis," in *England in the Twelfth Century: Proceedings of the 1988 Harlaxton Symposium*, ed. Daniel Williams (Woodbridge: Boydell Press, 1990),

The Anglo-Norman Civil War

Aelred had only been at Rievaulx for about a year when the death of King Henry I in December 1135 plunged England into turmoil. In November 1120 the White Ship had sunk in the cold waters of the English Channel, taking with it the flower of the Anglo-Norman nobility, including King Henry's only son and heir, William.[53] The widowed king had quickly taken a new bride in the hope of producing a male heir, but his marriage to Adeliza of Louvain remained childless. So in 1127 Henry had compelled his magnates, including David of Scotland, to swear to accept his daughter, Empress Matilda, the widow of Holy Roman Emperor Henry V, as his heir if he left no male child to succeed him.[54] Nevertheless, when Henry's death became known, his nephew Stephen of Blois violated his oath, dashed across the English Channel from Boulogne, where he was count, and, with the assistance of his younger brother, Bishop Henry of Winchester, seized the treasury at Winchester and had himself crowned king in Westminster Abbey on Christmas Day, 1135.[55]

31–49. See also Pierre-André Burton, "Aux origines de l'expansion anglaise de Cîteaux: La fondation de Rievaulx et la conversion d'Aelred," *Collectanea Cisterciensia* 61 (1999): 186–214, 248–90, here 186–214; Pierre-André Burton, "Aelred face à l'histoire et à ses historiens: Autour de l'actualité Aelrédienne," *Collectanea Cisterciensia* 58 (1996): 161–93, here 164–69.

[53] Hugh the Chanter, *History of the Church of York*, 164–65; Orderic Vitalis, *Ecclesiastical History*, 6:296–301; John of Worcester, *Chronicle*, 3:146–49; Henry of Huntingdon, *Historia Anglorum: The History of the English People*, ed. and trans. Diana Greenway (Oxford: Clarendon Press, 1996), 466–67; Simeon of Durham, *Opera Omnia*, 2:259; William of Malmesbury, *Gesta Regum*, 760–63; *Liber Monasterii de Hyda*, ed. Edward Edwards, RS 45 (London: Longmans, 1866), 321; Judith A. Green, *Henry I: King of England and Duke of Normandy* (Cambridge: Cambridge University Press, 2006), 164–67; C. Warren Hollister, *Henry I*, edited and completed by Amanda Clark Frost (New Haven, CT: Yale University Press, 2001), 276–79.

[54] John of Worcester, *Chronicle*, 3:166–67; Simeon of Durham, *Opera Omnia*, 2:281; William of Malmesbury, *Historia Novella*, ed. Edmund King, trans. K. R. Potter (Oxford: Clarendon Press, 1998), 6–9; Henry of Huntingdon, *Historia*, 706–9; *Anglo-Saxon Chronicle*, AD 1127; *Gesta Stephani*, ed. and trans. K. R. Potter, rev. R. H. C. Davis (Oxford: Clarendon Press, 1976), 10–11.

[55] *Liber Eliensis*, ed. E. O. Blake, Camden 3rd ser. 92 (London: Royal Historical Society, 1962), 285–86; William of Malmesbury, *Historia Novella*, 26–29; *Gesta Stephani*, 4–13.

David I invaded England for the first time in early 1136, capturing an assortment of castles and the major city of Carlisle in southern Cumbria. Years later, when Aelred came to write his *Lament for David I*, he acknowledged that when David invaded England in support of his niece's claim to the throne, he was being faithful to the oath that he had sworn in 1127.[56] Modern historians, however, have rightly questioned how much David was motivated by loyalty to Empress Matilda, suggesting instead that the overriding consideration was the desire for territorial gain.[57] In any case, Stephen responded to David's aggression by taking the earldom of Huntingdon into his own hands. When the Treaty of Durham ended the hostilities, however, David's son Henry was granted the earldom of Huntingdon and allowed to remain in possession of Carlisle. Henry subsequently attended Stephen's court and was warmly received by the king, but after Archbishop William of Canterbury and Earl Ranulf II of Chester accused Henry of treason, David called him home to Scotland.[58]

The insult to the young Henry was not forgotten, and David invaded Northumberland again in early 1137. This time Archbishop Thurstan of York managed to negotiate a six-month truce, allowing Stephen time to return from an expedition to the continent aimed at securing his Norman lands. When the truce expired in November, David renewed his demand that the earldom of Northumberland be awarded to Henry, a request Stephen refused to grant.[59] In January 1138 David renewed the conflict for the third time.

---

[56] Aelred, Lam D V; CCCM 3:11; (not in PL 195); CF 56:54.

[57] Oram, *David I*, 127, 154–55, 167–89; Marjorie Chibnall, *The Empress Matilda: Queen Consort, Queen Mother and Lady of the English* (Oxford: Blackwell, 1991), 77; Keith J. Stringer, *The Reign of Stephen: Kingship, Warfare and Government in Twelfth-Century England* (New York: Routledge, 1993), 13; Keith J. Stringer, "State-building in Twelfth-Century Britain: David I, King of Scots and Northern England," in *Government, Religion and Society in Northern England, 1000–1700*, ed. John C. Appleby and Paul Dalton (Stroud: Sutton Publishing, 1997), 40–62.

[58] John of Hexham, *Historia*, in *Symeonis Monachi opera omnia*, ed. Thomas Arnold, 2 vols., RS 75 (London: Longmans, 1882–1885), 2:287; Oram, *David I*, 122–25; Oram, *The Lordship of Galloway* (Edinburgh: John Donald, 2000), 65.

[59] John of Hexham, *Historia*, 2:288; Oram, *David I*, 127.

Aelred's home in the north of England suffered severely during these invasions. In an account of the devastation wrought by the Scots, Richard of Hexham wrote that they murdered the old, the sick, pregnant women, and children without distinction, and that in crossing the Tyne River they laid waste the greater part of the territory of Saint Cuthbert of Durham. He also noted that these attacks completely destroyed the newly founded Cistercian monastery of Newminster, near Morpeth. According to him, the church of Hexham itself was preserved by the power of its saints, Andrew the apostle, Wilfrid, Acca, Alchmund, and Eata, and became a haven for refugees fleeing the attacks.[60]

With Stephen occupied in the south, Thurstan of York rallied the English forces to withstand the invasion. The climactic battle, fought August 22, 1138, took place less than twenty miles from Rievaulx. David I made a crucial error in allowing lightly armed Galwegian foot soldiers to lead the charge, because they proved no match for mounted English knights supported by archers. The Scots, however, remained in possession of much of Carlisle, Cumberland, and Northumberland,[61] and despite his loss, David continued his siege of Walter Espec's castle at Wark. The garrison was reduced to desperate straits, the inhabitants eventually eating their horses, before the castle surrendered.[62]

A second treaty was concluded at Durham early in 1139, one that handed over the earldom of Northumberland to David's son Henry and confirmed him in possession of Carlisle, Cumberland,

---

[60] Richard of Hexham, *De Gestis Regis Stephani et de Bello Standardo*, in *Chronicles of the Reigns of Stephen, Henry II., and Richard I.*, ed. Richard Howlett, 4 vols., RS 82 (London: Longmans, 1884–1890), 3:151–59; Oram, *David I*, 129–36.

[61] John of Hexham, *Historia*, 2:292–95; Richard of Hexham, *De Gestis*, 159–60; Robert of Torigny, *Chronica*, in *Chronicles of the Reigns of Stephen, Henry II., and Richard I.*, ed. Richard Howlett, 4 vols., RS 82 (London: Longmans, 1884–1890), 4:135; Henry of Huntingdon, *Historia*, 712; John of Worcester, *Chronicle*, 3:252–57; Donald Nicholl, *Thurstan, Archbishop of York (1114–1140)* (York: Stonegate Press, 1964), 221–28; Ritchie, *Normans in Scotland*, 256–70; John Beeler, *Warfare in England, 1066–1189* (Ithaca, NY: Cornell University Press, 1966), 84–95; Oram, *David I*, 137–41.

[62] Oram, *David I*, 142; Richard of Hexham, *De Gestis*, 171–72; Powicke, Introduction to Vita A, xlvi.

and Huntingdon. Even though certain key fortresses, notably Bamburgh and Newcastle, remained in Stephen's hands, the treaty gave David almost everything he had set out to achieve by his invasion, despite the trouncing that he had received in the battle of the Standard.[63] From this time forward, the north enjoyed relative peace, at least on the secular front.

Aelred was only a young monk at Rievaulx during these years, but even then he may have been more than a bystander at some of these tumultuous events. Walter Daniel recorded that because Aelred "revealed an unexpected ease in the solution of hard, difficult, and important problems," Abbot William "determined to admit him to the intimacies of his counsel and to the discussion of matters closely affecting the household of Rievaulx."[64] The details of these important matters remain unknown, but Richard of Hexham recorded Aelred's presence along with William at Durham when Eilaf surrendered his property at Hexham to the Augustinians.[65] Of course his presence was only to be expected, since Aelred was the son who might have expected to inherit the benefice if the old ways had prevailed. A much more telling sign of Aelred's involvement in public affairs is the possibility that he also accompanied William to Wark to negotiate the surrender of Walter Espec's castle there in 1138.[66]

At least on the secular front, northern England enjoyed relative peace for some years after the conclusion of the Treaty of Durham in 1139, but fighting continued in the south. The forces of Empress Matilda captured King Stephen at the battle of Lincoln in February 1141, and for a brief time the English church under the leadership of Henry of Winchester accepted her as queen.[67] However, when

[63] John of Hexham, *Historia*, 2:300; Oram, *David I*, 143–44.

[64] Vita A 14, p. 23; CF 57:106.

[65] Richard of Hexham, *Church of Hexham*, 1:55–56.

[66] Richard of Hexham, *Bello Standardo*, 171–72; Powicke, Introduction to Vita A xlvi; Oram, *David I*, 142.

[67] John of Hexham, *Historia*, 2:307–8; Orderic Vitalis, *Ecclesiastical History*, 6:538–47; William of Malmesbury, *Historia Novella*, 80–89; *Gesta Stephani*, 110–19; John of Worcester, *Chronicle*, 3:292–95; Henry of Huntingdon, *Historia*, 724–39; Gervase of

Matilda arrived in London for her coronation in June, things immediately began to go wrong. When Stephen's queen, Matilda of Boulogne, appeared before the city gates with an army of Flemish mercenaries, the Londoners, traditionally loyal to Stephen, rose in rebellion, and the empress and her advisors fled to Oxford.[68]

In a battle fought on September 14, the queen's forces captured Earl Robert of Gloucester, the empress's half brother, chief advisor, and commander of her forces.[69] Henry of Winchester once again took the lead in brokering peace negotiations, with the result that the two sides exchanged their prisoners in November.[70] In December, Bishop Henry, again acting in his capacity as papal legate, called a council at which the church returned its allegiance to Stephen.[71] The situation was now essentially the same as it had been at the beginning of the year, before the battle of Lincoln. From this point forward, Stephen and the empress settled down to a siege warfare contest in which each tried to capture the castles controlled by the other, primarily in the central and western parts of the country.[72]

Robert of Gloucester died on October 31, 1147, and finding it impossible to remain in England without his leadership and sup-

---

Canterbury, *Chronica*, in *Chronicles of the Reigns of Stephen, Henry II.*, and Richard I., ed. William Stubbs, 2 vols., RS 82 (London: Longmans, 1879–1880), 1:113–18; *Liber Eliensis*, 320–21; H. A. Cronne, "Ranulf de Gernons, Earl of Chester, 1129–53," *Transactions of the Royal Historical Society*, 4th ser. 20 (1937): 103–34; Chibnall, *Empress Matilda*, 97–98; Edmund King, "A Week in Politics: Oxford, Late July 1141," in *King Stephen's Reign, 1135–1154*, ed. Paul Dalton and Graeme J. White (Woodbridge: Boydell Press, 2008), 61–63.

[68] See Jean Truax, "Winning over the Londoners," *Anglo-Norman Studies* 8 (1996): 43–61, here 50–59. William of Malmesbury, *Historia Novella*, 96–99; *Gesta Stephani*, 122–27; R. H. C. Davis, *King Stephen, 1135–1154*, 3rd ed. (London: Longmans, 1990), 54–57.

[69] William of Malmesbury, *Historia Novella*, 100–107; *Gesta Stephani*, 126–37; John of Worcester, *Chronicle*, 3:298–303; Gervase of Canterbury, *Chronica*, 1:120–21.

[70] William of Malmesbury, *Historia Novella*, 118–21; Gervase of Canterbury, *Chronica*, 1:122; Paul Dalton, "Churchmen and the Promotion of Peace in King Stephen's Reign," *Viator* 31 (2000): 87–88.

[71] William of Malmesbury, *Historia Novella*, 108–11; *Councils and Synods*, vol. 1, pt. 2, no. 143, pp. 792–94; Gervase of Canterbury, *Chronica*, 1:122.

[72] William of Malmesbury, *Historia Novella*, 126–33; *Gesta Stephani*, 138–205; Davis, *King Stephen*, 63–95.

port, Empress Matilda returned to Normandy at the beginning of 1148.[73] While her campaign in England had been largely unsuccessful, her husband, Geoffrey of Anjou, had gained complete control of Normandy, so providing a base for a renewed invasion of England at some future date.[74] Matilda's son Henry invaded England in 1149 and received his knighthood from David I at Carlisle on May 22.[75] The Cistercian archbishop, Henry Murdac of York, visited David at Carlisle during this time for the knighting of the young prince.[76] Henry, David, and Earl Ranulf of Chester then joined forces for an attack on York. Stephen's lightning response foiled their plans, but Henry escaped to Hereford and wreaked considerable havoc in the western counties before departing for Normandy in January 1150.[77]

When Henry invaded England for the third time in 1153, the English barons forced the warring factions to make peace.[78] The resulting Treaty of Winchester provided that Stephen would remain king for his lifetime, with Henry then succeeding to the crown as King Henry II.[79] Stephen died less than a year later, putting an end to the nineteen-year-long civil war.

[73] John of Hexham, *Historia*, 2:321; *Gesta Stephani*, 210–11; Gervase of Canterbury, *Chronica*, 1:131, 133; Davis, *King Stephen*, 94–95.

[74] Davis, *King Stephen*, 95.

[75] *Gesta Stephani*, 214–17; Henry of Huntingdon, *Historia*, 754–55; John of Hexham, *Historia*, 2:323; Gervase of Canterbury, *Chronica*, 1:140–41; Emily Amt, *The Accession of Henry II in England: Royal Government Restored, 1149–1159* (Woodbridge: Boydell Press, 1993), 7–9; Dalton, "Churchmen," 89–90.

[76] Oram, *David I*, 155, 187–89.

[77] John of Hexham, *Historia*, 2:22–23; *Gesta Stephani*, 216–25; Henry of Huntingdon, *Historia*, 754–55.

[78] William of Newburgh, *Historia Rerum Anglicarum*, in *Chronicles of the Reigns of Stephen, Henry II., and Richard I.*, ed. Richard Howlett, 4 vols., RS 82 (London: Longmans, 1884–1890), 1:88–90; Gervase of Canterbury, *Chronica*, 1:151–56; Robert of Torigny, *Chronica*, 4:171–74; *Gesta Stephani*, 230–39; Henry of Huntingdon, *Historia*, 764–71; Z. N. and C. N. L. Brooke, "Henry II, Duke of Normandy and Aquitaine," EHR 61, no. 239 (1946): 86–88; Amt, *Accession of Henry II*, 11–15; Graeme J. White, "The End of Stephen's Reign," *History* 75, no. 1 (1990): 5–10; Donald Matthew, *King Stephen* (London: Hambledon Press, 2002), 207–13.

[79] *Regesta Regum Anglo-Normannorum 1066–1154*, vol. 3, *Regesta Regis Stephani ac Mathildis Imperatricis ac Gaufridi et Henrici Ducum Normannorum 1135–1154*, ed.

Chaos in the Northern Church

Though the north enjoyed several years of relative freedom from secular disturbance after the Scottish invasion of 1138, ecclesiastical affairs were not so peaceful. When Bishop Geoffrey Rufus of Durham died in 1141, the Scottish chancellor, William Cumin, intruded himself into the bishopric and took over the administration of the see. Supported by King David and many of the northern barons, he attempted to force the monks of the cathedral chapter to elect him as bishop, but they refused on the grounds that a full canonical election could not be held without the permission of the archbishop of York and the papal legate, Henry of Winchester.[80] This response effectively left the decision to Henry of Winchester, since the archbishopric of York was technically vacant at the time.[81] King David personally accompanied a delegation from Durham to the English court, arriving just as his niece, the Empress Matilda, celebrated her triumphal entry into London after capturing Stephen at the battle of Lincoln. Henry of Winchester decreed that Cumin could not become the bishop without a canonical election by the Durham monks, but in spite of this decree, the empress prepared to invest Cumin with his ring and staff in defiance of the agreement on investitures concluded between Henry I and Saint Anselm in 1105.[82] On the very day that the ceremony was to take

---

H. A. Cronne and R. H. C. Davis (Oxford: Clarendon Press, 1968), no. 272; John of Hexham, *Historia*, 2:331; Robert of Torigny, *Chronica*, 4:177; *Gesta Stephani*, 238–41; Gervase of Canterbury, *Chronica*, 1:156; William of Newburgh, *Historia*, 1:90–91; King, "Week in Politics," 75–79; White, "End of Stephen's Reign," 11–13.

[80] Simeon of Durham, *Opera Omnia*, 1:143–45, 161–63; John of Hexham, *Historia*, 2:312; Alan Young, *William Cumin: Border Politics and the Bishopric of Durham 1141–1144*, Borthwick Papers 54 (York: York University Press, 1978), 11–15; Alan Young, "The Bishopric of Durham in Stephen's Reign," in *Anglo-Norman Durham, 1093–1193*, ed. David Rollason, Margaret Harvey, and Michael Prestwich (Woodbridge: Boydell Press, 1994), 357–61.

[81] See below, 56–58.

[82] Eadmer, *Historia Novorum*, 164–66; Saint Anselm, *Epistolae*, nos. 364, 388–89; Vaughn, *Anselm of Bec and Robert of Meulan*, 289–92; Sally N. Vaughn, *St. Anselm and the Handmaidens of God: A Study of Anselm's Correspondence with Women* (Turnhout: Brepols, 2002), 244–46; R. W. Southern, *St. Anselm and His Biographer: A Study in Monastic Life and Thought, 1059–c. 1130* (Cambridge: Cambridge University Press,

place, however, the irate Londoners drove Matilda out of the city.[83] Cumin and his supporters returned to Durham with a letter from the empress endorsing Cumin's election, but a substantial number of the monks, including Archdeacon Rannulf and Prior Richard, remained adamantly against him. When King David returned to Scotland, he left Cumin in charge as castellan of the fortress at Durham, but Cumin began to act as though he were the bishop, among other things by receiving the homage of the barons who held land of the bishop and expelling his chief opponent, Archdeacon Rannulf. The archdeacon made his way back to Henry of Winchester, who responded by excommunicating Cumin.[84]

In 1143 an embassy to Rome returned with a mandate from Pope Innocent II ordering an election to be held within forty days of receipt of the letter. The election was duly held at York, despite Cumin's efforts to capture the electors on the road, and William de Sainte-Barbe, the dean of York, was elected bishop. Henry of Winchester consecrated him on June 20.[85] As the new bishop traveled to Durham, he acquired an army made up of a number of the barons of the bishopric who had become disillusioned with Cumin by this time.

There might have been a battle before the walls of Durham had Count Alan of Richmond not come to Cumin's aid, driving off Bishop William and his supporters.[86] Cumin discovered that

1963), 176–77; Lynn Barker, "Ivo of Chartres and Anselm of Canterbury," *Anselm Studies* 2, no. 2 (1988): 16–17; Norman F. Cantor, *Church, Kingship and Lay Investiture in England 1089–1135* (Princeton, NJ: Princeton University Press, 1958), 202–27; A. L. Poole, *From Domesday Book to Magna Carta, 1087–1216*, 2nd ed. (Oxford: Clarendon Press, 1955), 179; Henry Mayr-Harting, *Religion, Politics and Society in Britain, 1066–1272* (London: Longmans, 2011), 53–54.

[83] Simeon of Durham, *Opera Omnia*, 1:145; Young, *William Cumin*, 15–17; Chibnall, *Empress Matilda*, 138.

[84] Simeon of Durham, *Opera Omnia*, 1:145–46; Young, *William Cumin*, 18–20.

[85] Simeon of Durham, *Opera Omnia*, 1:148–50, 163; John of Hexham, *Historia*, 2:313–14; *Päpsturkunden in England*, ed. Walther Holtzmann, 3 vols. (Berlin: Weidmannsche Buchhandlung, 1930–1952), vol. 2, nos. 30–31; Young, *William Cumin*, 20–21, 41; Dalton, "Churchmen," 92–93.

[86] Simeon of Durham, *Opera Omnia*, 1:151–52, 163–66; John of Hexham, *Historia*, 2:314–15; Young, *William Cumin*, 21–22; Young, "Bishopric of Durham," 357–61.

some of the monks had been in communication with William, so he expelled them from the monastery and turned the cathedral itself into a barracks for his soldiers. Open violence broke out in the countryside around Durham until Archbishop William fitz Herbert of York arranged a truce dividing the revenues of the bishopric between William Cumin and William de Sainte-Barbe pending a further appeal to Rome.[87] In the meantime William de Sainte-Barbe enlisted the aid of Earl Henry of Northumberland, who, together with his father King David, finally convinced Cumin to abandon his now hopeless claim to the bishopric. William de Sainte-Barbe was finally able to take possession of his see on October 18, 1144.[88] Aelred does not seem to have played any direct role in the disputed episcopal election at Durham, but his family's long-standing ties with the cathedral chapter undoubtedly caused him to follow the situation closely.

However, the Cistercian Order took a leading role in another disputed episcopal election during this period, and Aelred himself played at least a small part in the affair. After the death of Archbishop Thurstan of York in 1140, King Stephen and Bishop Henry of Winchester wanted to place their nephew, Henry de Sully, abbot of Fécamp, in the position, but Pope Innocent II would not approve the election unless Henry de Sully resigned his abbacy, as he refused to do. The next candidate was Aelred's close friend Prior Waldef of Kirkham, who, as the stepson of King David of Scotland, could hardly have expected to meet with royal approval. Finally the choice lit upon another royal relative, the archdeacon of the East Riding and treasurer of York Minster, William fitz Herbert. King Stephen invested the archbishop-elect with the temporalities of the see right before his own capture at Lincoln on February 2, 1141, but the consecration did not take place.[89]

---

[87] Simeon of Durham, *Opera Omnia*, 1:152–55; Lawrence of Durham, *Dialogi Laurentii Dunelmensis Monachi ac Prioris*, Surtees Society 70 (Durham: Andrews and Co., 1880), 3–31; Young, *William Cumin*, 22–23.

[88] Simeon of Durham, *Opera Omnia*, 1:159–60, 167; John of Hexham, *Historia*, 2:316; Lawrence of Durham, *Dialogi*, 38–40; Young, *William Cumin*, 24–25.

[89] John of Hexham, *Historia*, 2:306–7; Gervase of Canterbury, *Chronica*, 1:123; R. L. Poole, "The Appointment and Deprivation of St. William, Archbishop of

By the end of the year, significant opposition to William fitz Herbert had surfaced, spearheaded by Abbots William of Rievaulx and Richard II of Fountains and including Priors Cuthbert and Waldef of the Augustinian houses of Guisborough and Kirkham and Master Robert of the Hospital of Saint Peter in York.[90] Henry of Winchester, as papal legate, heard the charge of simony that the group brought against William at the legatine council held in December 1141 and then referred the case to Rome. Bernard of Clairvaux entered the fray at this time, firing off an intemperate series of letters against William, one of which described him as "rotten from the soles of his feet to the crown of his head."[91] William fitz Herbert made his case to the pope in person, while his opponents were represented by one of the York archdeacons, Walter of London, and Aelred of Rievaulx.

As Walter Daniel told the story, when Aelred arrived in Rome he "expounded the business and brought it to conclusion with such energy, that the esteem and admiration which he won after his return was widespread."[92] Certainly this mission afforded Aelred the opportunity to make himself known to the powerful churchmen of his time, not only in Rome but also within his own order, since it is likely that he and Archdeacon Walter stopped off at Clairvaux to confer with Bernard on their way home. Perhaps it was at this time that Bernard, undoubtedly impressed with his order's new young recruit, commanded him to write his treatise

---

York," EHR 45, no. 178 (1930): 276–77; Christopher Norton, *St. William of York* (York: York Medieval Press, 2006), 80–81; Derek Baker, "*Viri Religiosi* and the York Election Dispute," in *Councils and Assemblies*, ed. G. J. Cuming and Derek Baker (Cambridge: Cambridge University Press, 1971), 87–100.

[90] John of Hexham, *Historia*, 2:311; David Knowles, "The Case of Saint William of York," *Cambridge Historical Journal* 5, no. 2 (1936): 162–65; Norton, *St. William*, 82; Poole, "Appointment," 277–78.

[91] Bernard, Ep 346 (SBOp 8:288–89; J187); C. H. Talbot, "New Documents in the Case of St. William of York," *Cambridge Historical Journal* 10, no. 1 (1950): 1–5; Christopher Holdsworth, "St. Bernard and England," *Anglo-Norman Studies* 8 (1986): 149–51; Norton, *St. William*, 82–83; Janet Burton, *The Monastic Order in Yorkshire, 1069–1215* (Cambridge: Cambridge University Press, 1999), 112–13.

[92] Vita A 14, p. 23; CF 57:107; P.-A. Burton, *Aelred*, 170–73.

The Mirror of Charity.[93] The journey, however, cannot be termed quite the unqualified success that Walter Daniel made it, for when Pope Innocent II returned his decision in April 1142, he said that he could not decide a case based on secondhand evidence and invited the five leaders of the northern religious houses to present their case in person during the next Lent.[94]

Nevertheless, Aelred's efforts seem to have been satisfactory to his superiors, since upon his return he was entrusted with the position of novice master at Rievaulx.[95] It was also at this time that, in Walter Daniel's words, "he began to write to various personages letters most lucid in sense and distinguished in style."[96] We do not know whether these letters concerned the still-disputed York election or something else entirely, but Walter's statement confirms that by this time, Aelred had begun to broaden his horizons and to look beyond the walls of Rievaulx to the role that he might play in the church at large. Within a bit more than a year Aelred moved up to yet another position of increased responsibility as the first abbot of Rievaulx's third daughter house, Saint Laurence of Revesby.[97] There is no evidence that Aelred played a further role in the York election dispute, but it is likely that he continued to follow the events, at least at a distance.

At any rate the pope heard the case again in March 1143 and referred it to his legate, Henry of Winchester, assisted by Bishop Robert of Hereford, for a final settlement, with certain guidelines. On the charge that William had been intruded into the see by order of the king, he decreed that the election should stand if the dean and two or three other chapter members would swear that William had been elected without royal coercion. On the further charges that William was guilty of fornication and simony, the

---

[93] Vita A 17, pp. 25–26; CF 57:109; Charles Dumont, Introduction to Aelred of Rievaulx, *Mirror of Charity,* trans. Elizabeth Connor, CF 17 (Kalamazoo, MI: Cistercian Publications, 1990), 55–58; P.-A. Burton, *Aelred,* 170–73.

[94] John of Hexham, *Historia,* 2:311; Norton, *St. William,* 83.

[95] Vita A 14, p. 23; CF 57:107.

[96] Vita A 17, p. 25; CF 57:108.

[97] Vita A 19, p. 27; CF 57:110.

pope ruled that if no one came forward with formal charges, the archbishop-elect could clear himself by swearing an oath on the gospels in company with four honorable men.[98] On the way home to England Abbot Richard of Fountains stopped off at Clairvaux, where he collected another batch of letters from Bernard to Henry of Winchester, Robert of Hereford, and the king and queen, urging the condemnation of William fitz Herbert.[99]

Henry of Winchester heard the case again at a legatine council held at Winchester in September 1143, and the appropriate oaths exonerating William fitz Herbert were sworn. The dean of the York cathedral chapter, however, William de Sainte-Barbe, was not present because, as was discussed above, he was on his way to assume his own new episcopal seat at Durham.

One final hurdle remained, for Archbishop William still had to obtain his pallium from the pope. The news, however, had not yet reached England that Innocent II had died and that a new pope, Celestine II, had been enthroned on the very day that William was consecrated, September 26, 1143. Celestine died in March 1144 and was succeeded by Lucius II. Bernard of Clairvaux appealed furiously against William fitz Herbert to both men, using as his excuse the fact that although other members of the York cathedral chapter had sworn that William's election had not been forced on the chapter by the king, William de Sainte-Barbe had not done so.[100] No response from Celestine is recorded, perhaps because he died before receiving Bernard's letter. Lucius II seems to have ignored Bernard, for he dispatched Cardinal Imar of Tusculum to England with William's pallium. Lucius died in February 1145, however, bringing the cardinal's legation to an end before his mission could be carried out.

---

[98] John of Hexham, *Historia*, 2:313; *Päpsturkunden in England*, vol. 2, no. 32; Knowles, "Saint William," 168–70; Norton, *St. William*, 83–85.

[99] Bernard, J195–98; Talbot, "New Documents," 6–7, 12–13. Not in SBOp. Also Norton, *St. William*, 85.

[100] Bernard, Epp 235–36 (SBOp 8:108–12; J202–3); also J204; not in SBOp.

William fitz Herbert made a third journey to Rome in an attempt to clear himself before the new pope, Eugenius III, a former monk of Clairvaux. Bernard immediately returned to the fray, writing furiously to his protégé.[101] In February 1146 Eugenius ruled that William fitz Herbert was to be suspended from office pending the oath of William de Sainte-Barbe validating his free election.[102] When this oath was not forthcoming, the pope ordered a new election, and when the electors were divided between Master Hilary, a canon lawyer with ties to Henry of Winchester, and Abbot Henry Murdac of Fountains, Eugenius conferred the appointment on his fellow Cistercian, Henry Murdac, performing the consecration himself.[103] William fitz Herbert therefore retired to Winchester, where he had grown up, taking refuge with Bishop Henry and the monks of the cathedral chapter.[104] Murdac was initially unable to take possession of his see, for King Stephen refused to accept him and retained the temporalities of the see in his own hands, while the king's deputy in the north, William of Aumâle, barred him from the city of York.[105] But a reconciliation was eventually achieved, and Henry Murdac was formally enthroned as archbishop of York on January 25, 1151.[106]

Relative peace endured for two years until the death of the bishop of Durham, William de Sainte-Barbe. The monks elected in his place Hugh du Puiset, William fitz Herbert's successor as

---

[101] Bernard, Epp 238–40, 252 (SBOp 8:115–24, 148–49; J205–8). For Bernard's relationship with Eugenius, see above, chap. 2:29–32.

[102] John of Hexham, *Historia*, 2:318; *Päpsturkunden in England*, vol. 2, no. 50; *Regesta Pontificum Romanorum*, no. 8863.

[103] John of Hexham, *Historia*, 2:320–21; Gervase of Canterbury, *Chronica*, 1:134–35; William of Newburgh, *Historia*, 1:56; *Vita Sancti Willelmi*, in *Historians of the Church of York and its Archbishops*, ed. James Raine, 3 vols., RS 71 (London: Longmans, 1879–1894), 2:272; Hugh of Kirkstall, *Narratio de Fundatione Fontanis Monasterii in Comitatu Eboracensis*, in *Memorials of the Abbey of St. Mary of Fountains*, ed. John Richard Walbran (London & Edinburgh: Andrews and Co. for the Surtees Society, 1863), 103.

[104] *Vita Sancti Willelmi*, 2:272–73; John of Hexham, *Historia*, 2:320; Norton, *St. William*, 124–27.

[105] John of Hexham, *Historia*, 2:322; William of Newburgh, *Historia*, 1:56; Hugh of Kirkstall, *Narratio*, 103.

[106] John of Hexham, *Historia*, 2:325; Norton, *St. William*, 127–31.

treasurer of York Minster and archdeacon of the East Riding, and a longtime supporter of the deposed archbishop. Because Henry Murdac could not stomach this insult, he overturned the election on the grounds of Hugh's youth and worldly character and excommunicated the prior of Durham and others. The citizens of York rose up against Murdac and drove him from the city, appealing to Archbishop Theobald of Canterbury as papal legate. While Murdac assented to his request to lift the excommunications, he refused to accept the election itself. First obtaining a letter of recommendation from Theobald, Hugh du Puiset appealed to Rome. While it is not likely that Eugenius III would have overturned the decision of Henry Murdac, Eugenius died in the fall of 1153, along with Bernard of Clairvaux and Murdac himself. The new pope, Anastasius IV, upheld the election and himself consecrated Hugh du Puiset.[107]

When the news of Murdac's death reached the royal court, a chapter meeting was hastily summoned, probably at Winchester, where the treaty between King Stephen and Duke Henry had just been concluded. With the approval of both the king and the duke, William fitz Herbert was elected archbishop of York and immediately set off for Rome, where he finally received his pallium from Anastasius IV. He then returned to York, where he made a ceremonial entry into the city on May 9, 1154. Archbishop William celebrated his first pontifical Mass on May 30, only to fall ill of a fever immediately thereafter.[108] After he died on June 8, his

[107] John of Hexham, *Historia*, 2:328–29; Gervase of Canterbury, *Chronica*, 1:157; William of Newburgh, *Historia*, 1:78–79; Simeon of Durham, *Opera Omnia*, 1:167; Geoffrey of Coldingham, *Historia Dunelmensis Scriptores Tres, Gaufridus de Coldingham, Robertus de Graystanes, et Willielmus de Chambre*, ed. James Raine (London: J. B. Nichols & Son, 1839), 6; Geoffrey V. Scammell, *Hugh du Puiset, Bishop of Durham* (Cambridge: Cambridge University Press, 1956), 12–16; Young, "Bishopric of Durham," 362–67.

[108] Gervase of Canterbury, *Chronica*, 1:158; William of Newburgh, *Historia*, 1:80–81; Robert of Torigny, *Chronica*, 4:178–79; *Chronica Pontificum Ecclesiae Eboracensis*, in *Historians of the Church of York and its Archbishops*, ed. James Raine, 3 vols., RS 71 (London: Longmans, 1879–1894), 2:397; *Vita Sancti Willelmi*, 2:277; Roger of Hoveden, *Chronica Magistri Rogeri de Houedene*, ed. William Stubbs, 4 vols., RS

chaplain, Symphorian, accused Osbert, the archdeacon of Richmond and one of William's bitterest enemies, of having poisoned the wine in the communion chalice. The case was initially heard in the royal court, but King Stephen died before rendering a decision, and Archbishop Theobald succeeded with some difficulty in having the case transferred to his own court because of Osbert's clerical status. The accused archdeacon appealed to Rome, and the case dragged on into the papacy of Alexander III (1159–1181). The details of the proceedings are lost, but Osbert lost his archdeaconry in 1157 and lived out the rest of his life as a layman.[109]

As a young monk, Aelred had little direct involvement in the stirring events of the mid-twelfth century, beyond a possible appearance at the surrender of Wark castle in 1138 and a brief role in the beginning stages of the York election dispute. Nevertheless, these occasions set his feet on the path of increased public responsibility and had profound effects on the northern church. The Scottish invasions of the mid-1130s devastated his homeland, and the climactic battle of the Standard took place only a few miles from his own monastery. At the same time, the death of Archbishop Thurstan in 1140 deprived the Cistercians and the other reformed religious orders of a faithful friend and patron, and the lack of stable authority at York and Durham thereafter

---

51 (London: Longmans, 1868–1871), 1:213; Hugh of Kirkstall, *Narratio*, 109–10. See Norton, *St. William*, 135–37, for the view that this was a new election and consecration rather than a restoration to the see and a repudiation of the actions of Eugenius III.

[109] Hugh of Kirkstall, *Narratio*, 110; William of Newburgh, *Historia*, 1:80–81; Roger of Hoveden, *Chronica*, 1:213; John of Salisbury, *The Letters of John of Salisbury, Volume One, The Early Letters (1153–1161)*, ed. and trans. W. J. Millor, S. J. Butler, and H. E. Butler, rev. C. N. L. Brooke (Oxford: Clarendon Press, 1986), nos. 16, 18, 25–26; Gilbert Foliot, *The Letters and Charters of Gilbert Foliot*, ed. Z. N. Brooke, Adrian Morey, and C. N. L. Brooke (Cambridge: Cambridge University Press, 1967), no. 127; Norton, *St. William*, 146–47; Knowles, "St. William," 175–77; Avrom Saltman, *Theobald, Archbishop of Canterbury* (New York: Greenwood Press, 1969), 122–25; Adrian Morey, "Canonist Evidence in the Case of St. William of York," *Cambridge Historical Journal* 10, no. 3 (1952): 352–53; *English Lawsuits from William I to Richard I*, ed. R. C. Van Caenegem, 2 vols. (London: Selden Society, 1990–91), vol. 2, no. 520, pp. 571–78.

threatened their continued peace and prosperity. It is against this unsettled background that Aelred began his abbatial career, first at Revesby and then at Rievaulx itself.

Chapter 4

Friends and Rivals

Aelred and His Neighbors

*Aelred. Come here now, brother, and tell me why you were sitting
all alone a little while ago at some distance from us, when I was
dealing with material affairs with those men of the flesh.*

*Walter. Who could preserve his patience through a whole day
seeing those agents of Pharaoh getting your full attention, while
we, to whom you are particularly indebted, were not able to gain
even so much as a word with you?*

*Aelred. But we must show kindness to such people, too, for either
we expect benefits from them or we fear their enmity.*[1]

In this conversation with the monk Walter at the beginning of
the second book of *Spiritual Friendship*, Aelred pictured himself
as occupied with the business of the monastery while his monks
waited impatiently for his attention. The tension is echoed in several of his sermons, in which he announced that he was bringing
his talk to a close because of the need to deal with secular business,
mentioning in one case that he was called away to meet with the

---

[1] Aelred, Spir amic 2:1–3; CCCM 1:302; CF 5:69; J. Stephen Russell, "The Dialogic
of Aelred's Spiritual Friendship," CSQ 47, no. 1 (2012): 50–52. Similarly Aelred,
Anima 1.1; CCCM 1:685; CF 22:35; Marsha L. Dutton, Introduction to *The Life of
Aelred of Rievaulx and the Letter to Maurice*, ed. and trans. Frederick M. Powicke,
CF 57 (Kalamazoo, MI: Cistercian Publications, 1994), 81. Note that Walter Daniel
identifies the monk Walter with himself in the *Vita Aelredi* (Vita A 32, p. 41; CF
57:121), but Aelred does not identify him as such in *Spiritual Friendship*.

archbishop.[2] These comments reflect the frustration that Aelred and his monks must often have felt as the affairs of the outside world intruded on the peace and quiet of their abbey. But they must also have realized that they, and all cloistered religious, relied for their support on the generosity of the believing laity. In a sermon for the birthday of Saint Benedict, certainly a model for monastic conduct, Aelred remarked that a good bishop or abbot had to be concerned with both temporal and spiritual things.[3] The example of Saint Benedict illustrates that this dual concern had been true since the earliest days of Christian monasticism, but the times in which Aelred lived were unusual for several reasons.

Twelfth-Century Religious Ferment

The twelfth century was a time of great religious fervor, not just in England but throughout Europe.[4] A complete study of the reasons behind the extraordinary efflorescence of religious life during the period is well beyond the scope of this book; however, a few possibilities can be mentioned. On one hand, a booming economy made more funds available to support a variety of religious lifestyles, while at the same time the lesser demands of the new orders opened religious sponsorship to less wealthy members of society.[5] In addition, people living in an uncertain time were naturally concerned not only with their own salvation but also with establishing a personal spiritual stronghold where they

---

[2] Aelred, S 73.19, CCCM 2B:240–45, here 245; Oner 3.23, CCCM 2D:40–46, here 46; Oner 4.18, CCCM 2D:47–52, here 52.

[3] Aelred, S 117.16, CCCM 2C:183–88, here 188.

[4] David Knowles, *The Monastic Order in England: A History of its Development from the Times of St. Dunstan to the Fourth Lateran Council*, 2nd ed. (Cambridge: Cambridge University Press, 1963), 296–98; Gert Melville, *The World of Medieval Monasticism: Its History and Forms of Life*, trans. James D. Mixon, CS 263 (Collegeville, MN: Cistercian Publications, 2016), 89–124.

[5] Frank Barlow, *The English Church: 1066–1154* (London: Longmans, 1979), 207; Bennett D. Hill, *English Cistercian Monasteries and Their Patrons in the Twelfth Century* (Urbana: University of Illinois Press, 1968), 44–52; Constance Brittain Bouchard, *Holy Entrepreneurs: Cistercians, Knights, and Economic Exchange in Twelfth-Century Burgundy* (Ithaca, NY: Cornell University Press, 1991), 164–74.

would be remembered even if they subsequently lost everything they possessed, up to and including their very lives.[6] Bennett Hill went so far as to argue that the barons were motivated to found Cistercian monasteries as a means of reducing the amount of military service owed to the king.[7] Regardless of the donors' motives, Aelred was able to take full advantage of these natural desires when he became the first abbot of the new monastery at Revesby.[8]

The most obvious evidence of this religious fervor was the sudden and rapid growth of new religious orders in the twelfth century. The Augustinians, Cistercians, Savigniacs, Premonstratensians, and Gilbertines, all nonexistent or virtually unknown in 1100, exploded across Europe over the next fifty years. Dom David Knowles counted seventy houses of Benedictine monks, five of Augustinian canons, and thirteen for women in England in 1100. He determined that by 1155 fourteen new Benedictine monasteries for men had been established, certainly a respectable rate of growth. The number of houses of Augustinian canons had, however, mushroomed to an astonishing ninety, and there were fifty new monasteries for women. In addition, there were fifty-three Cistercian monasteries, six houses of Premonstratensian canons, and eleven Gilbertine houses. These three orders had all been unknown in England at the beginning of the reign of Henry I.[9] A later study by Christopher Holdsworth uncovered

[6] Christopher Holdsworth, "The Church," in *The Anarchy of King Stephen's Reign*, ed. Edmund King (Oxford: Clarendon Press, 1994), 228.

[7] Hill, *English Cistercian Monasteries*, 60.

[8] Vita A 19–20, pp. 27–29; CF 57:110–11; Dutton, Introduction to *Life of Aelred*, 28–29.

[9] Knowles, *Monastic Order*, 227–47, 296–98, 711; also Barlow, *English Church*, 193–94, 205–25; Denis Bethell, "English Black Monks and Episcopal Elections in the 1120s," EHR 84, no. 333 (1969): 687–94. For Europe as a whole, see Giles Constable, *The Reformation of the Twelfth Century* (Cambridge: Cambridge University Press, 1996), 44-50, 89–93. For the growth of the Cistercian Order, see C. H. Lawrence, *Medieval Monasticism: Forms of Religious Life in Western Europe in the Middle Ages*, 3rd ed. (Harlow, Essex, UK: Longman, 2001), 180; Melville, *World*, 155. On monasteries for women see Sally Thompson, *Women Religious: The Founding of English Nunneries After the Norman Conquest* (Oxford: Clarendon Press, 1991), esp. 161–210, on the wide variety of people who founded these monasteries. Also

even more new foundations during the period. He counted one hundred seventy-one new foundations in England and four in Wales during King Stephen's reign alone. Of these, only twenty-four were Benedictine, including Cluniacs, while thirty-nine were Cistercian.[10]

The religious fervor of the age manifested itself not only in the establishment of new monasteries but also in the variety of new forms of religious life that individuals undertook during the period. Even the ancient role of the recluse was subject to reinterpretation. Before the eleventh century, the majority of recluses had been monks or nuns who sought a higher level of asceticism by having themselves enclosed in a cell attached to the monastery church. Thereafter an increasing number of ascetics bypassed the monastic phase and occupied cells in urban settings, perhaps attached to a parish church or the city gates.[11] In an extensive statistical survey of the anchoritic lifestyle, Ann Warren identified ninety-six recluses in twelfth-century England;[12] there were undoubtedly many more who did not leave a trace in the records. Furthermore, all these endeavors, of whatever size, from the mighty abbeys of Fountains and Rievaulx to the recluse in a cell attached to the village church, needed the charity and support of the pious laity.

On the one hand, Rievaulx benefited from the new religious fervor with an increase of its endowment and an influx of new members. However, while the uncertainty of the day may have fueled religious giving in general, the increased number and

---

Henry Mayr-Harting, *Religion, Politics and Society in Britain, 1066–1272* (London: Longmans, 2011), 179–82. Even the small number of Augustinian houses that Knowles counted in 1100 may be too large, as it is notoriously difficult to date the early foundations. See J. C. Dickinson, *The Origins of the Austin Canons and Their Introduction into England* (London: SPCK, 1950), 97–98, 148–49.

[10] Holdsworth, "The Church," 215–28.

[11] Jean Leclercq, "Solitude and Solidarity: Medieval Women Recluses," in *Peace Weavers*, ed. John A Nichols and Lillian Thomas Shank, Medieval Religious Women, 3 vols., CS 72 (Kalamazoo, MI: Cistercian Publications, 1987), 2:69–70.

[12] Ann K. Warren, *Anchorites and Their Patrons in Medieval England* (Berkeley and Los Angeles: University of California Press, 1985), 18–41.

variety of institutions placed Rievaulx in competition with a growing number of rivals for a slice of the charitable pie.[13] Furthermore, that same uncertainty affected the abbey's claims to the lands given to it. As King Stephen and Empress Matilda battled for control of England, they often rewarded their followers with lands seized from the adherents of the other side. If some of those lands were subsequently donated to a monastery, the institution's claim might be disputed by the previous owners. Thus Aelred and his fellow abbots were increasingly occupied with securing not just donations of new property but also confirmations and guarantees of their claim to existing lands.

Building Rievaulx's Endowment

Walter Daniel indicated in a general way that Aelred was rewarded with an avalanche of donations at Revesby and later at Rievaulx. At Revesby, he said, the great landowners of the area "load it with possessions, heap gifts upon it and defend it by their peace and protection."[14] Similarly, he pointed to Aelred's accumulation at Rievaulx, writing that "Aelred doubled all things in it—monks, *conversi*, laymen, farms, lands, and every kind of equipment." By the time of the abbot's death, he said, the monastery was home to 140 monks and 500 laymen and *conversi*.[15] The *Peterborough Chronicle* echoed Walter's words, noting that "in his time [Aelred] doubled the lands, territory, wealth and ornaments of his church."[16] The painstaking process by which this growth took place is evident in the cartulary of Rievaulx, which has been extensively analyzed by Emilia Jamroziak and Janet Burton. A few examples illustrate the complex activities that would have

---

[13] Janet Burton, "The Estates and Economy of Rievaulx Abbey in Yorkshire," *Cîteaux: Commentarii Cistercienses* 49 (1998): 44.

[14] Vita A 20, p. 28; CF 57:111.

[15] Vita A 30, p. 38, CF 57:118–19; Janet Burton, "Rievaulx Abbey: The Early Years," in *Perspectives for an Architecture of Solitude*, ed. T. N. Kinder (Turnhout: Brepols, 2004), 50–51.

[16] *Chronicon Angliae Petriburgense*, ed. John Allen Giles (London: D. Nutt, 1845), 99.

consumed so much time for Aelred and the other early abbots; much more complete accounts are found in their works.[17]

The foundation charter of the abbey, as it survives in the cartulary, is a composite document recording two separate transactions by the founder, Walter Espec. The first gift consisted of nine carucates of land in the vills of Griff and Tilston, for the foundation of the abbey in 1132. The second donation, which conveyed Bilsdale to the monastery, took place between 1145 and 1153, when Walter Espec died at Rievaulx.[18] The document records the consent of King Henry I, Archbishop Thurstan of York, and Pope Innocent II. Perhaps because Walter Espec had no direct heirs, the nine sons of his three sisters witnessed the charter. A group of tenants and neighbors also witnessed, including Eustace fitz John, who served along with Espec as a royal justice.[19] King Henry I and Archbishop Thurstan issued their own confirmations of the foundation, and Henry also issued a separate charter freeing the monks of Rievaulx from the payment of Danegeld for these lands. If the foundation charter itself seems primarily a local and family affair, the royal confirmation charter is anything but that. It may have been issued at the Christmas court of 1132 and was witnessed by the archbishop of Canterbury, eight bishops, and four earls, including the king's eventual successor, Stephen of Blois. Eustace fitz John and his brother also witnessed the document.[20]

[17] J. Burton, "Estates and Economy," 29–93; Emilia Jamroziak, *Rievaulx Abbey and its Social Context, 1132–1300*, Medieval Church Studies 8 (Turnhout: Brepols, 2005).

[18] *Cartularium Abbathiae de Rievalle*, ed. J. C. Atkinson, Surtees Society 83 (Durham: Andrews and Co., 1889) [CAR], no. 42; J. Burton, "Estates and Economy," 30; Jamroziak, *Rievaulx Abbey*, 32–36; Janet Burton, *The Monastic Order in Yorkshire, 1069–1215* (Cambridge: Cambridge University Press, 1999), 99–103.

[19] *Pipe Roll 31 Henry I*, ed. Joseph Hunter (London: Record Society, 1833), 131; *Regesta Regum Anglo-Normannorum 1066–1154*, vol. 2, *Regesta Henrici Primi 1100–1135*, ed. Charles Johnson and H. A. Cronne (Oxford: Clarendon Press, 1956), nos. 1557, 1560–61, 1604, 1662, 1679, 1685, 1891; Judith A. Green, *The Government of England Under Henry I* (Cambridge: Cambridge University Press, 1986), 245–46, 250–52; Jamroziak, *Rievaulx Abbey*, 36–37.

[20] CAR no. 196. See also nos. 194, 218; *Regesta Regum Anglo-Normannorum 2*, nos. 1740–41; *English Episcopal Acta* [EEA] 5, no. 59.

The foundation of Rievaulx also entailed some remodeling of the holdings of Walter Espec's other foundation, the Augustinian priory at Kirkham, notably the transfer of the tithes of Griff and Tilston, which had previously been granted to Kirkham.[21] There seems indeed to have been some thought of turning Kirkham into a Cistercian house. A charter survives stating that the property at Kirkham would be surrendered to the Cistercians and that the Augustinians who chose to remain there would be received into the Cistercian Order. The prior and the rest of the canons would establish a new home at Linton and would be permitted to take their books, sacred vessels, vestments, and stained glass from the windows at Kirkham with them. The agreement, however, was never fulfilled.[22]

These charters illustrate several trends of the age. First, the initial endowment was not very large, showing that the austere lifestyles of the new religious orders brought monastic foundation within reach of less wealthy patrons.[23] Particular care seems to have been taken to obtain the consent of Walter Espec's nephews, because they, rather than a son, would be his heirs. Anxiety over the succession to the Espec estates was undoubtedly also responsible for the care taken to obtain the royal and archiepiscopal confirmation charters. This concern was well founded, for after Espec's death the role of primary patron and protector of Rievaulx passed to the de Ros family, the descendants of Walter's sister Adelina, and as Jamroziak has demonstrated, they did not show nearly the care for the abbey that Walter Espec had.[24]

---

[21] CAR nos. 234–35.

[22] CAR no. 149; Emilia Jamroziak, "Considerate Brothers or Predatory Neighbors: Rievaulx Abbey and Other Monastic Houses in the Twelfth and Thirteenth Centuries," *Yorkshire Archaeological Journal* 73 (2000): 34; Derek Baker, "Patronage in the Early Twelfth-Century Church: Walter Espec, Kirkham and Rievaulx," in *Traditio, Krisis, Renovatio aus theologischer Sicht: Festschrift Winfried Zeller zum 65. Geburtstag*, ed. Bernd Jaspert and Rudolf Mohr (Marburg: Elwert, 1976), 92–100.

[23] Knowles, *Monastic Order*, 246–47; Martin Brett, *The English Church under Henry I* (Oxford: Oxford University Press, 1975), 138.

· [24] Jamroziak, *Rievaulx Abbey*, 43–52; Jamroziak, "Rievaulx Abbey and Its Patrons: Between Cooperation and Conflict," *Cîteaux: Commentarii Cistercienses* 53 (2002): 59–71; J. Burton, "Estates and Economy," 44–45.

In addition, changes to Kirkham's endowment when Rievaulx was founded and especially its contemplated conversion into a Cistercian house illustrate the uncertainty that was bound to prevail when religious houses competed for limited charitable resources. Thus Aelred and the other early abbots of Rievaulx were faced with several pressing tasks: securing new patrons, increasing the monastery's initial small endowment, and defending its interests in uncertain times.

Even before Walter Espec's death, the Mowbray family had stepped to the fore as important patrons of Rievaulx. Gundreda, the widow of Nigel d'Aubigny, began her family's connection to the abbey in 1129–1138 with a donation of land at Welburn, which would become the foundation of one of the abbey's important granges. During Aelred's tenure as abbot, she increased her gift with additional lands and also included an important clause granting her automatic confirmation of any further gifts her tenants at Welburn might make to Rievaulx in the future.[25] But Gundreda's initial grant was only the beginning of the story, for the abbey had a strong interest in rounding out its holdings at Welburn. More than a dozen charters followed, recording additional grants, quitclaims, and confirmations by various other individuals involving either Welburn alone or in combination with other properties.[26] In one of these, Bertram de Bulmer donated a single carucate of land at Welburn that he had acquired from his tenant, Asketil son of Gospatric, by exchanging eleven bovates of land in Flockton for it. A separate document was drawn up to record the exchange; the fact that Aelred himself witnessed the charter indicates the abbey's strong interest in seeing that their rights would not be disputed in the future.[27] Between 1160 and

[25] CAR nos. 55–56; *Charters of the Honour of Mowbray, 1107–1191*, ed. Diana E. Greenway (Oxford: Oxford University Press for the British Academy, 1972), nos. 232, 235; Jamroziak, *Rievaulx Abbey*, 68–69.

[26] CAR nos. 64, 104–5, 130, 132–33, 152–55, 203, 214, 350; *Charters of the Honour of Mowbray*, nos. 236–37, 242, 245–48.

[27] CAR nos. 104, 214. A bovate is the amount of land an ox could plow in one season, about twenty acres. One carucate is equal to eight bovates.

1169, a disagreement occurred between Gundreda's son Roger de Mowbray and his tenant Alan de Ryedale over pastureland near Welburn that Roger had donated to the abbey and that Alan claimed belonged to his own demesne. An attempt was eventually made to settle the matter with a trial by battle, but when the Mowbray champion began to win, Alan de Ryedale agreed to submit the matter to the judgment of a group of twelve knights, who eventually decided in favor of Roger de Mowbray and Rievaulx.[28]

Roger de Mowbray was also a devoted patron of Rievaulx in his own right. In addition to the Welburn grants, he made several other gifts of new rights and property to the abbey.[29] Like Welburn, the vill of Hovedon also illustrates the complexity of building up the abbey's lands by piecemeal acquisition and of securing its claims for the future. Roger de Mowbray's initial grant was soon followed by a confirmation, with the specific inclusion of four bovates of land there that Samson of Cornwall and his wife had received as a gift from Roger's mother Gundreda and that Roger had subsequently purchased from the couple for twenty marks. There must have been particular concern that the pair would seek to reclaim the lands, for Roger's son Nigel issued a separate confirmation of his father's charter, and the dean and chapter of York issued yet another charter recording the couple's release of their claim.[30] The York dean and chapter also issued similar charters recording quitclaims by Ralph Beler, Peter of Hovedon, and Sunniva, the widow of Lambert of Hovedon, and her two daughters.[31] Archbishop Roger of Pont L'Évêque himself also confirmed Ralph Beler's quitclaim.[32]

---

[28] CAR nos. 61, 153; *Mowbray Charters*, no. 247–48; Jamroziak, *Rievaulx Abbey*, 115.

[29] CAR nos. 62, 64, 66–67, 70, 154; *Mowbray Charters*, nos. 238, 241, 243. On Roger de Mowbray's career, see Hugh M. Thomas, "Mowbray, Sir Roger (I) de (d. 1188)," DNB 19458, accessed February 12, 2011; Janet Burton, "*Fundator Noster*: Roger de Mowbray as Founder and Patron of Monasteries," in *Religious and Laity in Western Europe 1000–1400: Interaction, Negotiation, and Power*, ed. Emilia Jamroziak and Janet Burton (Turnhout: Brepols, 2006), 23–39.

[30] CAR nos. 66–68, 232; *Mowbray Charters*, nos. 243, 249–50.

[31] CAR nos. 230–31, 239.

[32] CAR no. 224; EEA 20, no. 75.

Janet Burton and Emilia Jamroziak have suggested that special care had to be taken over this particular parcel because of its possible involvement in a long-running quarrel between the Stuteville and Mowbray families over lands that King Henry I took from the Stutevilles after the battle of Tinchebrai in 1106 and gave to the Mowbrays. King Henry II subsequently restored some of the lands to the Stutevilles, but in the meantime portions of them had been given to various religious institutions, including Rievaulx.[33] Sometime between 1170 and 1180 Pope Alexander III issued a mandate to Bishop Bartholomew of Exeter, Abbot Clement of Saint Mary's York, and Dean Robert Butevilain of York ordering them to investigate and correct injustices done to Rievaulx properties in Hovedon, which may also have been part of this dispute.[34]

Perhaps equally important were the confirmations that Roger issued, not only of his own and his mother's donations to Rievaulx but also of the grants by Peter of Thirsk, Benedict fitz Gervase, Stephen de Meinil, and Hugh de Malebisse.[35] Roger's active involvement in the abbey's affairs is also shown by his confirmation of an agreement defining the boundary between the abbey's property in Welburn and the lands of Robert de Dalville.[36] Aelred and Roger de Mowbray were often together on such matters of business, and on two occasions Aelred confirmed charters of Roger de Mowbray that had nothing to do with Rievaulx: a confirmation of Gundreda's donation of one carucate of land in Hovingham to the Augustinians at Newburgh and a gift to Hugh de Cramaville in Sleningford, Grantley, and Skelden for the fourth part of the service of one knight.[37] The picture that emerges is one of constant interaction between Aelred and his monastery's patrons as new lands were acquired and old rights secured.

---

[33] Jamroziak, *Rievaulx Abbey*, 47, 70; J. Burton, "Estates and Economy," 44–45.
[34] CAR no. 262; Jamroziak, *Rievaulx Abbey*, 70–71.
[35] CAR nos. 57–58, 60, 63, 71, 156; *Mowbray Charters*, nos. 233–34, 240, 244.
[36] CAR no. 155; *Mowbray Charters*, no. 245.
[37] *Mowbray Charters*, nos. 201, 359.

Furthermore, a lord's importance to a favored institution did not end with his own personal donations, for his patronage often inspired other donations from his tenants, and Rievaulx benefited handsomely from this tendency in the case of the Mowbray family. Tenants of the Mowbray family who donated property to Rievaulx in Aelred's time included Bertram de Bulmer, Robert de Stuteville, William de Vescy, Hugh de Malebisse, Hugh de Flamvill, and Benedict fitz Gervase.[38] The Bulmers, Stutevilles, and Vescys were major landholders, holding land from other lords besides the Mowbrays and also as tenants-in-chief of the crown. Of course these magnates had tenants of their own, and among the benefactors of Rievaulx we find Adam de Boltby, a tenant of the Stutevilles.[39] As Jamroziak has demonstrated, this process created a tenurial tree of benefactors for the abbey, one that in some cases lasted for generations.[40]

Rievaulx's network of benefactors encompassed many lesser knightly families as well, of which one, the Lasceles, may serve as an example. In Aelred's time Robert de Lasceles made two small grants to the abbey, one carucate of land in Morton in the parish of East Harlsey and later the income of one mark from his mill in Bordelby.[41] His cousin William also donated a meadow in Cowton.[42] Another family member, Emma, the sister of John de Lasceles and the wife of Peter de Birkin, donated two carucates of land in Shitlington and Flockton to the abbey.[43] Her son Adam fitz Peter de Birkin followed up with additional grants in the same area. His generosity established Rievaulx in the ironworking business, for several of the grants included rights for mining iron ore and lands suitable for doing so, woods for producing charcoal,

---

[38] CAR Bulmer, nos. 104, 214; Stuteville, no. 131; Vescy, no. 190; Malebisse, nos. 73–75; Flamvill, no. 311; fitz Gervase, no. 69.

[39] CAR nos. 76–77.

[40] Jamroziak, *Rievaulx Abbey*, 73–80.

[41] CAR nos. 87, 289; Jamroziak, *Rievaulx Abbey*, 106–10.

[42] CAR no. 293.

[43] *Early Yorkshire Charters*, ed. William Farrer, 6 vols. (Edinburgh: Ballantyne, 1916), vol. 3, no. 1724.

and sites for building furnaces.[44] His brother Roger also made a donation of additional land in Shitlington and Flockton.[45] Adam and Roger also confirmed a charter issued by Matthew son of Saxe granting a number of benefits to the abbey, including land in Blacker for the construction of smithies and iron and wood to supply the smithies from his part of Shitlington and Flockton.[46] Adam also witnessed a grant by Adam fitz Orm of ten acres in Pilley to Rievaulx.[47] Adam fitz Peter's own charters are unique because several of them contain an unusual, recurring phrase, praying for the salvation of those who "may have sinned for me and because of me." This suggests that there was something in Adam fitz Peter's past for which he sought to do penance, perhaps something connected to the civil war between King Stephen and Empress Matilda, but no details have survived.[48] The donations of the Birken family, though smaller than those of the Mowbrays, were nevertheless significant, especially because they established a source of revenue for the abbey that would endure for centuries.

The generosity of the patrons of Rievaulx extended far beyond that single monastery. The Mowbrays also made donations to the Cistercian houses at Combe, Fountains, Garendon, Pipewell, and Vaudey in England and to Saint-André-en-Gouffern in France, near Caen.[49] They were also major patrons of the Order of Savigny,

---

[44] CAR nos. 91–95, 99, 100, 345, 356; *Early Yorkshire Charters*, vol. 3, nos. 1725–28, 1737; Coburn V. Graves, "The Economic Activities of the Cistercians in Medieval England," *Analecta Sacri Ordinis Cisterciensis* 13 (1957): 17–18; J. C. Atkinson, "Existing Traces of Mediaeval Iron-working in Cleveland," *The Yorkshire Archaeological and Topographical Journal* 8 (1884): 30–48; R. W. Vernon, G. McDonnell, and A. Schmidt, "The Geophysical Evaluation of an Ironworking Complex: Rievaulx and Environs," *North Yorkshire Archaeological Prospection* 5 (1998): 181–201.

[45] CAR no. 97.

[46] CAR no. 101; *Early Yorkshire Charters*, vol. 3, no. 1753.

[47] CAR no. 111.

[48] CAR nos. 345, 356; *Early Yorkshire Charters*, vol. 3, nos. 1730, 1732, 1734–35, 1739, 1742; Jamroziak, *Rievaulx Abbey*, 93–95; J. Burton, "Estates and Economy," 35; J. Burton, *Monastic Order*, 210–15.

[49] *Mowbray Charters*, Combe, nos. 79, 84–85; Fountains, nos. 95, 98, 102–3, 110, 114–15, 118–19, 125–27, 129, 132, 134–37, 139–40, 145, 149; Garendon, nos. 155–56; Pipewell, no. 225; Vaudey, no. 278; Saint-André-en-Gouffern, nos. 162–63. For Roger

which united with the Cistercians in 1147. Roger founded a monastery for Savigniac nuns at Villers-Canivet.[50]

Roger and Gundreda might also be considered the founders of Byland Abbey, although they did not supply the original endowment. The story of Byland began in 1134 or 1135 when a group of monks was sent out from the Savigniac abbey of Furness to establish a daughter house at Calder. The house prospered until it was destroyed in the Scottish invasion of 1137. Left homeless, the monks attempted to return to Furness but were refused admittance, either because Abbot Gerald of Calder refused to give up his abbatial title or because the resources of Furness could not support the additional members. The refugees then turned to the Mowbrays, who settled them temporarily at Hood before giving them a permanent home at Byland.[51] The family also made donations to Furness and Jervaulx in England, although it is not possible to determine whether these donations were made before or after the union of the Cistercian and Savigniac orders.[52]

The generosity of the Mowbrays also extended to houses of other new religious orders. Roger's father, Nigel de Aubigny, founded an Augustinian monastery at Hirst, and Roger established another at Newburgh. He also made donations to the Augustinians at Bridlington, Kenilworth, and Nostell; the Gilbertines at Malton and North Ormsby; the Premonstratensians at Welford; and the Hospitallers and the Templars.[53] Perhaps the care of the

---

de Mowbray's relationship with Fountains Abbey, see Jean Wardrop, *Fountains Abbey and Its Benefactors, 1132–1300*, CS 91 (Kalamazoo, MI: Cistercian Publications, 1987), 137–41.

[50] *Mowbray Charters*, no. 279.

[51] *The Foundation History of the Abbeys of Byland and Jervaulx*, ed. and trans. Janet Burton, Borthwick Texts and Studies 35 (York: University of York, 2006), 1–14; *Mowbray Charters*, no. 32–44, 47–49, 52–56, 64, 66–67, 69; Burton, *Monastic Order*, 110–12.

[52] *Mowbray Charters*, Furness no. 150; Jervaulx, nos. 172, 174.

[53] *Mowbray Charters*, Hirst, nos. 15, 215–21; Newburgh, nos. 194–95, 197–203, 208, 210–11; Bridlington, nos. 21–22; Kenilworth, nos. 176, 179–80; Nostell, nos. 215–18, 220; Malton, nos. 185–87; North Ormsby, nos. 223–24; Welford, nos. 281–83; Hospitallers, no. 170; Templars, nos. 271–76. An additional gift of land and rights

sick was a particular interest of the family, for they also gave to Saint Leonard's hospital in York, which was run by the Augustinians, and Roger established a leper hospital at Burton Lazars.[54] Gundreda gave a gift of two bovates of land in Hovedon to Saint Michael's hospital in Whitby.[55] The traditional Benedictine houses and the cathedral chapters were not neglected, either; Roger also made gifts to the cathedral priories at Durham and York and to the Benedictine abbeys of Selby, Whitby, and Saint Mary's York.[56]

Like the Mowbrays but on a smaller scale, Adam fitz Peter de Birkin patronized a variety of other religious houses besides Rievaulx, including the Cistercian nuns at Hampole, Cluniacs at Monk-Bretton and Pontefract, Saint Peter's Hospital in York, Selby Abbey, and Saint Mary of Headley.[57] He also donated lands in Horsforth and Keighley to the Gilbertine house at Haverholme when his daughter Juliana and his granddaughter Matilda became nuns there.[58] The magnitude of this generosity at multiple levels in society testifies to the strength and vitality of the twelfth-century reform movement.

Building the Abbey

While all of these acquisitions were taking place, the buildings of Rievaulx Abbey were also being constructed. The church was the first permanent structure to be completed, perhaps before 1140. The chapter house was probably built between 1150 and 1160, and the dorter and reredorter between 1160 and 1180. All the rest of the

---

in Westwood were given to "Master Gilbert and the order of Sempringham" and later held by the priory of Newstead, no. 264.

[54] *Mowbray Charters*, St. Leonard's, nos. 294, 299–300, 306–8, 311–12; Burton Lazars, nos. 23–31.

[55] *Mowbray Charters*, no. 287.

[56] *Mowbray Charters*, Durham, no. 92; St. Peter's York, nos. 318–19; 322, 324–327A; Selby, nos. 254–61; Whitby, nos. 288–89; St. Mary's York, nos. 317–19.

[57] *Early Yorkshire Charters*, vol. 3, Hampole, no. 1732; Monk-Bretton, nos. 1729, 1735; Pontefract, nos. 1730–31, 1734, 1739–41; Saint Peter's Hospital, no. 1742; Selby, no. 1738; Saint Mary of Headley, no. 1733.

[58] *Early Yorkshire Charters*, vol. 3, no. 1871.

administrative buildings were finished by the end of the twelfth century.[59] Describing the growth of Rievaulx under Aelred's direction, Walter wrote, "He doubled all things in it—monks, *conversi*, laymen, farms, lands and every kind of equipment."[60] After noting that when Aelred died, there were one hundred forty monks and five hundred *conversi* and laymen at Rievaulx, Walter commented, "His material legacy was great enough, under prudent management, to feed and clothe a still greater number."[61] Walter really preferred to talk about Aelred's other accomplishments, especially his writing and his miracles. Speaking metaphorically, he contrasted the brick and wood of earthly concerns with the precious metals and stones of Aelred's writings and miracles: "For I deem it unjust to show to the readers of this work the brick, wood, brass and iron in which the father abounded in external things, and to be silent about the silver, gold and precious stones in which his spirit exceeded."[62]

Walter clearly gave Aelred credit for bringing material prosperity to Rievaulx, but it has been left to modern investigators to describe the magnitude of his accomplishment. Peter Fergusson and Stuart Harrison give Aelred credit for enlarging the original church, completing the east range, rebuilding the chapter house, and constructing the infirmary, novitiate, and abbot's residence.[63] Two of these buildings are worthy of special mention. The chapter house constructed during Aelred's tenure replaced an earlier one built by Abbot William. The original chapter house was a single story, about seven meters by ten meters, with the dormitory overhead, clearly based on Cistercian houses on the continent.

---

[59] C. R. Peers, "Two Relic-holders from Altars in the Nave of Rievaulx Abbey, Yorkshire," *Antiquaries Journal* 1, no. 4 (1921): 272; Peers, "Rievaulx Abbey: The Shrine in the Chapter House," *The Archaeological Journal* 86 (1929): 21.

[60] Vita A 30, p 38; CF 57:118–19.

[61] Vita A 30, p. 38; CF 57:119.

[62] Vita A 33, p. 42; CF 57:122. For the scriptural reference see Dan 2:45.

[63] Peter Fergusson and Stuart Harrison, *Rievaulx Abbey: Community, Architecture, Memory* (New Haven: Yale University Press, 1999), 66; Pierre-André Burton, *Aelred de Rievaulx (1110–1167), De l'homme éclaté à l'être unifié: Essai de biographie existentielle et spirituelle* (Paris: Éditions du Cerf, 2010), 323.

By contrast, Fergusson and Harrison consider Aelred's building a radical departure from the norms of Cistercian architecture. It was a large, freestanding, two-story structure terminating in an apse and surrounding ambulatory, well lit from the clerestory. Its vastly greater size meant that the new chapter house could accommodate the lay brothers along with the choir monks on feast days and other special occasions, a characteristic that Fergusson considers a reflection of the inclusiveness of the community in Aelred's time.[64] Fergusson has also suggested that the unique features of the building were based on the mortuary basilicas of Christian antiquity, which Aelred would have seen during his 1142 trip to Rome.[65] Fergusson noted that as part of the reconstruction, the shrine of Abbot William was moved to the center of the apse, which suggests that devotion to the memory of the founding abbot may have played a role in the structure's design.[66]

The second building meriting special attention is the abbot's residence. The very existence of such separate quarters for the abbot contradicted the Benedictine rule, which specified that the abbot should sleep in the dormitory with his monks.[67] Walter Daniel referred to the structure as a *mausoleum* and emphasized that it was constructed as a special favor for Aelred as he became more and more infirm toward the end of his life. Walter described the warmth and intimacy of gatherings in this room as the monks clustered around their beloved abbot, and perhaps because of this description the reader tends to think of the building as some small, perhaps temporary, structure.[68]

As Fergusson and Harrison have pointed out, however, Walter also noted that as many as twenty or thirty monks might be there at a time and that in fact the entire community, well over a hundred

---

[64] Peter Fergusson and Stuart Harrison, "The Rievaulx Abbey Chapter-House," *Antiquaries Journal* 74 (1994): 240; Fergusson and Harrison, *Rievaulx Abbey*, 95–97.

[65] Fergusson and Harrison, *Rievaulx Abbey*, 66–67, 99.

[66] Fergusson and Harrison, "Rievaulx Chapter-House," 235–45; Ferguson and Harrison, *Rievaulx Abbey*, 99.

[67] RB 22; *RB 1980*, 49.

[68] Vita A 31, pp. 39–40; CF 57:120.

people, gathered there as Aelred lay dying.[69] The structure was therefore quite large, and examination of the ruins reveals that it consisted of three rooms: a main hall, a chapel, and an antechamber connecting it with the infirmary. They have suggested that it closely resembled the domestic hall in a medieval house and that the complex was in fact a place where Aelred and his successors could conduct the business of the abbey in privacy, without disturbing the rest of the monks.[70] The building reflects Aelred's solution to the tension between the pure observance of the Rule and the practical necessities of running the abbey. The vast building program undertaken during his tenure illustrates both his fundraising ability and his organizational skill. The unusual features of the chapter house and the addition of an abbatial residence to the standard monastery complex reflect both his practical and his artistic vision.

Old Friends at Hexham and Durham

As busy as Aelred must have been with the affairs of his abbey, he also made time for an ever-increasing network of friends and colleagues. It is especially clear that he maintained a close relationship with the monks of Durham, an institution with which his family had long been associated and where he himself may have been educated.[71] Bishop Hugh du Puiset of Durham became an active supporter of the abbey, even though his past history indicated that he would be anything but a friend to the Cistercians. He had been a supporter of William fitz Herbert and succeeded to his positions as treasurer of York Minster and archdeacon of the East Riding when fitz Herbert began his long battle to become archbishop of York. Fitz Herbert's opponent, Archbishop Henry

---

[69] Vita A 31, 49, 53, pp. 40, 57, 59; CF 57:120, 134, 136; Fergusson and Harrison, *Rievaulx Abbey*, 128–29.

[70] Fergusson and Harrison, *Rievaulx Abbey*, 67, 128–29; Fergusson, "Aelred's Abbatial Residence at Rievaulx Abbey," *Studies in Cistercian Art and Architecture* 5, ed. Meredith Parsons Lillich, CS 167 (Kalamazoo, MI: Cistercian Publications, 1998), 42.

[71] See above, chap. 3:39.

Murdac, the former abbot of the Cistercian abbey of Fountains, bitterly opposed Hugh du Puiset's election at Durham, and it is likely that Hugh would never have been able to take possession of the see if Murdac, along with Bernard of Clairvaux and Pope Eugenius III, had not all died in 1153. Furthermore, Rievaulx would have seemed to be one of the last Cistercian houses that the bishop of Durham would choose to patronize, given that Abbot William had been one of the leaders of the opposition to fitz Herbert and that the current abbot, Aelred, had been part of the first group sent to Rome in 1142 to seek the archbishop's deposition.[72]

Nevertheless, Bishop Hugh soon proved himself a generous patron and a stout defender of Rievaulx. He granted three carucates of land in Crosby, including a mill, a marsh, and a meadow, to Rievaulx and later confirmed an agreement between the abbey and the parish church of Leake regarding the payment of tithes there.[73] He issued another charter ratifying Geoffrey of Ottrington's quitclaim of the Crosby lands. This charter stated that the land had been "surrendered by rod" to Hugh and Aelred.[74] Hugh also granted lands in Cowton to the abbey in return for a rent of sixty shillings, stating in his charter that he was doing so because of the "special affection that we feel for our son Abbot Aelred."[75] Later he both witnessed an agreement between Rievaulx and the monks of Durham regarding payment of tithes there and also issued his own separate charter confirming the agreement.[76] Confirmation charters issued by Henry II and Richard I mention that the boundaries of the lands in Crosby and Cowton were perambulated and sworn in the bishop's presence.[77]

Hugh also witnessed a donation by Everard de Ros of additional land in Helmsley, supplementing Walter Espec's original

---

[72] See above, chap. 3:60–61.

[73] CAR nos. 49–50; EEA 24, nos. 125, 128; EEA 20, no. 79; Jamroziak, *Rievaulx Abbey*, 184–91.

[74] CAR no. 51; EEA 24, no. 130.

[75] CAR no. 53; EEA 24, no. 126.

[76] CAR nos. 54, 236; EEA 24, no. 129.

[77] EEA 24, no. 127.

grant.[78] Pope Alexander III also recognized Hugh as a protector of the abbey and addressed several mandates to him and others commanding them to stop those who were encroaching on the abbey's lands.[79] Hugh's generosity in granting new lands to Rievaulx is remarkable considering his past history with the Cistercians in general and Rievaulx in particular. But the bishop was doing more than just initialing documents—several of the charters reveal his active participation in the affairs of Rievaulx, establishing him as one of the key promoters and protectors of the abbey.

Prior Laurence was one particularly important friend of Aelred's at Durham. His earliest known work is the *Vita Brigidae*, a life of Saint Brigid of Kildare. In his dedicatory letter to Aelred, he noted that Aelred's father Eilaf had requested that he undertake the work, a rewriting of an earlier prose version. Since he mentions in his letter that Aelred was at King David's court, the letter can be dated to 1132–1133.[80]

Aelred especially encouraged the monks of Durham who were interested in historical writing to pursue these interests. Reginald of Durham wrote that Aelred suggested that he write his *Libellus de Admirandis Beati Cuthberti Virtutibus*, and he dedicated the work to Aelred.[81] Moreover, Aelred probably supplied several examples of Cuthbert's powerful intercession from his own experience. During

[78] CAR no. 44.

[79] CAR nos. 253–54, 256.

[80] Anselm Hoste, "A Survey of the Unedited Work of Laurence of Durham, with an Edition of his Letter to Ailred of Rievaulx," *Sacris Erudiri* 11 (1960): 260–65; Frederick M. Powicke, "The Dispensator of King David I," *The Scottish Historical Review* 23, no. 89 (1925): 35–37; Mia Münster-Swendsen, "Irony and the Author: The Case of the Dialogues of Lawrence of Durham," in *Modes of Authorship in the Middle Ages*, ed. S. Rankovic and others (Toronto: Pontifical Institute of Mediaeval Studies, 2005), 159–60; Mia Münster-Swendsen, "Setting Things Straight: Law, Justice and Ethics in the *Orationes* of Lawrence of Durham," *Anglo-Norman Studies* 27 (2012): 152–54.

[81] Reginald of Durham, *Libellus de Admirandis Beati Cuthberti Virtutibus*, Surtees Society 1 (London: J. B. Nichols and Sons, 1835), 1–4, 32; Frederick M. Powicke, *Ailred of Rievaulx and his Biographer Walter Daniel* (Manchester: Manchester University Press, 1922), 33; Sally Crumplin, "Modernizing St. Cuthbert: Reginald of Durham's Miracle Collection," *Studies in Church History* 41 (2005): 179–91; Victoria Tudor, "The Cult of St. Cuthbert in the Twelfth Century: The Evidence of Reginald of Durham," in *St. Cuthbert: His Cult and His Community to A.D. 1200*,

one of Aelred's trips home from the Cistercian general chapter at Cîteaux, a miracle occurred that illustrated Aelred's devotion to Cuthbert, Durham's patron saint.[82] According to Reginald, Aelred meditated upon Cuthbert's life and miracles as he traveled to Cîteaux and even began to compose a poem in his honor. Once he arrived at Cîteaux, however, the press of other duties caused him to neglect this work. After the general chapter, Aelred and a group of other abbots gathered at the coast on their way back to England but were unable to embark because of stormy seas. Soon Aelred recognized that the problem was due to his failure to complete his work in honor of Cuthbert. No sooner had he resumed his writing than the seas miraculously calmed and the abbots were able to set sail.[83]

Reginald of Durham mentioned another miracle that took place as Aelred passed through the village of Kirkcudbright in Galloway on Saint Cuthbert's Day, March 20, 1164. A penitent arrived at the village church wearing an iron belt around his naked flesh as a punishment for his crimes. The sinner began to pray and beg Cuthbert for mercy, and in answer to his prayers the iron belt miraculously fell from his waist.[84] Similarly, in his *Libellus de vite et miraculis S. Godrici heremitae de Finchale*, Reginald wrote that Aelred sent him to visit the hermit and convinced him to write Godric's life story, including in it a tale that Aelred had told him about an angelic vision that Godric had received.[85] He also mentioned that Aelred himself had visited Godric in the company of an unnamed young monk of Durham.[86]

---

ed. Gerald Bonner, David Rollason, and Clare Stancliffe (Woodbridge: Boydell Press, 1989): 447–67.

[82] Janet Burton and Julia Kerr, *The Cistercians in the Middle Ages* (Woodbridge: Boydell Press, 2011), 134; Ann Lawrence Mathers, *Manuscripts in Northumbria in the Eleventh and Twelfth Centuries* (Cambridge: D. S. Brewer, 2003), 240.

[83] Reginald of Durham, *Libellus de Beati Cuthberti*, 176–77.

[84] Reginald of Durham, *Libellus de Beati Cuthberti*, 178; Powicke, *Aelred and his Biographer*, 32, 70. For another possible visit, see *Beati Cuthberti*, 188.

[85] Reginald of Durham, *Libellus de vita et miraculis S. Godrici heremitae de Finchale*, Surtees Society 20 (London: J. B. Nichols and Sons, 1847), 19, 173, 269; Tom Licence, *Hermits and Recluses in English Society, 950–1200* (Oxford: Oxford University Press, 2011), 187.

[86] Reginald of Durham, *Libellus de vita Godrici*, 176–77.

It is clear from these examples that Aelred maintained his family ties with Durham, that he visited Durham frequently, and that he was liked and respected by the clergy there. In a pattern that was repeated over and over, however, Aelred was more than just a friendly and welcome visitor at Durham, for on two occasions he took part in resolving a conflict involving the brothers there. In the first case, he presided over a board of arbitrators convened to settle a dispute over the status of the prior. The settlement confirmed that the prior was to have the first place after the bishop in all things and would occupy the seat of an abbot in synod.[87] On the second occasion, Aelred's role in the proceedings is unclear, but his attestation appears on a charter settling a dispute between York and Durham over a number of points. The charter specified that the prior of Hexham would be ordained by the bishop of Durham and would attend the Durham synod, and that the church of Hexham would receive its chrism from Durham, as had been the custom. It upheld the rights of Durham to various churches in Yorkshire and exempted certain churches from paying synodal dues to the archdiocese. Clerics of these churches accused of wrongdoing would be corrected by the archbishop after a summons enabling the bishop of Durham or his representative to be present.[88] In this case, Aelred's long-standing ties with Durham seem to have made him an ideal outside arbiter when conflicts involving the community arose.

This agreement between York and Durham was not restricted to concerns over the priory of Hexham, but it did involve these other old friends of Aelred in significant ways. Aelred's presence

[87] *Feodarium Prioratus Dunelmensis*, ed. William Greenwell (Durham: Andrews and Co. for the Surtees Society, 1872), lx–lxiii; Powicke, *Ailred and his Biographer*, 33; Dom Alberic Stacpoole, "The Public Face of Aelred, 1167–1967," *Downside Review* 85 (1967): 193; Geoffrey V. Scammell, *Hugh du Puiset, Bishop of Durham* (Cambridge: Cambridge University Press, 1956), 140–41.

[88] EEA 24, no. 167; EEA 20, no. 15; Roger of Hoveden, *Chronica Magistri Rogeri de Houedene*, ed. William Stubbs, 4 vols., RS 51 (London: Longmans, 1868–1871), 2:70–71; *Historians of the Church of York and its Archbishops*, ed. James Raine, 3 vols., RS 71 (London: Longmans, 1879–1894), 3:79–81; Scammell, *Hugh du Puiset*, 265–66; Powicke, *Ailred and his Biographer*, 47n1; Stacpoole, "Public Face of Aelred," 193.

at the negotiations is one example of his continued involvement in the affairs of his old home. As was noted earlier, Aelred was apparently invited to preach at the translation of relics of the five holy bishops of Hexham in 1155, and his reminiscences on that occasion show his continuing affection for the priory and the canons living there. John of Hexham wrote admiringly of Aelred, stating that he was "one who had obtained from the Lord an excellent grace in the preaching of wisdom."[89] The remarks could have been occasioned by Aelred's preaching at the great occasion of the translation, by some other occasion, or by his reputation in the larger neighborhood. In any case his remarks indicate that Aelred's affection for his old home was returned by the canons who currently lived there.

The Union of Savigny and Citeaux

In the same way Aelred also became involved in the politics of the union of Savigny with the Cistercians as agreed upon at the general chapter in 1147 and ratified by Pope Eugenius III the following year.[90] As Christopher Holdsworth has demonstrated,

[89] John of Hexham, *Historia*, in *Symeonis Monachi Opera Omnia*, ed. Thomas Arnold, 2 vols., RS 75 (London: Longmans, 1882–1885), 2:317; Mather, *Manuscripts*, 244.

[90] *Foundation History*, 25–34; *Regesta Pontificum Romanorum ad Annum post Christum Natum 1198*, ed. P. Jaffé and others, 2 vols. (Leipzig: Veit, 1885–1888), no. 9235; *Calendar of Documents Preserved in France Illustrative of the History of Great Britain and Ireland*, vol. 1, *A.D. 918–1206*, ed. John Horace Round (London: Eyre and Spottiswoode, 1899), nos. 813–15, pp. 294–96; Léopold Delisle, "Documents Relative to the Abbey of Furness, Extracted from the Archives of Savigny," *Journal of the Archaeological Association* 6 (1851): 419–24; R. H. C. Davis, *King Stephen, 1135–1154*; 3rd ed. (London: Longmans, 1990), 99–101; Janet Burton, "English Monasteries and the Continent in the Reign of King Stephen," in *King Stephen's Reign, 1135–1154*, ed. Paul Dalton and Graeme J. White (Woodbridge: Boydell Press, 2008), 101–9; Janet Burton, "The Abbeys of Byland and Jervaulx, and the Problems of the English Savigniacs, 1134–1156," in *Monastic Studies* 2, ed. Judith Loades (Bangor: Headstart History, 1991), 119–31; Christopher Holdsworth, "The Affiliation of Savigny," in *Truth as Gift: Studies in Honor of John R. Sommerfeldt*, ed. Marsha L. Dutton, Daniel M. La Corte, and Paul Lockey, CS 204 (Kalamazoo, MI: Cistercian Publications, 2004), 57–61, 82–83; Béatrice Poulle, "Savigny and

however, combining the orders was a complex process requiring much advance planning.[91] Even if Aelred's interactions with the Savigniac houses took place before the formal affiliation with the Cistercians, they are still important and in fact take on additional significance if they were part of the initial negotiations. Conflicts between monasteries that were close together were inevitable, especially if they were suddenly thrust together in one order. Neighboring houses like Rievaulx and the Savigniac house at Byland competed for lands, privileges, and new members. Aelred and Abbot Roger of Byland eventually negotiated a complex agreement clarifying the property rights of their two houses and regulating the use of nearby rivers, bridges, ponds, roads, and mineral resources.[92]

Aelred went much further, however, becoming a friend and counselor to the newly incorporated Savigniac houses. Shortly after his election as abbot of Rievaulx, he sent a mission of advice and instruction in the Cistercian way of life to the former Savigniac abbey of Swineshead.[93] The union of the two orders may have been part of the impetus for the composition of *Mirror of Charity*. Aelred probably met Bernard of Clairvaux in the spring of 1142 on his way back from Rome following his mission regarding the election of William fitz Herbert to the see of York, and Bernard may have asked him to write the work at that time. As Charles

---

England," in *England and Normandy in the Middle Ages*, ed. David Bates and Anne Curry (London: Hambledon Press, 1994), 165–66; Francis R. Swietek, "The Role of Bernard of Clairvaux in the Union of Savigny with Cîteaux: A Reconsideration," *Cîteaux: Commentarii Cistercienses* 42 (1991): 289–302; Knowles, *Monastic Order*, 250–51. Constance Berman has argued, however, that the actual union of the orders took place much later than 1147 (Constance Hoffman Berman, *The Cistercian Evolution: The Invention of a Religious Order in Twelfth-Century Europe* [Philadelphia: University of Pennsylvania Press, 2000], 142–48).

[91] Holdsworth, "Affiliation of Savigny," 83–84.

[92] CAR no. 243; J. Burton, "Estates and Economy," 45–47; Jamroziak, "Considerate Brethren," 32–33.

[93] Vita A 28, p. 35; CF 57:116; Charles Dumont, Introduction to *The Mirror of Charity*, trans. Elizabeth Connor, introduction and notes by Charles Dumont, CF 17 (Kalamazoo, MI: Cistercian Publications, 1990), 30.

Dumont pointed out, however, while their acquaintance probably did begin at this time, there is no reason Bernard could not have communicated with Aelred at any time thereafter by letter.[94] Emero Stiegman has gone further, suggesting that Bernard wrote the letter after he had read the completed work and intended his letter to be an introduction and endorsement of the book.[95] It is certainly suggestive that Bernard asked Aelred to write "a little something for me in reply to the complaints of certain [monks] who are struggling from more remiss to stricter ways."[96] If the composition of the work in its final form spanned several years, *Mirror of Charity* may well have been strongly influenced by the author's firsthand experience of the difficulties of incorporating the Savigniacs into the stricter Cistercian way of life.

Aelred also became directly involved in the controversy between the abbeys of Furness and Savigny over possession of the abbey of Byland. The monks of Byland, who had been sent from Furness to Calder, were concerned that Furness might try to reassert its authority over them, so Abbot Gerald of Byland traveled to the continent in 1141 to ask for his abbey to be placed directly under the authority of Savigny, a request that was freely granted.[97] In the meantime, the monks of Furness, having realized that the monks now at Byland were not going to return to Calder, established a new colony at Calder under the direction of Abbot Hardred.[98] The new abbot of Calder immediately attempted to claim jurisdiction over Byland as a daughter house, but the abbot of Savigny, who was visiting the English houses of his order, convinced him to relinquish his claims.[99]

---

[94] Dumont, Introduction to *Mirror of Charity*, 55–59.

[95] Emero Stiegman, " 'Woods and Stones' and 'The Shade of Trees' in the Mysticism of Saint Bernard," in *Truth as Gift: Studies in Honor of John R. Sommerfeldt*, ed. Marsha L. Dutton, Daniel M. La Corte, and Paul Lockey, CS 204 (Kalamazoo, MI: Cistercian Publications, 2004), 321–54, here 338–47.

[96] Spec car 1; CCCM 1:3; CF 17:69; Dumont, Introduction to *Mirror of Charity*, 28–29.

[97] *Foundation History*, 9; J. Burton, "Byland and Jervaulx," 121–25.

[98] *Foundation History*, 10.

[99] *Foundation History*, 25–28.

Not satisfied with this solution, the monks of Furness eventually took the complaint to the general chapter at Cîteaux, which appointed Aelred to look into the matter. He speedily resolved the conflict, concluding that Byland should remain a daughter house of Savigny.[100] The case had wider implications for the relationship between the two orders, for the abbot of Savigny had argued that the chief reason that the claim of Furness to Byland should be denied was that "those things which had been done, presented, ordained, and established according to custom in the annual general chapter at Savigny ought not now to be retracted in any way or weakened by the authority of the general chapter of Cîteaux."[101] By thus concluding that the early decision regarding Byland taken at the Savigny general chapter should stand, Aelred established an important precedent for the handling of matters undertaken before the union between the two orders.

Aelred may also have involved himself in another controversy surrounding the foundation of the abbey of Jervaulx. Brother Peter, who was a Savigniac monk learned in medicine, and his companions established a house at Jervaulx in Wensleydale with the support of both Count Alan of Richmond and Roger de Mowbray. When Count Alan traveled to visit his lands in Brittany, he stopped off at Savigny to report the news of the new foundation to the abbot and the brothers there and to request that an abbot and additional monks be sent to strengthen Brother Peter's small community. The abbot of Savigny refused to accede to this request, citing previous difficulties with the English foundations of the Order. Abbot Roger of Byland carried a second petition to the general chapter in 1147, with the result that Abbot Gervase of Quarr was delegated to investigate the situation and determine whether the monastic site at Jervaulx was able to support

---

[100] *Foundation History*, 28–32; J. Burton, *Monastic Order*, 116–17, 200–201; *Calendar of Documents Preserved in France*, no. 819, p. 297; Frederick M. Powicke, "Maurice of Rievaulx," EHR 36, no. 141 (1921): 23, 25; Powicke, *Ways of Medieval Life and Thought: Essays and Addresses* (London: Odhams Press, 1950), 23; Powicke, Introduction to Vita A, lxiii; Stacpoole, "Public Face of Aelred," 193; Knowles, *Monastic Order*, 250–51.

[101] *Foundation History*, 31.

a community. If so, the abbot was authorized to grant Jervaulx to Byland as a daughter house; otherwise the property itself was to be maintained for the use and profit of Savigny. The following year, with the merger between Savigny and Cîteaux now complete, the abbot performed his inspection and granted Brother Peter's community to Byland.[102] Aelred's role in the negotiations over Jervaulx is not detailed in the *Foundation History* of the two abbeys, but he witnessed the resulting charter, so it appears that he may have had a hand in resolving this conflict as well.

Aelred's early assistance to Byland and Jervaulx seems to have endeared him to the Savigniacs, and Abbot Roger of Byland became a close friend. Walter Daniel wrote that Roger was present at Aelred's deathbed, anointed him as he lay dying, and anointed the body again after death.[103] Aelred was also beloved at Swineshead, where, upon hearing of his death, Abbot Gilbert of Hoyland included a eulogy of Aelred in his Sermon 40 on the Song of Songs.[104] Very little is known of Gilbert's life, but the warmth of his words indicated that he loved and admired Aelred. Lawrence Braceland, who translated Gilbert's works, suggested that Gilbert entered Clairvaux during Bernard's lifetime, in time to be part of the expedition that led to the founding of Rievaulx in 1132. If so, he could also have been part of the group that Aelred sent to Swineshead shortly after his own election as abbot of Rievaulx in 1149 to help the Savigniacs adapt to the stricter customs of the Cistercians.[105] Dumont, however, considered the evidence too slim to support this conclusion and maintained that Gilbert was originally a Savigniac at either Furness, Byland, or Swineshead itself. Particularly if this is the case, then the warmth of his eulogy

---

[102] *Foundation History*, 36–44; Burton, "Byland and Jervaulx," 125–28.

[103] Vita A 52–59, pp. 59–63; CF 57:135–39.

[104] Gilbert of Hoyland, S 40.4 [=PL S 41.4]; PL 184:216; Gilbert of Hoyland, *The Works of Gilbert of Hoyland: Sermons on the Song of Songs, III*, trans. Lawrence Braceland, CF 26 (Kalamazoo, MI: Cistercian Publications, 179), 493–99, here 495.

[105] Lawrence Braceland, Introduction to Gilbert of Hoyland, *Sermons on the Song of Songs, I–III*, trans. Lawrence C. Braceland, CF 14, 20, 26 (Kalamazoo, MI: Cistercian Publications, 1978–79), CF 14:6.

for Aelred testifies to the latter's tact and skill as he welcomed the Savigniacs into the Cistercian Order.[106]

When the news of Aelred's death reached Swineshead, Gilbert's exposition of the *Song* had reached the verse "I have gathered my myrrh with my spices, I have eaten the honeycomb with my honey, I have drunk my wine with my milk. Eat, friends, and drink and be inebriated, most dearly loved" (Song 5:1). Playing on the theme of the honeycomb, Gilbert described Aelred as "a busy bee, fashion[ing] the honeycombs of the divine word," and being "busy to gather a knowledge of morals, he stored it in the well-fashioned cells of his words."[107] His eulogy is particularly significant because it includes testimony to Aelred's skills as a mediator: "He was lucid in interpretation, not hasty in speech. He questioned modestly, replied more modestly, tolerating the troublesome, himself troublesome to no one. Acutely intelligent, deliberate in statement, he bore annoyance with equanimity." Gilbert then described the way in which Aelred reacted to being interrupted, waiting patiently until the other speaker had exhausted himself: "[Then] he would resume his interrupted discourse with the same calmness with which he had waited, for he both spoke and kept silent as the occasion demanded. Quick to listen, slow to speak, but not slow to anger. How is he to be described as slow to anger? I would rather say he was not in the race!"[108]

New Friends

Other surviving examples also show Aelred reaching out to monastic houses outside the Cistercian orbit. One such case is

[106] Charles Dumont, Review of Gilbert of Hoyland, *Sermons on the Song of Songs*, vol. 1, CF 14, in *Bulletin de Spiritualité* n. 749, *Collectanea Ordinis Cisterciensium Reformatorum* 41 (1979): 470.

[107] Gilbert of Hoyland, SC 40.4; PL 184:217; CF 26:497; Dutton, Introduction to *The Life of Aelred of Rievaulx and the Letter to Maurice*, ed. and trans. Frederick M. Powicke, CF 57 (Kalamazoo, MI: Cistercian Publications, 1994), 39; Powicke, Introduction to Vita A, xxxii–xxxiii.

[108] Gilbert of Hoyland, SC 40.4; PL 184:216–17; CF 26:496; Dumont, Introduction to *Mirror of Charity*, 47–48.

a short treatise ascribed to Aelred and appended to a surviving manuscript of *Mirror*. It is an answer to a letter written by an Augustinian on the subject of the variety of monastic rules. According to this canon, the essence of all monastic rules was the triple obligation of stability, conversion, and obedience; all the individual details could be dispensed with and were merely aids to salvation. Aelred disagreed, pointing out that failure to observe the details of the rule was contrary to obedience. The cause that united all monastic rules was charity, and any requirement could be dispensed with if it was profitable to that cause.

Both André Wilmart, who published the piece, and Sir Maurice Powicke date the work to the early 1140s, when Aelred was either novice master at Rievaulx or abbot of Revesby, which would make its composition contemporary with the presumed early stages of Aelred's composition of *Mirror*, and Wilmart noted that similar ideas appear in both works.[109] This dating also places it at the same time as a controversy involving Waldef, the stepson of King David I and Aelred's close friend from his days at the Scottish court. Waldef had become the prior of Kirkham, but in 1143 he decided to leave the Augustinians and become a Cistercian, entering the novitiate at Warden. The Augustinians were angry at his departure and enlisted the support of their patron, Earl Simon of Northampton, whose hostility was felt to be so dangerous to the monks at Warden that Waldef took refuge at Rievaulx itself.[110] Aelred would naturally have been interested in the dispute centered on his friend, and it is possible that his communication with the unnamed Augustinian canon was occasioned by the conflict. In any case, the exchange, whether related to the disagreement between Rievaulx and Kirkham or not, shows Aelred corresponding with and advising a member of a religious order other than his own at a very early stage in his own monastic career.

---

[109] André Wilmart, "Un court traité d'Aelred sur l'étendue et le but de la profession monastique," *Revue d'ascétique et de mystique* 23 (1947): 259–73; Powicke, Introduction to Vita A, lxxiii–lxxiv.

[110] Jocelin of Furness, *Vita S. Waltheni Abbatis, Acta Sanctorum*, August 3, 257.

Perhaps Aelred also made friends at the Benedictine abbey of Peterborough, for the chronicle written there contains several notices of his activities. The chronicle continues to the year 1368, with composition probably beginning in the second half of the thirteenth century.[111] The author of the work was generally interested in the Cistercians, carefully noting the foundation of each English house. Perhaps the tie between the two monasteries dated from Aelred's time at Revesby, for the two houses were both in Lincolnshire, about forty-five miles apart.[112] The writer recorded Aelred's selection as the first abbot of Revesby, noted his writing of the *Lament for David I*, and stated that the papal schism of 1159 was resolved in favor of Alexander III largely through the efforts of Aelred of Rievaulx and Bishop Arnulf of Lisieux. He also recorded that Aelred wrote a new life of Edward the Confessor and preached at the translation of his relics to the new shrine in Westminster Abbey in 1163. Finally he noted Aelred's death, remarking that he had doubled the monastery's property and wealth during his tenure.[113]

Of course the *Peterborough Chronicle* is not a contemporary source for Aelred's activities, but as Powicke remarked, its statements are accurate where they can be checked.[114] Furthermore, under the year 1153 a puzzling statement occurs: *Hic finit Chronica Alredi*.[115] Does this refer to some lost work of Aelred, the abbot of Rievaulx, or to another writer by the same name? Perhaps Aelred corresponded with a monk of Peterborough who, like Reginald of Durham, was interested in writing history. It is even possible that Aelred supplied his correspondent with information about the growth of the Cistercian Order in England, information that survived to be incorporated into the fourteenth-century chronicle. There is no way to know the truth of the matter, but the

---

[111] *Chronicon Angliae Petriburgense*, xii.

[112] Aelred Squire, "Aelred and King David," *Collectanea Ordinis Cisterciensium Reformatorum* 22 (1960): 371–72.

[113] *Chronicon Angliae Petriburgense*, 91, 96, 98–99.

[114] Powicke, Introduction to Vita A, xlviii, n4.

[115] *Chronicon Angliae Petriburgense*, 95.

Peterborough Chronicle's unusual interest in Aelred testifies if not to friendship, then at least to the extent of Aelred's reputation outside his immediate environs.

Aelred and the Hierarchy

Aelred also numbered some of the leading ecclesiastics of his time among his friends. Charter evidence shows that Aelred was part of the administrative machinery of the diocese of York. He witnessed four charters by Archbishop Henry Murdac; however, Murdac's only action regarding Rievaulx itself was to issue a notification that Robert de Ros, Walter Espec's son-in-law and successor at Helmsley, had confirmed his predecessors' gifts to Rievaulx in the archbishop's presence.[116] Aelred also witnessed four charters of the next archbishop, Roger of Pont L'Évêque: a confirmation of the rights of the prior and monks of Durham, a notification to diocesan personnel of his confirmation of the church of Kirklevington to the prior of Guisborough, a notification that the abbot of Rufford was to pay one mark annually to Canon Paulinus of York, and the record of the settlement of a dispute over the church at Sheriff Hutton.[117] We do not know what role Aelred played in any of these negotiations, but the charter attestations confirm his presence at the archbishop's court and suggest that he had at least the opportunity to exercise his talent for mediation there as well. The regularity with which the archbishop added his own confirmation to grants and agreements involving the abbey is an indication of the esteem in which Roger held Aelred and the abbey of Rievaulx.[118] In addition to Ralph Beler's quitclaim of lands at Hovedon mentioned above, Archbishop Roger also confirmed the original Mowbray grant at Welburn, Hugh du Puiset's grant in Crosby, Bernard de Balliol's grant of pasturage rights in his forest of Teesdale, and a grant by

[116] EEA 5, nos. 110, 118, 127, 130, 132.
[117] EEA 20, nos. 15, 39, 88, 94.
[118] Jamroziak, *Rievaulx Abbey*, 177–80.

William de Vescy.[119] He also ratified agreements over tithes between the abbey and the churches of Scawton and Leake.[120] Perhaps most important, Archbishop Roger issued a charter taking the abbey under his special protection and ordering his rural deans to uphold justice against any who persecuted the monks.[121] Furthermore, the York cathedral chapter was also actively involved in Rievaulx's affairs.[122] Dean Robert Butevilain witnessed four charters in the abbey's favor and also issued his own charter confirming the arrangement over tithes from the church of Scawton.[123] He and the chapter also issued seven charters of their own confirming the actions of others who had made donations to the abbey or released their claims upon its property.[124]

Another of Aelred's friends who occupied a high ecclesiastical position was Gilbert Foliot, the bishop of Hereford and later of London. Ties between the two men may have originated either at the court of King David of Scotland or through the association of the Foliot family with the Cistercian Order. Bishop Gilbert's family origins are unclear, but it is likely that his father was Robert Foliot I, who had been the steward of David I and his son Henry as earls of Huntingdon. His son, Robert II, married Margery, the heiress of Richard de Raimbeaucourt, Lord of West Warden in Northamptonshire, where the family founded Warden Abbey. Robert II died clothed in the habit of a Cistercian monk.[125] A Helias Foliot witnessed two charters in favor of Rievaulx, both confirmations of grants by the Gant family and their retainers of lands at Hunmanby.[126]

Aelred dedicated his *Sermons on the Prophetic Burdens of Isaiah* to Gilbert Foliot, and in return Foliot dedicated his own *Book of*

---

[119] EEA 20, nos. 75–76, 80–82; CAR nos. 222–24, 237–38; EEA 24, nos. 125, 130.

[120] EEA 20, nos. 78–79; CAR nos. 221, 225.

[121] EEA 20, no. 77; CAR no. 220.

[122] Jamroziak, *Rievaulx Abbey*, 191–202.

[123] CAR nos. 82, 86, 161, 167, 226; C. T. Clay, "Notes on the Early Archdeacons in the Church of York," *Yorkshire Archaeological Journal* 36 (1946–1947): 280–81.

[124] CAR nos. 227–33.

[125] Adrian Morey and C. N. L. Brooke, *Gilbert Foliot and His Letters* (Cambridge: Cambridge University Press, 1965), 32–49.

[126] CAR nos. 80, 159.

Homilies to Aelred.[127] Sadly, the only surviving correspondence between the two is Aelred's dedicatory letter to Bishop Gilbert at the beginning of his sermon collection. In this letter Aelred cast himself as the humble suppliant, begging Bishop Gilbert in his greater wisdom to review and pass judgment on his work. It is evident that the two men had met in person at least once, for Aelred mentioned that Gilbert's "mere notice of me was a great thing for me" and that he had "obtained a greeting that was like a loving embrace."[128]

The picture that emerges from the scattered documentation shows Aelred at the center of a complex web of friends, patrons, and allies. He built up Rievaulx's resources through constant interaction with the lay patrons of the abbey while directing the design and construction of the monastery's permanent buildings. He carefully maintained his relationships with old friends at Hexham and Durham, all the while reaching out to neighboring monasteries, especially those of the other new religious orders.

Furthermore, Aelred developed relationships with members of the hierarchy, and both Archbishop Roger of Pont L'Évêque and Bishop Hugh du Puiset of Durham became strong supporters of Rievaulx. Other monastics in the north may well have envied Rievaulx's success and Aelred's growing reputation, but it is clear that in many cases they also relied on his advice and mediation.

---

[127] Morey and Brooke, *Gilbert Foliot and His Letters*, 70 and n1; Stacpoole, "Public Life," 186; Charles Dumont, "Autour des sermons *De Oneribus* d'Aelred de Rievaulx," *Collectanea Ordinis Cisterciensium Reformatorum* 19 (1957): 114–21.

[128] CCCM 2D:3–5; R. Jacob McDonie, trans., "Abbot Aelred of Rievaulx's Letter to Gilbert, Venerable Bishop of London," CSQ 45, no. 2 (2010): 119–24, here 124; see App. 2:242–49. See CCCM 2D:188 for a mention of this interaction in one of the sermons.

Chapter 5

Brothers and Sisters in Christ
Aelred and the Care of Women

It is by now well known that many of the most famous churchmen from ancient times forward have enjoyed particularly close spiritual friendships with women. To cite only a few examples, Saint Jerome was devoted to the Roman noblewoman Paula and her daughter Eustochium, writing to Pope Theophilus that when Paula died he was so overcome with grief that he was unable to work, because "I have suddenly lost the comforter whom I have carried about with me."[1] It is evident that Saint John Chrysostom enjoyed a similar relationship with the deaconess Olympias.[2] Such relationships between churchmen and wealthy female patrons have been known throughout the history of the church. For the twelfth century Sally Vaughn has devoted a book to an analysis of Saint Anselm's correspondence with noblewomen such as Adela of Blois, Ida of Boulogne, and even Queen Edith (Matilda), the wife of King Henry I; in all cases the bonds of affection are similarly clear.[3] Bernard of Clairvaux himself wrote to Countess Ermengarde

[1] Saint Jerome, Ep 99, PL 22:813. For other letters to and about Paula and Eustochium, see Ep 39, PL 22:465–73; Ep 45, PL 22:480–84; Ep 54, PL 22:550–60; Ep 108, PL 22:878–906; Ep 143, PL 22:1181–82.

[2] John Chrysostom, Epp 1–17, PG 52:549–680; J. N. D. Kelly, *Golden Mouth: The Story of John Chrysostom—Ascetic, Preacher, Bishop* (Ithaca, NY: Cornell University Press, 1995), 112–14.

[3] Sally N. Vaughn, *St. Anselm and the Handmaidens of God: A Study of Anselm's Correspondence with Women* (Turnhout: Brepols, 2002).

of Brittany, a wealthy patroness, "If you could but read in my heart how great an affection for you the finger of God has there inscribed, then you would surely see how no tongue could express and no pen describe what the spirit of God has been able to inscribe there."[4] As Jean Leclercq has pointed out, Bernard's tone of sincere affection sets this correspondence apart from any of his other letters to women.[5]

There is, however, no evidence of a woman in Aelred's life. Brian Patrick McGuire wrote, "Like many of the early Cistercians, he lived in a world so centered on good and attractive men that women remained on the periphery."[6] Similarly, "For him the world of men was far more important than that of women. Here he reflected the official Cistercian attitude in the early years of the order, according to which the new monasticism was for men only."[7] But something is being overlooked here. It is the letters of Jerome, John Chrysostom, Anselm, and Bernard that reveal the depth of the affection and respect that they felt for their female correspondents—letters that are lacking in Aelred's case. Without the lost letter collection, no correspondents, male or female, can be identified with whom Aelred may have felt a particular closeness. Aelred's other writings, however, provide important clues to his attitude toward women, especially *On the Formation of Anchoresses* and the sad tale of the nun of Watton.

---

[4] Bernard, Ep 116 (SBOp 7:296; J119). Also Ep 117 (SBOp 7:297; J120).

[5] Jean Leclercq, *Women and St. Bernard of Clairvaux*, CS 104 (Kalamazoo, MI: Cistercian Publications, 1989), 45–52.

[6] Brian Patrick McGuire, *Brother and Lover: Aelred of Rievaulx* (New York: Crossroad Publishing Co., 1994), 31.

[7] McGuire, *Brother and Lover*, 34. For contrary views on the Cistercian Order, see Brigitte Degler-Spengler, "The Incorporation of Cistercian Nuns into the Order in the Twelfth and Thirteenth Century," in *Hidden Springs: Cistercian Monastic Women*, ed. John A. Nichols and Lillian Thomas Shank, *Medieval Religious Women*, 3 vols., CS 113A (Kalamazoo, MI: Cistercian Publications, 1995), vol. 3, bk. 1, 87–99; Constance H. Berman, "Men's Houses, Women's Houses: The Relationship Between the Sexes in Twelfth-Century Monasticism," in *The Medieval Monastery*, Medieval Studies at Minnesota 2, ed. Andrew MacLeish (St. Cloud, MN: North Star Press of St. Cloud, 1988), 43–52.

Women in Holy Scripture

Nevertheless, brief mentions of women occur in most of Aelred's works, often as examples drawn from the Bible. Such examples tell us more about his mastery of Scripture than they do about his attitude toward women; nevertheless, they are worth collecting and considering in Aelred's case. Five examples in *Spiritual Friendship* involve women, three portrayed favorably and the other two unfavorably. As an example of friends who gave up their lives for one another, Aelred offered the story of a soldier who rescued a girl from a brothel and later became her companion in martyrdom.[8] In discussing the responsibility to correct a friend engaged in wrongdoing and certainly not to fall into sin oneself at a friend's urging, Aelred gave four examples, including among them Adam, who ate the forbidden fruit rather than correct Eve.[9] Similarly, discussing the great sin of slandering a friend, Aelred mentioned the case of Miriam, who was stricken with leprosy for having done so.[10] Aelred also cautioned his readers against allowing friendship to trump love of family and responsibility for dependents, offering the example of the wife of Heber the Klenite, Jael, who executed the family friend Sisera.[11] Finally Aelred discussed the need to anticipate the needs of one's friends and to offer help in such a way that the friend is not embarrassed. He offered the example of Boaz, who saw the poverty of Ruth the Moabite, who was gleaning in his fields, and instructed his reapers to leave ears of corn behind for her to collect without shame.[12] The point here is not that Eve and the leprous Miriam are portrayed unfavorably, but that men and women are used equally and apparently without differentiation as examples of both good and bad behavior. And while Ruth the Moabite was the beneficiary

---

[8] Aelred, Spir amic 1:29; CCCM 1:294; CF 5:57. The reference is to the story of Didyme and Theodora of Alexandria, which occurs in Saint Ambrose, *De Virginibus*, PL 16:212–16.

[9] Aelred, Spir amic 2:40; CCCM 1:310; CF 5:79; Gen 3:6.

[10] Aelred, Spir amic 3:28; CCCM 1:322; CF 5:98; Num 12:1-15.

[11] Aelred, Spir amic 3:47; CCCM 1:326; CF 5:102; Judg 4:17-22.

[12] Aelred, Spir amic 3:100; CCCM 1:339–40; CF 5:119; Ruth 2:1-22.

rather than the initiator of a friendly gesture, it is significant that
Aelred portrayed her as a worthy friend for Boaz rather than as
the passive recipient of a charitable donation.

Adding Women to the Story

Aelred also mentioned women in several of his historical works.
In the *Life of Saint Ninian*, there are three such incidents. The first
concerns a young woman, pregnant out of wedlock, who decided
that she would be judged less harshly by her neighbors if she said
that she had been forced by some important man. She therefore
accused the village priest of fathering her son. When the baby,
only one day old, was brought to Ninian for baptism, the saint
commanded him to declare who his real father was. Speaking in
an adult voice, the infant pointed to his real father and declared,
"This is my father! He begot me; he committed the wrongdoing
with which the priest is charged."[13] In crafting his *Life of Ninian*,
Aelred said that he worked from an earlier source, which is now
lost.[14] An eighth-century poem survives, however, which probably
used the same source, and it is interesting to compare Aelred's
interpretation with the earlier work. The poem considers the story
solely from the point of the view of the accused priest, but Aelred
changed the viewpoint, focusing instead on the woman and her
situation.[15]

It is particularly remarkable the other two incidents involving
women do not occur in the eighth-century poem at all. The second
mention of a woman occurs in the course of a visit that Ninian
made to inspect his dairy herds. When the animals had all been

---

[13] Aelred, Vita N V; Pinkerton, *Lives*, 23–25; CCCM 3:123; CF 71:46–48.

[14] John MacQueen, "The Literary Sources for the *Life of St. Ninian*," in *Galloway: Land and Lordship*, ed. Richard D. Oram and Geoffrey P. Stell (Edinburgh: Scottish Society for Northern Studies, 1991), 17–25; Ann W. Astell, "To Build the Church: Saint Aelred of Rievaulx's Hexaemeral Miracles in the *Life of Ninian*," CSQ 49, no. 4 (2014): 456–57. For more on the Life of Ninian, see below, chap. 7:157–62.

[15] John MacQueen, *St Nynia, with a translation of the Miracula Nynie Episcopi and the Vita Niniani by Winifred MacQueen* (Edinburgh: Birlinn Ltd., 2005), 92–93; Astell, "To Build the Church," 470–71.

gathered in one place, he drew a furrow around them with his staff and invoked divine protection upon them for the night. He then withdrew to "a certain honorable matron's house" for the night. That night, thieves came and tried to steal the animals, but the cattle resisted, and one great bull attacked and gored one of the men to death. When Ninian and his companions returned the next morning, they found the dead man lying on the ground and his fellow thieves milling around aimlessly as though they had lost their reason. Through Ninian's prayers the dead man was restored to life and the madmen regained their reason.[16] The mention of the matron whose hospitality Ninian had enjoyed shows that Ninian had a woman friend with whom he felt comfortable spending the night and that neither he nor Aelred considered it improper to seek hospitality in the home of a woman of good reputation. The third miracle in this work involving a woman occurred after Ninian's death and is a classic healing miracle in which a blind girl named Deisuit had her sight restored after praying at Ninian's tomb.[17] Perhaps these two miracles were recent additions to the saint's legend and so were unavailable to the eighth-century poet, or maybe Aelred simply liked them for his own reasons. Nevertheless, their inclusion in his work resulted in women's having a larger place in Ninian's story than had previously been allotted to them.

As in the *Life of Ninian*, in the *Life of Saint Edward the Confessor* Aelred followed an earlier source, an account written by Osbert of Clare. A still earlier anonymous life of King Edward, dating to shortly after the Norman Conquest, had been written for Edward's queen, Edith. The text waxed eloquent about the queen's virtues and those of her family, the Godwins.[18] Osbert of Clare and Aelred both toned down the effusive praise of the Godwins, and

---

[16] Aelred, Vita N VIII; Pinkerton, *Lives*, 28–30; CCCM 3:124–26; CF 71:50–52.

[17] Aelred, Vita N XIV; Pinkerton, *Lives*, 38; CCCM 3:132–33; CF 71:61–62.

[18] Frank Barlow, Introduction to *The Life of King Edward Who Rests at Westminster*, ed. and trans. Frank Barlow, 2nd ed. (Oxford: Clarendon Press, 1992), xviii–xxviii; Frank Barlow, *Edward the Confessor* (Berkeley and Los Angeles: University of California Press, 1970), xxii–xxiii.

Aelred inserted a long passage about Earl Godwin's traitorous rebellion and miserable death into his own work.[19] The originally praised virtues of the queen herself, however, remained unaltered by the later authors, both of whom emphasized her seriousness and modesty and the chastity that the couple preserved throughout their marriage.[20] Aelred in fact added a passage defending Edith against charges that Edward had avoided marital relations with her because he did not want to beget children who would also have ties to his enemies, the Godwin family, writing, "But if the love by which they were encompassed be considered, such an opinion is easily discredited."[21]

By the time that Edward's great project, the building of Westminster Abbey, was completed and ready to be dedicated, the king lay ill, but he still took part in the ceremony. Aelred, however, noted that "the queen made all the arrangements, attended to everything, was concerned for all, and thought of all. She filled the place of them both."[22] Both authors noted the queen's presence at Edward's deathbed, with only Osbert recording the homely little detail that Edith held Edward's feet in her lap to warm them.[23] Both authors recorded that at the end Edward admonished his queen not to weep or be sad at his death. Aelred also inserted a passage in which the king praised his wife for her modesty, obedience, and chastity and also commanded that everything she had brought into the marriage as her dowry should remain hers forever.[24]

---

[19] Aelred, Vita E 1.24–25; PL 195:765–67; CCCM 3A; CF 56:188–92.

[20] Aelred, Vita E 1.8; PL 195:747–48; CCCM 3A; CF 56:145–49; Marc Bloch, "La vie de s. Édouard le Confesseur par Osbert de Clare," *Analecta Bollandiana* 41 (1923): 74–75.

[21] Aelred, Vita E 1.8; PL 195:748; CCCM 3A; CF 56:148; Bloch, "La vie de s. Édouard le Confesseur," 104–5.

[22] Aelred, Vita E 1.28; PL 195:771; CCCM 3A; CF 56:202.

[23] Aelred, Vita E 1.29; PL 195:773; CCCM 3A; CF 56:206; Bloch, "La vie de s. Édouard le Confesseur," 108.

[24] Aelred, Vita E 1.31; PL 195:774; CCCM 3A; CF 56:210; Bloch, "La vie de s. Édouard le Confesseur," 110–11.

One other significant difference between the two works with regard to their treatment of women occurs in the story that both Aelred and Osbert told of a vision received by King Edward and Earl Leofric of Mercia in which Jesus appeared to them during Mass, standing on the altar at the moment of the consecration.[25] Earl Leofric and his wife Godgiva were well known for their piety and generosity, and perhaps because of this fact Aelred took the opportunity to add a passage praising Godgiva, writing, "She wonderfully fulfilled the meaning of her name, 'a good gift,' by the way she carried out her affairs, either because Christ had brought her to benefit the church as a kind of good gift or because she was continually offering to God the acceptable gift of faith and devotion. With such a companion at his side, the holy earl was always intent on the work of God."[26] Aelred did not go so far as to include Godgiva as a recipient of the vision, but he did recognize her goodness and charity and gave her credit for supporting and inspiring the earl's pious life, which provided the background for the vision that he received.

Both Aelred and Osbert concluded their treatises with accounts of the miracles performed at Edward's tomb. Aelred added a new miracle involving a nun at Barking Abbey who was troubled by a recurring fever. In a dream she saw herself on a journey with a group of friends to visit her parents. Along the way, a stranger advised her to seek healing at the tomb of King Edward at Westminster. When she awakened the nun went to the chapel and prayed to Edward, saying that the labor of a journey was too great for her and that if he so willed, he could certainly heal her where she was. The fever never troubled her again.[27] By her faith the nun therefore became the equal of the Roman centurion who said to Jesus that he did not need to come to his home, telling him, "Only

[25] Aelred, Vita E 1.18; PL 195:760–61; CCCM 3A; CF 56:176–78; Bloch, "La vie de s. Édouard le Confesseur," 91–92.

[26] Aelred, Vita E 1.18; PL 195:760; CCCM 3A; CF 56:176. For more on Earl Leofric and his wife, the legendary Lady Godiva, see Simeon of Durham, *Opera Omnia*, ed. Thomas Arnold, 2 vols., RS 75 (London: Longmans, 1882–1885), 2:173.

[27] Aelred, Vita E 2.41; PL 195:787–88; CCCM 3A; CF 56:238–40.

say the word and my servant will be healed" (Matt 8:8; Luke 7:6). As in the *Life of Ninian*, Aelred's *Life of Edward* accords women a larger position in the story than does that of his predecessor. Rather than being uninterested in the spiritual lives of women, these two cases in which Aelred worked from an earlier text show that he was actually more interested in women's spiritual lives than were the earlier authors.

References to women also occur in works that Aelred constructed without the use of an earlier model. Two of these are found in *The Saints of the Church of Hexham*, which Aelred wrote to celebrate the translation of the relics of the five holy bishops, Eata, Acca, Frethbert, Alchmund, and Tilbert, in 1155. During Aelred's own lifetime, Edric, the leader of the first group of Augustinian canons sent to Hexham in 1112, had discovered two chests containing the bones of Acca and Alchmund and had effected the healing of a blind woman by washing her eyes with water in which one of the bones of Acca had been dipped.[28] In a second case, a young woman traveling with her brother to the Holy Land was a protagonist in another story, as part of a group of international pilgrims that included two devout young men from Hexham who were fond of extolling the virtues of their hometown saint, Acca. The brother, never having heard of Acca, began to mock the saint and continued to blaspheme until he suddenly fell on the ground in a fit, foaming at the mouth. His sister begged for the help of her fellow pilgrims, and one of the men from Hexham took pity on her and prayed to Acca, who then healed his detractor.[29]

The Genealogy of the Kings of the English includes the stories of two notable royal women. The first, Aethelflaed, the sister of King Edward the Elder, was known as the Lady of the Mercians. She was a warrior queen who fought the Danish invaders, capturing Derby from them and constructing numerous fortified cities. Her story was recorded in the *Anglo-Saxon Chronicle* and repeated by

---

[28] Aelred, SS Hag XIb; Raine, *Priory*, 1:187–88; CCCM 3:91; CF 71:83–84.
[29] Aelred, SS Hag XIII; Raine, *Priory*, 1:188–89; CCCM 3:92–93; CF 71:85–87.

most twelfth-century English chronicles, always with high praise.[30] Curiously, Aelred only mentioned the empress Matilda briefly, as Henry II's mother, but perhaps the inclusion of Aethelflaed's story is a backhanded compliment to the warrior queen of his own time.[31]

The second woman who received special notice in the *Genealogy* was Henry I's wife, Matilda, the sister of King David I of Scotland. Aelred especially praised her for her saintliness and charity, recounting a story that he had heard from David himself. One evening while David was at the English court, Matilda summoned him to attend her in her apartments. When he arrived there he found her surrounded by lepers, washing and kissing their feet. David remonstrated with her, saying that her husband would be so repulsed by her actions that he would never kiss her again. Matilda replied, "Who does not know that the feet of the eternal king should be preferred to the lips of a king who will die?" She went on to encourage David to follow her example, but too repulsed to do so, he retreated in confusion to his own chambers.[32] At a minimum miracle stories involving women show Aelred's belief that women were as worthy of God's mercy and favor as men. Examples praising women like Godgiva, Aethelflaed, and Queen Matilda prove that far from ignoring or denigrating

[30] Aelred, Gen Angl XIV; PL 195:723; CCCM 3:32–33; CF 56:87; *The Anglo-Saxon Chronicle*, ed. and trans. Michael Swanton (New York: Routledge, 1998), 909D, 910C, 912–18C, 913D, 918E, 922A; Henry of Huntingdon, *Historia Anglorum: The History of the English People*, ed. and trans. Diana Greenway (Oxford: Clarendon Press, 1996), 304–9; John of Worcester, *The Chronicle of John of Worcester*, ed. R. R. Darlington and P. McGurk, trans. P. McGurk and Jennifer Bray, 3 vols. (Oxford: Clarendon Press, 1995–1998), 2:294–97, 366–81; William of Malmesbury, *Gesta Regum Anglorum: The History of the English Kings*, ed. and trans. R. A. B. Mynors, R. M. Thomson, and M. Winterbottom, 2 vols. (Oxford: Clarendon Press, 1998), 1:199; Simeon of Durham, *Opera Omnia*, 2:120, 122–23, 234.

[31] Aelred, Gen Angl Pref, XIII; PL 195:716, 736; CCCM 3:23, 55; CF 56:72, 120–21; Dutton, Introduction to *Northern Saints*, 30.

[32] Aelred, Gen Angl XIII; PL 195:736; CCCM 3:55; CF 56:119–20; Lois L. Huneycutt, *Matilda of Scotland: A Study in Medieval Queenship* (Woodbridge: Boydell Press, 2003), 104–6; Freeman, *Narratives of a New Order: Cistercian Historical Writing in England, 1150–1220*, Medieval Church Studies 2 (Turnhout: Brepols, 2002), 81–85; Dutton, Introduction to *Northern Saints*, 27–29.

women, Aelred recognized and celebrated them as capable of virtuous and sometimes heroic behavior.

Women as Equals

The theme of equality becomes even more pronounced when we turn from Aelred's historical works to a consideration of his sermons and works of spiritual direction. Aelred's liberal use in *Spiritual Friendship* of both men and women drawn from Scripture to illustrate the proper behavior of friends toward one another indicates that Aelred considered women both capable and worthy of spiritual friendship. Aelred offered clear and moving statements on the equality of women and the possibility of true friendship between men and women. Discussing the creation of Eve from Adam's rib, Aelred stated, "How beautiful it is that the second human being was taken from the side of the first, so that nature might teach that human beings are equal and, as it were, collateral, and that there is in human affairs neither a superior nor an inferior, a characteristic of true friendship."[33]

Aelred often performed a balancing act in his prescriptive works, taking pains to indicate that his advice applied to both men and women. For example, in *Mirror*, he discussed how one type of attachment could turn into another, less virtuous, type. He first offered the example of how admiration for a holy nun because of her faith and virtues might, as a man sought closer acquaintance with her, turn into something sinful. He then immediately balanced this example with the case of experienced monks becoming inappropriately attached to virtuous young men within the monastery.[34]

This theme of equality is most pronounced in Aelred's *Formation*, a work that, on the surface at least, was specifically directed toward women. He seems to have composed this treatise late

[33] Aelred, Sp amic 1:57; CCCM 1:298–99; CF 5:63; Gen 2:21-24; Elizabeth A. Freeman, *Narratives*, 84–85; Marsha L. Dutton, "Aelred of Rievaulx on Friendship, Chastity and Sex: The Sources," CSQ 29.2 (1994): 184.

[34] Aelred, Spec car 3.28.66–68; CCCM 1:136–37; CF 17:266–67.

in life, 1160–1162, at the request of a sister who was a recluse. He stated that they were siblings, born of the same parents, but because this work contains the only mention of a sister and does not even give her name, it has been suggested that she is only a literary construct.[35] The treatise begins with a discussion of external observances and the recluse's way of life, moves on to her interior, spiritual life, and concludes with a threefold meditation on the past, the present, and the future. The past considers the life of Christ, the present the recluse's own spiritual state, and the future the Last Judgment.[36] Throughout his work, Aelred sometimes tailored his remarks specifically to women, while at other times he addressed recluses in general or included religious men and women living in monasteries as well. He began by explaining, "The monks of old chose to live as solitaries for several reasons: to avoid ruin, to escape injury, to enjoy greater freedom in expressing their ardent longing for Christ's embrace."[37] He then moved on to a consideration of temptations to which women might be subject, especially gossip and curiosity, which might lead to unchaste behavior.

The interpretation of Aelred's stereotypical assumptions is problematic. On the one hand, Brian Patrick McGuire has remarked that his statements about religious women "indicate either contempt for them in what he imagines to be a gossipy world, or else belief that they will be subject to violent sexual

[35] Aelred, Inst incl 32; CCCM 1:673–74; CF 2:93; also Inst incl 1; CCCM 1:637; CF 2:43; Marsha L. Dutton, "The Conversion and Vocation of Aelred of Rievaulx: A Historical Hypothesis," in *England in the Twelfth Century: Proceedings of the 1988 Harlaxton Symposium*, ed. Daniel Williams (Woodbridge: Boydell, 1990), 32n3; Elizabeth A. Freeman, "Aelred of Rievaulx's Pastoral Care of Religious Women, with Special Reference to the *De institutione inclusarum*," CSQ 46, no.1 (2011): 23–24.

[36] Marsha Dutton-Stuckey, "Getting Things the Wrong Way Round: Composition and Transposition in Aelred of Rievaulx's *De institutione inclusarum*," in *Heaven on Earth, Studies in Medieval Cistercian History* IX, ed. E. Rozanne Elder, CS 68 (Kalamazoo, MI: Cistercian Publications, 1983), 90–101; Pierre-André Burton, *Aelred de Rievaulx (1110–1167), De l'homme éclaté à l'être unifié: Essai de biographie existentielle et spirituelle* (Paris: Éditions du Cerf, 2010), 235–39.

[37] Aelred, Inst incl 2; CCCM 1:637; CF 2:45.

temptations."[38] This interpretation, however, overlooks Aelred's concluding statement: "Evidence abounds that misfortunes of this kind are only too common today among both men and women."[39] Later Aelred warned, "But as in this life we are all prey to inconstancy, as we never remain long in the same state of mind, we will best avoid idleness by the alternation of exercises and safeguard our peace by varying our occupations."[40] It should also be noted that Aelred issued similar warnings against undue curiosity in *Mirror* and his first sermon on the feast of Saints Peter and Paul, works not specifically directed to women.[41] As Aelred described the recluse's daily round of prayer, reading, meditation, and manual labor, he relied heavily on the Rule of Saint Benedict, which was of course written for men.[42] Several times he used monks rather than nuns or recluses to illustrate the struggle necessary to preserve chastity in thought as well as deed.[43]

As Aelred moved to a discussion of the recluse's interior life, he waxed eloquent on the glory of her virginity, but he was careful to specify that his praise applied to both men and women: "Let her contemplate the most blessed Mary [Miriam] as with the timbrel of virginity she leads the dance of the virgins and entones that sweet song which none may sing but the virgins of both sexes."[44] He suggested that the recluse place pictures of the Virgin Mary and Saint John the Apostle on either side of her cell's altar so that she might "consider how pleasing to Christ is the virginity

[38] McGuire, *Brother and Lover*, 30.

[39] Aelred, Inst incl 2; CCCM 1:638; CF 2:47.

[40] Aelred, Inst incl 9; CCCM 1:644; CF 2:55. Similarly Inst incl 11; CCCM 1:647; CF 2:58.

[41] Aelred, Spec car 2.24.72–73; CCCM 1:100–101; CF 17:213–15. Also S 17; CCCM 2A:136; Aelred of Rievaulx, *The Liturgical Sermons: The First Clairvaux Collection*, trans. Theodore Berkeley and M. Basil Pennington, CF 58 (Kalamazoo, MI: Cistercian Publications, 2001), 248.

[42] Aelred, Inst incl 11–13; CCCM 1:647–49; CF 2:58–61; Freeman, "Pastoral Care," 15–16.

[43] Aelred, Inst incl 18, CCCM 1:653–54, CF 2:66–67; Inst incl 22, CCCM 1:655–56, CF 2:69–70.

[44] Aelred, Inst incl 15; CCCM 1:651; CF 2:64.

of both sexes."[45] He concluded by praising his sister for having preserved her virginity while he himself had failed to safeguard his own.[46] McGuire interpreted Aelred's interchangeable use of monks and nuns as a sign of Aelred's basic lack of interest in the world of a female recluse: "He was curious about it, projected his self upon it, and had strong opinions, but he was an outsider to its inhabitants and their inner lives."[47] A more positive understanding of the same material is that Aelred considered men and women spiritually equal and believed that the same rules of conduct and way of life would be beneficial to both. Evidently his fellow monks thought so too, for as Elizabeth Freeman has observed, the extant manuscripts of *Formation* were preserved in male Cistercian houses.[48]

Aelred also spoke in one of his sermons on the prophet Isaiah about the ecstatic visions received by a nun at the Gilbertine priory generally thought to be Watton. He described how she was "daily transmitted to the heavens" and remarked (following Paul's words in 2 Cor 5:16) that she who had once known Christ according to the flesh now knew him according to the truth.[49] His remarks show that he was conversant with and interested in events at the priory, and furthermore that he considered the nun's piety a worthy example for his own brethren at Rievaulx. But as

[45] Aelred, Inst incl 26; CCCM 1:658–59; CF 2:73–74. Similarly on Saint John, Inst incl 31; CCCM 1:668; CF 2:87.

[46] Aelred, Inst incl 32; CCCM 1:674–77; CF 2:93–96; Marsha Dutton-Stuckey, "A Prodigal Writes Home: Aelred of Rievaulx's *De institutione inclusarum*," in *Heaven on Earth, Studies in Medieval Cistercian History* IX, ed. E. Rozanne Elder, CS 68 (Kalamazoo, MI: Cistercian Publications, 1983), 35–42.

[47] McGuire, *Brother and Lover*, 30–31.

[48] Freeman, "Pastoral Care," 15; Burton, *Aelred*, 233.

[49] Aelred, Oner 2; CCCM 2D:36–37; Sharon K. Elkins, *Holy Women of Twelfth-Century England* (Chapel Hill, NC: University of North Carolina Press, 1988), 100; Giles Constable, "Aelred of Rievaulx and the Nun of Watton: An Episode in the Early History of the Gilbertine Order," in *Medieval Women*, ed. Derek Baker (Oxford: Basil Blackwell for the Ecclesiastical History Society, 1978), 210–11; Elias Dietz, "Ambivalence Well Considered: An Interpretive Key to the Whole of Aelred's Works," CSQ 47, no. 1 (2012): 82; Burton, *Aelred*, 508; Dutton, Introduction to *Northern Saints*, 29.

Elizabeth Freeman has pointed out, his statements are noteworthy for another reason. Beginning with Augustine and throughout the Middle Ages, it was common to make distinctions between various types of mystical experiences. A vision in which the recipient saw or heard manifestations of the divine was considered a corporeal vision. It was thought to be inferior to an intellectual vision, in which the person experienced an inward knowledge of the presence of God without any sensory component. It was often thought that women, as essentially carnal beings, were incapable of experiencing the higher type of vision. Thus when Aelred referred to the nun as having previously known Christ according to the flesh but now according to the truth, he was clearly stating that she had experienced the higher type of purely intellectual vision and was thereby holding her up as spiritually equal to the monks to whom he spoke.[50]

Aelred also preached a number of sermons at Rievaulx to celebrate the various feasts of the Virgin Mary: her Nativity, Purification, Annunciation, and Assumption.[51] Occasionally these sermons portray the Mother of Jesus in an imaginative new light, made all the more striking by the fact that they were spoken by a man to other men. For example, in a sermon on the Annunciation Aelred speculated, "Perhaps at the time the angel came . . . [Mary] was holding [the text of] Isaiah in her hands; perhaps she was then studying the prophecy which declares: *Behold a virgin shall conceive and bear a son and his name will be called Emmanuel.*"[52] Aelred here portrayed Mary in the guise of a literate woman, practicing *lectio divina* as she waited, hoping and fearing that she

---

[50] Freeman, "Pastoral Care," 20–21; Rosalynn Voaden, *God's Words, Women's Voices: The Discernment of Spirits in the Writing of Late-Medieval Women Visionaries* (York: York Medieval Press, 1999), 7–40. J. Stephen Russell, "Vision and Skepticism in Aelred's *De Oneribus*," CSQ 49, no. 4 (2014): 483–97. For Aelred's three types of visions, see Spec car 2.8.20–21; CCCM 1:75; CF 17:176; and for his list of six types, see Oner, Hom 2.2-14; CCCM 2D:31–36.

[51] Aelred, SS 5, 9, 19–24; CCCM 2A:46–52, 70–80, 147–203; CF 58:119–28, 155–69, 263–345.

[52] Aelred, S 9; CCCM 2A:75; CF 58:161–62; Isa 7:14.

might be the one to receive the privilege of giving birth to the savior. By the fact that Mary waited and hoped, carefully guarding her virtue, she appears very much in charge of her own destiny, not a passive vessel.

The same sense of control is present in a sermon on the Assumption in which Aelred used the motif of a spiritual castle in which Mary carefully prepared to receive the Lord, with a moat of humility, walls of chastity, and a tower of charity. He remarked that "if the Blessed Mary had not prepared this castle within herself, the Lord Jesus would not have entered her womb or her spirit."[53] Again, by her own virtue, he showed Mary as having made herself worthy to become the Mother of Jesus. In another sermon on the Assumption, he preached on the strong woman "whose worth is beyond pearls" described in the book of Proverbs, saying, "This strength shone forth exceptionally in the ever blessed Mary, Mother of God, who without any previous example despised the delights of this world, abhorred the lewdness of the flesh and—something no one before her had done—chose the purity of virginity."[54] He made Mary's strength an example for everyone, both men and women, remarking, "I see a *strong woman*—a strong soul, that is—in Paul, who is stoned, who is beaten with rods, who is afflicted with *hunger, thirst and cold.*"[55]

Aelred also preached a sermon for the feast of Saint Katherine of Alexandria, an unusual choice for a Cistercian abbot since her feast day was not part of the Cistercian liturgical calendar at the time. Marie Anne Mayeski, whose translation of the sermon appears in Appendix 3 below, has therefore suggested that the sermon was preached outside of Rievaulx, perhaps at some occasion involving religious women, such as the consecration of a nun or an enclosure ceremony for an anchoress.[56] Aelred began

---

[53] Aelred, S 19; CCCM 2A:148; CF 58:264.

[54] Aelred, S 21; CCCM 2A:166; CF 58:290–91.

[55] Aelred, S 21; CCCM 2A:166; CF 58:291; 2 Cor 11:24-27.

[56] Aelred, S 174; CCCM 2C:573–79; App. 3:250–59; Marie Anne Mayeski, "'The Right Occasion for the Words': Situating Aelred's Homily on St. Katherine," CSQ 33, no. 1 (1998): 45–60.

with the text from the Gospel of Matthew: "This is the wise virgin whom the Lord found watching."[57] He noted that mere physical virginity was not enough—it had to be accompanied by wisdom. He described the union of virginity and wisdom as "a decoration beyond every necklace, every earring, every collar, or any ornament whatever that is precious and most beautiful to women." From the two together a "precious ring is made, a seal of love and chastity."[58] As Mayeski suggested, this is perhaps an allusion to the ring with which consecrated religious women were invested,[59] one of a number of images making this sermon especially appropriate for an occasion involving religious women.

Mayeski also drew attention to Aelred's likening of Katherine to "a wise business woman . . . [who] sold earthly things and bought heavenly ones." Aelred noted that Katherine found "a treasure hidden in a field . . . through the study of heavenly discipline." Having found this treasure she "sold all that she had and bought that field"—again the wise and prudent business woman.[60] This would have been a particularly appropriate simile for an audience including laywomen who had retired to a convent or anchorhold after a life spent running or working in a family business. Furthermore anchorites themselves, existing outside the support of a religious community, often engaged in some type of business, such as copying books or embroidering vestments and church linens.[61]

Throughout his account of Saint Katherine's life and martyrdom, Aelred presented her as the active agent of her own salvation: "But I have said too little in saying that the Lord found her watching; I say more, I say truly that the prudent and watchful

---

[57] Aelred, S 174; CCCM 2C:573–74; App. 3:250; Matt 25:1-13.

[58] Aelred, S 174; CCCM 2C:573–74; App. 3:251.

[59] Mayeski, "Right Occasion," 58–59.

[60] Aelred, S 174; CCCM 2C:574; App. 3:252–53; Mayeski, "Right Occasion," 59.

[61] Tom Licence, *Hermits and Recluses in English Society, 950–1200* (Oxford: Oxford University Press, 2011), 67, 106–7; C. H. Lawrence, *Medieval Monasticism: Forms of Religious Life in Western Europe in the Middle Ages*, 3rd ed. (Harlow, Essex, UK: Longman, 2001), 149.

virgin, by persistent and ardent seeking, arrived at and found the Lord."[62] Even in martyrdom Aelred showed Katherine as being far from the innocent victim of her persecutors. Aelred pictured her "fearlessly present[ing] herself for immolation to an idol by a cruel tyrant" and noted that "this innocent virgin debated against rhetoricians and grammarians, taught faith in Christ, and produced worthy martyrs for the Lord."[63] Of course by Aelred's time the era of physical persecution was long past, but his audience may well have included women who had faced the displeasure of their families and perhaps even the ecclesiastical hierarchy in order to undertake a religious life. For example, Christina of Markyate (ca. 1096–ca. 1155) defied her parents by rejecting marriage in order to become a recluse and then encountered strong resistance from two bishops. The first, Ranulf Flambard of Durham, having failed in his attempt to seduce Christina, engineered the forced marriage. The second, Robert Bloet of Lincoln, at first agreed to dissolve the union but then accepted a bribe to deny Christina's petition.[64]

Overall the sermon indicates that Aelred had a deep understanding of and respect for religious women. He skillfully portrayed Katherine, and by extension all religious women, as actively seeking their own path to God, employing the skills that they had learned in the world. Like the sermons on the Blessed Virgin, Aelred's sermon for the feast of Saint Katherine portrays a woman as a worthy role model for both men and women and is a further indication of Aelred's belief in the spiritual equality of women. The work concludes, "Let us imitate this glorious virgin, O brothers, and if we cannot [travel] that admirable way through which the Lord God led her, let us at least, after her example, seek our beloved on our couch. This means, let us see God through a

[62] Aelred, S 174; CCCM 2C:575; App. 3:254.

[63] Aelred, S 174; CCCM 2C:577–78; App. 3:257.

[64] *The Life of Christina of Markyate, A Twelfth Century Recluse*, ed. and trans. C. H. Talbot (Oxford: Clarendon Press, 1959), 40–45, 67–73, 112–13, 118–19; Katharine Sykes, *Inventing Sempringham: Gilbert of Sempringham and the Origins of the Role of the Master* (Zurich and Berlin: LIT Verlag, 2011), 38.

pure conscience, quiet contemplation, and a holy manner of life so that when the Lord comes, he will find us watching."[65]

This equality between men and women is also an underlying feature of Aelred's account of the sordid affair of the nun of Watton, in which his main concern was to rescue the convent from the consequences of the incident. Before he got down to the details of the case, he was at great pains to stress the holiness of the nuns at Watton. He praised the love within the community, writing, "They showed so much love and concern for one another that when one died, the others did not cease praying until something certain enlightened them about either her punishment or her glorification." He continued with an account of a vision that one of the nuns received during Mass, in which her dear friend who had just died appeared to her encased in a beam of light.[66] Aelred's praise of the love within the Watton community reflects his own great interest in spiritual friendship and demonstrates that he believed that friendship was open to everyone, men and women alike.[67]

Women as Temptresses

A special subset of Aelred's stories about women involve those who either succumbed to sexual temptation themselves or inspired it in men. It is especially noteworthy that in these cases he seemed to go out of his way to avoid painting the women as harlots and temptresses.[68] For example, in the *Life of Ninian*, when Aelred told the story of the young woman who falsely accused the village priest of fathering her illegitimate son, he kept the focus squarely upon the man who had actually seduced her and fathered her child. As Aelred told it, when commanded by the saint, the day-old baby pointed out his real father and declared that he had committed

[65] Aelred, S 174; CCCM 2C:579; App. 3:259.

[66] Aelred, Mira I; PL 195:790–91; CCCM 3:138; CF 71:110–11; Elizabeth Freeman, "Nuns in the Public Sphere: Aelred of Rievaulx's *De sanctimoniali de Wattun* and the Gendering of Authority," *Comitatus* 27 (1996): 62–63.

[67] Freeman, "Nuns in the Public Sphere," 62–64.

[68] Dutton, Introduction to *Northern Saints*, 29.

the wrongdoing with which the priest had been charged.[69] Thus although Aelred made it clear that the young woman had sinned twice, first sexually and second in making the false accusation, at the climax of the story he blamed the man as seducer, not the woman.

A second tale of sexual sin is found in *Hexham*. In this story a villain kidnapped a beautiful young woman and murdered her brother, only to have the hand holding the spear that stabbed the brother struck withered and useless. Aelred attributed the sudden, miraculous atrophy of the murderer's hand to the fact that the evil deed had taken place in the courtyard of a church at Hexham. In any case, the blame is once more clearly attached to the seducer, not to his victim.[70]

A third woman, this time an evil one, goes unnamed in Aelred's *Genealogy of the Kings of the English*, though Eadmer of Canterbury does name her in his *Life of Saint Dunstan*. Eadmer reports that King Eadwig (955–957) was so enamored of a woman named Aethelgifu that he left his own coronation feast to enjoy a romantic interlude with her and her daughter Aelfgifu. Archbishop Dunstan of Canterbury surprised them in the bedroom and made Eadwig return to the feast. The king was so angry that he exiled Dunstan to Flanders, where he remained until a rebellion forced the king from his throne in favor of his brother Edgar.[71] Aelred was clearly unsympathetic to the temptress, referring to her variously as Herodias and Jezebel and blaming her for giving the king bad counsel. By omitting the details of the affair and leaving the woman unnamed, however, he transferred the blame to Eadwig.[72] Aelred did not blame any of the women for inspiring lust in the men who attacked or seduced them but rather sought to mitigate their faults and highlight those of the men.

---

[69] Aelred, Vita N V; Pinkerton, *Lives*, 23–25; CCCM 3:121–23; CF 71:46–48.

[70] Aelred, SS Hag VII; Raine, *Priory*, 1:181–82; CCCM 3:84; CF 71:74–75.

[71] Eadmer of Canterbury, *Lives and Miracles of Saints Oda, Dunstan, and Oswald*, ed. and trans. Andrew J. Turner and Bernard J. Muir (Oxford: Clarendon Press, 2006), 96–99.

[72] Aelred, Gen Angl VII; PL 195:725–76; CCCM 3:37–38; CF 56:94–95; Freeman, *Narratives*, 81.

The Cistercians and the Gilbertines

In no case is Aelred's reluctance to blame women in matters of sexual sin more apparent than his treatment of the scandal of the nun of Watton, which he recounted in a work with the interesting title *A Certain Wonderful Miracle*. Watton was a Gilbertine house; the relationship between the Cistercians and the Gilbertines explains the role Aelred played in the events. The founder of the Gilbertines, Gilbert of Sempringham, was the son of a well-to-do Lincolnshire knight named Jocelin. When Gilbert inherited his father's two demesne churches at Sempringham and West Torrington, he wanted his goods to be used in God's service, so he tried to establish a male community of anchorites at Sempringham. He was unable, however, to find any men willing to live the strict life he envisioned, so in 1131 he acted on the request of seven young women from the parish and enclosed them as anchoresses instead.[73]

Since the women were strictly confined to their cells, they at first depended on women from the village to bring them their meals and handle other necessities. Fearing the temptations that such contact with secular women might bring, however, Gilbert soon decided to act on the advice of William, the first abbot of Rievaulx, and incorporated into the community an order of lay sisters, modeled on the *conversi* of the Cistercians.[74] Their presence was soon followed by the addition of a group of lay brothers to perform necessary manual labor and handle the community's business affairs.[75] By 1139, a second community had been established at

[73] *The Book of St Gilbert*, ed. and trans. Raymonde Foreville and Gillian Keir (Oxford: Clarendon Press, 1987), 30–35; Brian Golding, *Gilbert of Sempringham and the Gilbertine Order, c. 1130–c. 1300* (Oxford: Clarendon Press, 1995), 17–22.

[74] *Institutes of the Gilbertine Order*, in William Dugdale, *Monasticon Anglicanum*, ed. John Caley, Henry Eales, and Bulkeley Bandinel, 6 vols. (London, 1846), vol. 6, pt. 2, insert after p. 945. For the Cistercian abbot's advice, xix. For the identification of the abbot as William, xxxvi. See *Book of St Gilbert*, 34–35, for Gilbert's receiving advice on the lay sisters. Also see Golding, *Gilbert of Sempringham*, 22–23; Elkins, *Holy Women*, 80; Brian Golding, "St. Bernard and St. Gilbert," in *The Influence of St. Bernard*, ed. Benedicta Ward (Oxford: SLG Press, 1976), 44.

[75] *Book of St Gilbert*, 36–39; Golding, *Gilbert of Sempringham*, 23.

Haverholme on land granted by Bishop Alexander of Lincoln, with their foundation charter noting that the women followed "the Cistercian way of life."[76]

Seeing the growth of the communities, Gilbert began to doubt his worthiness to oversee them; by this time he was approaching sixty years of age and rightfully feared for the future of the Order after his death. He therefore requested help from the Cistercians, feeling that "because he had often received hospitality from them, he was more at home with these men than with others."[77] It is possible that Aelred began his relationship with the Gilbertines by taking part in some preliminary negotiations at this point. At some time in 1147 Gilbert witnessed a charter recording the resolution of a dispute between Nicholas, a canon of Lincoln cathedral, and Bishop Alexander over two bovates of land belonging to the canon's church of South Scarle. Aelred himself also witnessed the charter as abbot of Revesby, along with three other Cistercian abbots, Gervase of Louth Park, Walter of Kirkstead, and Richard of Leicester. It has been suggested that the Cistercian abbots, and perhaps Gilbert as well, were together for the founding of the abbey of Vaudey on May 23, 1147.[78] In September of that year Gilbert traveled to Cîteaux for the annual general chapter, at which he formally petitioned the Cistercians to take over the supervision of his order. His request was turned down because "the lord Pope and the Cistercian abbots said that monks of their own Order were not permitted authority over the religious life of others, least of all that of nuns."[79]

Modern historians have occasionally considered this decision a prime example of the Cistercians' supposed distaste for wom-

---

[76] *Book of St Gilbert*, 38–41; EEA 1, no. 37; Golding, *Gilbert of Sempringham*, 24–25.

[77] *Book of St Gilbert*, 40–41.

[78] *The Registrum Antiquissimum of the Cathedral Church of Lincoln*, ed. C. W. Foster, 3 vols. (Hereford: Hereford Times for the Lincoln Record Society, 1931–1935; reprinted Woodbridge: Boydell, 2008), 3:921, pp. 262–64; H. E. Salter, "Two Lincoln Documents of 1147," EHR 35, no. 138 (1920): 212–14.

[79] *Book of St Gilbert*, 42–43; Elizabeth A. Freeman, "Gilbert of Hoyland's Sermons for Nuns: A Cistercian Abbot and the *cura monialium* in Twelfth-Century Lincolnshire," CSQ 50, no. 3 (2015): 280.

en;[80] however, recent scholarship has provided a more nuanced interpretation. Most obviously, the same general chapter that rejected the Gilbertines admitted the congregations of Savigny and Obazine, both of which included communities of nuns. Brian Golding and others have pointed out that there were only two Gilbertine communities at the time, and they were neither generously endowed nor well organized. Their rule had not been fully formalized, and it was not clear that the group's funds were sufficient to support the strict enclosure of the nuns on which the Cistercians insisted. The general chapter may also have believed that the incorporation of the Gilbertines, along with the congregations of Savigny and Obazine, would stretch the resources of the Cistercians beyond their limit.[81]

Marsha Dutton, however, has pointed out that Gilbert of Sempringham asked for something quite different from what the congregations of Savigny and Obazine wanted. While these two groups were asking for incorporation into the Cistercian Order, Gilbert intended for the Cistercians merely to supervise his monasteries. According to the thirteenth-century treatise *The Book of St Gilbert*, he felt that oversight by the Cistercians "would ensure that the pattern of life which he himself had devised should be more strictly observed."[82] The Gilbertine monasteries would not

---

[80] Sally Thompson, "The Problem of the Cistercian Nuns in the Twelfth and Early Thirteenth Centuries," in *Medieval Women*, ed. Derek Baker (Oxford: Blackwell, 1978), 227–52; Thompson, *Women Religious: The Founding of English Nunneries after the English Conquest* (Oxford: Clarendon Press, 1991), 94–95; Freeman, *Narratives*, 84; Constance H. Berman, "Were there Twelfth-Century Cistercian Nuns?" *Church History* 68 (1999): 824–64; Lawrence, *Medieval Monasticism*, 227–28.

[81] Golding, *Gilbert of Sempringham*, 26–28; Golding, "Bernard and Gilbert," 46; Golding, "Hermits, Monks and Women in Twelfth-Century France and England: The Experience of Obazine and Sempringham," in *Monastic Studies: The Continuity of Tradition*, ed. Judith Loades (Bangor: Headstart History, 1990), 127–45; Degler-Spengler, "Incorporation," 99–105; Berman, "Twelfth-Century Cistercian Nuns," 848; Sykes, *Inventing Sempringham*, 8–9, 48; Peter King, *Western Monasticism, A History of the Monastic Movement in the Latin Church*, CS 185 (Kalamazoo, MI; Cistercian Publications, 1999), 205–6.

[82] *Book of St Gilbert*, 40–41; Marsha L. Dutton, "Were Aelred of Rievaulx and Gilbert of Sempringham Friends? Speculating from a Close Reading of *A Certain Wonderful Miracle*," unpublished paper, 2012.

become Cistercian but would retain their own organization as double monasteries of men and women. Therefore, the Cistercian abbots' statement that they were not permitted to supervise the religious life of others was not merely an excuse to avoid dealing with nuns, for the *Charter of Charity* states the same thing.[83]

Furthermore, the fact that the Cistercians refused to exercise formal supervision over Gilbert's monasteries did not mean that they completely abandoned them.[84] It is unclear from the sources exactly what role Bernard of Clairvaux played in the formulation of the Gilbertine rule, but it is evident that he and Gilbert of Sempringham became friends. The *Book of St Gilbert* states, "Gilbert also became so intimate with St. Malachy, archbishop of Ireland, and St. Bernard, abbot of Clairvaux, during his visit that in the presence of those men alone he too was present when it is recorded that through their prayers health was restored to a sick man."[85] Gilbert also received the gift of a pair of pastoral staffs from the two men.[86]

Malachy did not arrive at Clairvaux until October 1148, so if Gilbert returned with Bernard to Clairvaux after the general chapter at Cîteaux in September 1147, he had to have remained there for over a year in order to meet the Irish bishop. Furthermore Malachy died only a month after his arrival, so there was little time for the two men to become fast friends.[87] Malachy, however, also visited Clairvaux in 1140, traveling through Yorkshire on his way.[88] Gilbert could have met the Irishman at that time and

---

[83] "Carta caritatis prior: *De morte et de electione abbatum. XI,*" *Narrative and Legislative Texts from Early Cîteaux,* ed. and trans. Chrysogonus Waddell (Cîteaux: Commentarii Cistercienses, 1999), 450–51; Dutton, "Were Aelred of Rievaulx and Gilbert of Sempringham Friends?"

[84] Freeman, "Gilbert of Hoyland's Sermons for Nuns," 281–83; Elizabeth Freeman, "Nuns," in *The Cambridge Companion to the Cistercian Order,* ed. Mette Birkedal Bruun (Cambridge: Cambridge University Press, 2013), 100–111; Sykes, *Inventing Sempringham,* 172–74.

[85] *Book of St Gilbert,* 44–45.

[86] *Book of St Gilbert,* 44–45; Elkins, *Holy Women,* 132–33.

[87] Bernard, V Mal 74; SBOp 3:377; CF 10:91; Golding, "Bernard and Gilbert," 47–48.

[88] Bernard, V Mal 34–54; SBOp 3:341–46; CF 10:49–54; Richard D. Oram, "A Family Business? Colonisation and Settlement in Twelfth- and Thirteenth-Century

even traveled to Clairvaux with him, though no documentation supports this conjecture. In any case, after spending some time with Bernard at Clairvaux, Gilbert returned home to England, where he completed the rule for his order and brought in groups of Augustinian canons to care for the nuns and the lay brothers and sisters.[89]

The *Historia* of William of Newburgh is similarly obscure regarding the interaction between Bernard and Gilbert: "Instructed by his [Bernard's] respected counsel and strengthened in his purpose he did not cease to pursue more fervently and confidently what had been devoutly begun."[90] A privilege from Pope Alexander III to the priory of Alvingham dating from 1178 stated that the Gilbertine nuns' way of chanting the Divine Office had been "first approved by blessed Bernard along with many other religious persons."[91] The inconclusive state of the evidence has led several modern historians to conclude that the degree of Bernard's influence over the Gilbertine rule has been overstated and that the statements in the *Book of St Gilbert* are an exaggeration designed to enlist Bernard's prestige in order to protect the Order from criticism and further the cause of Gilbert's canonization, which took place in 1202.[92] Even if Bernard and Gilbert did not sit across the table from each other, working out the details of the

---

Galloway," *The Scottish Historical Review* 72, no. 194, pt. 2 (1993): 115; James Wilson, "The Passages of St. Malachy through Scotland," *The Scottish Historical Review* 18, no. 70 (1921): 73–77. On Saint Malachy generally, see J. A. Watt, *The Church and the Two Nations in Medieval Ireland* (Cambridge: Cambridge University Press, 1970), 19–28; A. Gwynn, "St. Malachy of Armagh," *The Irish Ecclesiastical Record* 70 (1948): 961–78; Marie Therese Flanagan, *The Transformation of the Irish Church in the Twelfth and Thirteenth Centuries* (Woodbridge: Boydell, 2010), 120–28.

[89] *Book of St Gilbert*, 44–51; Golding, *Gilbert of Sempringham*, 31–33.

[90] William of Newburgh, *Historia Rerum Anglicarum*, in *Chronicles of the Reigns of Stephen, Henry II., and Richard I.*, ed. Richard Howlett, 4 vols., RS 82 (London: Longmans, 1884–1890), 1:54.

[91] Golding, *Gilbert of Sempringham*, 28–31; C. R. Cheney, "Papal Privileges for Gilbertine Houses," in *Medieval Texts and Studies* (Oxford: Clarendon Press, 1973), 59–60.

[92] Golding, *Gilbert of Sempringham*, 28–31; Sharon K. Elkins, "All Ages, Every Condition, and Both Sexes: The Emergence of a Gilbertine Identity," in *Distant Echoes*, ed. John A. Nichols and Lillian Thomas Shank, Medieval Religious Women, 3 vols., CS 71 (Kalamazoo, MI: Cistercian Publications, 1984), 1:169–82.

Gilbertine rule, it is still evident that Gilbert was friends not only with Bernard but with other Cistercian abbots as well and that the rules and customs of the new order were strongly influenced by the Cistercian example.

Aelred himself would have been familiar with the affairs of the Gilbertines, for during his tenure as abbot of Revesby he was a close neighbor of both Sempringham and Haverholme.[93] In 1164 Aelred led a delegation of English Cistercians to a meeting at Kirkstead with Gilbert of Sempringham and his followers where an agreement was drawn up regulating relationships between houses of the two orders established in close proximity to one another. They agreed that new buildings would be kept at least two leagues from those of the other order and that neither order would accept members from the other.[94] He seems to have been personally known at Watton as well, for, as was noted earlier, one of his sermons on Isaiah included an account of an ecstatic vision received by one of the nuns there.[95] The involvement of Bernard, Aelred, and other Cistercians in the affairs of the Gilbertines accords well with the findings of Brigitte Degler-Spengler, who has convincingly demonstrated that even though the Cistercians did not officially incorporate nuns into the Order in the twelfth century, Cistercian abbots did found nunneries and care for nuns in less formal ways.[96]

It is difficult to know exactly what a Gilbertine house looked like in this early period, as both written descriptions and archaeological remains date from the thirteenth century and after,[97] when enclosure was more strictly enforced. In this later period, the

---

[93] Freeman, "Pastoral Care," 20.

[94] CAR no. 246; Frederick M. Powicke, *Ailred of Rievaulx and His Biographer Walter Daniel* (Manchester: Manchester University Press, 1922), 70; Dom Alberic Stacpoole, "The Public Face of Aelred, 1167–1967," *Downside Review* 85 (1967): 194; Golding, "Bernard and Gilbert," 49; Constable, "Nun of Watton," 211; Emilia Jamroziak, *Rievaulx Abbey and its Social Context, 1132–1300*, Medieval Church Studies 8 (Turnhout: Brepols, 2005), 159.

[95] Aelred, Oner 2, CCCM 2D:36–37; Elkins, *Holy Women*, 100; Constable, "Nun of Watton," 210–11; Freeman, "Pastoral Care," 20–21; Dietz, "Ambivalence," 82.

[96] Degler-Spengler, "Incorporation," 87–99. Also Berman, "Men's Houses, Women's Houses," 43–52; King, *Western Monasticism*, 212–15.

[97] Sykes, *Inventing Sempringham*, 162–65.

men and women had completely separate facilities, with only the church in common, and even that was separated by a wall down the middle so that the two sexes could not see each other. A passageway connected the two walled compounds, but it was closed off by a wall in the middle, preventing access to the quarters of the opposite sex. A window in the wall was fitted with a turntable so that food and other necessities could be passed between them, and only two particularly trusted members of each sex had access to the window.[98] Unfortunately, whatever restrictions were in place in the early days proved insufficient to prevent at least one particularly tragic breach, a situation with which Aelred himself became involved.

The Nun of Watton

The facts of the case are known from a letter that Aelred wrote to an unnamed, distant friend. A young nun at the Gilbertine monastery of Watton became pregnant by one of the lay brothers. When her situation came to light, the nuns beat her, imprisoned her in a cell, loaded her with chains, and fed her on bread and water. They apprehended the guilty brother, who had fled the monastery, and forced the young nun to castrate her former lover. After she had done so, the enraged nuns flung the severed organs into the young girl's face. After this horrifying experience she remained in her lonely prison until she was about to deliver. Then, after receiving visions of Henry Murdac, the archbishop who had placed her in the monastery, she was miraculously relieved of her pregnancy, and some of the chains with which she had been bound fell off. As Brian Golding has noted, Gilbert of Sempringham often showed himself unconcerned and impatient with the management of details,[99] and so at that point he called on Aelred

[98] Freeman, "Nuns in the Public Sphere," 70–71; Golding, *Gilbert of Sempringham*, 127–31; W. H. St. John Hope, "The Gilbertine Priory of Watton, in the East Riding of Yorkshire," *The Archaeological Journal* 58 (1901): 1–34; Elkins, *Holy Women*, 138–44.

[99] Golding, *Gilbert of Sempringham*, 37. See also Sykes, *Inventing Sempringham*, 39–40, 66.

of Rievaulx to investigate. Upon Aelred's recommendation, the young nun was left alone to await further developments, and soon after he had returned to Rievaulx, he received a letter telling him that the other chain had dropped off as well.[100]

The long-standing ties of the Gilbertines to the Cistercians in general and to Aelred in particular, in addition to Aelred's own position as the head of the premier Cistercian monastery in Yorkshire, made it perfectly logical for Gilbert to call on him for advice in this moment of crisis.[101] Furthermore, Aelred was bound to Watton and the Gilbertines as part of the Yorkshire network of religious patronage. Watton's founder, Eustace fitz John, was a neighbor of Rievaulx and had witnessed its foundation charter.[102] The land that formed Watton's initial endowment had come from the *maritagium* of his wife Agnes, so it is likely that she instigated the foundation of the new monastery. She was a cousin of the Gant family, who were also major patrons of Rievaulx.[103]

The larger question is why Aelred would later choose to publicize such a distasteful and ultimately tragic event, which did nothing to enhance the reputation of the Gilbertines and which they would certainly have preferred to keep secret. Furthermore, Aelred's own attitude in the work seems strange, almost callous, showing little sympathy for the young woman, who in modern minds, at least, stands at the center of the story. Katharine Sykes has offered the interesting suggestion that Aelred's account of Henry Murdac's miraculous intervention at Watton was part of an abortive attempt by the monks of Fountains Abbey to produce a *vita* of Murdac, their former abbot.[104]

---

[100] Aelred, Mira 12–13; PL 195:791–96; CCCM 3:145–46; CF 71:112–22; Constable, "Nun of Watton," 206–12; Elkins, *Holy Women*, 106–11; Dietz, "Ambivalence," 80–85.

[101] Jamroziak, *Rievaulx Abbey*, 158.

[102] CAR no. 42.

[103] CAR nos. 78–79, 159–60, 359; Golding, *Gilbert of Sempringham*, 214–17; Jamroziak, *Rievaulx Abbey*, 81–84; *Early Yorkshire Charters*, ed. William Farrer, 6 vols. (Edinburgh: Ballantyne, 1916), vol. 2, nos. 1107–11.

[104] Sykes, *Inventing Sempringham*, 52–53.

Another clue to this question is offered by the timing of the event. The letter itself is undated, but Aelred stated that the young woman was placed in the monastery when she was four years old by Henry Murdac, who was elected archbishop of York in 1147, not enthroned until 1151, and died in 1153. If the little girl was four years old in 1151–1152, she could not have been old enough to have a baby much before 1160.[105] It is more likely that the event took place several years later, around 1164–1165. This dating places the affair of the nun of Watton only a few years before a crucial event in the history of the Gilbertines, the revolt of the lay brothers.[106] In 1164–1165, a group of lay brothers appealed to Pope Alexander III, complaining among other things about the lack of separation of the nuns from the canons and lay brothers of the monasteries, which resulted in scandalous behavior.[107] Archbishop Thomas Becket of Canterbury wrote to Gilbert several times demanding the reform of the Order.[108] Meanwhile King Henry II, Archbishop Roger of Pont L'Évêque of York, Bishops William de Turbe of Norwich, Henry of Winchester, and Robert of Lincoln, and Prior Gregory of Bridlington sent letters in support of Gilbert, testifying to the strict separation of the sexes within the monasteries.[109] Eventually the pope appointed as judges-delegate Roger of York and Hugh du Puiset for the province of York and

[105] Constable, "Nun of Watton," 210n14.

[106] Constable, "Nun of Watton," 222–23; Golding, *Gilbert of Sempringham*, 36.

[107] *Book of St Gilbert*, 76–85; Elkins, *Holy Women*, 111–12; Golding, *Gilbert of Sempringham*, 40–42; Janet Burton, *The Monastic Order in Yorkshire, 1069–1215* (Cambridge: Cambridge University Press, 1999), 175–76; David Knowles, "The Revolt of the Lay Brothers of Sempringham," EHR 50, no. 199 (1935): 465–87; Constable, "Nun of Watton," 222–24; Lawrence, *Medieval Monasticism*, 226; Sykes, *Inventing Sempringham*, 61–66; King, *Western Monasticism*, 207–8.

[108] *Book of St Gilbert*, 346–48; Thomas Becket, *The Correspondence of Thomas Becket, Archbishop of Canterbury 1162–1170*, ed., and trans. Anne J. Duggan. 2 vols. (Oxford: Clarendon Press, 2000) [CTB], vol. 1, nos. 44, 89; Golding, *Gilbert of Sempringham*, 43–44; Elkins, *Holy Women*, 112–17; Raymonde Foreville, "La crise de l'ordre de Sempringham au XIIIe siècle: Nouvelle approche du dossier des frères lais," *Anglo-Norman Studies* 7 (1983): 46.

[109] *Book of St Gilbert*, 134–57; Golding, *Gilbert of Sempringham*, 44–45; Sykes, *Inventing Sempringham*, 67–73.

William of Norwich and Henry of Winchester for Canterbury. The investigation generally vindicated the Gilbertine Order but did result in stricter separation between the sexes.[110]

The timing of the two events makes the affair of the young nun and her lover the prelude to a crisis within the Gilbertine Order. The letter that King Henry II wrote to Pope Alexander III makes it clear that the very future of the Order was at stake in the matter, for he stated that if the pope did not uphold Gilbert, he and the other benefactors of the Order would take back their donations.[111] Aelred's account also shows that the nuns were terrified of the consequences. Aelred wrote that the nuns, "fearing for their own honor, dreaded that the offense of one would be held against all. They felt as if they were exposed to all eyes to be mocked, given to all teeth to be mangled."[112] This fear makes Aelred's handling of the case more understandable, for his focus throughout the work was on the miraculous nature of the events at Watton, to the point that he seemed almost to neglect the plight of the young people involved.[113]

When Aelred recounted the facts of the case, everyone came in for a share of blame. He noted that the young woman had been placed in the monastery at the request of Archbishop Henry Murdac when she was only four years old. She turned out to be a wanton at heart and ill-suited to the monastic life, and Gilbert of Sempringham and the older nuns failed to give her the necessary supervision, with the result that she gave way to temptation with disastrous results.[114] Aelred's attempt to spread the blame in this case accords well with his reluctance to cast women as temptresses discussed above.[115] Furthermore, he also sought to

---

[110] *Book of St Gilbert*, 82–85; Golding, *Gilbert of Sempringham*, 45–51; Christopher Harper-Bill, "Bishop William Turbe and the Diocese of Norwich 1146–74," *Anglo-Norman Studies* 7 (1984): 148–49.

[111] *Book of St Gilbert*, 162–63; Foreville, "La crise de l'ordre de Sempringham," 42–43.

[112] Aelred, Mira V; PL 195:793; CCCM 3:141; CF 71:115.

[113] Constable, "Nun of Watton," 211, 217.

[114] Aelred, Mira II–IV; PL 195:791–92; CCCM 3:138–43; CF 71:111–14.

[115] McGuire, *Brother and Lover*, 32–33, Dietz, "Ambivalence," 81–85; Dutton, Introduction to *Northern Saints*, 26–27.

defend the brutal mutilation of the young man, writing, "I praise not the deed but the zeal; I do not approve the shedding of blood, but I extol the fervor of the holy virgins against such infamy."[116] After the sin had been thus avenged, the nuns "wept and prayed that . . . [Christ] would spare their place."[117] The very harshness of the nuns' response suggests that there was no general laxity in the community and that they reacted out of shock and horror at the event.[118]

From this point in the narrative, Aelred emphasized the miraculous events that followed, describing how the young nun, now penitent, was miraculously relieved of her pregnancy following a vision of the now-deceased Archbishop Henry Murdac. Shortly thereafter a second miracle occurred as the chain that bound her waist and the fetter around one of her ankles were miraculously loosed. At this point Gilbert of Sempringham himself came to the monastery to investigate and called upon Aelred to consult with him on the matter.[119] In conclusion Aelred wrote that he "understood that the Lord is pleased with those who fear him, especially with those who hope in his mercy."[120] He returned to Rievaulx, "praising and glorifying the Lord for all we had heard and seen."[121] Aelred's account ends triumphantly, praising God for the great miracle that had occurred. While he briefly excoriated Gilbert of Sempringham and the nuns of Watton for their failure adequately to supervise the unfortunate young woman, his emphasis throughout the work was far more on the basic holiness of the inhabitants of Watton and on God's favor to them manifested in the miraculous resolution of the case.

It is clear that one of Aelred's concerns in writing the account was to rescue the Gilbertine Order from the consequences of the unfortunate affair at Watton.[122] It would be helpful in this regard

---

[116] Aelred, Mira VII; PL 195:794; CCCM 3:142; CF 71:117.

[117] Aelred, Mira VIII; PL 195:794; CCCM 3:143; CF 71:117.

[118] Golding, *Gilbert of Sempringham*, 35.

[119] Aelred, Mira XII; PL 195:794–96; CCCM 3:145–46; CF 71:118–21.

[120] Aelred, Mira XIII; PL 195:796; CCCM 3:146; CF 71:121; Ps 146:11.

[121] Aelred, Mira XIII; PL 195:796; CCCM 3:146; CF 71:121; Luke 2:20.

[122] Golding, *Gilbert of Sempringham*, 36; P.-A. Burton, *Aelred*, 511–13.

to know the recipient of Aelred's letter, whom he described as "my dearest friend . . . far removed from this region."[123] Powicke suggested that the most likely candidates were John, prior of Hexham, where the only copy of the letter survives, or Aelred's fellow Cistercian, Abbot Simon of Warden.[124] Elizabeth Freeman has pointed out that the letter is not mentioned by Walter Daniel as one of Aelred's works and does not appear in the Rievaulx library catalogue. These facts, coupled with the lack of manuscripts, suggests that Aelred meant to address only a limited audience that had reason to be interested in the case or in the Gilbertines generally.[125]

Archbishops Roger of Pont L'Évêque and Thomas Becket, a number of the English bishops, and King Henry II himself, however, became involved in the lay brothers' accusations. Of the four bishops appointed as papal judges-delegate to investigate the allegations, only Hugh du Puiset of Durham had not previously shown himself a supporter of the Gilbertines.[126] It is tempting to think that Aelred's letter was written to Bishop Hugh, and perhaps some of the others who had become involved in the case, to attempt to defuse a volatile situation and build sympathy for the Gilbertines.

Katharine Sykes has suggested an alternative explanation for Aelred's letter, which also turns on the date of the affair. His account states that the girl was only four years old when she was placed at Watton. If *quatuor* in the sole surviving manuscript is a scribal error for *quatuordecim*, then the incident could have occurred as much as ten years earlier, perhaps in 1151–1153, about the time that Gilbert of Sempringham introduced groups of canons into his monasteries. In this case Aelred's account can be seen as a call for greater supervision within the Gilbertine houses.[127]

[123] Aelred, Mira XIII; PL 195:796; CCCM 3:146; CF 71:122.

[124] Powicke, Introduction to Vita A, lxxxi–lxxxii n4; P.-A. Burton, *Aelred*, 501–2.

[125] Freeman, "Nuns in the Public Sphere," 57–58.

[126] Golding, *Gilbert of Sempringham*, 45; Geoffrey V. Scammell, *Hugh du Puiset, Bishop of Durham* (Cambridge: Cambridge University Press, 1956), 71–72.

[127] Sykes, *Inventing Sempringham*, 55–57.

Either explanation of *Miracle* shows Aelred providing help and advice to religious women.

Spiritual Friendship

It is evident from the foregoing material that Aelred had great respect for religious women and that he worked actively on behalf of female religious houses, especially the Gilbertines, in a variety of ways. One issue remains, however. Although he was clearly supportive of religious women in the abstract, the question remains open as to whether Aelred himself ever enjoyed a close personal relationship with a woman. As was noted above, Aelred's own words indicate that he admitted the possibility of true spiritual friendship between men and women, but did he himself ever experience a relationship like that of Saint Jerome and Paula or Saint John Chrysostom and the deaconess Olympias? One thing that these women had in common is that they were wealthy noblewomen who were patrons as well as friends of these churchmen. For example, one need look no further than the prefaces to Saint Jerome's scriptural translations and commentaries to realize the tremendous debt that he owed to Paula and Eustochium, not only for their financial support but also for their linguistic and analytical skills.[128] Likewise Olympias supported Saint John Chrysostom's career and personal needs with her own considerable wealth.[129] Adela of Blois intervened on behalf of Saint Anselm during his conflict with her brother King Henry I of England, setting up the crucial meeting between the two in 1105 that led to the resolution of the English investiture controversy.

---

[128] Jerome, *Commentariorum in Aggaeum Prophetam ad Paulam et Eustochium, Liber Unis, Prologus*; PL 25:1387–88; *Commentarius in Ecclesiasten, ad Paulam et Eustochium, Praefatio*; PL 23:1009–12; *Praefatio Hieronymi in Librum Psalmorum*; PL 29:117–20; *Translatio Homiliarum XXXIX Origenis in Evangelium Lucae, ad Paulam et Eustochium: Prologus*; PL 26:219–20. See also Jerome, Ep 108; PL 22:878–906, in which Jerome discusses Paula's linguistic skills and the way her astute questions helped form his own thinking.

[129] Kelly, *Golden Mouth*, 112–14.

Anselm's correspondence with Queen Edith (Matilda) indicates that she also attempted to mediate the controversy.[130] Rievaulx too had its share of wealthy female patrons, and perhaps one or more of these women came to enjoy this kind of personal friendship with Aelred. Of course when charters were issued by a husband and wife acting together, it is impossible to determine who was the driving force behind the donation. Women, however, also made donations in their own right, perhaps as widows or from their dower lands, and in these cases it is can be assumed that they acted on their own initiative. Of the women who made such donations to Rievaulx, the most significant was Gundreda de Mowbray. Her most significant charitable donations, both to Rievaulx and to other institutions, were made between 1129 and 1138, after her husband died and before her son Roger came of age. Her donation of a part of her demesne in Welburn formed the nucleus of the abbey's grange.[131] Perhaps most important, during Aelred's abbacy Gundreda made a further grant of lands at Skiplam, Farndale, and Bransdale that included the crucial permission for her tenants to make further donations to Rievaulx without seeking her assent each time.[132] The Gant

[130] For events at Laigle, see Eadmer, *Historia Novorum in Anglia*, ed. Martin Rule, RS 81 (London: Longmans, 1884), 164–66; Saint Anselm, *Epistolae*, in *Sancti Anselmi Cantuariensis Archiepiscopi Opera Omnia*, ed. F. S. Schmitt, 6 vols. (Stuttgart-Bad Canstatt: Friedrich Frommann Verlag, 1963–1968), nos. 364, 388–89; Sally N. Vaughn, *Anselm of Bec and Robert of Meulan: The Innocence of the Dove and the Wisdom of the Serpent* (Berkeley, CA: University of California Press, 1987), 289–92; Vaughn, *Handmaidens of God*, 244–46; R. W. Southern, *St. Anselm and His Biographer: A Study in Monastic Life and Thought, 1059–c. 1130* (Cambridge: Cambridge University Press, 1963), 176–77; Lynn Barker, "Ivo of Chartres and Anselm of Canterbury," *Anselm Studies* 2, no. 2 (1988): 16–17; Norman F. Cantor, *Church, Kingship and Lay Investiture in England 1089–1135* (Princeton, NJ: Princeton University Press, 1958), 202–27; A. L. Poole, *From Domesday Book to Magna Carta, 1087–1216*, 2nd ed. (Oxford: Clarendon Press, 1955), 179; Henry Mayr-Harting, *Religion, Politics and Society in Britain, 1066–1272* (London: Longmans, 2011), 53–54. For Anselm and Queen Matilda, see Anselm, Epp 242–43, 246, 288, 296, 317, 320–21, 323, 329, 346–47, 352, 384–85, 395, 400, 406; Vaughn, *Handmaidens*, 221–41.

[131] CAR no. 56. See CAR no. 57 for Roger's confirmation of Gundreda's grants after her death in 1154.

[132] CAR no. 55; Jamroziak, *Rievaulx Abbey*, 68–69.

family also allowed its tenants to make grants to Rievaulx, and Alice de Gant independently confirmed grants to Rievaulx made by men holding land from her, a fact that perhaps indicates that she shared her birth family's interest in the abbey.[133]

Among the lesser patrons of the abbey, Emma, the wife of Peter de Birkin, was the first of her family to take an interest in Rievaulx, donating two carucates of land in Shitlington and Flockton to the abbey. The subsequent generous donations of her son Adam de Birkin were mentioned in the previous chapter, and it was noted above that the unusual tone of Adam's charters suggests a guilty conscience.[134] Perhaps Aelred and Emma were friends, and Adam came to Rievaulx for spiritual counseling because of his mother's close relationship with the abbot, but without Aelred's letters this must remain pure speculation. It can safely be said, however, that if these women had felt ignored, slighted, or neglected by the abbot of Rievaulx, they would undoubtedly have taken their generosity elsewhere.

For a man supposedly ignorant of and uninterested in women, an amazing number of them appear in Aelred's works. In cases in which he worked from an earlier source, Aelred added examples including women to the text, and he frequently used women as praiseworthy examples in works meant for monks. He seldom, if ever, succumbed to a common tendency among medieval monastic writers to blame women as temptresses for the sexual thoughts that they inspired in men. We do not know if Aelred ever had a close female friend, but his portrayal of women in his writings and his acknowledgment of the possibility of such relationships in *Spiritual Friendship* suggest that he remained open to the possibility.

[133] CAR nos. 159–60; Jamroziak, *Rievaulx Abbey*, 83–84.
[134] *Early Yorkshire Charters*, vol. 3, no. 1724; Jamroziak, *Rievaulx Abbey*, 93–95; Janet Burton, "The Estates and Economy of Rievaulx Abbey in Yorkshire," *Cîteaux: Commentarii Cistercienses* 49 (1998): 35. See above, chap. 4:74–75.

Chapter 6

A Time for Peace

Aelred of Rievaulx and the End of the Anglo-Norman Civil War

Three of Aelred's political-historical works deal with current events: *Lament for David I of Scotland*, *Genealogy of the Kings of the English*, and *Report on the Battle of the Standard*.[1] Marsha Dutton and others have suggested that these pieces belong to the mirror of princes genre, intended to instruct the newly enthroned Henry II of England on the proper way to be a good lord and king to his new subjects,[2] and it is certainly true that they contain much good advice for the young ruler. In addition, these three works were written at a crucial time in English history, just as the Anglo-

---

[1] An earlier version of this chapter appeared with this title in CSQ 46, no. 2 (2011): 171–87.

[2] Marsha L. Dutton, Introduction to *Aelred of Rievaulx: The Historical Works*, trans. Jane Patricia Freeland, ed. Marsha L. Dutton, CF 56 (Kalamazoo, MI: Cistercian Publications, 2005), 10–31; Rosalind Ransford, "A Kind of Noah's Ark: Aelred of Rievaulx and National Identity," in *Religion and National Identity: Papers Read at the Nineteenth Summer Meeting and the Twentieth Winter Meeting of the Ecclesiastical History Society*, ed. Stuart Mews (Oxford: Basil Blackwell, 1982), 137–46; Martha G. Newman, *The Boundaries of Charity: Cistercian Culture and Ecclesiastical Reform, 1098–1180* (Stanford, CA: Stanford University Press, 1996), 178–79; Marie Anne Mayeski, "*Secundum Naturam*: The Inheritance of Virtue in Aelred's *Genealogy of the English Kings*," CSQ 37, no. 3 (2002): 221–28; Marsha L. Dutton, "*Sancto Dunstano Cooperante*: Collaboration Between King and Ecclesiastical Advisor in Aelred of Rievaulx's *Genealogy of the Kings of the English*," in *Religious and Laity in Western Europe 1000–1400: Interaction, Negotiation and Power*, ed. Emilia Jamroziak and Janet Burton (Turnhout: Brepols, 2006), 183–85; Elizabeth A. Freeman, *Narratives of a New Order: Cistercian Historical Writing in England, 1150–1220*, Medieval Church Studies 2 (Turnhout: Brepols, 2002), 61.

Norman civil war was drawing to a close, and it is likely that they have something to say about the times in which they were written. In fact it can be argued that taken together, *Lament, Genealogy,* and *Battle* constitute a powerful plea for peace and for the upholding of the Treaty of Winchester that ended the conflict.[3]

Aelred and the Anglo-Norman Civil War

Aelred's home in the north of England suffered severely during the conflict between King Stephen and Empress Matilda. King David of Scotland invaded England twice during the early years of the war, supporting Matilda's claim to the throne and perhaps using it as an excuse to claim lands to the south for himself. In his account of the devastation wrought by the Scots, Prior Richard of Hexham wrote that they murdered the old, the sick, pregnant women, and children without distinction and, crossing the Tyne River, laid waste the greater part of the territory of Saint Cuthbert of Durham. He also noted that during these attacks, the newly founded Cistercian monastery of Newminster near Morpeth was completely destroyed. The church of Hexham itself was preserved by the power of its saints, Andrew the apostle, Wilfrid, Acca, Alchmund, and Eata, and became a haven for refugees fleeing the attacks.[4]

This was the territory where Aelred's family had lived for generations. Aelred's roots were sunk deep in northern soil, and the events of 1135 to 1138 had to have brought him intense sorrow. The devastation of his homeland must have been especially wrenching for Aelred because it was carried out by King David

[3] Paul Dalton, "Churchmen and the Promotion of Peace in King Stephen's Reign," *Viator* 31 (2000): 109–18.

[4] Aelred, SS Hag III; Raine, *Priory*, 1:183; CCCM 3:79; CF 71:77–78; Richard of Hexham, *De Gestis Regis Stephani et de Bello Standardo*, in *Chronicles of the Reigns of Stephen, Henry II., and Richard I.*, ed. Richard Howlett, 4 vols., RS 82 (London: Longmans, 1884–1890), 3:151–59. Similarly, Henry of Huntingdon, *Historia Anglorum: The History of the English People*, ed. and trans. Diana Greenway (Oxford: Clarendon Press, 1996), 712–17.

of Scotland, the man whom he said that he "loved beyond all mortals."[5]

To make matters worse, the climactic Battle of the Standard was a conflict between old friends.[6] In his account Aelred assigned the leading role in organizing the English troops to Walter Espec, the founder of Rievaulx. He also listed Count William of Albemarle, Ilbert de Lacy, Walter de Gant, and Roger de Mowbray as leaders of the southern forces.[7] Robert de Bruce also played a leading role in the story, visiting the Scottish camp and urging King David to return to his former alliance with the Normans. When the king refused to make peace, Robert renounced his fealty and returned to the English lines.[8] Aelred also listed Malise, earl of Strathearn, Alan de Percy, and Eustace fitz John among King David's supporters.[9] William de Percy, Richard de Courcy, William Fossard, Robert de Stuteville, Bernard de Balliol, William Peverel, Geoffrey Halsalin, and Robert de Ferrers can be added to the list of English adherents from Richard of Hexham's account of the battle.[10]

One tragedy of this occasion was that these men had all known one another for years. Robert de Bruce's decision to fight with the southern forces must have been particularly painful, as he had served the Scottish king for a long time, even before David had ascended the throne.[11] Eustace fitz John and Alan de Percy, who had witnessed King David's grant of the honor of Annandale to

---

[5] Aelred, Gen Angl XIII; PL 195:757; CCCM 3:56; CF 56:121.

[6] Brian Patrick McGuire, *Brother and Lover: Aelred of Rievaulx* (New York: Crossroad Publishing Co., 1994), 68–69; Aelred Squire, *Aelred of Rievaulx: A Study*, CS 50 (Kalamazoo, MI: Cistercian Publications, 1981), 79–80; Pierre-André Burton, *Aelred de Rievaulx (1110–1167), De l'homme éclaté à l'être unifié: Essai de biographie existentielle et spirituelle* (Paris: Éditions du Cerf, 2010), 167–68.

[7] Aelred, Stand I; PL 195:182–83; CCCM 3:59–60; CF 56:248–49. It was actually Ilbert's grandson Gilbert who fought with the English forces.

[8] Aelred, Stand VI; PL 195:192–95; CCCM 3:68–70; CF 56:261–65.

[9] Aelred, Stand IV; PL 195:190–91; CCCM 3:66; CF 56:258–60.

[10] Richard of Hexham, *Bello Standardo*, 3:159–61.

[11] *The Charters of King David I: The Written Acts of David I King of Scots, 1124–53 and of his son Henry Earl of Northumberland, 1139–52*, ed. G. W. S. Barrow (Woodbridge: Boydell Press, 1999), nos. 1, 3, 7–8, 14, 16, 23–25, 27–28, 30–31, 34, 41, 45–46, 49, 60–62.

Robert de Bruce, faced Robert across the battlefield.[12] William Peverel, Walter de Gant, and Walter Espec had also appeared at the Scottish court at some time before 1138.[13] On the southern side, Robert de Bruce, William Peverel, Walter de Gant, and Walter Espec had all witnessed royal charters at some point between King David's accession and Aelred's departure for Rievaulx in 1134, as had Alan de Percy, Eustace fitz John, and Malise of Strathearn on the northern side.[14] These facts meant that Aelred probably knew most of the noble combatants from his years of service in David's household.

Many of these men were also friends of Durham, Hexham, and Rievaulx. Walter Espec was the founder of Rievaulx Abbey, and Eustace fitz John, now his opponent across the field of battle, had witnessed the foundation charter.[15] Roger de Mowbray and his mother Gundreda had also been early donors to the abbey.[16] Many of Rievaulx's charters are undated, but they show that a number of the other combatants would also become involved with the abbey's affairs at some point in their careers. Robert de Stuteville witnessed a grant to the abbey by Odo of Boltby along with Walter Espec.[17] Similarly, when Roger de Clera surrendered his rights in the waste below Pickering to Rievaulx, Roger de Mowbray, William de Stuteville, and William Fossard all witnessed the transaction.[18] It is perhaps a tribute to Aelred's personal ties to the local magnates that during his abbacy and that of his immediate successor, Walter de Gant's son Gilbert, Robert de Stuteville's son William, and Bernard de Balliol also became benefactors of Rievaulx.[19] King David himself was the founder of and a generous donor to Melrose

---

[12] *Charters of King David I*, no. 16.

[13] *Charters of King David I*: William Peverel, nos. 5–6, 28; Walter de Gant, no. 29; Walter Espec, no. 46.

[14] *Charters of King David I*: Robert de Bruce, nos. 16, 23–25, 27–28, 30–31, 34, 41, 45–46, 49; William Peverel, no. 28; Walter de Gant, no. 29; Walter Espec, no. 46; Alan de Percy, no. 16; Eustace fitz John, nos. 16, 29; Malise of Strathearn, nos. 33, 44.

[15] CAR no. 42.

[16] See above, chap. 4:71–74.

[17] CAR no. 76.

[18] CAR no. 163.

[19] CAR Gilbert de Gant, nos. 78–79; William de Stuteville, no. 89; Bernard de Balliol, nos. 114–15.

Abbey, a daughter house of Rievaulx, and Bernard of Clairvaux had commended David for his generosity to Rievaulx.[20] As the disorder in the north worsened and a pitched battle appeared imminent, Aelred would have feared equally for family at Hexham and Durham, friends from his days at the Scottish court, and the founder and other patrons of the abbey of Rievaulx.

The decisive battle, fought August 22, 1138, took place less than twenty miles from Rievaulx.[21] It is possible that Aelred had a small part to play in the aftermath of these events, for he may have accompanied Abbot William of Rievaulx when he arranged the surrender of Walter Espec's castle at Wark in November of that year.[22] In *Lament* and *Battle*, Aelred was describing events that he had experienced to some degree firsthand and that involved patrons and friends with whom he had strong ties of affection. These works are therefore more than collections of examples drawn from ancient history, intended to educate and inspire a new generation; they are firsthand, eyewitness accounts of recent happenings in which Aelred had a deep emotional investment.

The Treaty of Winchester and the Dating of Aelred's Works

Furthermore, the results of these events were still being played out as Aelred was writing around 1153. As time passed in the often-

---

[20] For Melrose, *Charters of King David I*, nos. 120–21. For Rievaulx, J172. Not included in SBOp.

[21] John of Hexham, *Historia*, in *Symeonis Monachi Opera Omnia*, ed. Thomas Arnold, 2 vols., Rolls Series 75 (London: Longmans, 1882–1885), 2:292–95; Richard of Hexham, *Bello Standardo*, 3:159–60; Robert of Torigny, *Chronica*, in *Chronicles of the Reigns of Stephen, Henry II., and Richard I.*, ed. Richard Howlett, 4 vols., RS 82 (London: Longmans, 1884–1890), 4:135; Henry of Huntingdon, *Historia*, 712; John of Worcester, *The Chronicle of John of Worcester*, ed. R. R. Darlington and P. McGurk, trans. P. McGurk and Jennifer Bray, 3 vols. (Oxford: Clarendon Press, 1995–1998), 3:252–57; Donald Nicholl, *Thurstan, Archbishop of York (1114–1140)* (York: Stonegate Press, 1964), 221–28; R. L. Graeme Ritchie, *The Normans in Scotland* (Edinburgh: Edinburgh University Press, 1954), 256–70; John Beeler, *Warfare in England, 1066–1189* (Ithaca, NY: Cornell University Press, 1966), 84–95; Richard D. Oram, *David I: The King Who Made Scotland* (Stroud, Gloucestershire, UK: History Press Ltd., 2004), 137–41.

[22] Richard of Hexham, *Bello Standardo*, 3:171–72; Powicke, Introduction to Vita A, xlvi.

stalemated conflict, Matilda's son Henry, duke of Normandy, gradually took over his mother's place as the leader of the Angevin forces. When he invaded England for the third time in 1153, the English barons, unwilling to continue the fight, forced their warring leaders to the conference table.[23] They were helped immeasurably in their task by the sudden death of Stephen's heir, Prince Eustace, on August 17, 1153.[24] By the Treaty of Winchester, concluded shortly thereafter, it was agreed that Stephen would remain king for his lifetime, with Duke Henry succeeding to the crown after his death.[25] Stephen died less than a year later, but of course at the time of the agreement, no one knew how long the uncomfortable transition period might last.

To make matters worse, although Stephen's eldest son and acknowledged heir had been removed from the scene, a rival still remained in the person of his second son, William of Blois. By the Treaty of Winchester, William had renounced his claim to the throne in return for a guarantee that he would inherit the lands that his father had held before becoming king. William remained

---

[23] William of Newburgh, *Historia Rerum Anglicarum*, in *Chronicles of the Reigns of Stephen, Henry II., and Richard I.*, ed. Richard Howlett, 4 vols., RS 82 (London: Longmans, 1884–1890), 1:88–90; Gervase of Canterbury, *Chronica*, in *Chronicles of the Reigns of Stephen, Henry II., and Richard I.*, ed. William Stubbs, 2 vols., RS 73 (London: Longmans, 1879–1880), 1:151–56; Robert of Torigny, *Chronica*, 4:171–74; *Gesta Stephani*, ed. and trans. K. R. Potter, rev. R. H. C. Davis (Oxford: Clarendon Press, 1976), 230–39; Henry of Huntingdon, *Historia*, 764–71; Z. N. and C. N. L. Brooke, "Henry II, Duke of Normandy and Aquitaine," EHR 61, no. 239 (1946): 86–88; Emily Amt, *The Accession of Henry II in England: Royal Government Restored, 1149–1159* (Woodbridge: Boydell Press, 1993), 11–15; Graeme J. White, "The End of Stephen's Reign," *History* 75, no. 1 (1990): 5–10; Donald Matthew, *King Stephen* (London: Hambledon Press, 2002), 207–13.

[24] *Gesta Stephani*, 238–39; Robert of Torigny, *Chronica*, 4:176; Gervase of Canterbury, *Chronica*, 1:155; William of Newburgh, *Historia*, 1:90; White, "End of Stephen's Reign," 10–11.

[25] *Regesta Regum Anglo–Normannorum 1066–1154, Vol. III, Regesta Regis Stephani ac Mathildis Imperatricis ac Gaufridi et Henrici Ducum Normannorum 1135–1154*, ed. H. A. Cronne and R. H. C. Davis (Oxford: Clarendon Press, 1968), no. 272; John of Hexham, *Historia*, 2:331; Robert of Torigny, *Chronica*, 4:177; *Gesta Stephani*, 238–41; Gervase of Canterbury, *Chronica*, 1:156; William of Newburgh, *Historia*, 1:90–91; Edmund King, "A Week in Politics: Oxford, Late July 1141," in *King Stephen's Reign, 1135–1154*, ed. Paul Dalton and Graeme J. White (Woodbridge: Boydell Press, 2008), 75–79; White, "End of Stephen's Reign," 11–13.

true to his word and faithfully served Henry II until his death in 1159,[26] but in 1153 no one could guarantee that an opposition party would not form around the young man.

Furthermore, affairs in Scotland were unsettled as well, for David I's son Earl Henry had died in 1152. Consequently, when David himself died a year later, he left only grandsons to succeed him. The eldest of these was Malcolm, who was only eleven years old.[27] The possibilities for violence were endless: would the northern barons take revenge for the events of the 1130s by invading the territory now controlled by a boy king? Or would Henry II, seeing the same opportunity, attempt to bring Scotland permanently under his rule? Alternatively, would the new king seek to punish those who had opposed him and his mother during the long civil war? Or would a new rebellion, perhaps spearheaded by William of Blois, carry the war into a second generation? No one knew the answers to these questions when the Treaty of Winchester was concluded in 1153.

Two of Aelred's historical works, *Lament* and *Genealogy*, were written exactly during this uncomfortable waiting period between the Treaty of Winchester and the death of King Stephen. The two works occur together in manuscripts prefaced by a dedicatory letter to Duke Henry. Because it addresses Henry as duke of Normandy rather than as king of England, we can date these works to the period between the death of David I on May 24, 1153, and that of Stephen on October 25, 1154.[28]

Battle does not contain any internal evidence that allows assigning a firm date for its composition, but Sir Maurice Powicke noted that references to Walter Espec in the past tense indicated that it was written after his death and therefore suggested a date of 1155–1157.[29] On the basis of literary similarities between Aelred's account and that of Henry of Huntingdon, the latest continuation

---

[26] Amt, *Accession of Henry II*, 16–17, 27–28.

[27] Squire, *Aelred of Rievaulx*, 88; Aelred Squire, "Aelred and King David," *Collectanea Ordinis Cisterciensium Reformatorum* 22 (1960): 365; P.-A. Burton, *Aelred*, 431.

[28] Powicke, Introduction to Vita A, xci–xcii.

[29] Powicke, Introduction to Vita A, xcix.

of which ends at the close of 1154 with the arrival of the young
Henry II, Aelred Squire suggested a date of 1155 for the work.[30]
He also pointed out, however, that there was a Rievaulx tradition
that Walter Espec died in 1155 after having spent the last two
years of his life as a monk there, and he suggested that perhaps
it was Espec himself who asked Aelred to write his account of the
battle.[31] This would mean that the work might at least have been
started a bit earlier, while the English succession was still in doubt.

Marsha Dutton has pointed out a puzzling statement in Aelred's
account of Walter Espec's speech before the battle in which he referred to previous glorious victories of "a few Celts, Angevins,
and Aquitanians."[32] This odd statement attempts to cast the Normans as allies of the Angevins and Aquitanians, when in fact
the Angevins were the contending party in the civil war, while
the Aquitanians had no interest in the conflict before Henry's
marriage with Eleanor of Aquitaine in 1152. In addition she has
noted that *Battle* contains a ringing endorsement of King Stephen's
right to rule,[33] which was hardly appropriate after his rival had
ascended the throne. Taken together, these two points would
indicate that the work was composed after 1152 and perhaps
during the same critical period as *Lament* and *Genealogy*, before
Henry's accession at the end of 1154.[34] In any case conditions in
England remained unsettled during the early years of Henry
II's reign, especially before the death of William of Blois in 1159.
Therefore these three works afford a unique glimpse of the hopes
and fears of Aelred and the English people as they waited to see

---

[30] Squire, *Aelred of Rievaulx*, 82. See also Aelred Glidden, "Aelred the Historian:
The Account of the Battle of the Standard," in *Erudition at God's Service: Studies in
Medieval Cistercian History*, XI, ed. John R. Sommerfeldt, CS 98 (Kalamazoo, MI:
Cistercian Publications, 1987), 176–77.

[31] Squire, *Aelred of Rievaulx*, 77; CAR no. 370.

[32] Stand III; CCCM 3:62; CF 56:252.

[33] Stand III; CCCM 3:63; CF 56:254.

[34] Dutton, Introduction to *Historical Works*, 29 and 252n13; P.-A. Burton, *Aelred*,
320, 417–21.

if the nineteen-year civil war would resume with a new generation of combatants.

Advice for Princes

Although it is very likely that Aelred had the political situation
on his mind during these critical years, he never explicitly stated
that he wrote any of these works to influence current events.
While hints about his particular concerns are present, it must be
admitted that much of what he offered would have been good
advice for a ruler, particularly a new one, at any point in history.
For example, he stated that a good lord was to be the defender of
the poor, the widows, and the orphans.[35] In *Lament* he wrote that
David I "always reserved the affairs of the poor and of widows
to himself. He was their advocate, he their defender, he their
judge."[36] Similarly, in *Genealogy* Aelred described King Aethelwulf
as "a father of orphans and a judge of widows."[37] A good king
was also the patron and protector of the church.[38]

Aelred also praised David I for "found[ing] monasteries neither
few nor small and filling them with brothers of the Cluniac, Cistercian, Tironensian, Arroaisian, Premonstratensian and Belvacensian
orders."[39] In fact David is credited with founding, reestablishing,
or assisting in the foundation of thirteen new monasteries, and
the sixty-four surviving royal documents concerning these institutions testify to the care and concern that David lavished on
them throughout his reign.[40] Similarly in *Genealogy* Aelred care-

---

[35] John R. Sommerfeldt, *Aelred of Rievaulx on Love and Order in the World and in
the Church* (New York: Newman Press, 2006), 127–29; Newman, *Boundaries*, 178.

[36] Aelred, Lam D IV; PL 195:272–73; CCCM 3:8; CF 56:50.

[37] Aelred, Gen Angl I; PL 195:718; CCCM 3:25; CF 56:75.

[38] Sommerfeldt, *Love and Order*, 129–32.

[39] Aelred, Lam D IV; PL 195:272; CCCM 3:8; CF 56:49.

[40] Squire, *Aelred of Rievaulx*, 85; Squire, "Aelred and King David," 362–63n29;
Dutton, Introduction to *Historical Works*, 49n3. In the list that follows, numbers in
parentheses refer to acts in favor of these institutions in *Charters of King David I*. For
the Cluniacs, May (nos. 117, 132–34, 165, 186–87). For the Cistercians, Dundrennan, Kinloss, and Newbattle (nos. 96–98, 114, 124–25, 164). For the Tironensians,
Lessmahagow (no. 130) and Kelso, originally founded as Selkirk (nos. 14, 70, 91,

fully listed the monasteries founded by King Henry's illustrious predecessors: Aethelney and Shaftesbury by Alfred; Winchester by Edward the Elder; and Abingdon, Peterborough, Thorney, Ramsey, and Wilton by King Edgar.[41] He singled out Walter Espec, the leader of the English forces at the Battle of the Standard, for founding the monasteries at Kirkham, Rievaulx, and Warden.[42] Care of widows and orphans and the defense of the church were all recognized duties of a good ruler, and Aelred's recommendations to Henry II in this regard were clearly to be expected.

A Just Judge

Aelred's frequent mention of the need for a good lord to administer justice faithfully and fairly is a significant sign of the times in which he wrote.[43] Naturally, any good king would be concerned with the administration of justice, but this issue would have been of particular interest to the people of England at this time because of the unusually large number of land disputes that the civil war had left in its wake.[44] Aelred himself said that he had witnessed King David turning aside from a hunting expedition to hear the case of a poor man who accosted him.[45] He also noted that the

---

130, 149–51, 180–81, 183–84). For the Arroaisians, Cambuskenneth (no. 99, 128, 159, 182, 213–14). For the Augustinians, Loch Leven (no. 208) and Holyrood (no. 115, 125, 147–48). For the Belvacensians, who were Augustinian canons from Beauvais, Jedburgh (nos. 167, 174–75). For the Benedictines, Dunfermline (nos. 17–22, 33, 35–39, 48–50, 99, 131, 137–38, 140–41, 152, 171–72, 189–90, 244). David is also credited with founding preceptories for the Knights Templar (nos. 234–35, 259) and the Knights Hospitaller (no. 233).

[41] Aelred, Gen Angl III, IV, VIII for Alfred, PL 195:722; CCCM 3:31; CF 56:85. For Edward the Elder, PL 195:723; CCCM 3:33; CF 56:88. For Edgar, PL 195:727; CCCM 3:39; CF 56:97.

[42] Aelred, Stand II; PL 195:183–84; CCCM 3:61; CF 56:249–51.

[43] Sommerfeldt, *Love and Order*, 123–27; Newman, *Boundaries*, 178–79.

[44] Henry of Huntingdon, *Historia*, 770–73; R. H. C. Davis, *King Stephen, 1135–1154*, 3rd ed. (London: Longmans, 1990), 119–23; Amt, *Accession of Henry II*, 17–21; Matthew, *King Stephen*, 213–15; J. C. Holt, "1153: The Treaty of Winchester," in *The Anarchy of King Stephen's Reign*, ed. Edmund King (Oxford: Clarendon Press, 1994), 291–316.

[45] Aelred, Lam D V; PL 195:273; CCCM 3:8–9; CF 56:51.

king often beat his breast and shed tears when forced to punish
the guilty, making it clear that he was "serving justice, not dis-
playing cruelty."[46] The statement finds an echo in a sermon that he
preached on the feast of the Nativity of the Virgin Mary, in which
he remarked, "We discover that a certain holy king rejoiced when
anyone appealed to him on behalf of someone whom by law he
was forced to punish, because then he could have a just cause
for pardoning him. This king, without a doubt, was imitating
our Lord, who, so that he can still justly pardon us, wills that his
intimate companions pray for us."[47]

Similarly, Aelred praised King Edward the Elder for his concern
for justice: "He ruled his subjects with such moderation and ad-
judicated between neighbor and neighbor with such justice that
I say, not that he was unwilling to do anything contrary to truth,
but rather that he was unable to do so."[48] He wrote that King
Edgar "was accustomed winter and spring to travel everywhere
throughout the various provinces of his kingdom, thoroughly
to investigate the judgments, practices, customs and deeds of
his ministers and noblemen, attentively to inquire how the written laws and the statutes he had decreed were being kept, and
carefully to guard lest the poor should suffer from prejudice and
oppression by the powerful."[49] Henry II's following the example
of his predecessors would clearly have been welcome to Aelred's
countrymen in the unsettled aftermath of the civil war.

The Justification of Warfare

Another clue to Aelred's concern with the civil war is his emphasis on that fact that a model king should wage only just wars.[50]
Regarding David I, Aelred wrote, "We know that he did not seek

[46] Aelred, Lam D III; PL 195:271; CCCM 3:7; CF 56:48.

[47] Aelred, S 23; CCCM 2A:184; Aelred of Rievaulx, *The Liturgical Sermons: The First Clairvaux Collection, Advent–All Saints*, trans. Theodore Berkeley and Basil Pennington, CF 58 (Kalamazoo, MI: Cistercian Publications, 2001), 319.

[48] Aelred, Gen Angl IV; PL 195:723; CCCM 3:33; CF 56:87.

[49] Aelred, Gen Angl IV; PL 195:727; CCCM 3:34; CF 56:97.

[50] Sommerfeldt, *Love and Order*, 132–34.

the kingship but shrank from it; he accepted it because of the needs of others rather than eagerly invading a conquered state out of a desire to dominate."[51] In *Genealogy*, Aelred was careful to note that William the Conqueror had not wantonly invaded England out of greed but had possessed a "right of consanguinity" to the throne and had made covenants with both his predecessor, Edward the Confessor, and with the usurper Harold Godwin. Thus, "by God's judgment" he had defeated his rival in battle and claimed the throne.[52] *Battle* includes a ringing endorsement of King Stephen as the rightful ruler of England as part of Walter Espec's speech before the battle: "But we are not undertaking an unjust war on behalf of our king, who has not invaded a kingdom not rightfully his, as enemies falsely claim, but has accepted it as an offering, he whom the people sought, the clergy chose, the pope anointed, and apostolic authority confirmed in his kingdom."[53] Remarkably, *Lament* included a similar justification for David I's invasion of England. Aelred noted that David did so because of the oath that he and the rest of the English barons, including Stephen himself, had sworn in 1127 to uphold the succession of Empress Matilda to the throne.[54] Aelred stopped short of absolving David of wrongdoing, but he did note, "Others may excuse him, calling attention to the oath he had made, claiming that this matter pertained to royal virtue, that he kept his trust, that he did not violate his oath, that he bore arms against perjurers, that he tried to reclaim for

[51] Aelred, Lam D II; PL 195:270–71; CCCM 3:6; CF 56:47.

[52] Aelred, Gen Angl XIII; PL 195:734; CCCM 3:52; CF 56:116; Marsha L. Dutton, "This Ministry of Letters: Aelred of Rievaulx's Attempt to Anglicize England's King Henry II," in *Monasticism Between Culture and Cultures: Acts of the Third International Symposium, Rome, June 8–11, 2011,* ed. Philippe Nouzille and Michaela Pfeifer, *Analecta Monastica* 14 (2013): 179.

[53] Aelred, Stand III; PL 195:187; CCCM 3:63; CF 56:254; P.-A. Burton, *Aelred,* 405–6.

[54] John of Worcester, *Chronicle,* 3:166–67; Simeon of Durham, *Opera Omnia,* ed. Thomas Arnold, 2 vols., RS 75 (London: Longmans, 1882–1885), 2:281; William of Malmesbury, *Historia Novella,* ed. Edmund King, trans. K. R. Potter (Oxford: Clarendon Press, 1998), 6–9; Henry of Huntingdon, *Historia,* 701–2; *The Anglo–Saxon Chronicle,* ed. and trans. Michael Swanton (New York: Routledge, 1998), AD 1127; *Gesta Stephani,* 10–11.

the heirs the kingdom that their father had given them and that the clergy and people had confirmed by sworn testimony."[55] This statement in *Lament* contrasts with the confirmation of Stephen's right to rule in *Battle*. Taken together, the two contrasting views would have reminded Aelred's readers that both sides in the civil war had fought with the belief that right was on their side.

A Time to Forgive

It is to be expected that *Lament* and *Battle* would offer the most direct evidence of Aelred's views on the current political situation, since these works directly concern the personalities and events of the civil war. It is evident that in both these works Aelred did everything he could to distance King David from the worst atrocities of the invasion.[56] An attentive reading of Richard of Hexham's account of the Scottish attacks leading up to the Battle of the Standard demonstrates the heterogeneous nature of David's army: "That infamous army received accessions from the Normans, Germans, and English, from the Northumbrians and Cumbrians, from Teviotdale and Lothian, from the Picts, commonly called Galwegians, and the Scots, and no one knew their numbers."[57] He specifically blamed the Galwegians for the attacks on Hexham that were thwarted by the power of its saints and recorded that finally King David and his son Earl Henry guaranteed Hexham immunity from further troubles.[58] He also noted that David's nephew, William fitz Duncan, led a force of Galwegians into Yorkshire, where they massacred the inhabitants indiscriminately before rounding up the women and carrying them off as slaves.[59] Richard also implied that David might not have enjoyed perfect control over his army: "The king with his retinue took up his abode near Durham, and there a serious mutiny

---

[55] Aelred, Lam D VI; PL 195:275; CCCM 3:11; CF 56:54.
[56] McGuire, *Brother and Lover*, 69; Glidden, "Aelred the Historian," 177–83.
[57] Richard of Hexham, *Bello Standardo*, 152.
[58] Richard of Hexham, *Bello Standardo*, 153–54.
[59] Richard of Hexham, *Bello Standardo*, 156.

having arisen on account of a certain woman, the life of the king and his suite was placed in jeopardy by the Picts."[60] In his *Life of Aelred*, Walter Daniel confirmed Richard of Hexham's viewpoint when he described disorders in Galloway: "Our father on a visit to the place found the princes of the province quarrelling among themselves. The King of Scotland could not subdue, or the bishop pacify, their mutual hatreds, rancor and tyranny."[61]

Aelred went much further than Richard of Hexham in blaming the Galwegians for the devastation that his homeland had suffered. John Bliese has noted that Aelred's descriptions of the atrocities committed by the Scottish army went well beyond the conventional remarks usually included in battlefield orations and carried all the force and vividness of a genuinely outraged eyewitness.[62] The prebattle oration that Aelred wrote for Walter Espec had him describe the Scottish atrocities vividly: "Little children, thrown into the air and caught on the lance's point, furnished an entertaining spectacle to the Galwegians. A pregnant woman was cut through, and a wicked hand dashed the tender fetus snatched from her womb against the rocks."[63] He portrayed the Galwegians as drinking human blood and described one of them seizing little children by a foot, swinging them around, and dashing their brains out against the doorpost of a house.[64]

Aelred recorded a dispute between the various contingents of David's army over who would have the honor of leading the charge against the English army. Despite the king's well-founded reservations about having the primitively equipped Galwegian foot soldiers face mounted knights, he gave in to their demands, with ultimately disastrous results.[65] Aelred also concocted a speech for Robert de Bruce in which he called on King David

---

[60] Richard of Hexham, *Bello Standardo*, 156.

[61] Vita A 38, pp. 45–46; CF 57:125.

[62] John R. E. Bliese, "Aelred of Rievaulx's Rhetoric and Morale at the Battle of the Standard, 1138," *Albion* 20, no. 4 (1988): 543–56.

[63] Aelred, Stand III; PL 195:187; CCCM 3:64; CF 56:255.

[64] Aelred, Stand III; PL 195:187–88; CCCM 3:64; CF 56:255.

[65] Aelred, Stand IV; PL 195:189–90; CCCM 3:66; CF 56:258–59.

to abandon his alliance with the Galwegians and return to his former friendship with the English. Addressing the atrocities that the Galwegians had committed, Robert exclaims, "You have seen, O King, the hideous abominations these men have done. You have seen, I repeat, you have seen; you have shuddered, you have wept, you have struck your breast, you have cried out that this was done against your orders, against your will, against your decree."[66] King David was so moved by Robert de Bruce's speech, Aelred said, that he was on the verge of abandoning the fight until his nephew William fitz Duncan intervened and accused Robert of treason, whereupon Robert de Bruce formally broke his bond of fealty with David and returned to the southern lines.[67] Aelred carried out this theme in *Lament*, in which he stated that these evil acts had taken place "even though he did not will it—indeed the deeds may even have been forbidden."[68] The message is clear that the worst of the atrocities committed against Aelred's homeland were the work of the godless Galwegians and took place over the protests of a king powerless to stop them.

Nevertheless, Aelred could not condone David's sin: "Yet he could have refused to lead the army; he could after one experience have refused to lead them a second time; he could perhaps have restrained them more."[69] Finally Aelred was forced to admit that David had indeed sinned grievously in not stopping the Galwegian rampage; however, he had repented of his sins and done penance for them. Aelred asserted that the king would have renounced his throne and gone on pilgrimage to Jerusalem to atone for his faults but was held back by the needs of his kingdom. Failing in this resolve, he became a patron of the Knights Templar: "Keeping with him the excellent brothers of the celebrated Knights of the Temple at Jerusalem, he made them the guardians

---

[66] Aelred, Stand VI; PL 195:194; CCCM 3:70; CF 56:264.

[67] Aelred, Stand VI; PL 195:195; CCCM 3:70; CF 56:265.

[68] Aelred, Lam D VI; PL 195:275; CCCM 3:10; CF 56:54.

[69] Aelred, Lam D VI; PL 195:275; CCCM 3:10; CF 56:54; Squire, "Aelred and King David," 361.

of his way of life by day and by night."[70] Thus Aelred was able to write, "These are the things that console me in my sorrow, good Jesus! Not that I can say he did not sin, but that he repented, that he wept, that he confessed, that he followed the counsel of holy Daniel when he said to Nebuchadnezzar, 'Atone for your sins by almsgiving, and from your iniquities by showing mercy to the poor.'"[71] The message is unmistakable—David I, as king and leader of the northern forces, was ultimately responsible for the actions of his subordinates, but he had abhorred their excesses and done penance for them.

There are many reasons for Aelred to have written as he did, perhaps including the need to work out his own grief for the man whom he had loved but who had done so much damage to his homeland. The powerful plea for understanding and forgiveness for King David of Scotland contained in *Lament* and *Battle*, however, could also have suggested to Aelred's readers that they should forgive and forget and allow the wounds left by the long civil war to heal.

King and Clergy

The relevance of *Genealogy* to the events of Aelred's time is less obvious than that of the other works because it does not concern the participants in the civil war but concentrates instead on Duke Henry's illustrious ancestors and the examples of proper lordship that they provided. This approach was obviously useful in establishing Henry's credentials as a legitimate successor to these mighty Anglo-Saxon kings,[72] and it can be argued that as well as flattering the new king, Aelred was concerned to prevent

---

[70] Aelred, Lam D VII; PL 195:275–76; CCCM 3:11; CF 56:55. For donations to the Templars, see *Charters of King David I*, nos. 234–35, 259.

[71] Aelred, Lam D VII; PL 195:276; CCCM 3:11; CF 56:55. The scriptural reference is to Dan 4:24.

[72] Marsha L. Dutton, "A Historian's Historian: The Place of Bede in Aelred's Contributions to the New History of His Age," in *Truth As Gift: Studies in Honor of John R. Sommerfeldt*, edited by Marsha Dutton, Daniel M. La Corte, and Paul Lockey, CS 204 (Kalamazoo, MI: Cistercian Publications, 2004), 420–22, 438–39;

challenges to his rule and a possible return to violence. In addition, there is something more to be gained from a close reading of the text. Of all the lessons that could be drawn from the careers of Henry's predecessors, one that stands out in *Genealogy* is the necessity that the ruler accept the guidance of the clergy.[73] In his portrayal of King Alfred (871–899), Aelred explained that, "The dignity of a ruler must recognize that in Christ's kingdom he is not a king but a citizen. Thus he must not govern priests by his laws but be humbly subject to the laws of Christ that the priests have established."[74] Following this maxim, King Edmund (939–946), "with the advice of the most holy Dunstan of Glastonbury . . . established what needed establishing and corrected what needed correcting."[75] The next king, Edmund's brother Eadred (946–955), "in everything obeyed the advice of blessed Dunstan, and he ruled his subjects by highly just laws."[76] King Edgar (957–975) entrusted the reform of the church to Dunstan, by then archbishop of Canterbury, and to Bishops Aethelwold of Winchester and Oswald of Worcester. Initiating the reform campaign, King Edgar articulated thoughts that Aelred gave him, exclaiming to Dunstan, "When have I not obeyed you? What treasure did I ever prefer to your counsels? What possessions did I not spurn at your command?"[77] Aelred introduced the ancient Gelasian doctrine of the two swords of secular and ecclesiastical justice into the speech, having Edgar urge the assembled clerics, "In my hands I have the sword of Constantine, and you the sword of Peter in yours. Let us join our right hands, let us unite sword and sword that we may put lepers

---

Dutton, "Ministry of Letters," 176–84; Ransford, "Noah's Ark," 142; P.-A. Burton, *Aelred*, 437.

[73] Dutton, "Historian," 418; Squire, *Aelred of Rievaulx*, 88–89; McGuire, *Brother and Lover*, 71–72; Dutton, "*Sancto Dunstano Cooperante*," 187–93; Newman, *Boundaries of Charity*, 180.

[74] Aelred, Gen Angl II; PL 195:719; CCCM 3:26–27; CF 56:78.

[75] Aelred, Gen Angl VI; PL 195:725; CCCM 3:37; CF 56:93.

[76] Aelred, Gen Angl VII; PL 195:725; CCCM 3:37; CF 56:93.

[77] Aelred, Gen Angl IX; PL 195:728–29; CCCM 3:42; CF 56:101.

out of the camp, that we may cleanse the sanctuary of the Lord."[78]
Again, the lesson is clear that in the past, the lay and secular authorities, especially the king and the archbishop of Canterbury,
had worked together for peace and good order in the realm.

Just at the time Aelred was writing these words, Archbishop
Theobald of Canterbury and Bishop Henry of Winchester, King
Stephen's brother, were spearheading the peace movement that
would culminate in the Treaty of Winchester.[79] Even after the
treaty was concluded, enormous problems regarding disputed
land tenure remained to be resolved, and King Stephen and Duke
Henry held a series of councils regarding the details of the settlement before Henry's return to Normandy in April 1154.[80] As the
young duke left England behind, he had no assurance that the
treaty would be honored other than the authority of the church,
which had guaranteed the terms of the settlement under pain of
excommunication.[81] As is the case with many of Aelred's other
suggestions for Henry II, the admonition to accept the guidance
of the clergy and to work together with the church for the peace
and stability of the kingdom would have been good advice at
any time. The timing of the work's composition further suggests
that these passages in Aelred's *Genealogy* can be read as a plea for
Stephen and Henry and their followers to accept the direction of
Archbishop Theobald and Bishop Henry and observe the new

[78] Aelred, Gen Angl IX; PL 195:728; CCCM 3:42; CF 56:100. On this incident, see
Freeman, *Narratives*, 65; Squire, "Aelred and King David," 366–67; P.-A. Burton,
Aelred, 439–40. On the two swords, see Jean Truax, *Archbishops Ralph d'Escures,
William of Corbeil and Theobald of Bec: Heirs of Anselm and Ancestors of Becket* (Al-
dershot: Ashgate, 2012), 9–10.

[79] Henry of Huntingdon, *Historia*, 770–71; Gervase of Canterbury, *Chronica*,
1:156; *Regesta Regum Anglo-Normannorum* 3, nos. 491, 796; Adrian Morey and
C. N. L. Brooke, *Gilbert Foliot and His Letters* (Cambridge: Cambridge University
Press, 1965), 88–90; David Crouch, *The Reign of King Stephen, 1135–1154* (Harlow,
UK: Pearson Education Ltd., 2000), 26–72; Avrom Saltman, *Theobald, Archbishop
of Canterbury* (New York: Greenwood Press, 1969), 39; Truax, *Archbishops*, 131–32.

[80] Henry of Huntingdon, *Historia*, 770–73; Davis, *King Stephen*, 119–23; Amt,
Accession of Henry II, 17–21; Matthew, *King Stephen*, 213–15; Holt, "1153," 291–316.

[81] Davis, *King Stephen*, 123–24; White, "End of Stephen's Reign," 13–22.

treaty, just as Kings Edmund, Eadred, and Edgar had listened to Dunstan of Canterbury.

Conclusion

Lament and *Genealogy*, known to have been written during the uncomfortable waiting period between the signing of the Treaty of Winchester and the accession of Henry II, contain advice for the new king that would have been appropriate at any time. Some of Aelred's specific concerns in these works, notably the emphasis on the proper administration of justice, the waging of just war, cooperation between king and clergy, and forgiveness and understanding for former combatants, were especially appropriate for the unsettled period in which he wrote. The fact that *Battle* clearly shares these concerns supports Dutton's contention that this work was also written during this critical period. Taken together, these three political-historical works suggest that, among other things, Aelred of Rievaulx intended to be a strong voice for peace and reconciliation at a crucial point in English history.

Chapter 7

Behind the Scenes

Aelred of Rievaulx, the Lords of Galloway, and the Kings of Scotland

Aelred of Rievaulx grew up and spent his young adulthood at the court of King David of Scotland, where he met many of the great magnates of the north and formed close friendships with the young men of the court, including the king's stepson Waldef.[1] In later years, Aelred's position as abbot obliged him to visit Rievaulx's daughter houses at Dundrennan and Melrose at least annually. It is clear from the writings of Reginald of Durham, Jocelin of Furness, and Aelred himself that these visits gave him the opportunity to maintain his ties with the friends of his youth.

On one occasion Reginald of Durham recorded that Aelred visited the abbot of Melrose, who wanted to consult him about certain miraculous events in the neighborhood attributed to the power of Saint Cuthbert.[2] Jocelin of Furness wrote that Aelred was with his friend Waldef at Melrose in 1159, shortly before the latter's death, when a deputation arrived to offer Waldef the bishopric of St. Andrews.[3] He also recorded two visits that Waldef made to Rievaulx.[4] In his *Lament for King David I* Aelred himself mentioned a visit that he made to the Scottish king on some

---

[1] See above, chap. 3:39–41.

[2] Reginald of Durham, *Libellus de Admirandis Beati Cuthberti Virtutibus*, Surtees Society 1 (London: J. B. Nichols and Sons, 1835), 188.

[3] Jocelin of Furness, *Vita S. Waltheni Abbatis, Acta Sanctorum*, August 3, 266–67.

[4] Jocelin of Furness, *Vita S. Waltheni*, 264–65.

unspecified urgent business of his abbey in 1153 during the last Lent of David's life and described finding the king living as a monk in the midst of his court, reciting the Psalms, engaging in manual labor in the gardens, and observing the monastic silence after sundown.[5] These visits enabled Aelred to sustain the friendships with King David and his stepson Waldef that had begun during the years that he lived at the Scottish court.

It might be assumed that these friendships also gave Aelred some degree of clout in court politics. The case for Aelred's political influence at the Scottish court, however, would be much stronger if one single charter or other document bearing his attestation had survived from these visits. The one clear instance of political activity on Aelred's part occurred not at the royal court but in the southwestern province of Galloway, whose ruler, Fergus, harbored notions of making himself equal to and independent of the Scottish king. Walter Daniel described a visit by Aelred to Galloway in which he mediated a quarrel between Fergus and his sons, but Walter provided no context for the incident.[6] When the personalities and events leading up to the event are investigated, it becomes clear that Aelred and the Cistercian Order had exercised a far greater influence over a much longer time than Walter indicated.

Fergus of Galloway and David I

David I had spent his early years at the Anglo-Norman royal court of Henry I, and in later years his most faithful supporters were the Anglo-Norman magnates who had been the friends of his youth. Once he became king, David rewarded them generously with lands and titles in Scotland. These men, who now held lands in both Scotland and England, crossed freely back and forth over the porous border between the two countries and appeared

---

[5] Aelred, Lam D VIII; PL 195:278; CCCM 3:13; CF 56:58–59; Aelred Squire, *Aelred of Rievaulx: A Study*, CS 50 (Kalamazoo, MI: Cistercian Publications, 1981), 83.

[6] Vita A 38–39, pp. 45–46; CF 57:125.

frequently at both royal courts.[7] The Scottish kingdom, however, was also home to a group of native magnates who maintained their independence, acknowledged only a loose bond with the royal court, and often looked askance at the customs introduced by the newcomers. Among them were the great lords of Galloway and Argyll, who were bound together by a network of marriage alliances that included the lords of the Western Isles, who in turn maintained a loose allegiance to the kings of Norway.[8]

Aelred's own work indicates that the area was turbulent throughout his own lifetime. He made it clear in *Lament* and the *Report on the Battle of the Standard* that the worst atrocities inflicted on the north by the Scots during the civil war had been perpetrated by Galwegian troops attached to David's army and that the king himself did not exercise full control over that part of his forces. The same theme recurs in his treatise on the *Saints of Hexham* and is corroborated by other contemporary writers.[9] In a speech that Aelred wrote in *Battle*, he had Robert de Bruce comment to King David: "This reliance on the Galwegians is new to you."[10] The implication is clear that the men of Galloway were an outside force with whom the king of Scots had made an alliance, not a group that he could summon as a matter of right. Furthermore, the Galwegians' insistence on leading the charge against the English forces at the Battle of the Standard pitted their poorly equipped forces against the heavily armed English knights and probably cost David his chance at victory.[11] Perhaps

---

[7] See above, chap. 3:41–43.

[8] R. Andrew McDonald and Scott A. McLean, "Somerled of Argyll: A New Look at Old Problems," *The Scottish Historical Review*, 71, nos. 191 and 192, pts. 1 and 2 (1992): 5–7.

[9] See above, chap. 6:142–45.

[10] Aelred, Stand VI; PL 195:192–93; CCCM 3:68; CF 56:262.

[11] Aelred, Lam D VI; PL 195:275; CCCM 3:10; CF 56:53–54; Stand VI, IX; PL 195:187–90; CCCM 3:68, 71; CF 56:254–58; SS Hag IX; Raine, *Priory*, 1:183–84; CCCM 3:86; CF 71:77–78; Richard of Hexham, *De Gestis Regis Stephani et de Bello Standardo*, in *Chronicles of the Reigns of Stephen, Henry II., and Richard I.*, ed. Richard Howlett, 4 vols., RS 82 (London: Longmans, 1884–1890), 3:151–59; Henry of Huntingdon, *Historia Anglorum: The History of the English People*, ed. and trans.

out of deference to a man who would loom large in the affairs of the northern church in later years, none of the accounts of the battle, including Aelred's own, mentions the leader of these forces, Fergus of Galloway, by name. One of his sons, however, became one of the hostages taken by King Stephen to ensure compliance when the peace was concluded, so it is almost certain that Fergus participated in the invasion and the battle.[12]

Fergus of Galloway first appeared at the Scottish court in 1136 along with his son Uchtred as a witness to several royal charters endowing the newly consecrated cathedral of Saint Kentigern in Glasgow.[13] His origin is unknown, and opinion is divided on whether he was an acquaintance of David I, perhaps from the English court, or a native lord, possibly related in some way to Somerled of Argyll.[14] The latter view seems more likely, since in addition to his independent stance at the Battle of the Standard, Fergus's early activities left no doubt about his view of himself as a sovereign magnate and his aspirations for the domain he had acquired. In a charter granting land to the Templar preceptory of Temple Hurste in the West Riding of Yorkshire, Fergus styled himself king of the Gallovidians (*Rex Galwicensium*). His association with this particular institution placed him in royal company, along with David of Scotland and Stephen of England. The house

---

Diana Greenway (Oxford: Clarendon Press, 1996), 712–19. On the situation in Galloway generally, see Keith Stringer, "Galloway and Abbeys of Rievaulx and Dundrennan," *Transactions of the Dumfriesshire and Galloway Natural History and Antiquarian Society,* series 3, 55 (1980): 176; Pierre-André Burton, "The Beginnings of Cistercian Expansion in England: The Socio-Historical Context of the Foundation of Rievaulx (1132)," CSQ 42.2 (2007): 179.

[12] Richard of Hexham, *Bello Standardo,* 3:178.

[13] *The Charters of King David I: The Written Acts of David I King of Scots, 1124–53 and of his son Henry Earl of Northumberland, 1139–52,* ed. G. W. S. Barrow (Woodbridge: Boydell Press, 1999), nos. 56–58; Daphne Brooke, *Wild Men and Holy Places: St. Ninian, Whithorn and the Medieval Realm of Galloway* (Edinburgh: Canongate Press, 1994), 78–79; Richard D. Oram, *The Lordship of Galloway* (Edinburgh: John Donald, 2000), 65–66.

[14] Richard D. Oram, "Fergus, Galloway and the Scots," in *Galloway: Land and Lordship,* ed. Richard D. Oram and Geoffrey P. Stell (Edinburgh: Scottish Society for Northern Studies, 1991), 117–22.

seems to have been a royal favorite, as it continued to be patronized by English royalty, including, eventually, Kings Henry II, John, and Henry III.[15]

The marriage alliances that Fergus negotiated for himself and his family provide additional insight into his hopes for his prospective Galwegian kingdom. It is now generally recognized that King Henry I of England used the marriages of his numerous illegitimate daughters to construct a network of defensive alliances along his borders,[16] and on a smaller scale, Fergus can be shown to have done the same thing. In the case of Fergus's own marriage, the strategies of the two rulers actually coincided, for Fergus married one of Henry I's illegitimate daughters. Her name is not known, and the evidence for the marriage rests on chronicle statements in which Fergus's known relatives are referred to as relatives or cousins of the English monarch. Indeed, Roger of Hoveden noted in 1175 that Henry II referred to Fergus's son Uchtred as his cousin.[17] Similarly Robert of Torigny recorded that Fergus's grandson, the king of Man, was related to Henry II.[18] A letter by King John in 1210 referred to another grandson, Gilbert's son Duncan, as his friend and relative.[19] Historian Richard Oram considers the marriage to have been in line with Henry's policy of consolidating his power around the Irish Sea by building alliances with client rulers in the area. He also notes that a date of about 1120 for the marriage coincides with the time when

---

[15] William Dugdale, *Monasticon Anglicanum*, rev. John Caley, Henry Ellis, and Bandinel Bulkeley (London: Harding and Longmans, 1830; reprinted Westmead, UK: Gregg International, 1970), 6:838; Brooke, *Wildmen*, 79; Daphne Brooke, *Fergus the King* (Whithorn: Friends of the Whithorn Trust, 1991), 2; Oram, *Lordship of Galloway*, 62.

[16] C. Warren Hollister and Thomas K. Keefe, "The Making of the Angevin Empire," in *Monarchy, Magnates and Institutions in the Anglo-Norman World* (London: Hambledon Press, 1986), 251–52.

[17] Roger of Hoveden, *Chronica Magistri Rogeri de Houedene*, ed. William Stubbs, 4 vols., RS 51 (London: Longmans, 1868–1871), 2:105.

[18] Robert of Torigny, *Chronica*, in *Chronicles of the Reigns of Stephen, Henry II., and Richard I.*, ed. Richard Howlett, 4 vols. RS 82 (London: Longmans, 1884–1889), 4:229.

[19] Brooke, *Fergus*, 5.

Ranulf Meschin, in order to become earl of Chester, surrendered Carlisle to the future David I, at that time prince of Cumbria.[20] Regardless of whether Henry or Fergus himself initiated the negotiations, the enhancement to the Galwegian ruler's prestige was unquestionable.

In the same way the marriage of Fergus's daughter Affrica to King Olaf of the Isle of Man was another alliance outside the Scottish orbit for the purpose of maintaining Galwegian independence.[21] Fergus, however, left no aspect to chance, and the marriage of his eldest son Uchtred to Gunnilda, the daughter of Waltheof of Allerdale, served two purposes at once. Since Waltheof was the younger brother of Earl Cospatric of Dunbar, this marriage forged an alliance with the neighboring Cumbrian nobility.[22] Oram, however, has noted that Gunnilda was also a distant kinswoman of David I's, so the marriage gave Uchtred a tie to the senior members of the royal court.[23] By his own marriage and those of his children, Fergus not only enhanced the prestige of his house but also ensured that if one of his neighbors attacked, another would come to his aid. His use of marriage alliances illustrates his carefully constructed strategy designed to elevate his status to that of royalty and to maintain his own freedom of action by playing the kings of Scotland and England against one another.

Fergus and the See of Whithorn

Fergus of Galloway was also fully aware of the way in which carefully placed donations to the church, and especially to reformed monasteries, might be used to elevate one's own status and perhaps in addition lay claim to unoccupied lands. And here, of course, his interests coincided with those of the Cistercians

---

[20] Richard D. Oram, "A Family Business? Colonisation and Settlement in Twelfth- and Thirteenth-Century Galloway," *The Scottish Historical Review*, 72, no. 194, pt. 2 (1993): 115–16; Oram, *Lordship of Galloway*, 59–61.

[21] Oram, "Colonisation and Settlement," 116.

[22] Oram, "Colonisation and Settlement," 117.

[23] Oram, *Lordship of Galloway*, 67–68.

and Aelred. Sometimes Fergus is credited with the foundation of the priory of Saint Mary's Isle for Augustinian canons, but it is possible that his contribution was to donate the isle to Holyrood Abbey and that the priory was established later.[24] Fergus also granted the Hospitallers the lands of Galtway near Kirkcudbright.[25] He was responsible for reestablishing the see of Whithorn, building a new cathedral, and possibly establishing a priory for Augustinian canons there.[26] Most important for our purposes, he founded two houses for Cistercians, one at Soulseat, and the other at Dundrennan with monks from Rievaulx itself.[27]

There has long been doubt about whether David I or Fergus actually revived the see of Whithorn in Galloway between 1125 and 1133 with the appointment of the first-known bishop in three centuries, Gilla-Aldan. It seems likely, however, that Fergus of Galloway should receive the credit for the reestablishment of the diocese, since it differed in one important respect from the other Scottish dioceses established or reinvigorated by David I. The see of Whithorn was quite alone in maintaining its allegiance to the see of York,[28] beginning with the consecration of Bishop Gilla-Aldan by Archbishop Thurstan. It is likely that this was part of Fergus's strategy for maintaining the independence of Galloway from the Scottish kings.[29] Richard Oram concludes on the basis of this fact that Fergus was the most likely candidate to

---

[24] Thomas Murray, *The Literary History of Galloway From the Earliest Period to the Present Time* (Edinburgh: Waugh and Inness, 1822), 38; Andrew McDonald, "Scoto-Norse Kings and the Reformed Religious Orders: Patterns of Monastic Patronage in Twelfth-Century Galloway and Argyll," *Albion* 27, no. 2 (1995): 198–99.

[25] *Regesta Regum Scottorum: Vol. 1, The Acts of Malcolm IV King of Scots 1153–1165 Together With Scottish Royal Acts Prior to 1153 not included in Sir Archibald Lawrie's Early Scottish Charters*, ed. G. W. S. Barrow (Edinburgh: Edinburgh University Press, 1960), 98; McDonald, "Monastic Patronage," 201.

[26] Brooke, *Wildmen*, 88; McDonald, "Monastic Patronage," 197–98.

[27] Murray, *Literary History*, 32, 47; McDonald, "Monastic Patronage," 193–97; James Wilson, "The Passages of St. Malachy through Scotland," *The Scottish Historical Review* 18, no. 70 (1921): 77–78.

[28] See above, chap. 3:43–47.

[29] Murray, *Literary History*, 62–64; Oram, "Colonisation and Settlement," 113.

have reestablished the see, for David I would have resisted the bishop's making a profession of obedience to York. He also suggested that Thurstan of York may have had a hand in the matter, because it would bolster his claim to authority over the rest of the Scottish dioceses and, most important, give him a critically useful additional suffragan bishop.[30]

Gilla-Aldan's successor Christian received his consecration in 1154 from Archbishop Hugh of Rouen, acting for Archbishop Roger of Pont l'Évêque of York, who had just been elected and had not yet received his pallium. Archbishop Roger, however, did attend the ceremony, which took place on the same day as Henry II's coronation.[31] Christian remained so loyal to York that he refused to attend a Scottish legatine council at Edinburgh in 1177 on the grounds that he belonged to the jurisdiction of York.[32] His defiance earned him a suspension from office and excommunication but, upheld by Archbishop Roger of York, he ignored the decree and continued in office. It is difficult to see how he could have done anything else, since the affair took place within the context of a recent rebellion by the lords of Galloway against the authority of King William the Lion.[33] In the same year Bishop Christian appeared at the court of Henry II, where he witnessed a charter confirming the resolution of a dispute between the kings of Castile and Navarre mediated by the English king.[34] Unlike his colleagues, who appeared regularly at the royal court, Christian

---

[30] Richard D. Oram, "In Obedience and Reverence: Whithorn and York c. 1128–c. 1250," *Innes Review* 42, no. 2 (1991): 83–90; Oram, *Lordship of Galloway*, 171–74.

[31] *Councils and Ecclesiastical Documents Relating to Great Britain and Ireland*, ed. Arthur West Haddan and William Stubbs, 3 vols. (Oxford: Clarendon Press, 1869–1878), vol. 2, pt. 1, 33; *Chronicle of Holyrood*, in *The Church Historians of England*, ed. and trans. Joseph Stevenson, 5 vols. in 8 (London: Seeleys, 1856), 4.1.74; Oram, *Lordship of Galloway*, 176.

[32] Benedict of Peterborough, *Gestis Regis Henrici Secundi Benedicti Abbas*, ed. William Stubbs, 2 vols., RS 49 (London: Longmans, 1867), 1:66–67; Roger of Hoveden, *Chronica*, 2:135.

[33] Benedict of Peterborough, *Gestis Regis Henrici*, 1:67; Roger of Hoveden, *Chronica*, 2:63; Oram, "Obedience and Reverence," 91–92.

[34] Roger of Hoveden, *Chronica*, 2:120–31; Murray, *Literary History*, 63.

witnessed only one charter of King Malcolm IV, a grant to Dunfermline between 1154–1159.[35]

Aelred's *Life of Saint Ninian* and the See of Whithorn

The adherence of the bishops of Whithorn to the see of York brought them into the same ecclesiastical orbit as the monastery of Rievaulx. Perhaps for this reason one of them commissioned Aelred to write his *Life of Saint Ninian*. Marsha Dutton has suggested that Aelred wrote for an important event in the life of the see of Whithorn, perhaps the consecration of the new cathedral around 1150 during the pontificate of Bishop Gilla-Aldan or the inauguration of his successor Bishop Christian on December 19, 1154.[36] Aelred remarked at the beginning of the work: "You say, moreover, that the clergy and people of your holy church, who hold in extraordinary affection this saint of God under whose patronage they live, will receive whatever we write with the greatest devotion, because, as you assert, the wishes of all have especially chosen me for this work."[37] This statement implies that Aelred was well known throughout the diocese of Whithorn and that his fame was not restricted to clerical circles. It is even possible that Aelred and Bishop Christian were close friends, for the bishop was an ardent admirer of the Cistercians. He had previously served in the diocese of Carlisle, and his appointment was supported by

---

[35] *Regesta Regum Scottorum*, 1:118.

[36] Marsha L. Dutton, Introduction to Aelred of Rievaulx, *The Lives of the Northern Saints*, trans. Jane Patricia Freeland, ed. Marsha L. Dutton, CF 71 (Kalamazoo, MI: Cistercian Publications, 2006), 11; Dutton, "A Historian's Historian: The Place of Bede in Aelred's Contributions to the New History of His Age," in *Truth As Gift: Studies in Honor of John R. Sommerfeldt*, ed. Marsha L. Dutton, Daniel M. La Corte, and Paul Lockey, CS 204 (Kalamazoo, MI: Cistercian Publications, 2004), 424–25; Squire, *Aelred of Rievaulx*, 115–16; Pierre-André Burton, *Aelred de Rievaulx (1110–1167), De l'homme éclaté à l'être unifié: Essai de biographie existentielle et spirituelle* (Paris: Éditions du Cerf, 2010), 480–85. For the date of the consecration of Whithorn Cathedral, see Brooke, *Fergus the King*, 9. See Brian Patrick McGuire, *Brother and Lover: Aelred of Rievaulx* (New York: Crossroad Publishing Co., 1994), 42–46, for the contrary view, placing this work before Aelred's entry into Rievaulx.

[37] Aelred, Vita N Prol.; Pinkerton, *Lives*, 10; CCCM 3:113; CF 71:36.

the Cistercian archbishop of York, Henry Murdac. He frequently involved himself in the affairs of the Cistercian abbey of Holm Cultram, where he later died and was buried.[38]

The source for the *Life of Ninian* is Bede,[39] who summed up the saint's career:

> The southern Picts who live on this side of the mountains had, so it is said, long ago given up the errors of idolatry and received the true faith through the preaching of the Word by that reverend and holy man Bishop Ninian, a Briton who had received orthodox instruction at Rome in the faith and the mysteries of the truth. His episcopal see is celebrated for its church, dedicated to St. Martin, where his body rests, together with those of many other saints. The see is now under English rule. This place which is in the kingdom of Bernicia is commonly called Whithorn, the White House, because Ninian built a church of stone there, using a method unusual among the Britons.[40]

The *Miracula Nynie Episcopi*, a Latin poem written at Whithorn toward the end of the eighth century, contains essentially the same information as Aelred's composition, differing only in the selection of a few of the miracle stories. It is likely that both derive from an earlier and now lost work, the information for which may have been supplied by an early bishop of the see named Pecthelm, perhaps an acquaintance of Bede.[41] Although Aelred was not

[38] *Register and Records of Holm Cultram*, ed. F. Grainger and W. G. Collingwood (Kendal: Titus Wilson and Son for the Cumberland and Westmorland Antiquarian and Archaeological Society, 1929), no. 141; J. G. Scott, "The Origins of Dundrennan and Soulseat Abbeys," *Transactions of the Dumfriesshire and Galloway Natural History and Antiquarian Society*, series 3, 63 (1988): 41; Emilia Jamroziak, "Holm Cultram Abbey: A Story of Success," *Northern History* 45, no. 1 (2008): 30–31.

[39] Murray, *Literary History*, 8.

[40] Bede, *Ecclesiastical History of the English People*, ed. and trans. Bertram Colgrave and R. A. B. Mynors (Oxford: Clarendon Press, 1969), 222–23.

[41] John MacQueen, "The Literary Sources for the *Life of St. Ninian*," in *Galloway: Land and Lordship*, ed. Richard D. Oram and Geoffrey P. Stell (Edinburgh: Scottish Society for Northern Studies, 1991), 17–25; John MacQueen, *St Nynia, with a translation of the Miracula Nynie Episcopi and the Vita Niniani by Winifred MacQueen*

inventing his narrative but working from an existing document, his treatment of the material can still reveal something about his motives and concerns in writing the work.

For example, Aelred began his account by stating that Ninian's native land of Galloway was "known to have had its own king right up to the most recent period of the English" and that Ninian himself was the son of the king.[42] This statement was certainly calculated to please Fergus of Galloway by highlighting the prestige and independence of his domain. Both Aelred's account and the eighth-century poem tell the story of Ninian's trip to Rome, the instruction that he received there, and his consecration as bishop by the pope himself.[43] In Ninian's time many young men from the outlying provinces made their way to Rome for an education, most notably Augustine of Hippo,[44] and thus the original narrator may not have attached too much significance to Ninian's Roman interlude. Aelred, however, personalized the story, noting that while in Rome, Ninian realized that "many things contrary to sound doctrine had been instilled in him and his fellow countrymen by incompetent teachers."[45] Following the account of Ninian's sojourn in Rome, the earlier poem moved directly to Ninian's mission to the Picts and the building of the cathedral at Candida Casa, the ancient name for Whithorn.[46] Aelred, perhaps moved by the dedication of the cathedral to Saint Martin of Tours, inserted at this point the story of a visit that Ninian paid to Saint Martin on his way home to Britain, explaining that Ninian obtained masons from the bishop of Tours so that "as he had determined to imitate

---

(Edinburgh: Birlinn Ltd., 2005), 3–6; Ann W. Astell, "To Build the Church: Saint Aelred of Rievaulx's Hexaemeral Miracles in the *Life of Ninian*," CSQ 49, no. 4 (2014): 456–57.

[42] Aelred, Vita N I; Pinkerton, *Lives*, 12; CCCM 3:116; CF 71:39.

[43] Aelred, Vita N I–II; Pinkerton, *Lives*, 15–16; CCCM 3:117–18; CF 71:40–42; *Miracula Nynie Episcopi*, ed. Karl Strecker, MGH *Poetae Latini Aevi Carolini*, vol. 4, pt. 3 (Berlin: Weidmannschen, 1978), 946–47; MacQueen, *St Nynia*, 89.

[44] W. Douglas Simpson, *St. Ninian and the Origins of the Christian Church in Scotland* (Edinburgh: Oliver and Boyd, 1940), 38, 45–49.

[45] Aelred, Vita N II; Pinkerton, *Lives*, 16; CCCM 3:119; CF 71:41.

[46] Strecker, *Miracula Nynie Episcopi*, 946–48; MacQueen, *St Nynia*, 89–90.

the faith of the holy Roman Church, he would also imitate its way of building churches and of establishing ecclesiastical offices."[47] Perhaps Aelred meant this part of the narrative to be interpreted as a plea for the diocese of Whithorn to align itself with the rest of the Scottish dioceses in seeking to report directly to Rome, without an English archbishop as intermediary. Alternatively, since the papacy was at this stage still determined that the Scottish bishoprics should be subject to York, these passages could also be read as an exhortation for the Scottish church to do what Rome actually wanted, to follow Bishop Christian's example. Either theory is pure conjecture, so perhaps it is safest to read Aelred's account as a general plea for adherence to Roman ways and for support of the reform of the diocese of Whithorn under Bishop Christian.

As Ninian's first miracle both Aelred and the eighth-century poet chose to recount an incident highlighting the saint's relationship with King Tuduvallus, a proud and lustful monarch who not only disregarded Ninian's warnings but also secretly disparaged his teaching and his way of life. In punishment for his sins, Tuduvallus was struck with a debilitating illness that rendered him blind. When Ninian touched the sick king's head and laid his hand upon his blind eyes, he was miraculously healed and became a devoted follower of the holy man.[48] Aelred asked, "who can doubt that someone who with sure faith and a sincere and humble heart asks the help of such a man in healing the wounds of the inner self will obtain a quick remedy through his holy merits?"[49] Perhaps by giving this miracle such a prominent place in his account, Aelred was calling upon Fergus of Galloway and his sons to submit themselves to Bishop Christian for spiritual healing. But the tale of King Tuduvallus was not original with Aelred, so it is also possible that he was simply following his source material here.

[47] Aelred, Vita N II; Pinkerton, *Lives*, 18; CCCM 3:119; CF 71:43.

[48] Aelred, Vita N IV; Pinkerton, *Lives*, 21–23; CCCM 3:120–21; CF 71:44–46; Strecker, *Miracula Nynie Episcopi*, 948–50; MacQueen, *St Nynia*, 90–92.

[49] Aelred, Vita N IV; Pinkerton, *Lives*, 23; CCCM 3:121; CF 71:46.

Similarly, for the rest of Ninian's story the two works follow the same path: the saint discerns the truth within the deceitful hearts of people, protects his lands and herds, raises the dead, and causes crops to flourish overnight.[50] Aelred added two additional miracles that occurred during Ninian's lifetime. In the first, rain refused to wet Ninian and his psalter as long as the saint remained focused on his meditations.[51] In the second, a young boy, fleeing from Galloway to Scotland to avoid punishment for some unnamed fault, stole Ninian's staff. The coracle that he chose for his journey was a common type of vessel, a basket woven of sticks and covered with cowhide. This particular boat, however, was not completely covered yet, and when it began to take on water, the terrified fugitive thrust the staff into one of the holes in his vessel, whereupon the leaking stopped. In this instance the reader has the impression that Aelred included the story because of his fascination with the characteristics of the boat itself, which he described at some length.[52]

Both works conclude with an account of Ninian's death and posthumous miracles. Aelred omitted a story from the earlier text concerning a pious priest who, while celebrating Mass at Ninian's tomb, received a vision of the Christ Child seated on the communion paten.[53] Perhaps feeling that this story demonstrated the sanctity of the pious priest who received the vision more than that of Ninian, Aelred substituted a story of two lepers healed by Ninian's power.[54] Except for Aelred's emphasis on Ninian's adherence to Roman customs, the differences between his work and the eighth-century poem seem to reflect personal taste rather than an overtly political agenda.

Nevertheless, by celebrating a great occasion in the life of the Galwegian church with a new *Life of Ninian*, Aelred placed before

[50] Aelred, Vita N V–VIII; Pinkerton, *Lives*, 23–30; CCCM 3:121–26; CF 71:46–52; Strecker, *Miracula Nynie Episcopi*, 950–53; MacQueen, *St Nynia*, 92–95.

[51] Aelred, Vita N IX; Pinkerton, *Lives*, 31; CCCM 3:126–27; CF 71:53–54.

[52] Aelred, Vita N X; Pinkerton, *Lives*, 31–33; CCCM 3:127–29; CF 71:54–56.

[53] Strecker, *Miracula Nynie Episcopi*, 957–59; MacQueen, *St Nynia*, 98–100.

[54] Aelred, Vita N XV; Pinkerton, *Lives*, 38–39; CCCM 3:133–34; CF 71:62–63.

his readers a carefully crafted summary of the benefits accruing to them from the presence of a holy bishop. It was undoubtedly no accident that this bishop adhered to the correct, Roman model of ecclesiastical reform and cooperated harmoniously with the secular ruler in support of this goal. The material on which Aelred based his work may not have been new, and may even have been familiar to his audience, but by refurbishing it for this occasion, he presented his audience with a powerful plea for support for the reforming bishops of Galloway.

The Abbeys of Dundrennan and Soulseat

Glad as Aelred must have been to see the regularization of the diocesan organization in Galloway, it is likely that the matter closest to his heart was the growth of Cistercian monasticism in the province. The abbey of Dundrennan was founded around 1142, while memories of the Scottish invasion and the Battle of the Standard were still fresh. The founding of a new Cistercian abbey would have been a particularly appropriate form of expiation for crimes committed during the recent conflict, since the Cistercian house of Newminster had been destroyed by the invaders. Colonizing the new house from Rievaulx would also have been appealing, since the Battle of the Standard had been fought less than twenty miles away on lands belonging to the abbey. Such a munificent gesture would have appealed to Fergus of Galloway himself, as it would demonstrate his parity with David I, who had founded Melrose and was at that time in the process of establishing a second Cistercian abbey at Newbattle.[55]

The leading role in the negotiations for the foundation of the new abbey was usually assigned to Archbishop Malachy of Armagh, who visited Scotland and northern England in 1140 during the course of a journey to Rome to seek palliums for himself and the archbishop of Cashel. He visited York on his way to the continent, and although it is likely that he did not arrive in time to

---

[55] Brooke, *Wildmen*, 88–90; Brooke, *Fergus the King*, 9–11; Oram, "Colonisation and Settlement," 115.

meet with Archbishop Thurstan, who died in February, he did receive a visit from King David's stepson Waldef, at that time prior of Kirkham. This route of course brought him close to Rievaulx, the premier Cistercian house in the north, so perhaps he visited there as well. Such a visit is particularly likely because Malachy also stopped at Clairvaux, and he was so impressed with the way of life there that when he arrived in Rome he begged Pope Innocent II to allow him to resign his bishopric and retire to the abbey. Instead the pope sent him back to Ireland as papal legate.

On the way home to Ireland Malachy stopped again at Clairvaux before going on to Scotland, where he met King David, perhaps at Carlisle. He then made no fewer than three stops in Galloway: at Cruggleton, where he cured a mute girl; at Kirk Mochrum, about twelve miles away, where he healed a mad woman; and finally on the coast at Cairngarbh. He was forced to wait for several days for favorable weather before crossing to Ireland, so he had a small oratory of woven branches constructed there.[56] King David of Scotland, Bernard of Clairvaux, Abbot William of Rievaulx, and Fergus of Galloway all had an interest in the foundation of the new house, and Malachy's journeys among the principals suggest that he was the intermediary among the stakeholders in the new foundation.

At that time Aelred was a relatively new member of the Rievaulx community, still some two to three years away from his appointment as novice master. He was, however, clearly a young man on the way up, and Walter Daniel says that Abbot William had early on "determined to admit him to the intimacies of his counsel and to the discussion of matters closely affecting the household of Rievaulx."[57] Furthermore Aelred's connections with the Scottish court make it possible that he was involved in

---

[56] Bernard, V Mal 34–40; SBOp 3:341–46; CF 10:49–54; Wilson, "St. Malachy," 73–78. On Saint Malachy generally, see J. A. Watt, *The Church and the Two Nations in Medieval Ireland* (Cambridge: Cambridge University Press, 1970), 19–28; A. Gwynn, "St. Malachy of Armagh," *The Irish Ecclesiastical Record* 70 (1948): 961–78; Marie Therese Flanagan, *The Transformation of the Irish Church in the Twelfth and Thirteenth Centuries* (Woodbridge: Boydell Press, 2010), 120–28.

[57] Vita A 14, p. 23; CF 57:106.

planning for the new monastery and that he met Fergus of Galloway at this time.

Malachy traveled through Scotland on his way to the continent again in 1148, this time to meet Pope Eugenius III in France and once again to ask for palliums for the Irish archbishops. Upon landing in Scotland he went to a place called Viride Stagnum, or Green Lake, "which he had prepared beforehand so that he might establish an abbey there." Bernard of Clairvaux reported on Malachy's preparations, "There he left some of his sons—our brothers—as a convent of monks with an abbot."[58] After a visit with King David, Malachy embarked for the continent and Clairvaux, where he fell ill and died.[59]

There is some doubt as to the location of Viride Stagnum, but J. G. Scott has suggested that it can be identified with a monastery at Soulseat, which later became a house for Premonstratensian canons.[60] He postulates that during the visit to Cruggleton in 1140 Malachy also negotiated with Fergus for the foundation of a second Cistercian monastery on the site near the shore where he had erected his little oratory, leaving Fergus to construct the required buildings while Malachy returned to Ireland. Arrangements were completed by the time of Malachy's last visit in 1148, when he left some monks who had come with him from Ireland in the new monastery.[61] Presumably these monks came from the Irish Cistercian abbey of Mellifont, which would make Soulseat a daughter house of that monastery, subject to visitation by its abbot.

Mellifont, itself, however, had only been founded in 1142, with a combination of French monks from Clairvaux and Irish monks who had been sent to Clairvaux for training. A letter from Bernard to Malachy makes it clear that not all ran smoothly at the new

---

[58] Bernard, V Mal 68; SBOp 3:373; CF 10:87.

[59] Bernard, V Mal 74; SBOp 3:377; CF 10:91.

[60] *Wigtownshire Charters*, ed. R. C. Reid, Scottish Historical Society, ser. 3, no. 51 (Edinburgh: T. and A. Constable, 1960), 88–91.

[61] Scott, "Dundrennan and Soulseat," 36–38. For a contrary view, see Wilson, "St. Malachy," 77–78.

foundation in Ireland, for some of the French monks quickly returned to Clairvaux. Bernard suggested that they had been driven out by Irish hostility: "But perhaps those natives of your country who are little disciplined and who found it hard to obey observances that were strange to them may have been in some measure the occasion of their return." He went on to note that he was sending back Mellifont's first abbot, Christian, to whom he had given additional instruction in the customs of the Order, hoping that "in the future he will be more careful about them."[62] Clearly Mellifont was in no position to supervise another foundation, let alone one on the other side of the Irish Sea. Thus Scott has suggested that perhaps Soulseat was given over to Rievaulx, the mother of two other Scottish foundations, Melrose and Dundrennan.[63]

Aelred the Peacemaker

The existence of a smaller Cistercian foundation loosely tied to Rievaulx helps make sense of a puzzling incident related by Walter Daniel. He describes an abbot of a daughter house of Rievaulx who was so insolent on the occasion of his annual visit that Aelred prophesied his imminent death, which happened as soon as the abbot returned home.[64] Powicke identified the abbot as Philip of Revesby,[65] but in the *Vita Aelredi* this incident is followed immediately by the statement that Aelred went to Galloway in order to console the monks of a house whose abbot had just died. Furthermore, Walter Daniel then launched into a diatribe about Galwegian monks, who rarely achieved perfection because they were by nature "dull and brutal" and "always inclined to carnal pleasures."[66] These remarks would have been a strange criticism of Dundrennan, which had been populated with Rievaulx monks

---

[62] Bernard, Ep 357 (SBOp 8:301–2; J385); Roger Stalley, *The Cistercian Monasteries of Ireland* (New Haven: Yale University Press, 1987), 15.

[63] Scott, "Dundrennan and Soulseat," 38.

[64] Vita A 37; pp. 44–45; CF 57:123–24.

[65] Powicke, Introduction to Vita A, lxx.

[66] Vita A 38; p. 45; CF 57:124.

and subject to its supervision from the beginning. Scott suggested that the criticism was more likely to apply to Soulseat, a monastery filled with Irish and local recruits, and that the quarrel between Aelred and the unnamed abbot concerned the resulting lax standards there.[67]

In any case when Aelred arrived in Galloway he found the province in turmoil, as "sons rose against their father, the father against his sons and brother against brother."[68] Neither King David nor the local bishop proved able to control the situation. Walter Daniel provided no context for the event, but the *Chronicle* of John of Fordun enables us to place the incident in the early years of the reign of the young king Malcolm IV. The problem had begun in 1155–1156 with a rebellion led by Somerled of Argyll and Malcolm MacHeth, a possibly bastard son of King Alexander I. MacHeth's son Donald was captured at Whithorn in 1156, perhaps on his way to enlist support for his father's claim from Fergus of Galloway and his sons. This situation forced MacHeth to make peace with King Malcolm, and although Somerled continued his depredations, peace was generally restored.

Matters came to a head in 1160 as King Malcolm returned from accompanying Henry II of England on an expedition to Toulouse. Fearing the growing English influence in Scotland, a group of six earls sought to take King Malcolm prisoner, but he escaped them and promptly mounted an expedition into Galloway to destroy the rebels.[69] Daphne Brooke has pointed out that the chronicle ac-

[67] Scott, "Dundrennan and Soulseat," 39.

[68] Vita A 38; p. 46; CF 57:125.

[69] *Johannis de Fordun Chronica Gentis Scottorum*, ed. William F. Skene (Edinburgh: Edmonston and Douglas, 1871), 254–56; *John of Fordun's Chronicle of the Scottish Nation*, trans. William F. Skene (Edinburgh: Edmonston and Douglas, 1872), 249–51; *Chronica de Mailros, e Codice Unico*, ed. Joseph Stevenson (Edinburgh: Bannatyne Club, 1835), 77–79; *A Mediaeval Chronicle of Scotland: The Chronicle of Melrose*, trans. Joseph Stevenson (London: Seeleys, 1853; reprinted Lampeter: Llanerch Press, 1991), 11–13; *Chronicle of Holyrood*, 74; Roger of Hoveden, 1:217; Scott, "Dundrennan and Soulseat," 40; Murray, *Literary History*, 338–39; McDonald and McLean, "Somerled of Argyll," 10–18; Oram, *Lordship of Galloway*, 74; Barrow, Introduction to *Regesta Regum Scottorum*, 12–13; Sir Archibald Campbell Lawrie, *Annals of the*

counts are vague and that Fergus might not have been associated with the six earls but mounted a separate campaign against the king instead. But she provides no information accounting for this view.[70] Richard Oram notes Fergus's son Uchtred's independent presence at the Scottish court and speculates that he may have been drawn more into the royal orbit than was his father or brother and that this association was the source of the familial discord.[71] In any case King Malcolm seems to have considered Galloway the most serious threat to his rule, for he made two more forays into Galloway in the same year before Fergus, who was characterized as the leader of the revolt, abandoned his position and took the monastic habit at Holyrood, leaving his son as a hostage to ensure the peace.

Walter Daniel assigned Aelred a pivotal role in these negotiations: "Aelred the peacemaker met them all together and, with words of peace and goodness, bound together the angry sons by a firm peace in a single bond of affection." After this meeting, Walter said, Aelred further inspired Fergus of Galloway to retire to a monastery, leaving the province divided between his two sons Uchtred and Gilbert.[72] On his way home from his peacemaking mission, Walter went on, Aelred miraculously cured a man who had accidentally swallowed a frog, an event witnessed by "almost more persons in Galloway than can be numbered."[73] Aelred made at least one and perhaps two further visits to Galloway, including the one reported by Reginald of Durham about 1164, when

Reigns of Malcolm and William, Kings of Scotland A.D. 1153–1214 (Glasgow: Robert Maclehose and Co., 1910; reprinted Oswald Press, 2008), 11–13, 21, 26, 40–48, 54–57, 79–83; P. A. Burton, *Aelred*, 407–8.

[70] Brooke, *Wildmen*, 93–95; Brooke, *Fergus*, 13–16.

[71] *Charters of King David I*, no. 151; *Regesta Regum Scottorum*, vol. 1, no. 131; *Liber S. Maria de Calchou: Registrum cartarum abbacie Tironensis de Kelso 1113–1567*, 2 vols. (Edinburgh: Bannatyne Club, 1846), vol. 2, no. 375; Oram, *Lordship of Galloway*, 78–79.

[72] Vita A 38–39; pp. 45–46; CF 57:125; Ann Lawrence Mathers, *Manuscripts in Northumbria in the Eleventh and Twelfth Centuries* (Cambridge: D. S. Brewer, 2003), 246–48.

[73] Vita A 39, *Letter to Maurice*; pp. 46–47, 69; CF 57:125–26, 149.

Aelred visited Kirkcudbright on the feast of Saint Cuthbert and the saint's power caused the iron chain binding a penitent's waist to miraculously fall off.[74] In his *Letter to Maurice* Walter Daniel also recorded a visit to an unnamed daughter house in Galloway two years before the abbot's death. During this stay Aelred's bedding was miraculously preserved from being soaked by rainwater pouring through the monastery's leaky roof.[75] Neither author, however, provided further details about Aelred's other activities in Galloway.

Scott has placed Aelred's peacemaking efforts in 1156 during the rebellion of Somerled of Argyll and Malcolm MacHeth, suggesting that Aelred took advantage of the negotiations to arrange the transfer of the monks of Soulseat to the new foundation at Dundrennan, thereby placing the foundation date of the latter in 1156 rather than 1139–1142. Then, he suggests, Aelred arranged for the abandoned property at Soulseat to be turned over to the Premonstratensian canons.[76] John of Fordun and Walter Daniel, however, seem to place Aelred's intervention at the time of Fergus's entry into Holyrood, known to have taken place around 1160. It is also possible that the abbot-less monks of Soulseat were incorporated into an existing community at Dundrennan rather than being the founding congregation. In any case a possible decision by Aelred to turn over the unoccupied property at Soulseat to the Premonstratensians accords well with the traditional close relationship between the two orders.[77] Furthermore, the supposition that Aelred enjoyed a long-standing relationship with the ruling family in Galloway through his association with the monasteries at Dundrennan and Soulseat would explain how he was able to effect his timely and forceful intervention in the strife between Fergus and his sons.

---

[74] Reginald of Durham, *Beati Cuthberti*, 178.
[75] Vita A, *Letter to Maurice*, 4; pp. 74–75; CF 57:153–54.
[76] Scott, "Dundrennan and Soulseat," 41–43.
[77] See above, chap. 2:16.

The result of replacing Fergus with his two sons as the joint rulers of Galloway is also significant. Fergus's credentials as a religious patron cannot be questioned, but his independent stance toward the Scottish monarchy ensured that Galloway remained in turmoil. By contrast Uchtred, who ruled eastern Galloway, appears to have been much more open to royal and Anglo-Norman influence than either his father or his brother Gilbert.[78] He was devoted to Bishop Christian, who frequently appeared as a witness to his acts.[79] Uchtred's brother-in-law, Alan of Allerdale, founded the Cistercian priory of Holm Cultram, where Bishop Christian eventually died and was buried,[80] and Uchtred and his son Roland quickly became benefactors of the priory, frequently in cooperation with Bishop Christian.[81] Uchtred himself donated a grange with a saltworks and pasture for pigs to the priory.[82] Uchtred also founded a convent at Lincluden for Benedictine nuns[83] and worked with Bishop Christian to reorganize and reform the parish structure in the diocese of Whithorn.[84]

Several of Uchtred's acts indicate that he had become the first of his family to recognize the inevitability of the extension of royal authority into Galloway. At Stirling between 1141 and 1147, Uchtred had appeared as a witness to King David's charter granting a saltpan to Kelso Abbey.[85] In line with Christian's allegiance to York, Uchtred firmly established himself as a loyal son of the archdiocese with the donation of a carucate of land and a toft to Saint Peter's Hospital in York in a charter addressed to "his

---

[78] Oram, *Lordship of Galloway*, 90–91.

[79] *Register of Holm Cultram*, nos. 120, 120A, 121, 140A, 269, and p. 121; *Liber Cartarum Sancte Crucis: Munimenta ecclesie Sancte Crucis de Edwinesburg* (Edinburgh: Bannatyne Club, 1840), no. 25.

[80] *Register of Holm Cultram*, no. 260, and pp. 49, 118.

[81] *Register of Holm Cultram*, nos. 120, 120A, 121, 140A, 269, and p. 121.

[82] *Register of Holm Cultram*, nos. 120, 269; Brooke, *Wildmen*, 104–5; Oram, "Colonisation and Settlement," 122.

[83] Murray, *Literary History*, 48; McDonald, "Monastic Patronage," 200. Brooke judges this claim doubtful, *Wildmen*, 106.

[84] Brooke, *Wildmen*, 106–8.

[85] *Charters of King David I*, no. 151.

lord and father, Christian, bishop of the Gallovidians"; Christian also witnessed the charter. He made this donation for the souls not only of his parents and ancestors but also of King David of Scotland.[86] Uchtred also donated churches and other properties to the royal abbey of Holyrood.[87] Both brothers visited the Scottish court occasionally, with Uchtred appearing in the witness lists of royal charters slightly more frequently than his brother Gilbert.[88]

Kings Malcolm IV and William I were quick to extend their authority into Galwegian territory. Shortly after the replacement of Fergus by his two sons, Malcolm confirmed the earlier grants to Holyrood by Fergus and Uchtred and took under his protection travelers passing through this territory.[89] Similarly King William confirmed Uchtred's grant to Saint Peter's Hospital in York.[90] The case of the property in the parish of Kirkgunzeon, which Uchtred originally donated to Holm Cultram, is particularly telling. King William also issued his own confirmation of this donation. Later, under unclear circumstances, the abbey either surrendered the lands or was deprived of them, either by Uchtred himself or by Walter de Berkeley, so King William ordered Uchtred and Roger of Minto to investigate. The problem was solved after Uchtred's death when Walter returned the lands to Holm Cultram.[91] These charters show that after Fergus of Galloway's demise, the kings of Scotland were more willing to assert their authority in the formerly troublesome province, especially in the eastern part ruled by Uchtred. It appears that with the replacement of Fergus of Galloway by his son as the ruler in eastern Galloway, Bishop Christian gained a close collaborator in the work of ecclesiastical reform

---

[86] Robert Edgar, *An Introduction to the History of Dumfries*, ed. R. C. Reid (Dumfries: J. Maxwell and Sons, 1915), 218–19; Brooke, *Wildmen*, 104.

[87] *Liber Cartarum Sancte Crucis*, nos. 23–27, 49–50; *Regesta Regum Scottorum*: vol. 2: *The Acts of William I King of Scots 1165–1214*, ed. G. W. S. Barrow (Edinburgh: Edinburgh University Press, 1971), no. 39.

[88] For Uchtred, *Regesta Regum Scottorum*, vol. 1, nos. 131, 159, 265; vol. 2, no. 80. For Gilbert, *Regesta Regum Scottorum*, vol. 1, no. 254; vol. 2, no. 80.

[89] *Regesta Regum Scottorum*, vol. 1, no. 230.

[90] *Regesta Regum Scottorum*, vol. 2, no. 103.

[91] *Regesta Regum Scottorum*, vol. 2, nos. 88, 256, 540.

and King Malcolm an ally willing to accept his royal authority. In 1174, long after Aelred's beneficent influence had been removed, Uchtred and his brother Gilbert rebelled against King William the Lion,[92] but at least initially the abbot's efforts at mediation in Galloway held out the promise of peace and a more complete incorporation of the province into the larger Scottish realm.

In conclusion it must be admitted that much speculation and a great deal of reading between the lines has been necessary to build this case for Aelred's sustained political activity in the northern realm. At a minimum Cistercian monasticism certainly flourished in Scotland during this time, and it would have been strange indeed if the abbot of the major monastery in the north had not had a role to play in this. In addition Aelred's *Life of Saint Ninian* testifies to his longtime relationship with the reforming bishops of Galloway and perhaps to a personal friendship with Bishop Christian of Whithorn. The scattered notices of Aelred's travels to Scotland and Galloway that can be gleaned from contemporary sources do not permit establishing a chronology for his visits or proving that he engaged in some kind of shuttle diplomacy between Galloway and the royal court. Nevertheless, it seems clear that Aelred's frequent visits to the north were sufficient to establish and maintain a friendship network there and that these ties allowed him to intervene effectively in the internal affairs of Galloway when the time came.

---

[92] Benedict of Peterborough, *Gestis Regis Henrici*, vol. 1:67; Roger of Hoveden, *Chronica*, 2:63; *Regesta Regum Scottorum*, 2:8.

Chapter 8

Trusted Counselor
Aelred of Rievaulx and King Henry II

In one of his few comments on Aelred's public life, Walter Daniel noted that he corresponded with the great and near great of medieval society, including the kings of France, England, and Scotland.[1] Aelred was abbot of Rievaulx from 1147 until 1167, during the reigns of two English monarchs, Stephen (1135–1154) and Henry II (1154–1189). The relationship between Aelred and Stephen depends largely upon the word of Walter Daniel, who in addition to the statement noted above remarked that while Aelred was abbot of Revesby (1143–1147), he was "greatly beloved by all in the province, indeed by the whole realm and most of all by the king."[2] Stephen showed some generosity toward the abbeys under Aelred's care, for example, by confirming Walter Espec's foundation charter for Rievaulx.[3] No royal donations are recorded

---

[1] Vita A 34, p. 42; CF 57:121.

[2] Vita A 20, pp. 28–29; CF 57:111; Marsha L. Dutton, "*Sancto Dunstano Cooperante*: Collaboration Between King and Ecclesiastical Advisor in Aelred of Rievaulx's *Genealogy of the Kings of the English*," in *Religious and Laity in Western Europe 1000–1400: Interaction, Negotiation, and Power*, ed. Emilia Jamroziak and Janet Burton (Turnhout: Brepols, 2006), 194; Marsha L. Dutton, Introduction to *The Life of Aelred of Rievaulx and the Letter to Maurice*, ed. and trans. Frederick M. Powicke, CF 57 (Kalamazoo, MI: Cistercian Publications, 1994), 29–30; Pierre-André Burton, *Aelred de Rievaulx (1110–1167). De l'homme éclaté à l'être unifié: Essai de biographie existentielle et spirituelle* (Paris: Éditions du Cerf, 2010), 403.

[3] *Regesta Regum Anglo-Normannorum 1066–1154*, vol. 3, *Regesta Regis Stephani ac Mathildis Imperatricis ac Gaufridi et Henrici Ducum Normannorum 1135–1154*, ed. H. A. Cronne and R. H. C. Davis (Oxford: Clarendon Press, 1968), no. 716.

for Revesby, but Rufford, a second English daughter house of Rievaulx, received three royal confirmation charters and a gift from Stephen himself in the form of a release from paying tolls at Nottingham.[4]

Stephen and his wife were also major patrons of the Order of Savigny, which united with the Cistercians in 1147.[5] Between them the couple had founded the abbeys of Furness, Buckfast, and Coggeshall in England and Longvilliers in the county of Boulogne.[6] Relations between the Savigniacs and the Cistercians were complicated by the events of the civil war, for at about this time the mother house of Savigny fell under the control of the Empress Matilda's husband, Geoffrey of Anjou, after which the English abbeys loyal to Stephen refused obedience to Abbot Serlo of Savigny. This schism within the Order continued even after the union was complete, with Stephen's foundation at Furness being particularly adamant in resisting the new arrangement.[7]

---

[4] *Regesta Regum Anglo-Normannorum* 3, nos. 736–39.

[5] See above, chap. 4:85–86.

[6] *Regesta Regum Anglo-Normannorum 1066–1154*, vol. 2, *Regesta Henrici Primi 1100–1135*, ed. Charles Johnson and H. A. Cronne (Oxford: Clarendon Press, 1956), nos. 1545–46; *Regesta Regum Anglo-Normannorum* 3, nos. 207, 337; David Knowles and R. Neville Haddock, *Medieval Religious Houses, England and Wales* (London: Longmans, 1953), 105–6; *Lancashire Pipe Rolls and Early Lancashire Charters*, ed. W. Farrer (Liverpool: Henry Young and Sons, 1902), 301–3; Donald Nicholl, *Thurstan, Archbishop of York (1114–1140)* (York: Stonegate Press, 1964), 144; R. H. C. Davis, *King Stephen, 1135–1154*, 3rd ed. (London: Longmans, 1990), 100; James Tait, *Mediaeval Manchester and the Beginnings of Lancashire* (Manchester: Manchester University Press, 1904), 163.

[7] *Regesta Pontificum Romanorum ad annum post Christum natum 1198*, ed. P. Jaffé, rev. W. Wattenbach et al., 2 vols. (Leipzig: Veit, 1885–1888), no. 9235; *Calendar of Documents Preserved in France Illustrative of the History of Great Britain and Ireland*, Vol. 1: *A.D. 918–1206*, ed. John Horace Round (London: Eyre and Spottiswoode, 1899), nos. 813–15, pp. 294–96; Léopold Delisle, "Documents Relative to the Abbey of Furness, Extracted from the Archives of Savigny," *Journal of the British Archaeological Association* 6 (1851): 419–24; Davis, *King Stephen*, 99–101; Janet Burton, "English Monasteries and the Continent in the Reign of King Stephen," in *King Stephen's Reign, 1135–1154*, ed. Paul Dalton and Graeme J. White (Woodbridge: Boydell Press, 2008), 101–9; Burton, "The Abbeys of Byland and Jervaulx, and the Problems of the English Savigniacs, 1134–1156," in *Monastic Studies* 2, ed. Judith Loades (Bangor: Headstart History, 1991), 119–31; Christopher Holdsworth, "The

The king's sympathies probably lay with the monks of the abbey that he had founded, but there is no way to tell what if any opinion he may have had regarding Aelred's efforts on behalf of the Savigniac houses in Yorkshire.[8]

Aelred and Henry II

The evidence for a relationship between Henry II and Aelred is much more solid. As was noted in chapter 6, Aelred dedicated his *Lament for David I of Scotland* and his *Genealogy of the Kings of the English* to Henry. As well as containing much good advice for the young ruler, these works, together with the *Report on the Battle of the Standard*, were written as a plea for peace and, presumably, support of the Treaty of Winchester, which brought Henry to the throne. Aelred also dedicated a third work, *The Life of Edward the Confessor*, to the king, and designed this work as well as a gesture of support during a troubled time.

Fragmentary evidence also suggests that Aelred attempted to advise Henry II on several of the controversies of the day. In 1159 Aelred involved himself in matters of high ecclesiastical politics when the papal election split between two claimants, the imperial party supporting Victor IV and the anti-imperial forces Alexander III.[9] King Henry II's first act was to send a mandate to Archbishop Theobald of Canterbury and the English church forbidding any-

---

Affiliation of Savigny," in *Truth as Gift: Studies in Honor of John R. Sommerfeldt*, ed. Marsha L. Dutton, Daniel M. La Corte, and Paul Lockey, CS 204 (Kalamazoo, MI: Cistercian Publications, 2004), 57–61, 82–83; Béatrice Poulle, "Savigny and England," in *England and Normandy in the Middle Ages*, ed. David Bates and Anne Curry (London: Hambledon Press, 1994), 165–66; Francis R. Swietek, "The Role of Bernard of Clairvaux in the Union of Savigny with Cîteaux: A Reconsideration," *Cîteaux: Commentarii Cistercienses* 42 (1991): 289–302; David Knowles, *The Monastic Order in England: A History of Its Development from the Times of St. Dunstan to the Fourth Lateran Council*, 2nd ed. (Cambridge: Cambridge University Press, 1963), 250–51.

[8] See above, chap. 4:86–90.

[9] Robert of Torigny, *Chronica*, in *Chronicles of the Reigns of Stephen, Henry II., and Richard I.*, ed. Richard Howlett, 4 vols., RS 82 (London: Longmans, 1884–1890), 4:204–205; Anne Duggan, "Henry II, the English Church and the Papacy, 1154–76,"

one to recognize either candidate, banning appeals, and prohib-
iting travel outside the kingdom for any purpose connected with
the papal schism.[10] At this time Henry was on the continent, intent
on his war with Louis VII of France. In May 1160 Henry and Louis
made peace; shortly afterward they met at Beauvais and decided
together to recognize Alexander III.[11] Despite the fact that Henry's
decision was probably already made, he took the trouble of sum-
moning the English clergy to a council at London in June 1160 to
discuss the question of the schism. Henry had received documents
from both parties, which he sent along to the council to be used as
a basis for their deliberations. A long letter from Arnulf of Lisieux,
read out during the meeting, greatly influenced the conclusion.
To no one's surprise the council recommended the recognition

---

in *Henry II: New Interpretations*, ed. Christopher Harper-Bill and Nicholas Vincent
(Woodbridge: Boydell Press, 2007), 168–70.

[10] Avrom Saltman, *Theobald, Archbishop of Canterbury* (New York: Greenwood
Press, 1969), no. 131 and Suppl D, p. 543; John of Salisbury, *The Letters of John of
Salisbury, Volume One, The Early Letters (1153–1161)*, ed. and trans. W. J. Millor, S. J.
Butler, and H. E. Butler, revised by C. N. L. Brooke (Oxford: Clarendon Press, 1986),
no. 116; Mary Cheney, "The Recognition of Pope Alexander III: Some Neglected
Evidence," EHR 84, no. 332 (1969): 479; Raymonde Foreville, *L'Église et la royauté en
Angleterre sous Henri II Plantagenet (1154–1189)* (Paris: Bloud and Gay, 1943), 93–96.

[11] Arnulf of Lisieux, *The Letters of Arnulf of Lisieux*, ed. Frank Barlow, Camden
3rd ser. 61 (London: Royal Historical Society, 1939), no. 29; Arnulf of Lisieux, *The
Letter Collections of Arnulf of Lisieux*, trans. Carolyn Poling Schriber (Lewiston,
Queenston, and Lampeter: Edwin Mellen Press, 1997), no. 1.22. See also Barlow,
nos. 23–24, 27–28; Schriber, nos. 1.19–1.21, 1.32; Gilbert Foliot, *The Letters and
Charters of Gilbert Foliot, Abbot of Gloucester (1139–48), Bishop of Hereford (1148–63)
and London (1163–87)*, ed. Zachary N. Brooke, Adrian Morey, and Christopher N. L.
Brooke (Cambridge: Cambridge University Press, 1967), no. 133; *Regesta Pontificum*,
nos. 10653–54; Carolyn Poling Schriber, *The Dilemma of Arnulf of Lisieux: New Ideas
Versus Old Ideals* (Bloomington: University of Indiana Press, 1990), 40–45; Saltman,
Theobald, 45–52; Frank Barlow, "The English, Norman and French Councils Called
to Deal with the Papal Schism of 1159," EHR 51, no. 202 (1936): 266; Cheney, "Recognition of Pope Alexander III," 474–97; Foreville, *L'Église et la Royauté*, 95–96;
Marsha L. Dutton, "Aelred, Historian: Two Portraits in Plantagenet Myth," CSQ
28 (1993): 113–44; B. W. Scholz, "The Canonization of Edward the Confessor,"
Speculum 36, no. 1 (1961): 49–60; Henry Mayr-Harting, "Hilary, Bishop of Chichester (1147–1169), and Henry II," EHR 78, no. 397 (1963): 215; Aelred Squire, *Aelred
of Rievaulx: A Study*, CS 50 (Kalamazoo, MI: Cistercian Publications, 1981), 85.

of Alexander III but kept its answer secret, a clear recognition by the clergy of the king's right to make the final decision.[12] A similar council, with identical results, was held for the Norman church at Neufmarché.[13] Once Henry had formally transmitted the decision to Theobald, the archbishop issued a mandate to the English church ordering obedience to Pope Alexander.[14]

Martha Newman has detailed the way in which Alexander III used a network of Cistercian abbots, including Geoffrey of Clairvaux, Gilbert of Cîteaux, Philip of L'Aumône, and William of Morimond, in his negotiations with Emperor Frederick Barbarossa, Henry II of England, and Louis VII of France.[15] Aelred also interested himself in the dispute, for one of his sermons in the *De Oneribus Propheticis Isaiae* includes a passionate digression on the papal schism in which he characterized Alexander as the choice of the majority of the electors and described the few dissenters as heretics and schismatics belonging to the church of Satan instead of to the church of Christ.[16] Similarly, in *Spiritual Friendship*, Aelred used the example of the Cardinal Priest John of Saint Martin, who supported the anti-pope Victor IV out of friendship, as an example of a relationship that was false because it caused one of the participants to act in an evil way.[17] Aelred apparently also wrote a letter or tract condemning the participants in the council of Pavia in February 1160, which had recognized

---

[12] Arnulf of Lisieux, *Letters of Arnulf of Lisieux*, nos. 28–29; Schriber, *Letter Collection*, nos. 1.20, 1.22; Gilbert Foliot, *Letters*, no. 133; John of Salisbury, *Early Letters*, no. 125; Duggan, "Henry II," 168–70.

[13] William fitz Stephen, *Vita Sancti Thomae, Cantuariensis Archiepiscopi et Martyris*, in *Materials for the History of Thomas Becket, Archbishop of Canterbury*, ed. James Craigie Robertson, 7 vols., RS 67 (London: Longmans, 1875–1885) [MTB] 3:27; Saltman, *Theobald*, 51.

[14] John of Salisbury, *Early Letters*, no. 130. Also Cheney, "Recognition of Pope Alexander III," 474–97.

[15] Martha G. Newman, *The Boundaries of Charity: Cistercian Culture and Ecclesiastical Reform, 1098–1180* (Stanford, CA: Stanford University Press, 1996), 203–9.

[16] Aelred, Oner S 23; CCCM 2D:214–15.

[17] Spir amic 2.41; CCCM 1A:310; CF 5:79–80; Dutton, Introduction to *Life of Aelred*, 45.

Victor IV, but the text has been lost.[18] The fourteenth-century continuation of the *Peterborough Chronicle* notes that King Henry was induced to accept Alexander "by the letters of Arnulf, bishop of Lisieux, and greatly *viva voce* by the holy Aelred, abbot of Rievaulx."[19] Once again details are lacking, but this reference could mean that Aelred attended and spoke at the council in London. Alternatively, since Henry II was on the continent at this time, it could also mean that Aelred visited him there to discuss the schism, perhaps as part of an annual journey to the general chapter at Cîteaux.

Additional evidence for Aelred's intervention in the schism is provided by the fact that Rievaulx profited handsomely from the favor of Pope Alexander III, who issued a series of precepts, confirmations, and letters of protection in favor of the abbey, which continued long after Aelred's death.[20] The first of these, which took the abbey under the pope's special protection and confirmed all the gifts that had been made to Rievaulx, was specifically issued in Aelred's name. It was granted December 21, 1160, only six months after the councils at which Henry II had agreed to recognize Alexander as pope.[21] A second papal bull, which also mentioned Aelred by name, prohibited any other religious order from encroaching on the pastures and possessions of Rievaulx.[22] The abbey received one of its most significant signs of Alexander's favor after Aelred's death. In 1132 Pope Innocent II had freed the

[18] John Bales, *Index Britanniae Scriptorum*, ed. R. L. Poole and M. Bateson (Oxford: Clarendon Press, 1902), 13; Newman, *Boundaries*, 205; Aelred Squire, *Aelred of Rievaulx*, 94, 165n79; Squire, "Aelred and King David," *Collectanea Ordinis Cisterciensium Reformatorum* 22 (1960): 372–73.

[19] *Chronicon Angliae Petriburgense*, ed. J. A. Giles (London: Caxton Society, 1845; reprinted New York: Burt Franklin, 1967), 98. Also Frederick M. Powicke, *Ailred of Rievaulx and His Biographer Walter Daniel* (Manchester: Longmans, Green and Co., 1922), 41; Powicke, Introduction to Vita A, xlviii; Dom Alberic Stacpoole, "The Public Face of Aelred, 1167–1967," *Downside Review* 85 (1967): 185; Thomas Merton, "St. Aelred of Rievaulx and the Cistercians," pt. 5, CSQ 24, no. 1 (1989): 62–64.

[20] *Cartularium Abbathiae de Rievalle*, ed. J. C. Atkinson, Surtees Society 83 (Durham: Andrews and Co., 1889) [CAR], nos. 250–71.

[21] CAR no. 250.

[22] CAR no. 255.

Cistercians from paying tithes on the goods produced on their lands; however, in 1155 Pope Adrian IV had restricted this privilege to those goods produced on lands that had previously been uncultivated. When Pope Alexander III restored the former decree and exempted all Cistercian lands from the payment of tithes, Rievaulx was the first house to receive its privilege.[23]

Similarly in 1163 Aelred seems to have been involved in the case of Bishop Robert de Chesney of Lincoln, who had appealed to both the pope and the king regarding the claim of Abbot Robert of Gorham and the monks of Saint Alban's Abbey to be independent of episcopal jurisdiction. The case acquired huge significance because of the potential conflict between royal and papal authority. The king ordered an ecclesiastical commission to investigate the case, and at the same time a papal mandate arrived, appointing the bishops of Chichester and Norwich as judges-delegate to look into the matter. A great council was held at Westminster in March 1163 to discuss the matter. Initially the king was furious with Abbot Robert, thinking that he had instigated the appeal to Rome, but he was soon placated.[24] The king then proceeded to an examination of the abbey's charters and was suitably impressed, until he came to a charter of Pope Celestine II (1143–1144), which stated that the abbey was to pay an ounce of gold to Rome each year. He exclaimed, "This article, my lord abbot, is contrary to our dignity; you had no right to make my church tributary to the see of Rome, nor ought the pope to have required it."[25] This time

---

[23] *Regesta Pontificum*, no. 13846; Emilia Jamroziak, *Rievaulx Abbey and its Social Context, 1132–1300*, Medieval Church Studies 8 (Turnhout: Brepols, 2005), 180–81; Giles Constable, *Monastic Tithes from their Origins to the Twelfth Century* (Cambridge: Cambridge University Press, 1964), 251–54, 280–81, 295–99.

[24] *Gesta Abbatum Monasterii Sancti Albani*, in *Chronica Monasterii S. Albani*, ed. Henry T. Riley, 12 vols., RS 28 (London: Longmans, 1863–78), 4:137–45; *English Lawsuits From William I to Richard I*, ed. R. C. Van Caenegem, 2 vols. (London: Selden Society, 1990–1991), vol. 2, no. 405, pp. 368–82; David Knowles, "The Growth of Exemption," *Downside Review* 50 (1932): 213–18; Knowles, *Monastic Order*, 587–88; W. L. Warren, *Henry II* (Berkeley and Los Angeles: University of California Press, 1973), 439–42; Duggan, "Henry II," 165–67; R. E. Eyton, *Court, Household and Itinerary of King Henry II* (London: Taylor and Co., 1878), 59–60.

[25] *Gesta Abbatum Monasterii Sancti Albani*, 4:152.

Abbot Robert managed to mollify the king by pointing out that the agreement had been made by his predecessor. Overall the king was suitably impressed with the abbot's collection of documents and went so far as to tell Bishop Robert of Lincoln that the abbey should be restored to its birthright, noting, "It is the function of popes in such cases to intervene, and as they should see fit to restore, on the authority of St. Peter, each one to its pristine state."[26] The king settled the case with a compromise by which the bishop renounced his claims over the abbey in return for a vill of land worth ten pounds.

Aelred appears among the list of witnesses to the charter of Archbishop Thomas Becket that ratified the agreement.[27] Aelred also witnessed another of Becket's charters, by which the archbishop confirmed King Malcolm IV of Scotland's gift of the church of Great Paxton to the canons of Holyrood, and it is possible that this charter dates from the same period.[28] The only record of Aelred's participation in these discussions is his attestation of the charter that ended the dispute, but his record as a mediator and problem solver suggests that he may have had more than a passive role in the resolution of this conflict as well.

The evidence suggests that Aelred was a faithful supporter of the young Henry II and that he attempted to establish himself as an occasional royal adviser, within the bounds prescribed by his monastic vocation. In return, the cartulary of the abbey records the king's generosity. While Aelred was abbot, Henry II issued several charters taking Rievaulx under his special protection and granting the abbey forest privileges and freedom from certain dues.[29] Royal confirmations were an important means by which religious institutions secured their property against intrusions

[26] *Gesta Abbatum Monasterii Sancti Albani*, 4:154.

[27] *English Episcopal Acta* [EEA] 2, no. 37; *English Lawsuits*, vol. 2, no. 405, p. 379. For a complete account of the controversy between St. Alban's and Lincoln, see Brenda Bolton, "St. Alban's Loyal Son," in *Adrian IV, The English Pope, 1154–1159*, ed. Brenda Bolton and Anne J. Duggan (Aldershot: Ashgate, 2003), 75–103; Duggan, "Henry II," 165–68.

[28] EEA 2, no. 13.

[29] CAR nos. 198, 200, 202.

by rivals, and the king issued such confirmations of the grants at Welburn and Hovedon by Roger de Mowbray and the gifts of Everard de Ros, as well as a general confirmation listing all the gifts that had been made to the abbey since its foundation.[30] He also confirmed Bishop Hugh of Durham's grant at Cowton; a charter by Archbishop Roger of York confirming that donation states that the gift had been made at the king's suggestion.[31] The waste below Pickering was a particularly valuable property located to the east of the abbey, given to Rievaulx by the king and secured by no fewer than six royal charters.[32]

When Walter Daniel discussed Aelred's voluminous correspondence, he stated that the abbot wrote to "the most distinguished men in the Kingdom of England and especially to the Earl of Leicester."[33] The earl of Leicester was Robert de Beaumont, the younger of the twin sons of Count Robert of Meulan, the trusted friend and counselor of King Henry I. When the count died, his vast lands were split between the twins, with the elder son Waleran receiving the title of Count of Meulan and the ancestral lands in Normandy and Robert gaining his father's newly acquired earldom of Leicester in England. As one of the greatest magnates in England, Robert remained loyal to King Stephen during the long years of civil war, only switching his allegiance to the young Duke Henry of Normandy when the latter arrived in England on his third foray in 1153.[34] When Henry became king a year later, he rewarded Robert with the position of justiciar of England, an office that he held until his death in 1168.[35]

Earl Robert of Leicester and his family were great patrons of the Cistercians. Robert himself founded Garendon Abbey in Leices-

[30] CAR nos. 203, 211–12.

[31] CAR nos. 204; EEA 20, no. 80.

[32] CAR nos. 205–10; Jamroziak, *Rievaulx Abbey*, 117–19.

[33] Vita A 32, p. 42; CF 57:121.

[34] David Crouch, *The Beaumont Twins: The Roots and Branches of Power* (Cambridge: Cambridge University Press, 1986), 86–89.

[35] David Crouch, "Robert, Second Earl of Leicester (1104–1168)," DNB 1882, accessed October 11, 2013; John Guy, *Thomas Becket: Warrior, Priest, Rebel* (New York: Random House, 2012), 101; Crouch, *Beaumont Twins*, 89–94.

tershire, and his sister, nephew, and cousin endowed the abbey with additional lands. His steward Arnold de Bosco founded the daughter house of Bittlesden in Buckinghamshire. His son-in-law, Earl Simon of Northampton, established the abbey of Sawtry in Huntingdonshire, and his brother Waleran of Meulan founded Bordesley in Worcestershire.[36] His patronage, however, did not extend to Rievaulx or its daughter houses, so it is likely that Aelred's correspondence with the earl concerned public affairs rather than prospective donations to the abbeys under Aelred's stewardship.

The Life of Edward the Confessor

Aelred also sought to advise the king and to support his policies by his historical writings, *Lament, Battle,* and *Genealogy.* These works, written just as Henry II was about to ascend the throne, constituted a powerful plea for peace and the acceptance of the new king. In 1163 Aelred's kinsman, Abbot Laurence of Westminster,[37] commissioned him to write a new *vita* of Edward the Confessor to celebrate the translation of Edward's relics into the new shrine in Westminster Abbey after his canonization in 1161. Like *Genealogy, The Life of Edward the Confessor* emphasizes the English part of Henry's ancestry and carefully seeks to integrate the king into English culture and traditions.[38] It is thus another example of Aelred's efforts to advise and support Henry.

In writing the *Life of Edward,* Aelred was working within an existing framework established by an account of the Confessor's life written in 1138 by Osbert of Clare, a life that Abbot Laurence had given him to use as a basis for his own work. Osbert's work

---

[36] Bennett D. Hill, *English Cistercian Monasteries and Their Patrons in the Twelfth Century* (Urbana: University of Illinois Press, 1968), 33–34; Crouch, *Beaumont Twins,* 196–204.

[37] Vita A 32, pp. 41–42; CF 57:121. Walter Daniel referred to Laurence as Aelred's *cognatus,* but how they were related is unknown.

[38] Marsha L. Dutton, "This Ministry of Letters: Aelred of Rievaulx's Attempt to Anglicize England's King Henry II," in *Monasticism Between Culture and Cultures: Acts of the Third International Symposium, Rome, June 8–11, 2011,* ed. Philippe Nouzille and Michaela Pfeifer, *Analecta Monastica* 14 (2013): 184–86.

in turn was based on an earlier, anonymous *Life*, possibly commissioned by Edward's widow Edith.[39] All three works emphasize
God's great mercy to his people in working miracles through the
agency of the saintly king. The story of the foundation of Westminster Abbey as told by Osbert of Clare and Aelred contains an
important lesson for the young king. King Edward had vowed to
make a pilgrimage to the Holy Land, but once he became king,
he was afraid to leave his domain in the hands of others while he
made the long journey to the east, so upon the recommendation
of his nobles, he proposed to fulfill his promise by building a
magnificent church dedicated to Saint Peter instead. Edward is
shown anxiously sending multiple embassies to Rome to ask the
pope's permission for the change, which was willingly granted.[40]
The portrayal of the king cooperating with the Holy See to secure
his own salvation through the fulfillment of his vow may have
been a potent example for a young king about to defy the church
in the person of his own archbishop of Canterbury, but it is not
unique to Aelred and his time.

The changes that Aelred made in crafting his own work are significant in pointing up Aelred's intentions in writing for Henry.
Katherine Yohe has demonstrated that throughout his work
Aelred revised the miracle stories to emphasize love and personal relationships, undoubtedly a reflection of his own interests,
and that he focused more than the previous authors on the royal
virtues of chastity, humility, and simplicity, virtues anyone might
attain, which made the miracles possible. Thus Aelred's work is
much more a mirror for princes for Henry II to imitate than are
the two earlier *Lives*.[41]

[39] Frank Barlow, *Edward the Confessor* (Berkeley and Los Angeles: University of
California Press, 1970), 257–59; Burton, *Aelred*, 449–52.

[40] Aelred, Vita E 10–12, 15–17; PL 195:750–54, 757–60; CCCM 3A; CF 56:153–61,
169–75; John P. Bequette, "Aelred of Rievaulx's *Life of Saint Edward, King and
Confessor*: A Saintly King and the Salvation of the English People," CSQ 43, no.
1 (2008): 24–31.

[41] Kathleen Yohe, "Aelred's Recrafting of the Life of Edward the Confessor,"
CSQ 38, no. 2 (2003): 177–89.

Aelred, however, altered the portrayal of the Godwin family in an important way, transforming the favorable account in the anonymous *Life* and the neutral account in Osbert of Clare into his own distinctly anti-Godwin version: "For abusing the king's simplicity, for the sake of power he did many things in the kingdom against justice and right, and he often tried to bring the king's mind around to agreeing to his wickedness."[42] He also inserted a long passage in which King Edward foretold the coming quarrel between Earl Godwin's sons Harold and Tostig and an account of the earl's shocking death, choking on a piece of meat immediately after perjuring himself by swearing that he was not the murderer of King Edward's brother Alfred.[43] The lesson is clear: God worked through the king, his representative on earth, showing his mercy to his people through miracles. Those who interfered in the relationship by trying to usurp the king's power with the intent to bend it to their own needs would not be tolerated. Aelred issued a stern warning to the king's opponents with his analysis of right order in the kingdom as exemplified by the reign of Henry's saintly predecessor.

The Beginning of the Becket Controversy

In his *Life of Edward*, as in his other historical works, Aelred advised the king from a distance while safely tucked away in his monastery in the north of England. A further invitation from Abbot Laurence to preach at the ceremonies accompanying the translation of the saint's relics to the new shrine in Westminster Abbey, however, thrust Aelred into the center of the controversy brewing between the king and Thomas Becket, the recently enthroned archbishop of Canterbury. Becket had served as Henry II's chancellor, but despite the close friendship between the two men, disagreements arose almost as soon as Thomas became archbishop in 1162.

---

[42] Aelred, Vita E 25; PL 195:766; CCCM 3A; CF 56:190.
[43] Aelred, Vita E 25; PL 195:766–67; CCCM 3A; CF 56:190–92.

Every contemporary chronicler and modern historian has constructed his or her own list of the many disagreements between the two men. Specific sources of tension included differences over ecclesiastical appointments, jurisdictional disputes, and Becket's strenuous efforts to recover lost Canterbury lands, sometimes at the expense of the king's favored supporters. Thomas also defied the king in public at his court at Woodstock over the royal order that a traditional payment called sheriff's aid should be paid into the royal coffers rather than directly to the sheriffs. Furthermore, he violated a long-standing custom by excommunicating a royal tenant-in-chief for refusing to accept his appointment of a priest to serve in a church within the chief tenant's lands. Some of the matters in dispute predated Becket's primacy by many years. For example, the king supported Archbishop Roger of York's claim to parity with Canterbury, a source of contention that went back as far as Archbishop Lanfranc.

Perhaps no issue loomed larger in the struggle than that of "criminous clerks," that is, clerics, including men in minor orders, whose ecclesiastical status entitled them to be tried for their offenses in church courts, where they often escaped with little or no punishment. For example, Philip de Broi, a canon of Bedford accused of murder, suffered only the loss of his income for two years and a public whipping. This case came to symbolize the growing royal and public outrage over clerical criminals who received trifling punishments for serious offenses.[44] If Aelred

---

[44] Roger of Pontigny, *Vita Sancti Thomae, Cantuariensis Archiepiscopi et Martyris*, in MTB 4:22–25; William Fitzstephen, *Vita Sancti Thomae, Cantuariensis Archiepiscopi et Martyris*, in MTB 3:45–46; Michael Staunton, *The Lives of Thomas Becket* (Manchester: Manchester University Press, 2001), 75–79; William of Canterbury, *Vita, Passio et Miracula S. Thomae Cantuariensis Archiepiscopi*, in MTB 1:12–13; Herbert of Bosham, *Vita Sancti Thomae, Archiepiscopi et Martyris*, in MTB 3:250–52, 264–66; Edward Grim, *Vita Sancti Thomae, Cantuariensis Archiepiscopi et Martyris*, in MTB 2:371–76; Ralph of Diceto, *Radulphi de Diceto Decani Londoniensis Opera Historica*, in *The Historical Works of Master Ralph de Diceto, Dean of London (to 1202)*, ed. William Stubbs, 2 vols., RS 68 (London: Longmans, 1876), 1:311–13; Gervase of Canterbury, *Chronica*, in *Historical Works, The Chronicle of the Reigns of Stephen, Henry II., and Richard I., by Gervase, the Monk of Canterbury*, ed. William Stubbs, 2 vols., RS 73

heard of the matter, it must have reminded him of the earlier case of Archdeacon Osbert of York, accused of murdering Archbishop William fitz Herbert with poisoned communion wine during the latter's first Mass in York Minster.[45] Hovering over all these issues was the overarching question of appeals to Rome and the extent to which canon law and papal authority would be allowed to intrude themselves onto the English scene. The situation was ripe for an explosion by the time that the highest clergy and nobility of the land gathered for the celebration in honor of King Edward on October 13, 1163.[46]

Honoring Edward the Confessor

The sermon that Aelred preached on this occasion was long thought to have been lost. A reference to the sermon is found in a catalogue of the library of Bury, but the text remained unknown until Neil Ker discovered it in the Peterborough central library in 1992.[47] Peter Jackson published the text, with a translation by Tom Licence, in *Cistercian Studies Quarterly* in 2005.[48] This translation is reprinted here as Appendix 4. Jackson's extensive analysis presents strong evidence, based on both style and content, that this sermon is in fact Aelred's work.[49]

(London: Longmans, 1879–1880), 1:174; Guy, *Thomas Becket*, 152–65, 176–78; Anne Duggan, *Thomas Becket* (London: Arnold Publishing, 2004), 33–39; Frank Barlow, *Thomas Becket* (Berkeley and Los Angeles: University of California Press, 1986), 88–95; Warren, *Henry II*, 456–65. The sheriff's aid was a payment of two shillings per hide for the support of the local sheriff, originally paid directly to him. On the sheriff's aid, see Judith A. Green, "The Last Century of Danegeld," EHR 95, no. 379 (1981): 255–58.

[45] See above, chap. 3:61–62.

[46] Barlow, *Edward the Confessor*, 282–84.

[47] N. R. Ker and A. J. Piper, *Medieval Manuscripts in British Libraries 4: Paisley–York* (Oxford: Clarendon Press, 1992), 170; Peter Jackson, "*In translacione sancti Edwardi confessoris*: The Lost Sermon by Aelred of Rievaulx Found?" CSQ 40, no. 1 (2005): 46–47.

[48] Jackson, "*In translacione*," 45–83.

[49] Jackson, "*In translacione*," 50–63.

Jackson's analysis also sheds important light on another vexing question: whether or not Aelred preached the sermon in person or merely composed it for a cleric of Westminster to deliver on the anniversary of the translation every year. It has sometimes been suggested that Aelred's health was so poor during the last ten years of his life that he could not have made the journey to Westminster.[50] As was noted above, however, charter evidence proves that Aelred had made the journey to Westminster only six months earlier, when the Saint Alban's case was decided. He traveled to Scotland at least three times between 1159 and 1164 and also attended a meeting of Cistercian and Gilbertine abbots at Kirkstead in 1164.[51] When Walter Daniel described the event, his phrasing left open the possibility that Aelred wrote the sermon for someone else to deliver: "He expounded in honour of the same saint and to be read with the passage at his solemn vigils the gospel lesson which begins, 'No man, when he hath lighted a candle, putteth it under a bushel but on a candlestick.'"[52] Furthermore, the fullest account of the translation is that of Richard of Cirencester, which was written about 1400, and this narrative does not mention Aelred's having preached at the ceremony.[53] The *Peterborough Chronicle* specifically states, however, "The holy abbot Aelred was present at the translation, offering the life of the king and a sermon on 'No one lights a candle.'"[54] Jackson further suggests that the repeated use of the second person plural in such phrases as *patroni uestri* indicates that the speaker was someone who was not part of the Westminster community, thereby pro-

---

[50] Douglas Roby, "Chimera of the North: The Active Life of Aelred of Rievaulx," in *Cistercian Ideals and Reality*, ed. John Sommerfeldt, CS 60 (Kalamazoo, MI: Cistercian Publications, 1978), 158–59.

[51] See above, chap. 4:83; chap. 5:120–23; chap. 7:149, 166–68; chap. 8:174–79. For a more detailed discussion of Aelred's travels in the last years of his life, see below, chap. 10:225–28.

[52] Vita A 32, p. 41; CF 57:121; Luke 11:33.

[53] Richard of Cirencester, *Speculum Historiale de Gestis Regum Angliae*, ed. E. B. Mayor, 2 vols., RS 30 (London: Longmans, 1863–1869), 2:319–27.

[54] *Chronicon Angliae Petriburgense*, 98.

viding additional evidence that Aelred did deliver the sermon in person at the translation in 1163.[55]

When Aelred came to distill his work on Edward the Confessor into a sermon suitable for the great celebration of the translation of the saint's relics, which of the many possible topics was he to pick? There is little historical detail in the sermon that Aelred chose to preach. He focused on three of the saint's many miracles to illustrate Edward's humility, chastity, and justice: the cure of a crippled man while the king, at the direction of Saint Peter, carried him on his own back; Edward's vision on Easter of the Seven Sleepers of Mount Celion; and, most important, his prophecy of the drowning of King Sven of Denmark just as the Danish king prepared to invade England.[56]

The last miracle constitutes the largest part of the sermon; in it Aelred compares King Edward to Moses: "indeed the actions and total excellence of Moses most fittingly converge upon this Moses of ours, upon this our legislator."[57] He went on, "The Lord summoned Moses out of Midian to rule his people, and this our Moses, recalled from Neustria, was put in charge of the English people."[58] A closer parallel to current circumstances can hardly be imagined, for just as Edward the Confessor had been in exile on the continent before becoming king, Henry II had been duke of Normandy before his own accession.

Aelred drew a parallel between King Edward and Moses as rulers who had brought peace to their war-torn nations. Just as Moses had freed the Jews from Pharaoh's oppression, the drowning of King Sven had freed England from the fear of Danish invasion: "Our people . . . passed easy days and an age full of peace from

[55] Jackson, "*In translacione*," 63–64.

[56] Jackson, "*In translacione*," 66–83, App. 4:264–66. The Danish king was actually Magnus (1042–1047). Sven Estridsen, who succeeded him, contested the throne throughout Magnus's reign, a fact that undoubtedly explains the confusion. See *Historical Works*, CF 56:151–52n31.

[57] Jackson, "*In translacione*," 74–75, App. 4:267.

[58] Jackson, "*In translacione*," 74–75, App. 4:268.

then thereafter in great tranquility under this new Moses."[59] Later Aelred repeated the theme, saying that Edward had "announced that perpetual peace had been delivered unto every border of the English now that King Sven had been overwhelmed by the waves."[60] The further parallel with Henry II, whose accession had ended the Anglo-Norman civil war, could hardly have been lost on Aelred's listeners.

This story must have been one of Aelred's favorites, because it is found not only in his *Life of Edward* but also in *Genealogy*, in the latter case a version of the story attributed to Edward the Elder. In this case the Danish king did not drown, but rather a drunken brawl aboard ship resulted in so many casualties that the expedition was unable to continue. The story of the king's drowning also occurs in the earlier life of Edward by Osbert of Clare, which Aelred used as source material for his own work,[61] but none of these works contains the repeated comparisons between the king and Moses and the emphasis on Edward's having brought peace to England that Aelred seems to have added for the highly charged occasion on which he delivered the sermon.

Aelred referred frequently in the sermon to King Edward's administration of justice, asking rhetorically,

> Who assuredly protected God's people by law, armed them with faith, served them with good counsel, fortified them with prudence, with wisdom ruled them, defended them with arms, raised them up with prayers and, as much in times of peace as in times of war, devoted to God, undertook with paternal affection to nurture and love them, or more fiercely to convict and with harsher punishments to chastise the proud and the rebels?[62]

---

[59] Jackson, "*In translacione*," 74–75; App. 4:266.

[60] Jackson, "*In translacione*," 76–77; App. 4:268.

[61] Aelred, Vita E 9; PL 195:748–49; CCCM 3A; CF 56:149–51; Gen Angl IV; PL 195:723–24; CCCM 3:34; CF 57:89–90; Marc Bloch, "La vie de S. Édouard le Confesseur," *Analecta Bollandiana* 41 (1923): 75–77; Dutton, "Ministry of Letters," 183.

[62] Jackson, "*In translacione*," 74–75; App. 4:267.

Similarly, he wrote, "For this man appeared as the meekest among his people, filled with wisdom and the grace of God, and established a law and dictated justice for his nation (which he found as uneducated as she was untamed), according to which matters are settled and verdicts determined unto this day in the kingdom of the English."[63]

He waxed eloquent about King Edward's establishment of right order in a kingdom recently torn apart by the Danish invasions: "He calmly tempered the entire business of his realm so that the profligate would not evade their due punishment of condemnation and devout minds would find with him rewards befitting their integrity."[64] Aelred's repeated, carefully crafted, and obvious parallels between Edward the Confessor and Henry II appear to be veiled allusions to the king's efforts to reform the English judicial system generally and the ecclesiastical court system in particular, an effort that Archbishop Thomas Becket had recently opposed. This sermon was a tasteful and discreet comment on the current troubles, something that would not detract from the joyous celebration at hand. Nevertheless, the sermon placed Aelred squarely in Henry's corner in the upcoming controversy.

The Quarrel Worsens

After the festivities surrounding the translation, events rapidly spiraled out of control. The next day a royal council convened at which Henry demanded that the bishops swear to uphold the ancient customs of the realm. Archbishop Thomas Becket and the other bishops did so, adding the phrase "saving their order," which meant that they excluded from the promise anything contrary to canon law or to their positions within the church. This additional stipulation infuriated the king, who responded by seizing Becket's property and removing his son Henry from the

[63] Jackson, "*In translacione*," 74–75; App. 4:267.
[64] Jackson, "*In translacione*," 76–77, App. 4:269.

archbishop's household.[65] It is possible that Aelred was present for these events, but nothing about his participation is recorded.

In December Pope Alexander III sent the French Cistercian, Abbot Philip of L'Aumône, to attempt to make peace between the king and the archbishop. Henry told Philip that he would accept a simple verbal agreement to uphold the ancestral customs and would not require an oath from Thomas. Thus reassured, Becket met with the king at Woodstock and gave his promise.[66] Henry then, however, changed his mind, deciding that because Becket's initial refusal to accept the customs had been public, his subsequent assent to them should also be given in public. A new council at Clarendon was called for late January to settle the matter. Early in the conference Robert of Leicester and Reginald of Cornwall were sent to Thomas to advise him of Henry's great anger against him and to attempt to convince him to give way.

Eventually Thomas acquiesced, catching his fellow bishops off guard by saying that he would observe the customs of the realm, substituting "in all good faith" for the previous "saving my order." After the other bishops had reluctantly done the same, the king ordered a group of his barons to withdraw and make a written record of the customs to which they had just agreed. The memorandum was ready in a suspiciously short time, suggesting that it had been prepared in advance, and as it was being read

---

[65] *Summa Causae Inter Regem et Thomam*, in MTB 4:201–5; Staunton, *Lives*, 79–83; Herbert of Bosham, *Vita*, in MTB 3:266–75; Lambeth Anonymous, *Vita Sancti Thomae, Cantuariensis Archiepiscopi et Martyris*, in MTB 4:95–97; Gervase of Canterbury, *Chronica*, 1:174–75; Guy, *Thomas Becket*, 178–82; Duggan, *Thomas Becket*, 39–40; Barlow, *Thomas Becket*, 95; Warren, *Henry II*, 465–70; David Knowles, *The Episcopal Colleagues of Thomas Becket: Being the Ford Lectures Delivered in the University of Oxford in Hilary Term 1949* (Cambridge: Cambridge University Press, 1970), 56–58.

[66] Roger of Pontigny, *Vita*, in MTB 4:31–33; Staunton, *Lives*, 86–87; Edward Grim, *Vita*, in MTB 2:378–79; William of Canterbury, *Vita*, in MTB 1:15; Gervase of Canterbury, *Chronica*, 1:176; Roger of Hoveden, *Chronica Magistri Rogeri de Houedene*, ed. William Stubbs, 4 vols., RS 51 (London: Longmans, 1868–1871), 1:221; Guy, *Thomas Becket*, 185–86; Duggan, *Thomas Becket*, 43; Barlow, *Thomas Becket*, 97–98; Warren, *Henry II*, 472–73; Bennett D. Hill, "Archbishop Thomas Becket and the Cistercian Order," *Analecta Sacri Ordinis Cisterciensis* 27 (1971): 68–69; Knowles, *Episcopal Colleagues*, 59–60.

aloud, it became apparent that the clerics had been tricked into agreeing to something that they had not intended.[67]

While some of the provisions of the Constitutions of Clarendon were truly part of the ancient customs of the realm, others were radical innovations. To cite several of the most contentious issues, the Constitutions provided that a clerk accused of a crime would have his case registered in a royal court before being tried in a church court. If found guilty by the church court, he would be defrocked and turned over to the secular authorities for punishment. This approach had previously been allowed in exceptional cases, but it was now to become the rule in all cases. The Constitutions also prohibited appeals to Rome without the king's permission. Bishops and priests could not even travel to Rome without royal permission, and they were required to give security that they would not attempt anything against the king or his kingdom. Elections to vacant ecclesiastical positions could only be held with the king's permission and were to take place in his chapel.[68]

When the reading was complete, Henry demanded that Becket set his seal to the document. The archbishop hesitated, protesting that he needed more time to consider and take advice, and

---

[67] Roger of Pontigny, *Vita*, in MTB 4:33–36; Staunton, *Lives*, 87–91; John of Salisbury, *Vita Sancti Thomae, Cantuariensis archiepiscopi et martyri*, in MTB 2:311–12; Edward Grim, *Vita*, in MTB 2:379–83; William of Canterbury, *Vita*, in MTB 1:16–23; Herbert of Bosham, *Vita*, in MTB 3:278–80; Lambeth Anonymous, *Vita*, in MTB 4:99–103; *Summa Causae*, in MTB 4:206–8; Thomas Becket, *The Correspondence of Thomas Becket, Archbishop of Canterbury 1162–1170*, ed. and trans. Anne J. Duggan, 2 vols. (Oxford: Clarendon Press, 2000) [CTB], vol. 1, no. 109, pp. 508–11; Gervase of Canterbury, *Chronica*, 1:176–81; Roger of Hoveden, *Chronica*, 1:221–22; Guy, *Thomas Becket*, 190–96; Duggan, *Thomas Becket*, 44–45; Barlow, *Thomas Becket*, 98–100; Warren, *Henry II*, 473–75; Knowles, *Episcopal Colleagues*, 60–64.

[68] For the text of the Constitutions, see *Councils and Synods with other Documents Relating to the English Church*, ed. D. Whitelock, M. Brett, and C. N. L. Brooke, 2 vols. (Oxford: Clarendon Press, 1981), vol. 1, pt. 2, 877–83; William of Canterbury, *Vita*, in MTB 1:18–23; Staunton, *Lives*, 91–96; Gervase of Canterbury, *Chronica*, 1:178–80. For complete analyses of the Constitutions, see Duggan, *Thomas Becket*, 46–60; Barlow, *Thomas Becket*, 100–105; Warren, *Henry II*, 476; Graeme J. White, *Restoration and Reform 1152–1165: Recovery from Civil War in England* (Cambridge: Cambridge University Press, 2000), 196–98; Duggan, "Henry II," 172–74.

so the council session was adjourned for that day. The next day Becket announced that he would never seal the document. At that point Henry offered Thomas a way out, preparing a chirograph record of the council's proceedings. This document recorded the information three times on a single piece of paper, with the word *CIROGRAPHUM* in large block letters between each section. It was then cut in three pieces, making jagged edges through the word *CIROGRAPHUM*. One copy was given to Becket and one to Archbishop Roger of Pont L'Évêque of York, with the king retaining the third. By matching the cut edges of the parchment, each party could verify the authenticity of his piece of the document. Thomas later protested that he had taken the parchment only for information, but canon and civil lawyers had long before agreed that the acceptance of a chirograph was legally binding.[69]

By August Thomas's situation had become intolerable, and so he set off for the continent in a ship from Romney but was turned back, either by the weather or the sailors' fear of possible reprisals by the king.[70] A month later Becket refused a summons to the royal court to answer charges pertaining to his attempt to recover certain church lands from the king's loyal courtier, John the Marshal.[71] At a great council held at Northampton in October 1164, Thomas was accused of contempt of the royal court for refusing to comply with the earlier summons. Henry, however, was unable to obtain agreement from the other attendees on either that charge or the merits of John the Marshal's case. Balked of his objective, the king then switched course and accused Becket of financial malfeasance during his time as chancellor. Faced with

[69] Roger of Pontigny, *Vita*, in MTB 4:37; Staunton, *Lives*, 91; Edward Grim, *Vita*, in MTB 2:383; William Fitzstephen, *Vita*, in MTB 3:46–48; William of Canterbury, *Vita*, in MTB 1:23; Guy, *Thomas Becket*, 194–95.

[70] Edward Grim, *Vita*, in MTB 2:389–90; Staunton, *Lives*, 99–100; Alan of Tewkesbury, *Vita Sancti Thomae, Cantuariensis Archiepiscopi et Martyris*, in MTB 2:325; William of Canterbury, *Vita*, in MTB 1:29; Herbert of Bosham, *Vita*, in MTB 3:293; Roger of Pontigny, *Vita*, in MTB 4:40; Lambeth Anonymous, *Vita*, in MTB 4:104; Gervase of Canterbury, *Chronica*, 1:181–82; Guy, *Thomas Becket*, 199–200.

[71] William fitz Stephen, *Vita*, in MTB 3:50–51; Staunton, *Lives*, 101–2; Roger of Pontigny, *Vita*, in MTB 4:40–41; Guy, *Thomas Becket*, 200–201.

the confiscation of all his worldly goods and a further accusation of treason, Becket appealed to the pope, in direct defiance of the new Constitutions of Clarendon. He also ordered his bishops to excommunicate any secular officials who might lay hands upon him and not to take part in any further judgment against him. Efforts at mediation by Gilbert Foliot came to nothing, and Robert of Leicester was called upon to pronounce sentence upon the archbishop, an effort that failed when Becket jumped to his feet, forbade anyone to judge him, and swept from the room. Thomas then fled the city, taking a circuitous route to the southern coast and exile.[72] From the safety of the continent he directed an angry letter to Robert of Leicester, asking, "Has anyone ever abused his father and mother with insults, inflicted wrongs upon them, or sentenced them to punishment, without falling under the curse which came from the mouth of the Most High?" He admonished the earl to repent of his actions at Northampton: "Therefore, change your ways, dearest son; quickly do penance, so that the divine vengeance, which is already at the door, will not, God forbid, fall on you and on your sons."[73] The battle lines were now drawn, with Becket on one side and many of Aelred's friends and colleagues among the ranks of the higher clergy and the nobility on the other. There is no evidence to suggest that Aelred played a role in these developments, but at least he would have watched from the sidelines as the controversy between the king and the archbishop engulfed the British church and threatened the continued presence of the Cistercian Order in England.

---

[72] William fitz Stephen, *Vita*, in MTB 3:49–68; Roger of Pontigny, *Vita*, in MTB 4:41–55; Herbert of Bosham, *Vita*, in MTB 3:296–98; Staunton, *Lives*, 100–124; John of Salisbury, *Vita*, in MTB 2:312–13; Alan of Tewkesbury, *Vita*, in MTB 2:326–35; Edward Grim, *Vita*, in MTB 2:390–401; William of Canterbury, *Vita*, in MTB 1:29–42; Lambeth Anonymous, *Vita*, in MTB 4:104–6; *Summa Causae*, in MTB 4:209–10; Gervase of Canterbury, *Chronica*, 1:182–89; Roger of Hoveden, *Chronica*, 1:224–29; Guy, *Thomas Becket*, 202–16; Duggan, *Thomas Becket*, 61–83; Barlow, *Thomas Becket*, 108–14; Warren, *Henry II*, 485–89; Knowles, *Episcopal Colleagues*, 66–87, 163–66.

[73] CTB, vol. 1, no. 39, p. 153.

Chapter 9

The Wrong Side of History

Aelred, Rievaulx, and Thomas Becket

Aelred's strongly royalist sermon for the translation of the relics of Edward the Confessor was at most an indirect comment placing him on the side of Henry II during his quarrel with Archbishop Thomas Becket. It accorded well, however, with his long record of support for the king, as is documented in his various historical writings. If Aelred made any attempt to mediate the conflict, spoke out in favor of one side or the other, or even left a record of his opinion of the case, this information has been lost to history. Historians can only speculate and try to reconstruct Aelred's likely opinion through indirect evidence.

Aelred and His Friends

It is undoubtedly significant that Aelred's known close associates generally favored the king rather than the archbishop. Aelred had grown up at the court of David I of Scotland, a leading proponent of the Angevin cause.[1] Among the members of the English hierarchy, Aelred enjoyed particularly close relationships with Archbishop Roger of Pont L'Évêque of York, Bishop Hugh du Puiset of Durham, and Bishop Gilbert Foliot of London.[2] Hugh of Durham stayed largely clear of the Becket controversy, although he was suspended by the pope in 1170 for participating in the

---

[1] See above, chap. 3:39–41.
[2] See above, chap. 4:80–82, 93–95.

coronation of the young king.[3] Roger of Pont L'Évêque and especially Gilbert Foliot, however, led the opposition to the archbishop.[4] The one person singled out by name in Walter Daniel's discussion of Aelred's correspondence with notable members of English society, Earl Robert of Leicester, was a royal justiciar and a trusted advisor to Henry II.[5] These associations strongly suggest that Aelred would have favored the royal cause, but what, if any, practical effect this preference had remains undocumented.

Gilbert of Sempringham and the entire Gilbertine Order were other friends of Aelred who became caught up in the Becket controversy. When Becket fled Northampton for exile in 1164, Gilbertine canons acted as his guides, and he found refuge at the Gilbertine priories of Sempringham, Haverholme, and Chicksands along the way.[6] Later Gilbert himself had to appear before royal justices when he was falsely accused of sending large sums of money to Becket overseas. In this instance only the king's personal intervention saved Gilbert and his monks themselves from being sent into exile.[7] At about the same time, in 1164–1165, the Gilbertines were torn by the revolt of the lay brothers of Sempringham with their

[3] David Knowles, *The Episcopal Colleagues of Thomas Becket: Being the Ford Lectures Delivered in the University of Oxford in Hilary Term 1949* (Cambridge: Cambridge University Press, 1970), 14–15; Geoffrey V. Scammell, *Hugh du Puiset, Bishop of Durham* (Cambridge: Cambridge University Press, 1956), 30–31.

[4] For Roger of Pont L'Évêque, see Knowles, *Episcopal Colleagues*, 12–14, 91–100, 114–15; Frank Barlow, "Pont l'Évêque, Roger de (c. 1115–1181)," DNB 23961 accessed October 7, 2013. For Gilbert Foliot, see Knowles, *Episcopal Colleagues*, 37–49, 91–100, 115–27; C. N. L. Brooke, "Foliot, Gilbert (c. 1110–1187)," DNB 9792, accessed October 7, 2013; Adrian Morey and C. N. L. Brooke, *Gilbert Foliot and His Letters* (Cambridge: Cambridge University Press, 1965), 147–87; CTB vol. 1, no. 109, pp. 498–537; Thomas Merton, "St. Aelred of Rievaulx and the Cistercians," pt. 5, CSQ 24, no. 1 (1989): 67–68.

[5] On Robert of Leicester's role in the Becket controversy generally, see David Crouch, *The Beaumont Twins: The Roots and Branches of Power* (Cambridge: Cambridge University Press, 1986), 94–95.

[6] *The Book of St Gilbert*, ed. and trans. Raymonde Foreville and Gillian Keir (Oxford: Clarendon Press, 1987), 72–73; Brian Golding, *Gilbert of Sempringham and the Gilbertine Order, c. 1130–c. 1300* (Oxford: Clarendon Press, 1995), 38–40.

[7] *Book of St Gilbert*, 72–75.

accusations of laxity within the Order.[8] From his refuge at Pontigny Becket wrote angrily to Gilbert, demanding the correction of "very serious scandals . . . which have been broadcast through the greater part of the globe, to your shame." He demanded that Gilbert appear before him to explain why he could not carry out the reform of the Order mandated by the pope and threatened him with excommunication.[9] A second letter accused Gilbert of neglecting or defying papal mandates and again threatened him with severe punishment.[10] In the meantime Becket's opponents, including King Henry himself, lined up solidly behind the Gilbertines, dispatching numerous letters to the pope praising Gilbert and his order, interspersed with letters of encouragement to Gilbert himself.[11] Aelred had helped the Gilbertines to deal with the earlier affair of the pregnant nun at Watton, and it is likely that his sympathies lay with the Gilbertines during the difficulties with the lay brothers as well.

A Letter from Rievaulx

There is one further small indication of the direction in which Aelred's sympathy and that of his abbey lay. A thirteenth-century manuscript now belonging to Balliol College (Oxford MS. Balliol 65, fol. 48) contains a mysterious letter from "frater M. minimus pauperum Christi de Rieualle" to Archbishop Thomas Becket of Canterbury as part of a miscellaneous collection including works by Simon of Tournai, John of Cornwall, and the patriarch of Antioch. Frederick M. Powicke printed the Latin text of the letter in an article in the *English Historical Review* in 1935, along with the few facts that are known about its supposed author, Maurice, the

---

[8] See above, chap. 5:123–24.

[9] CTB vol. 1, no. 44, pp. 180–83.

[10] CTB vol. 1, no. 89, pp. 358–61.

[11] *Book of St Gilbert*, 134–67; Golding, *Gilbert of Sempringham*, 44; Giles Constable, "Aelred of Rievaulx and the Nun of Watton: An Episode in the Early History of the Gilbertine Order," in *Medieval Women*, ed. Derek Baker (Oxford: Basil Blackwell for the Ecclesiastical History Society, 1978), 223–25.

second abbot of Rievaulx.[12] Later, in his introduction to Walter Daniel's *Life of Aelred*, Powicke attributed the letter to Aelred on stylistic grounds.[13] Appendix 5 is an English translation of the letter. The text makes it clear that the author, whoever he was, wrote in response to a letter from the archbishop, but no such letter is included in the Becket correspondence.[14] Becket, however, did write to at least some members of the clergy to announce his election, since a congratulatory letter from Bishop Arnulf of Lisieux mentions having received such a letter.[15] Powicke supposed that the letter sent to Rievaulx was a general request for prayers and advice, sent out early in the pontificate. Bennett Hill viewed the letter in the same way, focusing on a passage in which the author urged Becket to correct evils in the church to support his contention that the Cistercians were responsible for the archbishop's spiritual transformation and for his high Gregorian ideals.[16]

By the time Thomas Becket became archbishop of Canterbury, Aelred had been abbot of Rievaulx for about fifteen years, so why would Becket have written to a simple monk of the abbey rather than to the abbot himself? Maurice began his monastic career at Durham, where he rose to the rank of sub-prior before deciding to take up the stricter Cistercian life at Rievaulx sometime after 1138.[17] He was apparently known for his literary skill, for Walter Daniel described him as "a second Bede."[18] None of his works survives, but the thirteenth-century catalogue of the Rievaulx library lists three volumes attributed to him: a book of sermons, a letter collection, and a volume of miscellaneous works, including an account of the translation of the relics of Saint Cuthbert at Durham

[12] Frederick M. Powicke, "Maurice of Rievaulx," EHR 36 (1921): 17–29.

[13] Powicke, Introduction to Vita A, xlix–lii.

[14] Powicke, "Maurice," 26; App. 5:275.

[15] CTB vol. 1, no. 2, pp. 10–11.

[16] Bennett D. Hill, "Archbishop Thomas Becket and the Cistercian Order," *Analecta Sacri Ordinis Cisterciensis* 27 (1971): 67–68. Also Frank Barlow, *Thomas Becket* (Berkeley and Los Angeles: University of California Press, 1986), 74–75.

[17] John of Hexham, *Historia*, in *Symeonis Monachi opera omnia*, ed. Thomas Arnold, 2 vols., RS 75 (London: Longmans, 1882–1885), 2:317.

[18] Vita A 25, p. 33; CF 57:115.

in 1104.[19] He was elected abbot of Rievaulx upon the death of Abbot William in August 1145 and served for about two years before resigning in 1147, when Aelred was elected in his place.[20] His initial retirement was brief, for Abbot Henry Murdac of Fountains was elected archbishop of York in December 1147 and selected Maurice as his successor. Maurice remained in his new position for only three months before once again resigning and returning to Rievaulx.[21]

During this period Thomas Becket was a young clerk serving in the household of Archbishop Theobald of Canterbury. He joined the archiepiscopal household in 1145 and may soon have been sent to the continent for legal studies at Bologna and/or Auxerre.[22] It is unlikely, but not completely impossible, that Thomas and Abbot Maurice could have met during this period. For example Archbishop Theobald visited Pope Eugenius III in Paris in the fall of 1147, and perhaps his young clerk took advantage of the occasion to travel north to meet his patron.[23] Abbot Maurice might then have encountered the pair on his way to or from a general chapter meeting at Cîteaux, but this is pure conjecture.

[19] Powicke, "Maurice," 19–20; for the edited catalogue, see David N. Bell, ed., "Rievaulx, Yorkshire N.R. *Cist. Abbey of B.V.M.*" in *The Libraries of the Cistercians, Gilbertines and Premonstratensians*, ed. David N. Bell, Corpus of British Medieval Library Catalogues 2 (London: The British Library in association with the British Academy, 1992), 87–140.

[20] Vita A 25, p. 33; CF 57:115; John of Hexham, *Historia*, 2:317.

[21] Hugh of Kirkstall, *Narratio de Fundatione Fontanis Monasterii in Comitatu Eboracensis*, in *Memorials of the Abbey of St. Mary of Fountains*, ed. John Richard Walbran (London and Edinburgh: Andrews and Co. for the Surtees Society, 1863), 104; Janet Burton, "Rievaulx Abbey: The Early Years," in *Perspectives for an Architecture of Solitude*, ed. T. N. Kinder (Turnhout: Brepols, 2004), 50; Pierre-André Burton, *Aelred de Rievaulx (1110–1167), De l'homme éclaté à l'être unifié: Essai de biographie existentielle et spirituelle* (Paris: Éditions du Cerf, 2010), 311–12.

[22] John of Salisbury, *Vita Sancti Thomae, Cantuariensis Archiepiscopi et Martyris*, in MTB 2:303–4; William fitz Stephen, *Vita Sancti Thomae, Cantuariensis Archiepiscopi et Martyris*, in MTB 3:17; Roger of Pontigny, *Vita Sancti Thomae, Cantuariensis Archiepiscopi et Martyris*, in MTB 4:10; John Guy, *Thomas Becket: Warrior, Priest, Rebel* (New York: Random House, 2012), 55; Anne Duggan, *Thomas Becket* (London: Arnold Publishing, 2004), 14–15; Barlow, *Thomas Becket*, 36–37; Avrom Saltman, *Theobald, Archbishop of Canterbury* (New York: Greenwood Press, 1969), 168.

[23] Guy, *Thomas Becket*, 57; Saltman, *Theobald*, 23–24.

There may also have been opportunities for Thomas Becket and Maurice of Rievaulx to have met after the latter's resignation from Fountains. It is a sign of Aelred's tact and managerial skill that he chose to involve his esteemed predecessor in the administration of Rievaulx, and two instances are known in which Maurice participated with Aelred in some public business. The Byland Abbey foundation history records that in 1151, when Aelred gave his judgment in the dispute between Savigny and Furness over possession of Byland, Maurice was among the monks of Rievaulx who accompanied him to the meeting.[24] Maurice's attestation also appears on a charter recording an exchange between Bertram de Bulmer and Aschetil fitz Gospatric in which the former acquired a carucate of land in Welburn, which he subsequently donated to Rievaulx.[25] As this property was included in a papal bull of protection issued in 1160, the original exchange had to have taken place before that date.[26]

Perhaps Maurice and Thomas Becket met at some other time when the former abbot accompanied Aelred to a public event or represented Aelred and Rievaulx at some function that the abbot was unable to attend. For example, Becket is known to have been present with Archbishop Theobald at the council of Rheims in 1148, when, among other matters, William fitz Herbert was deprived of the archbishopric of York. This would have been an occasion of deep interest to Rievaulx and to the Cistercians in general, given the involvement of Abbots William of Rievaulx and Richard II of Fountains in the early stages of the controversy.[27] It is possible that Rievaulx sent a delegation to the council, but none

---

[24] *Foundation History of the Abbeys of Byland and Jervaulx*, ed. Janet Burton, Borthwick Texts and Studies 35 (York: Borthwick Institute for Archives, University of York, 2006), 32.

[25] CAR no. 214.

[26] CAR no. 250.

[27] On William fitz Herbert, see above, chap. 3:56–62. For Becket's attendance, Roger of Pontigny, *Vita*, in MTB 4:10; Michael Staunton, *The Lives of Thomas Becket* (Manchester: Manchester University Press, 2001), 46; John of Salisbury, *Historia Pontificalis*, ed. and trans. Marjorie Chibnall (Oxford: Clarendon Press, 1986), 15–19; Guy, *Thomas Becket*, 59–60; Barlow, *Thomas Becket*, 34–35.

was recorded. Becket also visited Yorkshire in the company of the king in February 1155 and January 1158, so Aelred and Maurice could have met the future archbishop at one of those times.[28]

Thomas Becket attended the council at Tours in May 1163, where he campaigned vigorously, if unsuccessfully, for the canonization of his predecessor, Archbishop Anselm. This council would have been of vital interest to the Cistercians, since the canonization of Bernard of Clairvaux was also put forward at this time. Although monks were minor players at such gatherings, Ralph of Diceto made a point of recording that abbots and even priors were included in the English delegation to the council.[29] Robert Somerville stated that while it is likely that several hundred attended, he was able to identify only about forty monks, and even that number was doubtful, being based on the fact that their monasteries received papal letters and privileges during this time. His list included only three Cistercians, but it is worth noting that Aelred's neighbor Abbot Richard III of Fountains attended, along with the abbot of the Benedictine monks at Durham.[30] Adriaan Bredero counts a possible nine Cistercian abbots and four bishops as attendees.[31]

Ralf Lützelschwab has made an interesting proposal regarding Aelred's possible attendance at this council. One of Aelred's synodal sermons states that it was preached at Troyes, but there is no record of such a synod matching his admittedly sketchily known travel itinerary. Lützelschwab suggests that Troyes was a scribal

[28] R. E. Eyton, *Court, Household and Itinerary of King Henry II* (London: Taylor and Co., 1878), 5, 33–34.

[29] Ralph of Diceto, *Radulphi de Diceto Decani Londoniensis Opera Historica, The Historical Works of Master Ralph de Diceto, Dean of London (to 1202)*, ed. William Stubbs, 2 vols., RS 68 (London: Longmans, 1876), 1:310.

[30] Herbert of Bosham, *Vita Sancti Thomae, Archiepiscopi et Martyris*, in MTB 3:253–55; Staunton, *Lives*, 72–74; Barlow, *Thomas Becket*, 85–87; Robert Somerville, *Pope Alexander III and the Council of Tours* (Berkeley and Los Angeles: University of California Press, 1977), 29–31.

[31] Adriaan Bredero, "The Canonization of Bernard of Clairvaux," in *Saint Bernard of Clairvaux: Studies Commemorating the Eighth Centenary of His Canonization*, CS 28 (Kalamazoo, MI: Cistercian Publications, 1977), 85.

error for Tours in 1163 and notes that if Aelred came as a guest speaker but did not stay for the rest of the proceedings, he would not have been included on any of the participant lists.[32] So the great council at Tours may have given Aelred and other representatives of Rievaulx a further opportunity to meet Thomas Becket.

It can be shown, however, that Aelred was with Becket on two public occasions. As was discussed in the previous chapter, Aelred witnessed two of Becket's charters in March 1163, one recording the resolution of the dispute between the bishop of Lincoln and Saint Alban's Abbey and the other confirming a gift by King Malcolm IV of Scotland to the canons of Holyrood.[33] In October of the same year Becket would have been in attendance when Aelred preached at the translation of the relics of Saint Edward the Confessor to the new shrine in Westminster Abbey.[34] There is no written evidence that Maurice was present on either of these occasions, but if not, other similar public events could have brought the two together. But how likely is it that such a chance encounter produced a long-standing relationship between Becket and an aging, obscure monk from the northern archdiocese? Thomas Becket was not known for his piety before his election as archbishop,[35] and it does not seem that he would have found much in common with Maurice of Rievaulx.

---

[32] Ralf Lützelschwab, "*Vox de coelis originem ducitis:* Aelred of Rievaulx as Preacher at Synods," unpublished paper presented at the Cistercian Studies Conference, held within the 49th International Congress on Medieval Studies at the University of Western Michigan, Kalamazoo, MI, May 8–11, 2014. The sermon is S 28; CCCM 2A:229–38; Aelred of Rievaulx, *The Liturgical Sermons: The First Clairvaux Collection, Advent–All Saints,* trans. Theodore Berkeley and Basil Pennington, CF 58 (Kalamazoo, MI: Cistercian Publications, 2001), 380–94.

[33] EEA 2, no. 13; *Regesta Regum Scottorum: Vol. 1: The Acts of Malcolm IV King of Scots 1153–1165 together with Scottish Royal Acts prior to 1153 not included in Sir Archibald Lawrie's Early Scottish Charters,* ed. G. W. S. Barrow (Edinburgh: Edinburgh University Press, 1960), no. 197; Eyton, *Itinerary,* 59–61; see above, chap. 8:178–79.

[34] *Chronicon Angliae Petriburgense,* ed. John Allen Giles (London: D. Nutt, 1845), 98; Peter Jackson, "*In translacione sancti Edwardi confessoris:* The Lost Sermon by Aelred of Rievaulx Found," CSQ 40, no. 1 (2005): 63–64.

[35] William fitz Stephen, *Vita,* in MTB 3:20–21; Staunton, *Lives,* 50–51; Alan of Tewkesbury, *Vita Sancti Thomae, Cantuariensis Archiepiscopi et Martyris,* in MTB

The text of the letter itself is of little help in determining who wrote it and when. The anonymous salutation from "brother M" could refer to Maurice, or it might mean that the scribe who copied the letter into the thirteenth-century manuscript was not sure of its authorship, since both Aelred and his successor Sylvanus were abbots of Rievaulx during the pontificate of Thomas Becket. The author called himself "the poorest and most insignificant of all Christ's men at Rievaulx" and remarked that he viewed Becket's condescension to him as "something of a miracle."[36] His abject humility is of course a convention of medieval letter writing, but it does seem strange that if Aelred or Sylvanus wrote the letter he did not use his title of abbot.

At the end of these protestations of unworthiness, the author wrote, "So I am not what you think I am. You seek another under my title and you give me an importance that I do not have."[37] Is this merely a further declaration of humility, or did Becket actually think Maurice was still the abbot of Rievaulx? The latter seems highly unlikely, but not impossible, given that Rievaulx lay far to the north in the archdiocese of York and that Becket had had little involvement with the monastic life before his selection as archbishop. These peculiar statements, however, do make it seem that the letter writer was a simple monk of the abbey, responding to a letter that might more properly have been addressed to the abbot.

It is clear that the letter, whoever wrote it, was composed in answer to one from Becket, and it even reveals that the archbishop's letter was carried by Hugh de Morville, who "went more than

---

2:363–64; William of Canterbury, *Vita, Passio et Miracula S. Thomae Cantuariensis Archiepiscopi*, in MTB 1:5; Herbert of Bosham, *Vita*, in MTB 3:163–77; Cary J. Nederman and Karen Bollerman, "'The Extravagance of the Senses': Epicureanism, Priestly Tyranny, and the Becket Problem in John of Salisbury's Policraticus," *Studies in Medieval and Renaissance History*, 3rd ser. 8 (2011): 1–26; Guy, *Thomas Becket*, 78; Duggan, *Thomas Becket*, 18–19; Barlow, *Thomas Becket*, 44–48; L. B. Radford, *Thomas of London Before His Consecration* (Cambridge: Cambridge University Press, 1894), 228–29.

[36] Powicke, "Maurice," 26; App. 5:274.

[37] Powicke, "Maurice," 26–27; App. 5:275.

twenty mileposts out of his way"[38] to deliver it. De Morville was the lord of Knaresborough castle and so would have been within about thirty miles of Rievaulx on any visit home. But it is doubtful that this staunch supporter of King Henry II would have been carrying messages for Becket after the archbishop's open break with the king, so it is almost certain that the letter was composed before the archbishop went into exile in November 1164.

The text of the letter itself sends mixed signals with respect to the question of its date. The fulsome assurances that the letter writer would see to it that all the monks prayed for the archbishop would be an appropriate response to an introductory letter from the new archbishop asking for prayers and support.[39] On the other hand, the author mentioned that he had "examined the evidence from every angle"[40] and alluded to enemies and dangerous times. These references suggest a time a bit later, after trouble had developed between the archbishop and the king.

Much of the letter is vague and meandering, offering little concrete information about the author or his sympathies. One unifying feature, however, is that certain allusions in the text seem to echo criticisms of Becket that are found in other sources. For example, the author acknowledged that many things needed to be corrected in the church. He offered as a specific example the tendency for "men of proven virtue"[41] to be set aside while younger men were appointed to high ecclesiastical positions for which they were not qualified. This is similar to a complaint that Herbert of Bosham recorded regarding ecclesiastical appointees with an insufficient knowledge of Scripture.[42] Perhaps this was not the most tactful statement the Rievaulx author could have made, for Becket's critics considered him unqualified to become archbishop, and many thought that Aelred's friend Bishop Gilbert Foliot of

[38] Powicke, "Maurice," 26; App. 5:275.
[39] Powicke, "Maurice," 26; App. 5:275–76.
[40] Powicke, "Maurice," 26; App. 5:275, 277.
[41] Powicke, "Maurice," 28; App. 5:277.
[42] Herbert of Bosham, *Vita*, in MTB 3:207–8.

London would have been a better choice.[43] On the other hand, as Powicke has suggested, this comment could have been a veiled allusion to the case of William fitz Herbert of York, a debacle with which both Maurice and Aelred would have been thoroughly familiar because of Rievaulx's involvement in the early stages of the affair.[44] Or perhaps the author's inspiration merely failed him at this point, for the passage is based on Bernard of Clairvaux's *On the Office of Bishops.*[45]

Similarly the Rievaulx writer warned Becket that he had been "appointed the shepherd of the flock of Christ not arrogantly to dominate them but anxiously to watch over them."[46] He cautioned him against both vanity and ambition, two of the very charges leveled against Becket from the moment of his election, as recorded in the following passage from John of Salisbury's *Vita*:

> They falsely asserted that his zeal for justice was cruelty. They attributed to avarice the fact that he procured advantages for the church. They said that his contempt for worldly favor was the pursuit of glory, and the magnificence of his court was made out to be pride. That he followed a divinely instructed will . . . was branded a mark of arrogance. That he often seemed to surpass the goals of his predecessors in defending justice was judged to be a sign of rashness.[47]

---

[43] Lambeth Anonymous, *Vita Sancti Thomae, Cantuariensis Archiepiscopi et Martyris*, in MTB 4:84–85; Staunton, *Lives*, 61; Edward Grim, *Vita Sancti Thomae, Cantuariensis Archiepiscopi et Martyris*, in MTB 2:365–67; Roger of Pontigny, *Vita*, in MTB 4:16–17; Staunton, *Lives*, 63; Herbert of Bosham, *Vita*, in MTB 3:182–85; *Thomas Saga Erkibyskups: A Life of Archbishop Thomas Becket, in Icelandic, with English Translation, Notes and Glossary*, ed. M. Eirikr Magnusson, 2 vols., RS 65 (London: Longmans, 1875–1883), 1:73–83; CTB vol. 1, no. 93, p. 377; Guy, *Thomas Becket*, 146–48; Duggan, *Thomas Becket*, 23–25; Barlow, *Thomas Becket*, 70–71; W. L. Warren, *Henry II* (Berkeley and Los Angeles: University of California Press, 1973), 454; Radford, *Thomas of London*, 209–10; Knowles, *Episcopal Colleagues*, 44–46.

[44] Powicke, Introduction to Vita A, l. For William fitz Herbert, see above, chap. 3:56–62.

[45] Bernard, Ep 42; SBOp 7:122; CF 67:68–69; Powicke, "Maurice," 22.

[46] Powicke, "Maurice," 29; App. 5:280.

[47] John of Salisbury, *Vita*, in MTB 2:310; Ronald E. Pepin, trans., *Anselm and Becket: Two Canterbury Saints' Lives by John of Salisbury* (Toronto: Pontifical Institute of Medieval Studies, 2009), 82.

Similarly, Garnier of Pont-Sainte-Maxence wrote, "He was deeply humble at heart, yet arrogant in appearance; he was humble with poor people, proud-looking with the mighty, a lamb inwardly but outwardly a leopard. . . . Perhaps he may have been proud and given to vanities, as far as worldly cares go and in outward appearance, yet he was chaste in body and healthy in soul."[48]

These remarks were written after Becket's martyrdom had changed everything, and in the best hagiographical tradition, the authors portrayed their subject as having been holy and especially chaste on the inside even though outward appearances suggested something quite different. Nevertheless it is clear that before that tragic event, at the time the Rievaulx letter was written, many people considered Becket domineering and arrogant.

In the same way the Rievaulx author and many others acknowledged Becket's former privileged position with the king and seemed to feel that the archbishop should be able to take advantage of that friendship to accomplish great things for the church. Pointing out that Becket's most important task was "the management of the sovereign,"[49] the Rievaulx author warned that left to their own devices, lay lords were prone to "take shameful advantage of sacred things."[50] He urged Becket to work for the reform of the church, using "the power of the prince, with which you have the special grace of familiarity."[51] This echoes a statement in Edward Grim's biography, which had the king's representatives at the Canterbury election argue that it would be to the chapter's advantage to elect a candidate "who would have influence with royal majesty in all things."[52] Similarly William fitz Stephen at one point had Bishop Hilary of Chichester tell Becket, "Because of a chancellor's intimacy with the king, you know him

---

[48] Garnier de Pont-Sainte-Maxence, *La vie de Saint Thomas le martyr, archévêque de Canterbury*, ed. C. Hippeau (Geneva: Slatkine Reprints, 1969), 11–12; Staunton, *Lives*, 54.

[49] Powicke, "Maurice," 27; App. 5:277.

[50] Powicke, "Maurice," 27; App. 5:277.

[51] Powicke, "Maurice," 28; App. 5:278.

[52] Edward Grim, *Vita*, in MTB 2:366; Staunton, *Lives*, 62.

better than we do. Undoubtedly you will prevail over him more easily, whether you oppose him or yield."[53]

It would be nice to know which particular failing of the archbishop the Rievaulx author had in mind when he wrote, "You should have disproved the invader of the alien law."[54] The word *alienus* could mean "belonging to another, alien, foreign" or "strange" but also "unsuitable, inadequate," or "unreasonable." As the noun *alienatio* it could refer to the alienation of property. Perhaps the statement referred to Becket's initial acceptance of the Constitutions of Clarendon, which certainly contained enough radical provisions to be described as *alienus* in the sense of "unsuitable, unreasonable," or "strange."

Another intriguing possibility is that the reference is to the scutage collected in 1159, while Becket was chancellor, to finance Henry II's campaign across the channel in Toulouse. Not only was the assessment foreign in that it was intended for an overseas expedition, but it was also novel because it was a commutation of personal military service, falling on both lay and ecclesiastical tenants. The church particularly objected to the new assessment, and many held the chancellor personally responsible for betraying them by enforcing, if not actually inventing, the scheme.[55] Certainly Gilbert Foliot remembered these novel exactions with anger, describing them in his 1166 denunciation of Becket as "a sword plunged into the vitals of holy mother church."[56] John of Salisbury noted that Becket's enemies believed that he "directed the king in everything at his own whim and persuaded him to this as to much other wickedness." John stated that he knew this charge to be false but nevertheless noted that Becket deserved to be punished for being "the servant of wickedness."[57] In his

[53] William fitz Stephen, *Vita*, in MTB 3:55; Staunton, *Lives*, 104. Similarly *Thomas Saga*, 1:73.

[54] Powicke, "Maurice," 29; App. 5:280.

[55] Radford, *Thomas of London*, 99–100, 156–61; Saltman, *Theobald*, 44–45.

[56] CTB vol. 1, no. 109, pp. 504–5.

[57] John of Salisbury, *The Letters of John of Salisbury*, vol. 2, *The Later Letters (1163–1180)*, ed. and trans. W. J. Millor and C. N. L. Brooke (Oxford: Clarendon Press, 1979), no. 168, pp. 106–7.

Entheticus John made the intriguing statement that he hoped that Archbishop Theobald's successor would cancel the unjust laws that kings had made.[58] The statement could imply that the laws in question were made by King Henry II during the pontificate of Becket's predecessor, which of course included the period when Becket was Henry's chancellor and the scutage was levied.

Ingratitude is another recurring theme in the criticism of Becket during this period. A group of the English clergy writing to the archbishop in 1166 recalled that despite the opposition of the clergy, the king "strove by every means possible" to raise Becket to the archiepiscopal throne and counseled the archbishop to have a care for his own reputation, asking, "If therefore, [the king] receives a battle-axe where he was hoping for safety, what story of you will be on everyone's lips?"[59] The Rievaulx author described ingratitude as "a deadly thing"[60] and warned the archbishop to "beware that friendship does not turn into anger."[61] He remarked, "It is often thought that anger is greater because of former affection."[62] Later he wrote, "And to whom do you owe faith, to whom the duty of faith, if not to him who created you, raised you from the dust, lifted you up, advanced you, and placed you on the throne of glory? A short time after you were granted favor by your faithful benefactor, he demanded a return on his investment."[63] The phrase "him who created you" could refer to Becket's faithfulness to God and the church, or it could mean that the king's favor had been responsible for Becket's election to Canterbury.

The words are markedly similar to those which Roger of Pontigny placed in Henry II's mouth in his account of a meeting between the king and the archbishop at Northampton shortly after

---

[58] John of Salisbury, *John of Salisbury's Entheticus Maior and Minor*, ed. Jan van Laaroven, 3 vols. (Leiden: Brill, 1987), 1:188–89.

[59] CTB vol. 1, no. 93, pp. 376–77; Ralph of Diceto, *Opera Historica*, 1:322; Roger of Hoveden, *Chronica Magistri Rogeri de Houedene*, ed. William Stubbs, 4 vols., RS 51 (London: Longmans, 1868–1871), 1:264.

[60] Powicke, "Maurice," 27; App. 5:276.

[61] Powicke, "Maurice," 27; App. 5:276.

[62] Powicke, "Maurice," 27; App. 5:276.

[63] Powicke, "Maurice," 29; App. 5:279–80.

the council of Westminster: "Did I not raise you from a humble and poor rank to the highest peak of honor and distinction? And this did not seem enough to me, unless I also made you father of the realm, and even exalted you over myself. How is it then that so many favors, and such signs of my love for you, well known to all, could so suddenly be banished from your mind, so that not only do you turn out to be ungrateful, but even hostile to me in every way?"[64]

The Rievaulx author also pointedly counseled the archbishop against greed: "The duty of the bishop is to provide necessities for the poor, not brood over his own wealth. The minister is ordained a steward and a servant, not to watch out for his own profit and gain, but to give of himself."[65] Henry II seized Becket's revenues after the council of Westminster, and this statement seems indirectly to accuse the archbishop of having acquiesced to the king's wishes at Clarendon out of concern for his lost property. Gilbert Foliot wrote, "And are your annual revenues so important to you that you wish to acquire them by the blood of your brothers? But when Judas brought back the money, the Jews threw it out because they knew that it was the price of blood."[66]

The themes of betrayal, exile, and abandonment intertwine in the literature surrounding the Becket controversy, even among those who were generally favorable to the archbishop. The issue of betrayal naturally called up comparisons to the betrayal of Jesus by his disciples. For example, several sources compared the archbishop's actions at Clarendon to Saint Peter's denial of Jesus on the eve of the passion. Herbert of Bosham wrote, "Peter, taking it for granted that he would die rather than deny his Master, first denied him at the question of a serving-girl, but later led before kings and rulers did not cease in his righteousness." He went on to say that even though Thomas had fallen disgracefully, God would still be with him.[67]

---

[64] Roger of Pontigny, *Vita*, in MTB 4:27–28; Staunton, *Lives*, 83.
[65] Powicke, "Maurice," 29; App. 5:280–81.
[66] CTB, vol. 1, no. 109, pp. 526–27. The scriptural reference is to Matt 27:6.
[67] Herbert of Bosham, *Vita*, in MTB 3:290–91; Staunton, *Lives*, 98.

Herbert of Bosham also wrote that the bishops who sided with the king considered that Becket had "rashly and disgracefully exasperated the king, recklessly disturbed the peace of the crown and the priesthood, and foolishly and indiscriminately abandoned the Church by fleeing in the night."[68] Gilbet Foliot was less kind: "Therefore, with what effrontery, father, have you invited us to death, a death which you both feared and fled, as you have revealed more clearly than the day to the whole world by such obvious evidence? What affection urges you to lay on us the burden which you have thrown down? The sword which you fled is threatening us, against which you chose to throw stones, not fight hand to hand."[69]

Other criticisms seem to allude to Becket's decision to go into exile on the continent in November 1164. The Rievaulx author wrote, "It is considered easier to flee than to stand firm."[70] Hugh de Morville delivered the original letter, which makes it unlikely that the statement refers to Becket's actual flight in 1164. Becket's departure was not unexpected, however, but rather had been anticipated for at least a year. On two occasions he sought a refuge on the continent in case he was driven out of England, first sending John of Salisbury to look for a possible site in December 1163.[71] Later, in the spring of 1164, John of Canterbury, the bishop of Poitiers, recommended the Cistercian abbey of Pontigny as a refuge.[72] At about the same time he recruited the Cistercian abbots Guichard of Pontigny, Geoffrey of Clairvaux, and Gerard of Fossanova as emissaries to the papal curia on Becket's behalf.[73]

---

[68] Herbert of Bosham, *Vita*, in MTB 3:323; Staunton, *Lives*, 120. Similarly Alan of Tewkesbury, *Vita*, in MTB 2:337–38; Staunton, *Lives*, 129; CTB vol. 1, no. 45, pp. 188–89.

[69] CTB, vol. 1, no. 109, pp. 526–27. On the view that episcopal exile was dishonorable and a dereliction of duty in most cases, see Michael Staunton, "Exile in the *Lives* of Anselm and Thomas Becket," in *Exile in the Middle Ages: Selected Proceedings from the International Medieval Congress, University of Leeds, 8–11 July 2002*, ed. Laura Napran and Elisabet van Houts (Turnhout: Brepols, 2004), 159–80.

[70] Powicke, "Maurice," 28; App. 5:279.

[71] CTB, vol. 1, no. 24, pp. 66–67; Guy, *Thomas Becket*, 186–87.

[72] CTB vol. 1, no. 18, 46–47; Guy, *Thomas Becket*, 199.

[73] CTB vol. 1, no. 31, pp. 104–5, no. 34, pp. 132–33; Barlow, *Thomas Becket*, 124; Martha G. Newman, *The Boundaries of Charity: Cistercian Culture and Ecclesiastical Reform, 1098–1180* (Stanford, CA: Stanford University Press, 1996), 211.

John had been the treasurer of the church of York from 1153 until his consecration as bishop of Poitiers in 1162. His years at York undoubtedly meant that he knew the Yorkshire Cistercians well, and his regard for the Order is shown by the fact that he retired to Clairvaux in 1194.[74] John of Canterbury's ties with the Cistercians probably explain his identification of Pontigny as a haven for Becket and also make it likely that his recommendation became known within the Order. Finally, in August 1164 Becket made an abortive attempt to flee to France, only to be turned back by bad weather and recalcitrant sailors.[75]

Gilbert Foliot also expressed disapproval of Becket's earlier attempt to leave England: "With the north wind filling your sails, the voyage would surely have been completed, if the south wind had not prevented the attempt with a better breeze, which fortunately carried the ship to the shore from which it began its voyage."[76] Rumors about a possible retreat into exile would thus have been swirling around Becket for at least a year before his actual departure in 1164.

At the end of the letter the Rievaulx author counseled Becket:

> Above all, do not resist the will of the Lord, knowing to what he has appointed you, but, mindful of his commandments, be content when you bring it to a conclusion, just as your fathers were, who are clearly praised in the church of the saints. You imitate the example of such honorable endeavors, and assisted by the favor of friends, you will earn even more favor, for favor is not given up for nothing but, even better, will be returned to you abundantly in a miraculous exchange.[77]

---

[74] Jean Dunbabin, "Canterbury, John of (c. 1120–1204?)," DNB, accessed July 6, 2013; Charles Duggan, "Bishop John and Archdeacon Richard of Poitiers: Their Roles in the Becket Dispute," in *Thomas Becket: actes du colloque international de Sédières, 19–24 août 1973*, ed. Raymonde Foreville (Paris: Beauchesne, 1973), 72–83.

[75] Edward Grim, *Vita*, in MTB 2:389–90; Staunton, *Lives*, 99–100; Alan of Tewkesbury, *Vita*, in MTB 2:325; William of Canterbury, *Vita, Passio et Miracula S. Thomae Cantuariensis Archiepiscopi*, in MTB 1:29; Herbert of Bosham, *Vita*, in MTB 3:293; Roger of Pontigny, *Vita*, in MTB 4:40; Guy, *Thomas Becket*, 199–200.

[76] CTB vol. 1, no. 109, pp. 512–13.

[77] Powicke, "Maurice," 29; App. 5:281. On this point, see Newman, *Boundaries of Charity*, 210.

The advice seems to be a plea for reconciliation between the king and the archbishop. The reference to "your fathers, who are clearly praised in the church of the saints" is perhaps an allusion to the core issue separating the two—the king's demand that Becket accept what he considered the ancestral customs of the realm.

Powicke ultimately attributed the letter to Aelred rather than to Maurice on stylistic grounds, but in at least one respect the letter is very different from Aelred's usual writing. As Marie Anne Mayeski has pointed out, Aelred's sermons are replete with scriptural allusions, but as can be seen in Appendix 5, the Rievaulx letter contains few scriptural citations.[78] A useful comparison can be made with Appendix 2, R. Jacob McDonie's translation of Aelred's letter to Gilbert Foliot. In what is little more than a transmittal letter for Aelred's *De oneribus* sermon collection, a dozen footnotes to the Scriptures appear, many containing multiple citations.

To summarize, it must be admitted that there is no clear evidence in the Rievaulx letter to indicate whether it was written by Aelred or Maurice. The most that can be said is that it echoes certain statements made by the opponents of Thomas Becket, especially those made by Bishop Gilbert Foliot of London in his famous denunciation of the archbishop, *Multiplicem nobis*. This fact, however, does not necessarily mean that the Rievaulx letter was composed after Foliot's in 1166, since as was noted earlier, it is unlikely that Hugh de Morville would have delivered a letter from Becket after the latter left England in late 1164. Foliot, however, was a vociferous critic of the archbishop from early on and undoubtedly expressed opinions similar to those ultimately recorded in *Multiplicem nobis* on other occasions. Regardless of who wrote the Rievaulx letter, its tone suggests that Foliot's viewpoint found a ready hearing at the abbey and came to be shared by Aelred and his monks.

The clearest evidence that the writer was Maurice rather than Aelred is simply the salutation from "brother M" and the author's peculiar statement: "So I am not what you think I am." Arguing

[78] Personal communication July 16, 2013.

against his authorship is the lack of evidence that the two men had ever met one another. There is, however, at least one scenario that could reconcile these contradictions. Aelred's sermon for the translation of the relics of Saint Edward the Confessor placed him squarely in the royal camp, and it is possible that he expressed himself more directly in the council that followed. He might also have spoken against Becket on other occasions that are not recorded. Becket or his allies might have encountered Maurice in Aelred's entourage and recognized him as a senior monk of the abbey. Suspecting that he might have some influence with Aelred, the archbishop could have written to Maurice seeking his help in winning over the abbot. In this way the letter writer's odd statement would mean that Becket had wrongly assumed that Maurice had more influence with Aelred than he really did. Nevertheless this is pure speculation, one of many possibilities.

In some ways it does not matter whether Maurice or Aelred actually penned this letter to Thomas Becket. As Giles Constable and Michael Clanchy have insisted, medieval letters were public productions. They were conscious literary productions, meant not only to be shared, read aloud, and discussed but also to be copied and collected, not necessarily by the original author.[79] Regardless of whether Becket addressed his letter to Maurice or to Aelred, it is likely to have been discussed and debated within the walls of Rievaulx. Thus, regardless of who actually wrote it, the negative elements of the response placed the abbey of Rievaulx itself, not merely its abbot, among the opponents of Thomas Becket. The letter from Rievaulx to the archbishop is the last tangible evidence of the abbey's participation in the quarrel between Becket and Henry II during Aelred's abbacy. In view of Aelred's long-standing support for Henry II and his friendships with the

---

[79] Giles Constable, "Diplomats and Dictators in the Eleventh and Twelfth Centuries: Medieval Epistolography and the Birth of Modern Bureaucracy," *Dumbarton Oaks Papers* 46 (1992): 37–46; Constable, "On Editing the Letters of Peter the Venerable," *Quellen und Falschungen aus Italienischen Archiven und Bibliotheken* 54 (1974): 491–92; Michael T. Clanchy, *From Memory to Written Record: England 1066–1307* (London: Edward Arnold, 1979), 68.

king's supporters, however, it is possible that Aelred had some further involvement in the matter. In any case it is almost certain that he had definite opinions on the subject. Furthermore his views would have influenced the monks of his abbey and other members of his order, even beyond his own lifetime.

The Cistercians and Thomas Becket

Aelred's concern with the Becket affair was ending, and his death in January 1167 spared him the knowledge of the archbishop's martyrdom. The involvement of the Cistercian Order as a whole, however, was just beginning. This is not the place for a full account of the tortuous negotiations between Archbishop Thomas Becket, King Henry II, and Pope Alexander III, but the participation of various Cistercians in the affair had a significant impact on the Order, and the resulting divisions within the Order may well have affected Aelred's posthumous reputation.

When Thomas Becket crossed the channel on November 2, 1164, he first received hospitality at the Cistercian abbey of Clairmarais.[80] After a visit with the pope at Sens, he traveled on to the Cistercian abbey at Pontigny, which would become his home for the next two years.[81] In the meantime the infuriated King Henry confiscated his property and that of his clerks and drove his relatives and

[80] Herbert of Bosham, *Vita*, in MTB 3:329; Staunton, *Lives*, 124; Alan of Tewkesbury, *Vita*, in MTB 2:336; William fitz Stephen, *Vita*, in MTB 3:371; Roger of Pontigny, *Vita*, in MTB 4:57; Gervase of Canterbury, *Chronica*, in *Chronicles of the Reigns of Stephen, Henry II., and Richard I.*, ed. William Stubbs, 2 vols., RS 73 (London: Longmans, 1879–1880), 1:189–90; Guy, *Thomas Becket*, 218; Barlow, *Thomas Becket*, 119.

[81] Alan of Tewkesbury, *Vita*, in MTB 2:341–45; Staunton, *Lives*, 132–34; Herbert of Bosham, *Vita*, in MTB 3:340–58; Staunton, *Lives*, 136–37; John of Salisbury, *Vita*, in MTB 2:313; Edward Grim, *Vita*, in MTB 2:403–4; William fitz Stephen, *Vita*, in MTB 3:76; Roger of Pontigny, *Vita*, in MTB 4:61–64; Lambeth Anonymous, *Vita*, in MTB 4:109–10; Ralph of Diceto, *Opera Historica*, 1:314–17; Gervase of Canterbury, *Chronica*, 1:194–96; Guy, *Thomas Becket*, 222–25; Duggan, *Thomas Becket*, 95–96; Barlow, *Thomas Becket*, 121–24; Warren, *Henry II*, 490–92. For Pontigny as a refuge for other English archbishops and bishops at odds with their respective rulers, see William Chester Jordan, "The English Holy Men of Pontigny," CSQ 43, no. 1 (2008): 63–75.

supporters into exile. Becket's sister and her children initially took refuge at Clairmarais.[82] In March 1165 the abbot of the Cistercian monastery of Le Valasse, working through Empress Matilda, arranged a meeting between Henry II, Louis VII, and Pope Alexander III at Gisors. Becket traveled to the nearby Cistercian abbey of Notre-Dame du Val, hoping for a meeting with Henry II, but negotiations faltered and the opportunity was lost.[83] At about the same time Abbot Gilbert of Cîteaux met with Henry II at Rouen, where he tried to keep peace with the king by promising to prevent the English Cistercians from publicizing Becket's more inflammatory remarks.[84]

After more than a year of fruitless negotiations with the king, Becket received an appointment as papal legate from Alexander III. Armed with his new authority, he dispatched Abbot Urban of Cercamp-sur-Canche, a daughter house of Pontigny, with letters for the king, urging him (in a tone that enraged Henry) to repent and be reconciled or face the wrath of God.[85] Hearing of Henry's angry refusal, Becket chose to escalate the quarrel. He traveled to Vézelay, stopping at the Cistercian abbey of Reigny on the way.[86] On Pentecost, June 12, 1166, he celebrated High Mass in the great Benedictine abbey. He preached a sermon explaining his quarrel with the king to the packed congregation and followed this with a condemnation of

[82] William fitz Stephen, *Vita*, in MTB 3:75–76; Staunton, *Lives*, 135–36; John of Salisbury, *Vita*, in MTB 2:313–14; Edward Grim, *Vita*, in MTB 2:404; Herbert of Bosham, *Vita*, in MTB 3:358–89; Roger of Pontigny, *Vita*, in MTB 4:64–65; CTB vol. 1, no. 115, pp. 556–57; Gervase of Canterbury, *Chronica*, 1:196–97; Roger of Hoveden, *Chronica*, 1:240–41; Guy, *Thomas Becket*, 230–31; Barlow, *Thomas Becket*, 127.

[83] CTB vol. 1, no. 46, pp. 202–3; Newman, *Boundaries*, 212.

[84] MTB vol. 5, no. 188, p. 365; Newman, *Boundaries*, 212.

[85] Herbert of Bosham, *Vita*, in MTB 3:383–85; CTB vol. 1, no. 93, pp. 374–75; John of Salisbury, *Later Letters*, no. 168, pp. 108–11; Guy, *Thomas Becket*, 239–40, Duggan, *Thomas Becket*, 105–7; Barlow, *Thomas Becket*, 145; Hill, "Becket and the Cistercian Order," 74–75; Newman, *Boundaries*, 212–13. For the letters that Abbot Urban carried, see CTB vol. 1, no. 68, pp. 266–71, and no. 74, pp. 92–99. For King Henry's letter of protest to the Cistercian Order, see MTB, *Epistolae*, vol. 5, no. 188, pp. 365–66.

[86] John of Salisbury, *Later Letters*, no. 168, pp. 112–13; Barlow, *Thomas Becket*, 147; Hill, "Becket and the Cistercian Order," 75.

the Constitutions of Clarendon and a general excommunication of those enforcing or defending them. He released the English bishops from any obligation to observe the Constitutions and concluded with specific excommunications by name of the king's advisors. Becket did not himself excommunicate Henry but called upon him publicly to repent and followed up with a letter threatening to excommunicate him if a reconciliation was not achieved.[87]

The Cistercians were among the first to feel the lash of the king's anger at this news. Henry dispatched a letter to Abbot Gilbert of Cîteaux threatening to expel the Cistercians from England and seize all their property because they had offered the archbishop sanctuary at Pontigny and had otherwise assisted him.[88] Left with little choice in the matter, the abbot of Cîteaux requested that Becket leave Pontigny. He departed on November 11, 1166, and took refuge at the Benedictine abbey of Sainte-Colombe at Sens, where he was under the personal protection of King Louis VII.[89] According to Herbert of Bosham, as Becket was leaving Pontigny he feared for his own safety and told the abbot of the dreams that disturbed his rest. A few days later he told the same story to the abbot of the Cistercian monastery of Vauluisant, who was a particular friend.[90]

This was not the first time that Thomas Becket had brought trouble to the Cistercian Order. At about the same time as the

[87] Herbert of Bosham, *Vita*, in MTB 3:391–92; Staunton, *Lives*, 145; Lambeth Anonymous, *Vita*, in MTB 4:111; Ralph of Diceto, *Opera Historica*, 1:318; Guy, *Thomas Becket*, 241–42; Barlow, *Thomas Becket*, 147–48.

[88] CTB vol. 1, no. 79, pp. 316–17; no. 80, pp. 320–21; no. 115, pp. 556–59; no. 150, pp. 696–97; Edward Grim, *Vita*, in MTB 2:413–15; Staunton, *Lives*, 148; William fitz Stephen, *Vita*, in MTB 3:83; Herbert of Bosham, *Vita*, in MTB 3:397–404; Roger of Pontigny, *Vita*, in MTB 4:65; Gervase of Canterbury, *Chronica*, 1:200; Guy, *Thomas Becket*, 243; Barlow, *Thomas Becket*, 157; Marie-Anselme Dimier, "Henri II, Thomas Becket et les Cisterciens," in *Thomas Becket: Actes du colloque international de Sédières, 19–24 août 1973* (Paris: Beauchesne, 1975), 49–53.

[89] Edward Grim, *Vita*, in MTB 2:413–14; Staunton, *Lives*, 149; John of Salisbury, *Vita*, in MTB 2:314; William of Canterbury, *Vita*, in MTB 1:50–51; William fitz Stephen, *Vita*, in MTB 3:84; Roger of Pontigny, *Vita*, in MTB 4:65; Lambeth Anonymous, *Vita*, in MTB 4:110; Guy, *Thomas Becket*, 246; Barlow, *Thomas Becket*, 158.

[90] Herbert of Bosham, *Vita*, in MTB 3:405–6.

archbishop's departure from Pontigny, Geoffrey of Auxerre was forced to resign his position as abbot of Clairvaux. Geoffrey, who had made his monastic profession at Clairvaux, had served as Bernard's secretary and after his death composed the last three books of the *Vita Prima*. After serving as abbot of Igny for five years, he returned to Clairvaux as abbot in 1162, only to resign after about two years. On the basis of the coincidence in timing between his resignation and Becket's forced departure from Pontigny and on the fact that the initial impetus seems to have come from Pope Alexander III rather than from within the Order, Dom Séraphin Lenssen has suggested that the call for his resignation was prompted by his opposition to Becket's cause.[91] Of course there are many other reasons Geoffrey might have been asked to resign. For example, Robert Fossier suggests that the problem was opposition to the abbey's policy of aggressive land acquisition, which had been spearheaded by Bishop Godfrey of Langres, a Cistercian bishop who had retired at Clairvaux.[92] Joseph Gibbons notes that the effort to have Bernard of Clairvaux canonized at the council of Tours in 1163 had failed and that this failure may have fatally damaged Geoffrey's standing within the Order.[93] Similarly Bredero suggests that dissatisfaction with Geoffrey's initial version of the *Vita Prima* on the part of older members of the Order may also have played its part in the forced resignation.[94] Nevertheless the timing remains suggestive, and it is highly significant that Geoffrey became an advisor to Henry II in the later stages of the quarrel.

---

[91] CTB vol. 1, no. 101, pp. 480–83; Séraphin Lenssen, "À propos de Cîteaux et de S. Thomas de Cantorbéry: L'abdication du bienheureux Geoffroy d'Auxerre comme abbé de Clairvaux," *Collectanea ordinis cisterciensium reformatorum* 17 (1955): 98–110; Duggan, *Thomas Becket*, 172; Anne Duggan, CTB vol. 2. App. 1:1369–70; Bredero, "Canonization," 92–93; Newman, *Boundaries*, 213–14.

[92] Robert Fossier, "La vie économique de Clairvaux des origines à la fin de la guerre de Cent Ans: 1115–1471," Thèse, École des Chartes, 1949, 107–9. Cited by Newman, *Boundaries*, 315n61.

[93] Joseph Gibbons, Introduction to *Geoffrey of Auxerre: On the Apocalypse*, CF 42 (Kalamazoo, MI: Cistercian Publications, 2000), 11.

[94] Bredero, "Canonization," 86–91.

After Becket was forced to leave Pontigny, two more years of inconclusive negotiations followed. In 1167 two papal legates, William of Pavia, cardinal-priest of Saint Peter ad Vincula and a former monk of Clairvaux, and Otto of Brescia, cardinal-deacon of Saint Nicholas in Carcere Tulliano, conducted prolonged, if ineffective, negotiations with the archbishop and the king. Thomas and his followers complained bitterly in numerous letters that William was prejudiced against them.[95] In a particularly interesting letter, the English canonist Gerard Pucelle warned Becket against William of Pavia and suggested that the Cistercians and the king of France might be able to help, apparently feeling that the monks might be able to sway a member of their own order.[96] In a letter that Becket wrote directly to Cardinal William, he viciously rejected the legate's authority, remarking that the latter's letter offered "the semblance of honey in the beginning, poison in the middle, and oil at the end."[97] Even John of Salisbury considered Becket's letter "to have come from bitterness and rancor of spirit."[98] Finally, on April 13, 1169, Becket staged another piece of ecclesiastical drama, this time at Clairvaux itself, interestingly enough while the abbot was absent. Following the great public procession for Palm Sunday, which featured a statue of Christ mounted on a donkey, the archbishop ascended the pulpit in the abbey church and excommunicated Bishops Gilbert Foliot and Jocelin of Salisbury and an assortment of laymen.[99]

---

[95] Herbert of Bosham, *Vita*, in MTB 3:408; Staunton, *Lives*, 150; William of Canterbury, *Vita*, in MTB 1:64–69; Roger of Pontigny, *Vita*, in MTB 4:63; CTB vol. 1, nos. 116–18, pp. 562–71; no. 121, pp. 574–81; no. 123, pp. 586–93; nos. 133–34, pp. 624–29; nos. 139–41, pp. 640–55; no. 159, pp. 736–39; Barlow, *Thomas Becket*, 163–74.

[96] CTB vol. 1, no. 107, pp. 494–95.

[97] CTB vol. 1, no. 133, pp. 624–25.

[98] CTB vol. 1, no. 135, pp. 630–31. See also CTB vol. 1, no. 136, pp. 632–35; no. 138, pp. 638–39; no. 154, pp. 722–25.

[99] Herbert of Bosham, *Vita*, in MTB 3:413–15; Staunton, *Lives*, 153–54; William fitz Stephen, *Vita*, in MTB 3:87; Staunton, *Lives*, 164; CTB vol. 2, no. 195, pp. 850–55; nos. 196a–199, pp. 856–65; no. 201, pp. 870–73, no. 207, pp. 900–90; nos. 209–14, pp. 910–37; no. 216, pp. 950–51; Guy, *Thomas Becket*, 271–72; Duggan, *Thomas*

Following these dramatic events Pope Alexander III dispatched two nuncios, the canon lawyers Master Gratian of Pisa and Master Vivian of Orvieto, to command Henry II to make peace with Becket. In August and early September 1169, Henry summoned a council of French prelates to Domfort to support him in a series of meetings with the papal emissaries. Several Cistercians were present: Geoffrey of Auxerre, the abbots of Beaubec and Mortemer, and, most significantly, the abbot of Rievaulx, Aelred's successor Sylvanus, formerly the abbot of Dundrennan. The talks failed because of the nuncios' reluctance to travel to England to absolve the excommunicates who were there and of Henry's last-minute insertion of the phrase "saving the dignity of his realm" into the peace agreement with the archbishop.[100] The importance of the Cistercians to the king's cause is shown by the fact that Henry immediately drafted a letter presenting his case to be carried by Brother Geoffrey and the three abbots to the general chapter at Cîteaux, which met on September 14.[101]

At the beginning of 1170 an embassy from the Latin Kingdom of Jerusalem produced a fleeting agreement upon a joint Anglo-French crusade, and as part of the agreement, Henry declared his intention to make peace with Becket. Alexander of Cologne, who was the abbot of Cîteaux, along with Geoffrey of Auxerre and Geoffrey Foulquia, the master of the Temple, attempted to bring Becket to Chaumont to be reconciled with the king, but the venture came to nothing.[102] Later talks were more successful, and in July 1170 Henry II and Thomas Becket met at Fréteval and made peace.[103] Becket returned to his see of Canterbury on December

Becket, 155–56; Barlow, *Thomas Becket*, 184; Bredero, "Canonization," 95; Newman, *Boundaries*, 214–15.

[100] CTB vol. 2, no. 227, pp. 978–87; Herbert of Bosham, *Vita*, in MTB 3:441–44; MTB vol. 7, no. 564, pp. 82–85; Duggan, *Thomas Becket*, 167–71; Barlow, *Thomas Becket*, 189.

[101] MTB vol. 7, no. 568, pp. 90–92; Duggan, *Thomas Becket*, 172.

[102] CTB vol. 2, no. 265, pp. 1140–41, and n. 4, no. 269, pp. 1148–49; Duggan, *Thomas Becket*, 180–81; Barlow, *Thomas Becket*, 200.

[103] William fitz Stephen, *Vita*, in MTB 3:107–12; Staunton, *Lives*, 174–78; Edward Grim, *Vita*, in MTB 2:422; Herbert of Bosham, *Vita*, in MTB 3:466–67; Roger of

1, only to be murdered before the high altar of his own cathedral less than a month later, on December 29.[104] Abbot Walter of the Cistercian abbey of Boxley, together with Richard, prior of Dover, supervised the burial of the martyred archbishop.[105]

When news of the murder became public, King Henry, fearing that the archbishop of Sens was about to impose an interdict on his lands, dispatched an embassy to plead his case. Abbot Richard de Blosseville of the Cistercian abbey of Le Valasse was a member of the group.[106] Abbot Richard was also part of a similar mission to the pope in March 1171.[107] Eventually Alexander III agreed to lift the excommunications of the archbishop of York and the bishops of London and Salisbury, a decision that outraged Becket's supporters. Two papal legates were sent to resolve matters, and Abbot Richard was again used as an intermediary, this time as part of a delegation that went to summon Henry back from Ireland to answer for his conduct.[108] In May 1172 public ceremonies of reconciliation were held at Caen and Avranches.[109] On Ash Wednesday

---

Pontigny, *Vita*, in MTB 4:67; Lambeth Anonymous, *Vita*, in MTB 4:119–20; CTB, vol. 2, nos. 299–300, pp. 1258–79; Guy, *Thomas Becket*, 289–96; Duggan, *Thomas Becket*, 183–88; Barlow, *Thomas Becket*, 208–11; Warren, *Henry II*, 505–6.

[104] Herbert of Bosham, *Vita*, in MTB 3:476–80, 491–507; Staunton, *Lives*, 182–85; Edward Grim, *Vita*, in MTB 2:430–39; Staunton, *Lives*, 195–203; John of Salisbury, *Vita*, in MTB 2:319–20; Benedict of Peterborough, *Passio Sancti Thomae Cantuariensis*, in MTB 2:1–16; William of Canterbury, *Vita*, in MTB 1:129–35; William fitz Stephen, *Vita*, in MTB 3:132–42; Roger of Pontigny, *Vita*, in MTB 4:70–77; Lambeth Anonymous, *Vita*, in MTB 4:128–31; Ralph of Diceto, *Opera Historica*, 1:343–44; Guy, *Thomas Becket*, 310–22; Duggan, *Thomas Becket*, 208–13; Barlow, *Thomas Becket*, 235–50; Warren, *Henry II*, 509–11.

[105] William fitz Stephen, *Vita*, in MTB 3:148; Ralph of Diceto, *Opera Historica*, 1:345; Duggan, *Thomas Becket*, 215.

[106] Barlow, *Thomas Becket*, 253.

[107] Roger of Hoveden, *Chronica*, 2:26–28; Barlow, *Thomas Becket*, 255; Duggan, *Thomas Becket*, 220.

[108] Lansdowne Anonymous, "*Excerpta E Codice MS^{to} Lansdowniano 398*," in MTB 4:169; Barlow, *Thomas Becket*, 260.

[109] Lansdowne Anonymous, "*Excerpta*," in MTB 4:173–74; Staunton, *Lives*, 216–17; Lambeth Anonymous, *Vita*, in MTB 4:143–44; Ralph of Diceto, *Opera Historica*, 1:352; Roger of Hoveden, *Chronica*, 2:35–39; Guy, *Thomas Becket*, 327–29; Barlow, *Thomas Becket*, 261; Warren, *Henry II*, 530–34.

1173 Pope Alexander III issued the formal bull of canonization for Thomas Becket,[110] and on July 12, 1174, King Henry II did public penance for the murder at Canterbury cathedral.[111]

This brief account of the long and involved quarrel between King Henry II and Archbishop Thomas Becket is sufficient to show that Cistercians were involved at every step of the way, as messengers, negotiators, and providers of sanctuary. Of course it cannot be assumed that every monastery that opened its guesthouse to a traveler, provided a meeting place, or dispatched a messenger thereby became committed to one side or the other in the dispute. When the monks of Clairmarais took in the weary archbishop when he first arrived on the continent in 1164, they were surely bound as much by the duty of hospitality as by any particular partisanship in the affair. When Abbot Philip of L'Aumône attempted to mediate between the king and the archbishop in 1163, he was acting at the behest of the pope, not of either party to the quarrel. The monks of Clairvaux may not even have known what Thomas Becket was going to say on Palm Sunday 1169 when he mounted the pulpit in the abbey church to proclaim the excommunication of Bishops Gilbert Foliot of London and Jocelin of Salisbury. Nevertheless, at a minimum these interactions gave many members of the Order the opportunity to hear the issues at stake in the quarrel, to meet the adherents of both sides, and to form some opinion of the case.[112]

It is also clear that some houses and individual members of the Order did take sides. Becket's two-year residence at Pontigny surely places that house squarely on his side in the quarrel. Most obviously, King Henry's threat to expel the Cistercians from England because of Becket's continued presence at Pontigny creates the overwhelming impression that most of the Order sided with the archbishop. On the other side, however, the Cistercian

---

[110] Duggan, *Thomas Becket*, 229–30; Barlow, *Thomas Becket*, 268–69.

[111] Edward Grim, *Vita*, in MTB 2:445–47; Staunton, *Lives*, 217–19; Barlow, *Thomas Becket*, 269–70.

[112] Newman, *Boundaries*, 209–18.

cardinal William of Pavia was widely perceived as a friend of Henry II, even though his attempts at mediation were mandated by the pope. The presence of Geoffrey of Auxerre and the abbots of Beaubec, Mortemer, and Rievaulx with Henry II at Domfort in 1169 and their subsequent appearance on his behalf before the Cistercian general chapter indicates that they supported the king. Likewise Richard of Le Valasse acted as an emissary and negotiator for the king in the aftermath of the murder.

Thus even though on the one hand the Order was threatened with catastrophic punishment for its support of Becket, some Cistercians actively and publicly supported the king. The case of Geoffrey of Auxerre points to a split in the Order so severe that it may have cost one abbot his position. The use of Cistercian monks as messengers in the case was widespread, and it appears that in some cases their own abbots did not approve, for Pope Alexander III found it necessary to send a letter to all the Cistercian abbots warning them not to punish monks who aided the archbishop.[113]

As for Aelred himself, he was coming to the end of his life by the time the Becket affair erupted, and there is no direct evidence of his participation in the matter. Several bits of evidence, however, point to his probable opinion of the matter. His early career at the court of David of Scotland, his friendships with Gilbert Foliot and Roger of Pont L'Évêque, his correspondence with Robert of Leicester, and his literary works supportive of and dedicated to Henry II all suggest that he would have been very much predisposed to support the king over the archbishop. His sermon for the translation of the relics of Saint Edward the Confessor, while appropriate to the occasion, was certainly royalist in tone, and coming as it did immediately before the council at Westminster, at which the quarrel between Henry and Becket first burst into full view, it placed Aelred on the king's side in a very public way.

The letter from Rievaulx to the archbishop, probably written before Becket's exile in 1164, is largely negative in tone and echoes

---

[113] MTB, *Epistolae*, vol. 5, no. 150, pp. 262–63. See Newman, *Boundaries of Charity*, 216–17, regarding division within the Order over the Becket case.

criticisms made by Becket's enemies, especially Gilbert Foliot. If this letter was written by Aelred himself, it constitutes further evidence for Aelred's royalist inclinations and for his connection with Foliot, Becket's most formidable opponent. If written by former abbot Maurice or someone else at Rievaulx, it suggests that Aelred's probable viewpoint had come to be shared by others at the abbey. The presence of Aelred's successor Sylvanus among Henry's advisors in 1169 indicates that support for the king at Rievaulx had not perished with the death of its most influential abbot.

Chapter 10

Conclusion

Aelred of Rievaulx: Politician and Peacemaker

One thing about Aelred's public career should be very clear—the abbot of Rievaulx was a busy man. When Aelred portrayed himself occupied with the worldly affairs of the monastery while his monks waited impatiently for a moment of his time, he was undoubtedly describing a frequent situation. Rievaulx received a minimal grant from its founder, Walter Espec, and was soon left without a patron when Espec died without a direct heir. Therefore it fell to Aelred and the other early abbots to build that initial gift into an endowment sufficient to support the monks who soon flocked there. Rievaulx's estates were built up piecemeal amid the uncertainties of the Anglo-Norman civil war, and multiple grants, quitclaims, and confirmations underlay each bit of land that came into the abbey's possession. Aelred was thus responsible for the maintenance of a network of Rievaulx's secular friends and patrons, only a small number of whom have been identified in these pages. In addition, the construction of several of the major buildings of the abbey took place during his tenure in office.[1]

Aelred also became closely involved in the affairs of the church as a whole. He appeared at the court of Archbishop Roger of Pont L'Évêque of York, where he helped settle a disagreement regarding

---

[1] See above, chap. 4:68–80.

the relationship between York and Durham.[2] He maintained close relations with the monks of Durham, especially with Prior Laurence and the historian Reginald. There again Aelred was called upon to mediate a dispute within the community over the seat of the prior in the choir. Both Archbishop Roger of York and Bishop Hugh du Puiset of Durham became friends and patrons of Rievaulx.[3]

Aelred also became a special friend to neighboring monasteries. He was closely involved with the integration of the Savigniac houses into the Cistercian Order, sending representatives from Rievaulx to assist them in adjusting to the stricter rule of his order. He also stepped in to mediate disputes between Byland and Furness over Byland's claim to be a daughter house of Savigny and over its possession of the daughter house at Jervaulx.[4] Aelred was close to Gilbert of Sempringham and the Gilbertines, and the mention of a community of Gilbertine nuns in one of his sermons suggests that he was an honored visitor there. He earned the trust of his fellow religious, so making it logical for them to call upon him to investigate the scandalous affair of the young nun made pregnant by one of the lay brothers at Watton.[5]

Aelred was in demand as a preacher on special occasions, with Walter Daniel reporting that he had preached over two hundred sermons to various groups outside the monastery's walls. Of his surviving sermons, three are identified as having been preached *in synodo*, one of them at either Troyes or the council of Tours in 1163, perhaps when Aelred was on the continent attending the general chapter at Cîteaux. One, and probably two, sermons were delivered to monasteries of nuns. Aelred's *History of the Saints of Hexham* was a sermon composed and delivered at the translation of the relics of the saints of his home church at Hexham.[6] His relative, Prior Lawrence of Westminster, commissioned him to write

---

[2] See above, chap. 4:84–85.

[3] See above, chap. 4:80–84.

[4] See above, chap. 4:85–90.

[5] See above, chap. 5:108–9, 115–27.

[6] See above, chap. 1:8–9. For the possibility that the sermon at Troyes was actually preached at the council of Tours in 1163, see above, chap. 9:200–201.

a new *Life of Saint Edward the Confessor* for the translation of the saint's relics to a new shrine in Westminster Abbey, and Aelred probably preached a sermon derived from this work at the celebration on October 13, 1163.[7]

Such public activities made it necessary for Aelred to travel widely, and Walter Daniel portrayed him as telling his monks as he lay dying that he was now going away from them just as he had often been absent from them when he went to transact business at the royal court.[8] He traveled to general chapter meetings at Cîteaux, perhaps stopping to visit his friends at Durham on the way. He visited Rievaulx's two daughter houses in Scotland, Dundrennan and Melrose, and took the opportunity to call on King David at the royal court as well. He was a friend of Bishop Christian of Whithorn and was well enough known and respected in Galloway to settle a quarrel between Fergus of Galloway and King Malcolm IV that led to Fergus's retirement to the monastery at Holyrood.[9]

Aelred traveled to the English royal court as well, and he can be placed there twice in 1163. He was present at Westminster in March when the controversy over the right of St. Alban's Abbey to be independent of the bishop of Lincoln was settled.[10] He reportedly returned in October to preach at the translation of the relics of Saint Edward the Confessor.[11] According to the *Peterborough Chronicle* Aelred was instrumental in convincing Henry II to recognize Alexander III as pope in the schism of 1159. The chronicle states that his contribution was made *viva voce*, but it is not clear whether this meant that Aelred spoke at the council of Westminster where the English hierarchy gave its recommendation in favor of Alexander or whether Aelred met with Henry II

---

[7] See above, chap. 8:181–83.
[8] Vita A 50, p. 57; CF 57:134.
[9] See above, chap. 7:165–71.
[10] See above, chap. 8:178–79.
[11] See above, chap. 8:185–89.

in person on the continent, perhaps as Aelred traveled to the general chapter.[12]

These three trips illustrate another important point about Aelred's later life. It has sometimes been assumed that he became bedridden and unable to travel for as much as ten years before his death in 1167.[13] This view is based on Walter Daniel's statement that because of Aelred's infirmities the Cistercian general chapter granted him many freedoms in the way he conducted the business of his abbey.[14] Nowhere does he say that the chapter specifically exempted the abbot from travel, and Merton, McGuire, Squire, and Burton have all recognized this.[15] Many of the incidental notices of Aelred's travels contained in Walter Daniel's biography, other narrative sources, and charter evidence cannot be firmly dated, but enough examples that can be pinned down prove that the abbot actually continued to travel until almost the very end of his life. In 1159, in addition to a possible journey relating to the papal schism, Aelred witnessed a notification by Roger of Pont L'Évêque that the abbot of Rufford was to pay one mark annually to Canon Paulinus of York, a fact that probably indicates a trip either to Rufford, one of Rievaulx's daughter houses, or to the archiepiscopal court at York.[16]

Aelred also made two trips on matters relating to the Gilbertine Order. In 1164 he and several other English Cistercian abbots met with Gilbert of Sempringham at Kirkstead to draw up an agreement defining relationships between Cistercian and Gilbertine

---

[12] See above, chap. 8:174–78.

[13] Douglas Roby, "Chimera of the North: The Active Life of Aelred of Rievaulx," in *Cistercian Ideals and Reality*, ed. John Sommerfeldt, CS 60 (Kalamazoo, MI: Cistercian Publications, 1978), 158–59.

[14] Vita A 31, pp. 39–40; CF 57:119–20.

[15] Brian Patrick McGuire, *Brother and Lover: Aelred of Rievaulx* (New York: Crossroad Publishing Co., 1994), 119; Aelred Squire, *Aelred of Rievaulx: A Study*, CS 50 (Kalamazoo, MI: Cistercian Publications, 1981), 64–65; Thomas Merton, "St. Aelred of Rievaulx and the Cistercians," Pt. 5, CSQ 24, no. 1 (1989): 62; Pierre-André Burton, *Aelred de Rievaulx (1110–1167), De l'homme éclaté à l'être unifié: Essai de biographie existentielle et spirituelle* (Paris: Éditions du Cerf, 2010), 317–19.

[16] EEA 20, no. 88; see above, chap. 4:93.

houses established close to one another.[17] He also traveled to the neighboring monastery of Watton at the request of Gilbert of Sempringham to investigate the strange events surrounding the incident of the pregnant nun.[18]

Aelred also made at least three trips to Scotland toward the end of his life. Jocelin of Furness reported that Aelred visited his friend Waldef at Melrose in 1159, shortly before the latter's death.[19] Powicke suggested that this trip also included the visit to Godric of Finchale recorded by Reginald of Durham, during which the hermit prophesied the death of Saint Robert of Newminster, which occurred on June 7, 1159.[20] Aelred visited Galloway around 1160, when the cessation of hostilities between King Malcolm IV and Fergus of Galloway resulted in the latter's retirement to the monastery at Holyrood.[21] Reginald of Durham noted that Aelred was visiting in Kirkcudbright on the feast of Saint Cuthbert, March 20, 1164, where he witnessed the chain binding a penitent's waist being miraculously struck off.[22] Walter Daniel recorded a visit to an unnamed daughter house in Galloway two years before the abbot's death, during which Aelred's bedding was miraculously preserved from being soaked by rainwater pouring through a leaky roof.[23] This story may be a reference to the trip noted by Reginald of Durham. Similarly Reginald recorded that the abbot of Melrose consulted Aelred about certain miracles that had occurred in the neighborhood.[24] This consultation could also have taken place during the 1164 trip, but Powicke suggested that it

[17] See above, chap. 5:120.

[18] See above, chap. 5:121–27.

[19] Jocelin of Furness, *Vita S. Waltheni Abbatis, Acta Sanctorum*, August 3, 266–67.

[20] Reginald of Durham, *Libellus de vita et miraculis S. Godrici heremitae de Finchale*, Surtees Society 20 (London: J. B. Nichols and Sons, 1847), 169–77; Powicke, Introduction to Vita A, xcii.

[21] See above, chap. 7:166–68.

[22] Reginald of Durham, *Libellus de Admirandis Beati Cuthberti Virtutibus*, Surtees Society 1 (London: J. B. Nichols and Sons, 1835), 178; see above, chap. 7:167–68.

[23] Vita A, *Letter to Maurice*, 4, pp. 74–75; CF 57:153–54; see above, chap. 7:168.

[24] Reginald of Durham, *Beati Cuthberti*, 188.

might have taken place as late as the spring of 1166.[25] The last ten years of Aelred's life were also a period of extraordinary literary activity, during which he produced his sermons on Isaiah, *Spiritual Friendship, The Life of Edward, A Certain Wonderful Miracle, On the Soul,* and probably *On the Formation of Anchoresses* and *Jesus as a Boy of Twelve.*[26] Undoubtedly Aelred felt the aches and pains of old age during the last years of his life, but it does not seem that he was too incapacitated to travel or to fulfill his duties as abbot.

As for Aelred's historical writings, it becomes apparent that such writing was more than an idle hobby, or even an intellectual passion, for him. It has frequently been pointed out that these works are to be read on multiple levels. Aelred had a strong interest in the facts of history and a unique talent for organizing and recounting them. The same compositions taught spiritual truths, and the author delighted in drawing parallels between scriptural personalities and events and those of English history. It is also striking that many of his historical works addressed a contemporary situation and were written to support a particular point of view. This is least clear in the case of the *Life of Saint Ninian,* but even this work can be seen as a plea for support of the reforming Bishop Christian of Whithorn, perhaps on the occasion of his consecration to the see.[27] Three of Aelred's historical works, the *Battle of the Standard,* the *Lament for King David I,* and the *Genealogy of the Kings of the English,* were composed during the period between the Treaty of Winchester in 1153 and the death of King Stephen in 1154; taken together they constitute a plea for the upholding of the treaty and the acceptance of the new king, Henry II.[28] *The Life of Edward* and the sermon for the translation of the relics drawn from that work also came at a critical time in Henry's reign, just at the beginning of the king's long quarrel with

---

[25] Powicke, Introduction to Vita A, xciv.
[26] Powicke, Introduction to Vita A, xcii–xciv.
[27] See above, chap. 7:157–62.
[28] See above, chap. 6:134–38.

Archbishop Thomas Becket. The strongly royalist tone of these works placed Aelred on the side of the king in this bitter dispute.[29]

Miracle, the sad story of the nun of Watton, is perhaps more a record of current events than a work of English history, but the same characteristics are present. When it is considered in light of the revolt of the lay brothers of Sempringham, which came shortly afterward, it can be seen that Aelred's work was more than a naive recounting of some strange, reputedly miraculous events surrounding the termination of the nun's pregnancy. It was instead a concerted effort to highlight the general sanctity of the other nuns, to cast the affair in the best possible light, and to rescue the Gilbertines from the consequences of the unfortunate event.[30]

The picture of Aelred that emerges from this study of his public life leaves one in awe of his accomplishments. He built up the abbey's endowment, supervised the construction of its major buildings, advised the kings of two countries, and befriended neighboring monastic communities. Perhaps the most striking feature of his career is the frequency with which he participated in the settlement of disputes, both within and between local religious communities and in the world outside the cloister.[31] Despite the press of daily business and his frequent journeys away from Rievaulx, he found time to write both profoundly spiritual treatises and historical studies with a special relevance to the issues of his day.

If Aelred accomplished so much, why then was he under a cloud, his reputation in doubt, at the time of his death? As was discussed in chapter 1,[32] Walter Daniel indicated that Aelred had a number of critics and hoped that the prayers of the unknown Abbot H, to whom the work was dedicated, and his monks would "make truth prevail over the opinion of many."[33] The text itself contains several references to Aelred's critics, including those who

[29] See above, chap. 8:185–89.
[30] See above, chap. 5:115–27.
[31] Merton, "St. Aelred," pt. 5, 55.
[32] See above, chap. 1:4–8.
[33] Vita A 1, p. 1; CF 57:89.

accused him of ambition at the time of his election as abbot[34] and others who suspected a lack of discipline at Rievaulx.[35] As Aelred lay on his deathbed he told the monks gathered around him, "My soul calls God to witness that, since I received this habit of religion, the malice, detraction or quarrel of no man has ever kindled any feeling in me against him which has been strong enough to last the day in the domicile of my heart."[36] After Walter's work had circulated, he was forced to compose a letter directed to a Lord Maurice, probably the prior of the Augustinian house of Kirkham, answering criticisms of the *Vita*.[37]

Two reasons have been advanced for the apparent disapproval of Aelred at the end of his life. As was noted in chapter 1, Brian Patrick McGuire and others have suggested that the possibly homosexual Aelred played favorites, collecting a group of special friends about himself, and that this fact caused the other monks to become jealous.[38] This argument seems to fail on two points. It rests largely on Walter Daniel's description of a special group of monks gathered at Aelred's bedside in the little room that had been built beside the infirmary for him when he became ill at the end of his life. As Peter Fergusson has pointed out, the room that Walter Daniel called a *mausoleum* was in fact a large, permanent room, which accommodated the entire community during Aelred's final hours. Fergusson considered the room to have been built as a private office for the abbot so that he could attend to the monastery's business without disturbing the solitude of the cloister.[39] This suggestion would seem to challenge the idea of the private nature and intimacy of the gatherings that took place there.

Secondly, McGuire himself has described the evolution of the role of the abbot in relation to his monks. He pointed out that

---

[34] Vita A 26, pp. 33–34; CF 57:115; Dutton, Introduction to *Life of Aelred*, CF 57:30–31.

[35] Vita A 30–31, pp. 39–40; CF 57:119–20.

[36] Vita A 50, pp. 57–58; CF 57:134–35.

[37] Vita A, *Letter to Maurice*, p. 66; CF 57:147.

[38] See above, chap. 1:7.

[39] See above, chap. 4:79–80.

when monasticism took root in the East, the care and counseling of monks was looked upon as a distraction from the abbot's concentration on his own spiritual development. Under the Benedictine Rule, the abbot was indeed held responsible for the salvation of his monks, but McGuire describes this as a rather mechanistic accounting, with little detail given about exactly how the abbot would accomplish this role. Early Cistercian writing, however, advised the abbot to enter into a close relationship with his monks, so that he would learn how best to promote each man's personal spiritual growth.[40] How would Aelred have been able to achieve this without the opportunity for close, intimate conversations with his charges?

A second theory for Aelred's reportedly bad reputation suggests that Aelred did too good a job enlarging the abbey's property, that he spent too much time away from Rievaulx, especially at the royal court, and that he was too involved in secular affairs. His very success as an abbot acted against him by inspiring jealousy among his less capable colleagues.[41] There are problems with this suggestion as well. All monasteries were dependent upon the generosity of their benefactors, and if Aelred had not built up Rievaulx's endowment, or had allowed it to be jeopardized during the civil war, the abbey would have been condemned to poverty and ultimate failure. Proper attention to Rievaulx's financial affairs was simply part of his duty as abbot. Furthermore, while Aelred certainly developed a significant patronage network for Rievaulx and claimed his fair share of the charitable pie, he definitely did not monopolize the attention of his donors. As was noted in chapter 4, Rievaulx's benefactors also patronized other religious houses, especially other Cistercian houses and the monasteries of other reformed religious orders.[42]

---

[40] Brian Patrick McGuire, "Taking Responsibility: Medieval Cistercian Abbots as Their Brothers' Keepers," *Cîteaux: Commentarii Cistercienses* 39 (1988): 249–68. See also Thomas Merton, "St. Aelred of Rievaulx and the Cistercians," pt. 4, CSQ 23, no. 1 (1988): 51.

[41] See above, chap. 1:7–8.

[42] See above, chap. 4:75–77.

In the same way, Aelred's activities in the outside world reflected what other Cistercian abbots also did. Of course Bernard of Clairvaux involved himself in virtually every important event of his time, but as was discussed in chapter 2, a number of other Cistercian abbots did so as well.[43] Aelred's predecessor, Abbot William, spearheaded the opposition to the election of Archbishop William fitz Herbert of York and was involved in negotiations during the civil war.[44] Cistercians were involved at every step of the Becket controversy, as messengers, negotiators, and providers of hospitality.[45] Aelred's activities in the outside world also paid dividends for his abbey. His friendships with David of Scotland, Fergus of Galloway, King Henry II, Pope Alexander III, Archbishop Roger of Pont L'Évêque, and Bishop Hugh du Puiset all resulted in numerous benefits for Rievaulx and her daughter houses over the years.[46]

Since these two theories seem inadequate to explain the challenges to Aelred's good reputation, a third suggestion can be made. Perhaps Aelred became unpopular within his own order and even among members of other monastic communities because of one specific aspect of his public career: his support of Henry II in his quarrel with Archbishop Thomas Becket. The evidence for Aelred's stance in the matter is at best indirect, resting mainly upon his own writing in support of the king in other matters and upon his friendship with Becket's known enemies, especially Gilbert Foliot, Roger of Pont L'Évêque, and Robert of Leicester.[47] Two additional pieces of evidence also link Rievaulx itself with the forces that opposed Becket. The critical tone of the letter to the archbishop from an unknown author at Rievaulx, whether Aelred, Maurice, or someone else, certainly aligned the abbey with the

[43] See above, chap. 2:19–23, 30–31. See also Martha G. Newman, *The Boundaries of Charity: Cistercian Culture and Ecclesiastical Reform, 1098–1180* (Stanford, CA: Stanford University Press, 1996), 191–218.

[44] See above, chap. 2:18; chap. 3:51; chap. 5:115.

[45] See above, chap. 8:190; chap. 9:213–21.

[46] See above, chap. 3:39–41; chap. 4:80–82, 93–94; chap. 6:131–34; chap. 7:163–68; chap. 8:174–80.

[47] See above, chap. 4:93–95; chap. 8:180–81; chap. 9:194–95.

archbishop's opponents, as did the presence of Abbot Sylvanus among the king's supporters in 1169.[48] Becket's exile at Pontigny and Henry II's consequent threats against the Order create the impression that the Cistercian Order was overwhelmingly on the side of Thomas Becket in his quarrel with the king.[49] It is probably true that the majority of Cistercian houses did side with the archbishop, but with notable exceptions like Geoffrey of Auxerre and Richard of Le Valasse.[50] Nevertheless, if Aelred chose to align himself and his abbey with this group, he would certainly have been in the minority.

Aelred's support of Gilbert of Sempringham and his order may have been another cause of disagreement between Aelred and Thomas Becket. When Becket learned of the revolt of the lay brothers, he dispatched two scalding letters from Pontigny, one of them threatening Gilbert with excommunication. His opponents at home in England, including Roger of York and Hugh of Durham, as well as the king himself, rallied to the support of the Order.[51] Aelred was already involved in the possible early stages of this quarrel with his investigation at Watton and subsequent efforts on behalf of the nuns there.[52] Could this have been another occasion on which Aelred spoke out, this time on behalf of a cause for which the archbishop apparently had little sympathy?

In any case Becket's quarrel with Henry II was a subject upon which reasonable people might disagree during Aelred's lifetime. Everything, however, changed with Becket's martyrdom in 1170. In its aftermath Becket's memory began to acquire the trappings of sainthood—the prophetic signs at birth, the chaste lifestyle, and the hair shirt. Few had thought of the archbishop's clerk and the king's chancellor as holy at the time, but after his shocking death, his biographers began to explain away his failings, typically by

---

[48] See above, chap. 9:218.
[49] See above, chap. 9:215.
[50] See above, chap. 9:215–21.
[51] See above, chap. 5:123–24; chap. 9:195–96.
[52] See above, chap. 5:121–27.

suggesting a secret chastity and asceticism.[53] Perhaps the Cistercians themselves gloried in their principled support of the martyred archbishop. For example, Lawrence Braceland suggested that two sermons preached by Gilbert of Hoyland on Saint Stephen, the first martyr, contained numerous references that were more appropriate to Thomas Becket. An allusion to a previous, now lost, sermon on Saint Stephen suggests that the two surviving sermons would have been preached on December 27 and 28, the two days following the saint's feast day and preceding the anniversary of Becket's martyrdom on December 29.

Gilbert did not mention Becket by name but referred to him as "our famous protomartyr." It is clear that the term *protomartyr* referred to someone other than Saint Stephen, since Gilbert wrote, "It is a great sign of a protomartyr that he has something in common with them, for he suffered outside the gate with the Lord and the protomartyr Stephen."[54] In this passage Gilbert of Hoyland seems to have sought to associate his order more closely with the murdered archbishop. It is also clear that other religious orders had been impressed by the Cistercians' support of the martyred archbishop. Anne Duggan has pointed out that the first liturgy composed for Becket's first feast day in 1173, by Benedict of Peterborough, a Benedictine, contained a reference to Henry II's threats against the Cistercians: "The king, having sent threatening letters to the General Chapter of the Cistercian Order by certain abbots, procured his [Becket's] removal from Pontigny."[55]

When Aelred died in January 1167 he was probably the holder of a minority viewpoint within his order with regard to the quarrel between the archbishop and the king. Nevertheless, he was not alone in that position, and the subject was in any case still open for

[53] Michael Staunton, *The Lives of Thomas Becket* (Manchester: Manchester University Press, 2001), 1–6.

[54] Gilbert of Hoyland, *The Works of Gilbert of Hoyland IV: Treatises, Epistles, and Sermons with a Letter of Roger of Byland, The Milk of Babes*, trans. Lawrence C. Braceland, CF 34 (Kalamazoo, MI: Cistercian Publications, 1981), 158–61. For Braceland's analysis, see CF 34:192–96.

[55] Anne Duggan, *Thomas Becket* (London: Arnold Publishing, 2004), 230–32.

debate. Four years later, though, the archbishop's martyrdom stilled all criticism, and two years after that, in February 1173, Thomas Becket became England's most revered saint. It is possible that for those who had disagreed with Aelred, his opposition to Thomas Becket cast a strong shadow over an otherwise outstanding career. Today Aelred's view of the Becket controversy remains a matter of conjecture. If he did indeed side with the king instead of the archbishop, today's distance from the events enables us to ignore the aura of sainthood surrounding Becket and accept that neither party to the quarrel was wholly blameless. In any case, it cannot obscure Aelred's outstanding career as spiritual writer, historian, monastic administrator, builder, mediator, and royal counselor.

Aelred ceased to be a courtier and politician when he left the Scottish court and entered Rievaulx. His change in status, however, does not mean that he abandoned his concern for his country and his neighbors at that time. Whether he was securing a quit-claim of lands given to his abbey, counseling religious outside his own order, attending the archiepiscopal court at York, advising the king, or intervening in matters of high secular and ecclesiastical politics, Aelred never ceased working to ensure that other English subjects, both lay and clerical, could enjoy a life of peace, tranquility, and holiness. Thomas Merton said it best: "Ultimately Aelred's ideal for England was the same as his ideal for himself: an ideal of Christian perfection. His ideal of a free and autonomous and unified England united under the royal line descended from Alfred and the Saxon Kings, a Catholic England praising God in justice and truth and sending up to him the sweet incense of adoration from the great shrines of the English saints: all this corresponded to his own aspirations for interior peace and unity."[56] The first great commandment is to love God; the second is to love one's neighbor as oneself. This second imperative propelled Aelred, like Bernard of Clairvaux, out of his monastery into the wider world.

---

[56] Merton, "St. Aelred," pt. 5, 51.

Appendix 1

Chronological Table

1110	Aelred born at Hexham.
1112–1113	Church at Hexham given to Augustinian canons.
Nov. 25, 1120	Henry I's son William dies in the wreck of the White Ship.
Dec. 21, 1120	Thomas Becket born.
April 1124	David I becomes king of Scotland.
ca. 1124	Aelred joins the Scottish royal court.
1125–1133	Refoundation of the see of Whithorn in Galloway.
Jan. 1127	David of Scotland and the English barons swear to support the daughter of Henry I, Empress Matilda, as his successor if he dies without a male heir.
ca. 1131	Gilbert of Sempringham founds a community of nuns at Sempringham.
1132	Foundation of Rievaulx by Walter Espec.
ca. 1134	Aelred becomes a monk at Rievaulx.
1134–1135	Monks from Furness sent to establish a new monastery at Calder.
Dec. 1135	Death of Henry I and coronation of Stephen.
1136	David I invades England.
1137–1138	Monks from Calder move to Byland.
Aug. 22, 1138	Battle of the Standard. Afterward Aelred probably accompanies Abbot William of Rievaulx as he negotiates the surrender of Walter Espec's castle at Wark.

1138	Aelred present at Durham when his father Eilaf turns over his property at Hexham to the Augustinians.
Spring 1139	Treaty of Durham halts fighting in northern England.
Feb. 5, 1140	Death of Archbishop Thurstan of York.
1140	Saint Malachy visits Scotland, northern England, and Clairvaux.
Jan. 1141	William fitz Herbert elected archbishop of York.
Feb. 2, 1141	King Stephen captured at the Battle of Lincoln.
May 6, 1141	Death of Bishop Geoffrey Rufus of Durham. William Cumin illegally takes over the administration of the see.
Sept. 14, 1141	Robert of Gloucester captured at Winchester. King Stephen freed in prisoner exchange.
Dec. 1141	York election dispute referred to Rome by Bishop Henry of Winchester acting as papal legate. Aelred accompanies the anti–fitz Herbert delegation to Rome.
April 1142	Innocent II postpones a decision on the York election dispute. Aelred returns to Rievaulx.
ca. 1142	Foundation of Dundrennan Abbey.
1142–1143	Aelred serves as novice master at Rievaulx, possibly starts writing *Mirror of Charity*, begins correspondence outside the monastery.
March 1143	Innocent II refers the York election dispute to England.
June 20, 1143	William de Ste.-Barbe consecrated bishop of Durham.
Oct. 18, 1143	Bishop William de Ste.-Barbe takes possession of the see of Durham.
1143	Aelred becomes abbot of Revesby.
Feb. 15, 1145	Eugenius III, a Cistercian, is elected pope.

Aug. 2, 1145	Death of William, first abbot of Rievaulx. Maurice succeeds him.
1145	Thomas Becket joins the household of Archbishop Theobald of Canterbury.
1145–1146	Thomas Becket possibly sent to study law at Bologna and Auxerre.
Feb. 1146	Eugenius III suspends Archbishop William fitz Herbert from office.
Nov. 30, 1147	Aelred attests a charter recording the resolution of a dispute at Durham over the position of the prior, the first reference to him as abbot of Rievaulx.
Dec. 7, 1147	Abbot Henry Murdac of Fountains consecrated as archbishop of York.
1147	The congregations of Savigny and Obazine admitted to the Cistercian Order. Gilbert of Sempringham petitions for his order to receive supervision from the Cistercians but is denied.
March 1148	Archbishop Theobald of Canterbury at the council of Rheims, accompanied by Thomas Becket. William fitz Herbert deprived of office.
June 1148	Empress Matilda returns to Normandy.
Oct. 1148	Saint Malachy visits Galloway on his way to Clairvaux. Possible date for the foundation of a monastery at Soulseat.
Nov. 1148	Saint Malachy dies while visiting Clairvaux.
1148	Aelred sends a mission to assist the Savigniac community at Swineshead.
ca. 1150	Consecration of the new cathedral at Whithorn in Galloway. Possible date for Aelred's *Life of Saint Ninian*.
Jan. 25, 1151	Henry Murdac enthroned as archbishop of York.
1151	Aelred resolves the dispute between Savigny and Furness over Byland, concluding that Byland should remain a daughter house of Savigny.

Nov. 13, 1152	Death of Bishop William de Ste.-Barbe of Durham.
Jan. 22, 1153	Election of Hugh du Puiset as bishop of Durham.
Lent 1153	Aelred visits the court of David I.
May 24, 1153	Death of King David I of Scotland.
May 1153–Dec. 1154	Aelred writes *Lament for David I of Scotland*, *Genealogy of the Kings of the English*, and *Report on the Battle of the Standard*.
July 8, 1153	Death of Pope Eugenius III.
Aug. 20, 1153	Death of Bernard of Clairvaux.
Oct. 14, 1153	Death of Archbishop Henry Murdac of York and reelection of William fitz Herbert.
Nov. 1153	Treaty of Winchester ends the Anglo-Norman civil war.
Dec. 20, 1153	Consecration of Hugh du Puiset as bishop of Durham.
May 9, 1154	William fitz Herbert enthroned at York.
June 8, 1154	Death of Archbishop William fitz Herbert of York.
Oct. 10, 1154	Roger of Pont L'Évêque consecrated archbishop of York. Thomas Becket succeeds him as archdeacon of Canterbury.
Oct. 25, 1154	Death of King Stephen.
Dec. 19, 1154	Coronation of Henry II.
Dec. 19, 1154	Consecration of Bishop Christian of Whithorn. Alternative date for Aelred's *Life of Saint Ninian*.
Jan. 1155	Thomas Becket becomes royal chancellor.
March 3, 1155	Aelred preaches at the translation of the relics of the saints of Hexham. The sermon is the basis for his treatise *The Saints of the Church of Hexham*.
1158–1163	Aelred composes *Spiritual Friendship* and his sermons *On the Prophetic Burdens of Isaiah*, and perhaps also *On the Formation of Anchoresses* and *Jesus as a Boy of Twelve*.

Summer 1159	Aelred visits Abbot Waldef at Melrose.
Sept. 7, 1159	Papal election split between Alexander III and Victor IV.
Sept. 29, 1159	Aelred witnesses a charter of Archbishop Roger of Pont L'Évêque of York in favor of Rievaulx's daughter house at Rufford.
June 1160	Council of London recommends the recognition of Alexander III as pope.
Dec. 21, 1160	Pope Alexander III issues a letter taking Rievaulx Abbey under his special protection.
1160	Revolt of the Scottish earls, including Fergus of Galloway, against Malcolm IV. Aelred makes peace between the king and Fergus of Galloway, who retires to the monastery of Holyrood.
May 23, 1162	Thomas Becket elected archbishop of Canterbury.
Fall 1162	Becket resigns as chancellor.
March 8, 1163	Aelred at Westminster, where he witnesses the resolution of the dispute between the bishop of Lincoln and the abbot of St. Albans.
May 18, 1163	Becket present at the Council of Tours and petitions for canonization of Archbishop Anselm. Petition also put forward for the canonization of Bernard of Clairvaux.
Oct. 13, 1163	Aelred probably preaches in Westminster Abbey at the translation of the relics of Edward the Confessor and writes his *Life of Saint Edward the Confessor* for the occasion. The Council of Westminster follows, airing the disagreements between Becket and Henry II.
Jan. 25–27/28, 1164	Council of Clarendon.
March 20, 1164	Aelred visits Kirkcudbright in Galloway on the feast of Saint Cuthbert.
Oct. 6–13, 1164	Council of Northampton.
Nov. 2, 1164	Becket flees England.

Nov. 30, 1164	Becket arrives at Pontigny.
1164	Aelred at Kirkstead, where an agreement regulating relations between the Cistercians and the Gilbertines is drawn up.
1164–1165	Probable date for Aelred's investigation of the affair of the Gilbertine nun of Watton and the writing of *A Certain Wonderful Miracle*.
1164–1165	Revolt of the lay brothers of Sempringham.
1165–1166	Aelred writes *On the Soul*, which he leaves unfinished.
June 12, 1166	Becket excommunicates Henry's supporters at the Benedictine abbey of Vézelay.
Sept. 1166	Henry II writes to Abbot Gilbert of Cîteaux threatening to expel all the Cistercians from England.
Nov. 11, 1166	Becket expelled from Pontigny.
Jan. 12, 1167	Aelred dies.
April 13, 1169	Becket excommunicates Gilbert Foliot, Jocelin of Salisbury, and certain laymen at Clairvaux on Palm Sunday.
Aug. 31–Sept. 2, 1169	Negotiations take place between Henry II and papal nuncios Master Gratian of Pisa and Vivian of Orvieto at Domfort. Present are Abbot Sylvanus of Rievaulx and Geoffrey of Auxerre, the former abbot of Clairvaux.
July 20–22, 1170	Peace talks between Henry II and Becket at Fréteval are successful.
Dec. 1, 1170	Becket returns to England.
Dec. 29, 1170	Becket murdered in Canterbury Cathedral.
May 21 and 30, 1172	Henry II participates in reconciliation ceremonies at Avranches and Caen.
Feb. 21, 1173	Alexander III issues a bull of canonization for Becket.
June 12, 1174	Henry II does penance at Canterbury.

Appendix 2

Abbot Aelred of Rievaulx's Letter to Gilbert, Venerable Bishop of London[1]

Translated by R. Jacob McDonie

Translator's introduction:

Aelred of Rievaulx (1110–1167), abbot of Rievaulx and the most influential Cistercian in twelfth-century England, here writes a letter to Gilbert Foliot, bishop of London at the time. This letter, Aelred's only extant one, prefaces a group of thirty-one sermons—Sermons on the Burdens of the Prophet Isaiah—*which Aelred composed and timorously sends to Gilbert for his approval. The* Sermons *concern the prophetic visions of destruction of certain sinful tribes and nations as recorded in Isaiah 13–16. Burden* translates Latin onus, *which translates Hebrew* maśśā', *rendered in Greek as* ὅρασις, *"vision." Jerome, in his commentary on these passages of Isaiah, defends his translation as* onus, *"burden," because of the somberness of the visions. Likewise, in the* Sermons *Aelred often treats Isaiah's "burdens" literally, stressing a vision of oppression in a world weighed down by sin.*

[1] Reprinted from R. Jacob McDonie, "Abbot Aelred of Rievaulx's Letter to Gilbert, Venerable Bishop of London," CSQ 45, no. 2 (2010): 119–24, by permission from CSQ. Scriptural references appear here as marginal notes.

Metaphorically, burden *expresses the responsibility of Aelred and his audience to interpret the prophecies and incorporate their message into their spiritual lives. In the exegesis of the prophecies he undertakes for the education of his monks Aelred explores their literal, typological, moral, and anagogical senses, and applies the lessons of the types and consequences of sin to his own time.*

The letter, however, gives almost no information on the content of the sermons. It is valuable, rather, as a personal account of Aelred's Cistercian theology of love and friendship which he expresses to Gilbert, and of which he writes in several other works, especially The Mirror of Charity *and* Spiritual Friendship. *The presence of these works is everywhere felt in the letter. After employing the customary medieval* topos *of humility and protesting his unworthiness of Gilbert's attention, Aelred boldly professes that he will "lean on the laws of love* [legibus amoris], *in which there is nothing of humility or sublimity* [cui nihil humile, nihil sublime est]," *to bring a lowly creature like himself and a person of Gilbert's eminence to the same level, just as God and humankind were united in Christ. The rhetoric of ontological love and unity provides both the occasion for Aelred to write to Gilbert and the reason why Gilbert should read the sermons. Aelred stands knocking at the doors* (pulsantem fores) *of Gilbert's friendship hoping that his soul might be led into friendship's inner chamber* (cubiculum), *thus echoing the process-oriented and deliberative model of friendship that Aelred presents in* Spiritual Friendship. *In this letter, friendship is the supreme* captatio benevolentiae, *for it is through their mystically joined and charitable will that Aelred hopes Gilbert will approach the sermons.*

The translation of this letter is based on the following Latin edition: Aelredi Rieuallensis homeliae de oneribus propheticis Isaiae, *ed. Gaetano Raciti,* Corpus Christianorum Continuatio Mediaeualis 2 *D*

(Turnhout: Brepols, 2005) 3–5. To my knowledge, the best, though still only partial, critical discussion of the homeliae *appears in Aelred Squire,* Aelred of Rievaulx: A Study *(London: SPCK, 1969; repr., 1981) 134–45, with page references to the reprint. I have relied on Raciti's annotations of Aelred's allusions to Scripture and his own works. I have checked them for accuracy and transcribed them here. The use of italics within the text indicates a quotation of or reference to Scripture. Henceforth, notes of my own are indicated with an asterisk. Whenever possible I have tried to insert footnotes only at the end of clauses to make the reading smoother, while still trying to facilitate ease of reference. As a matter of habit, I always note what Latin words I am translating as* soul *and* mind, *for, in this letter, Aelred tends to use* anima *and* animus *interchangeably as* soul, *and* mens *as* mind. Spirit *and* spiritual *always translate some form of* spiritus *and* spiritalis, *respectively. I am grateful to Jesse Weiner, to an anonymous reviewer with* Cistercian Studies Quarterly, *and especially to Father Mark Scott for their very helpful comments on my translation.*
University of California, Irvine

Text

1. To the beloved and loving holy Father Gilbert, bishop of London, with all the sweetness of devotion embracing you: Brother Aelred, of the poor in Christ of Rievaulx, sending indebted service with all affection.[2]

---

[2] *Gilbert Foliot (ca. 1110–18 February 1187), abbot of Gloucester (1139–1148), bishop of Hereford (1148–1163), bishop of London (1163–1187).

*Aelred's notion of *affectus* is difficult to translate with complete precision. Some translate it simply as "affection" and others as "attachment." It is probably best to let Aelred speak for himself

2. Most blessed father, cultivator of wisdom, and friend of peace eager for spiritual knowledge: I have heard that between many tasks, imposed upon you by the authority of your regal dignity or the necessity of pastoral care, you still find time for reading and, moreover, that between the sweet delights of prayer, you assuage the burden of concerns related to your position with repeated meditation on holy Scripture. With this in mind, I have grown very fond of you not only because I hope to become acquainted with your serenity, but also—which *I say in foolishness*—because I dare to aspire to friendship itself.* *see Oner 15.28 (CCCM 2 D:139); 2 Cor 11:21

3. Forgetful, indeed, that you are as eminent as I am lowly, I lean on the laws of love in which there is nothing of humility or sublimity.[3] It is the same love that, leveling heaven and earth, placed the Lord of heaven into mortal limbs, so that *the Word became flesh and dwelt among us;** the same love that pulled down the Lord and raised up humankind, so that misery and mercy would meet each other, as if in a kind of middle;** the same love that caused power to unite itself with infirmity,** so that they would be *in the flesh one* Word and soul, in which God and human would be one person.*[4] Therefore, what most exalted

*John 1:14

*see Ps 84:11

*see 2 Cor 12:9; 13:4

*see Gen 2:24; Eph 5:31

---

on this matter: *Est igitur affectus spontanea quaedam ac dulcis ipsius animi ad aliquem inclinatio* ("Therefore, affection is a kind of spontaneous and sweet inclination of the spirit toward someone"); Spec car 3.11.31 (CCCM 1:119). Those who translate *affectus* as "attachment" usually claim that "affection" makes *affectus* seem too ephemeral, when it is in fact for Aelred a much more committed bond. "Attachment," however, to my mind, is less accurate because it takes the sweetness out of *affectus*. For Aelred, friendship is a happy marriage of reason and pleasant, committed *affectus*, and I have chosen to emphasize the pleasantness of *affectus* in translating this letter.

[3] *For this very Cistercian and Pauline idea, see Gal 3:28 and 1 Cor 12:13.

[4] *Soul* translates *anima* here and below.

things would love not abase, or base things exalt, in order to be one? For by means of the soul such a love, whose natural property remains sound and ordered, so wonderfully mixes heaven with earth, the Lord with flesh, and spirit with dust.

4. Moreover, I see in every creature, even in those lacking reason or comprehension, a certain vestige of love through which the diverse are joined, the dissident come together in concord, and the contrary are united.[5] To be sure, this image of love appears in other creatures too, for its truth operates in the rational mind.[6] Indeed, to love is common to God, angels, and men. Therefore love, not inclined toward anything outside of nature, joins nature with nature so that there is *one heart and soul* for those brought together, for whom there is one faith, one hope, and one charity.* 5. In the same manner, my soul follows an impulse of love,*[7] which tells me that there is more to you than just you, and that everything about you is neither all yours nor all you.[8] My soul passes through you by a spiritual motion, crossing through the very substance of the body by means of its subtlety, pouring all of itself into the very bosom of your mind, mixing affection with affection, sense with sense, and spirit with spirit, so that my spirit is renewed from the sharing of your spirit, so that my

*Acts 4:32;
cf. Eph 4:4-5

*see Ezek
1:12

---

[5] The negation of *comprehension* translates the technical Latin term *insensibili*.

[6] *Image* translates *similitude; mind* translates *mente.* For the previous two sentences, see Aelred, S 68.3–4 (CCCM 2:191–92); Spec car 1.21.59 (CCCM 1:37); Spir amic 1.53–55 (CCCM 1:298).

[7] *Soul* translates *animus*, which cannot here mean "mind."

[8] The Latin, which I have translated as an independent clause structured by a finite verb, followed by indirect discourse in a relative clause, defies literal translation. It reads, *Animus proinde meus, amoris impetum sequens, omnia quae tua sunt non tu, omnia quae circa te sunt, quae nec tua sunt nec tu . . . se totus infundit.*

sense borrows light from the light of your sense of wisdom, so that, above all, my affection is warmed by the sweetness of your affection.[9] Thereupon I admire how good you are; thereupon I grasp and perceive how wise you are; thereupon I delight in and taste how worthy to be loved you are.[10]

6. Hence, most loving father, since my recent study concerns holy Scripture I have thought it prudent to entrust it to you so that you might refer it to the judgment of your discretion. It is my hope that when I savor something sound your authority may confirm me; that when I hesitate you may teach me and let the truth shine upon me; that when I falter your holy exactingness may correct me. And so, when some time ago in a meeting with the brethren I had summarily discussed the burdens of the prophet Isaiah, touching briefly on each one, and was asked by many of the brethren to describe them in more detail and at greater length, I was obedient to the will of them whose progress it is my duty to serve. 7. Beginning, therefore, with the burdens of Babylon, and thence passing through the burden of the Philistines to the secrets of the burden of Moab, I delivered thirty-one homilies in writing.* Then, *lest perhaps I should run or had run in vain,* I suspended my pen until your own *countenance* could pronounce *judgment* on what I had written, until *your own eyes* could see the reason behind all of these things, and until all that I had written could have the chance, by the

*see
Isa 13:1–16,
14

---

[9] *Its subtlety* translates *sua subtilitate,* and therefore the antecedent of *sua* is the subject of the clause, *animus,* which I have translated as *soul.*

[10] *Perceive* translates *sentio. Sentio* has a broad range of meaning in Cistercian vocabulary, but in this context Aelred seems to be discussing a knowledge based on the senses and perception.

*Gal 2:2; cf.
Ps 16:2

*cf. Prov
25:27

*Ps 20:4; Acts
9:6; cf. Mark
5:33

will of your discretion, to be destroyed, corrected, or approved.*[11] Although they seem unworthy to be read by one of such great wisdom, may you nonetheless venture to examine them with the vehemence of love, which embraces charity, so that in reading them you almost irreverently approach majesty.*[12]

8. Beyond this, the memory of your humility and kindness inspires me. For it was you, I remember, who once *welcomed* your position in London *with blessings of sweetness*, you whose mere notice of me was a great thing for me, you from whom I, *stupefied and trembling* before such great dignity, obtained a greeting that was like a loving embrace.* This explains whence my presumption derives. It makes me want to follow through with what started when I first became acquainted with your serenity; to hope that after knocking on the door of your friendship my soul might be led into its inner chamber.[13]

9. Therefore, while a wise man should be allowed some measure of time for leisure, however long or short, I hope it will not bother him, my Lord, to give up a small amount of that time. When you read what I have written, you can trim the excess, supply me with words, or delete the entire thing. Having sent these sermons I now have time to write other things. I have combined nineteen homilies on the burden of Babylon, three on the burden of the Philistines, and nine on the burden of Moab, and am prepared,

---

[11] For the previous two sentences, cf. Oner 31.26 (CCCM 2D:288).

[12] *Licet igitur tantae sapientiae horum lectio uideatur indigna, audet eam tamen amoris exigere uehementia, qui ita amplectitur caritatem, ut fere irreuerenter irruat in maiestatem.*

[13] **Soul* translates *animum*, which cannot here mean "mind." The antecedent of *its* (*eius*) is *friendship* (*amicitiae*), not *soul* (*animum*).

according to your will, to stop there or to proceed
further.[14]

---

[14] For the previous two sentences, cf. Oner 31.26 (CCCM
2D:288); Aelred ends the *homeliae* just as he ends his prefatory
letter, urging Gilbert to advise him whether to destroy, stop, or
continue his work.

Appendix 3

Aelred's Homily for the Feast of Saint Katherine of Alexandria

Translated by Marie Anne Mayeski

Translator's note:

This translation is based on the text in the Paris manuscript, nouv. acq. lat 294. Sister Felicitas Corrigan, OSB (1908–2003), a nun of Stanbrook Abbey in England, made this translation possible. Knowing my own paleographic skills to be minimal, Dame Felicitas enlisted the services of one of her sisters to transcribe the Latin text, of which I had excellent photographic copies. She would neither tell me the name of the nun who did the work nor accept any remuneration for it. She called it a work of friendship, and for the friendship of these gracious and scholarly women I am forever grateful.

Text

This is *the wise virgin* whom the Lord [*found*] *watching* etc.*

*Matt 25:1-5

Today we celebrate the birthday and glorious victory of the blessed virgin Katherine. Let us celebrate in such a way that we may find profit in celebrating, recalling that it is written to sing psalms wisely. Let us praise her wisely, this wise, eminent virgin. Who does praise wisely? The one who imitates what he praises, who completes by deed what he preaches in word. Wisely does one praise who praises both by voice and in the heart. Thus our celebration of the feast of the saints will make progress if—and only if—we are zealous to imitate the lives, behavior, and virtues of those we preach about.[1] If the deed is discordant with the speech, it may be said of us what was said of lost and perverse people by the Lord: *This people honor me with their lips, but their heart is far from me.** Therefore let your charity pay attention to what has been proposed to us in the praise of the glorious virgin.

*Matt 15:8; Mark 7:6

This is a wise virgin, etc. We have spoken briefly and [yet] said much, and in this one [verse], we have, in fact, said everything. Indeed, three things are put forward here: that she is a virgin, that she is wise, and that the Lord found her watching. [To say] that she is a virgin is incomplete praise, or rather, it is great praise when added to that which follows, that she is wise. Without wisdom, virginity is not [really] virginity but a foolish and confused virginity, nor does [a virginity without wisdom] make her a virgin but more powerfully corrupts her because it makes her a foolish virgin. When therefore you say that she is a virgin, the soul of hearing is as yet ambiguous. Judgment is suspended up to this point since there are both foolish and prudent virgins.

When you say that she is a virgin, it is as if you have jewels. Virginity may indeed rightly be compared to a jewel because it is refulgent but in itself

---

[1] The same thought is to be found in Sermon 44 of the Second Clairvaux Collection, CCCM 2A:54–63; CF 77:136–44. Aelred repeats *if* before all three direct objects of the infinitive *to imitate*. I have tried to capture his intensive language with the phrase between dashes.

so fragile that it may be easily destroyed unless it is encircled with some more solid material such as gold or silver or another medium and thereby protected from harm. Therefore you seek to surround your gem with gold and say that it is wise [to do so]. O, how well do these things fit together, one with the other, jeweled things and such gold. Behold, virginity and wisdom are a decoration beyond every necklace, every earring, every collar, or any ornament whatever that is precious and most beautiful to women. From such a jewel and this gold that precious ring is made, a seal of love and chastity dug up, in which the wise virgin glories when she says, *With his ring, my Lord Jesus Christ has dug me up.*[2] This is that treasure hidden in a field to which the kingdom of heaven is likened; the one who finds it hides it, and for the joy of it he hastens and sells all

Matt 13:44 that he has and buys that field.

The field in which that precious treasure is found is the discipline of heavenly study. In that field, this blessed virgin has found that most desirable treasure, because through the study of heavenly discipline she arrived at love, knowledge, and the desire for virginity and wisdom and came to embrace the one who is the virgin son of the Virgin, the spouse of virgins, the Lord Jesus Christ, who is the Wisdom of God the Father. Having found this treasure in this field, she sold all that she had and bought that field; to concentrate on heavenly discipline she renounced every physical pleasure and all worldly

---

[2] This is a difficult sentence. The verb *subaro*, "to plough," in its participial form, modifies *signaculum*, "seal," and the verb is repeated as the action of Christ toward the wise virgin (*anulo suo subarravit me dominus meus Jesus Christus*). The subsequent sentence reveals that Aelred is thinking of the gospel verse that he then quotes about the treasure hidden in a field.

desires, all magnificent possessions and delights for the Kingdom in order that she might truly say, "I have despised the kingdom of the world and every worldly adornment for love of the Lord Jesus Christ whom I have seen, whom I have loved, in whom I have believed, whom I have chosen."

Pay attention to her prudence, virgins. Consider what this wise businesswoman has done. See what she sold and what she bought. She sold earthly things and bought heavenly ones, she has exchanged an earthly kingdom for a heavenly one, for her spouse she cast her lot with the Son of God instead of with the son of a man; she has provided herself with unending glory and joys in place of false glories and momentary joys. Let therefore this prudent virgin speak: *I chose, and understanding was given to me; I asked, and the spirit of wisdom came upon me; I preferred her to kingdoms and thrones, and I counted riches to be as nothing in comparison to her.** Behold how truly, how rightly, how worthily it may be said of this blessed virgin, *blessed is the wise virgin whom the Lord finds watching.** *Matt 25:1-5

Behold, what is the conclusion, what the full completion of this praise? It is the praise of perseverance. Who is the one found watching by the Lord if not the one who persevered right up to the end in the true faith, in good works, and in holy meditation? Often in the divine Scripture, the end of this present life is signified by the coming of the Lord, so that the Lord is said to come to those whom he calls through the death of the flesh from sojourn in the world, either to a punishment or to rest according to their works. O how cautiously, how providently this virgin has ordered her life. She has equipped her lamp appropriately, she has stored oil in its vessel, she has spent the whole night of this present life awake in order that the Lord when he came might find her watchful. What am I saying, "she had stored"? Rather she had filled her vessel with such an abundance of oil that the oil did not fail in the vessel of her body up to this very day, and not just any old oil, but sweet oil, holy oil, the oil of salvation, as has been sung on this day: *A stream of healing oil flowed over the members of this virgin,* beginning from the head. Therefore let us say, *This is the wise virgin whom the Lord found watching.*

But I have said too little in saying that the Lord found her watching; I say more, I say truly that the prudent and watchful virgin, by persistent and ardent seeking, arrived at and found the Lord who was making as if absent, as if delayed. She could not do otherwise, she who had been wounded by charity, she who was languishing in love, she who was clamoring all the day, *When shall I come and appear before the face of my God? O daughters of Jerusalem, announce to my beloved that I languish from love; she was not able to endure the delay of the spouse.* It was as if she was saying in her heart, *arising, I will go around the city through districts and the streets, seeking him whom my* *Song 3:2 *soul loves.*[3]

Consider the life of this virgin before her passion and you will see that she completed a wondrous journey in a brief time while with ardent study and vehement desire she sought her beloved, her spouse, her God. Pay attention to her life and to its holy habits before the passion. See from where she proceeds; proceed and see the stages of her passion. Behold how she has crossed over. Raise your eyes and see her in heaven, positioned at the right hand of her spouse as a bride adorned with her necklace. Be-

[3] There is a parallel in another of Aelred's sermons, S 20.32–35, CCCM 2A:295–97, CF 58:286–88.

hold at what place she has arrived. She has crossed
over from quietness to quietness through labor, from
the quietness of contemplation to the quietness of
fruition by means of the labor of the passion. The
fire of longing to see God burned in her heart from
unremitting meditation of contemplation. For the
power and the nature of contemplation is [such] that
to the degree that someone makes progress in it, the
more ardently does she thirst to enjoy the presence
of the reality. Having attained it through longing by
the vision of the mind alone, she then feels herself to
be delayed from full enjoyment of that reality, and
she sighs, *I shall cross over into that place nevertheless
and shall go up even to the house of God.**   *Ps 122:1

Behold how she has crossed over, even to the
house of God, to the presence of God, to the glory
of God. But by what [path] did that eager virgin
cross over, hastening on the way, except by a hard
and troublesome path, a rough way filled with abuse
and envy;[4] she crossed through the hands of sinners,
through excessive and exquisite kinds of torments.
That is why she was able to say, *All of your heights and
your waves have passed over me.** The high ones and   *Ps 41:8
those in control who were tormenting her were being
watched. Those who oppressed her with torments
and destroyed her completely were being watched.
But they will go across, they will disappear, they will
lose their efficacy and gain no advantage against her.
They will cross over having failed; she will cross
over having succeeded. But by what leader, by what
helper did she cross over and conquer those invin-
cible ones? God helped her by his countenance, by
his presence: *God being in her midst, she will not be*

---

[4] Latin *inviam*. Perhaps *invidiam*.

*Ps 46:6
*moved.** God is in her, God is with her, God is for her.
In her, strengthening her; with her, leading her forth;
for her, protecting her, as is written in the psalms:
You have protected me from the mob of evildoers, from a
*Ps 64:2 *multitude of wicked intrigues.**

I find this crossing over sufficiently expressed in
the Canticle so that I seem to see this daughter—
whether by herself or with some sweet companions—conversing about her beloved and about his
absence and complaining loudly about his delay:
On my couch through the night, I have sought him whom
*Song 3:1 *my soul loves.** What does it mean that she sought
him on her couch if not that the peace and quiet of
contemplation is signified by the couch that is empty
for God alone; there she sighs for him with the whole
intention of her heart, *desiring to be dissolved and to
be with Christ*, just as described in the words of the
apostle. Not without meaning does it say "through
the night," because she herself passed the night in
good works and holy conversation while others were
lulled to sleep in the pleasure of vices. Therefore she
deserves to be called a prudent and watchful woman.

I sought and did not find him. She sought him on
her couch and did not find him because he had
already turned away, as if by suddenly depriving
her of his presence she might [be moved] to seek
more ardently. For her spouse had prepared for her
another way of seeking and finding him than the
one of quiet and peace—the way of the passion, a
harsher and more difficult but more glorious way.
It is as if her spouse had said to her, "In vain do
you seek me on your couch where in truth you will
not find me. *But arise and go forth, my love, my dove,*
*Song 2:10 *and come.** Follow the way described above if you
wish to come to me." And, as if she would unite in
one the warnings and invitations from her beloved,
she responds, *I will arise, and I will go around the city*

through the districts and through the streets seeking the one whom my soul loves.

When, you ask, did she do this? When did she arise from her secret couch and go out into the public, laden as she was with both maidenly fearfulness and similar modesty? It was at a certain time when a furious anger had been enkindled against the Christian religion that she who was inflamed by the love of her spouse, having abandoned her father's dominion, showed herself in the midst of a sinful people and fearlessly presented herself for immolation to an idol by a cruel tyrant. At that time, she cried out with a loud voice, *these are demons.* At that time, this innocent virgin debated against the rhetoricians and grammarians, taught faith in Christ, and produced worthy martyrs for the Lord. *I sought and did not find him.* Truly she did not yet find her spouse, because she had not yet completed her course. She was making a stand against the great ones on her difficult way.

Go forward, therefore, O blessed virgin, and show us those whom you found on the way or, rather, those who had found you before you found your beloved. *Those vigilant ones who guard the city have found me; they have struck me; they have wounded me.** This is not in need of explanation. Who doubts this except the one who has not heard or read or understood the passion of the glorious virgin? *The watchmen of the walls have stripped off my cloak.** The sequence is right and true: according to the truth of the story as first discovered, *they struck, they wounded,* and presently *they took* her *cloak.* By beheading her, they had robbed her of the cloak of her flesh, as it is written: *After many punishments, this kind virgin was led to the beheading.*[5]

*Song 5:7

*Song 5:7

---

[5] This seems to be a citation from the narrative life of Saint Katherine.

But the meaning of *the watchmen of the walls* must
not be passed over in silence. Who are those *watchmen of the walls*? They are those who preside in public
custody over the prison and other places of punishments, deputized to guard and torment the holy
confessors of the name of Christ who are stable and
firm as walls, because the holy ones founded on the
firm rock of Christ the Savior are strong for escaping
every attack of torments and persecutors. Christ is
called by the prophets a wall: *our Sion*, our Savior,
*Isa 26:1 is *a strong city placed on that wall and on that rampart.**
Was not this girl of whom we speak, whom neither
the wheel-machine nor carefully thought-out species
of torments were able to break down or penetrate
in any degree, was she not an impregnable wall?
And what more had been done against a wall of
stone or bronze? She remained constant, not car-
ing for the enticements or severities. The queen and
noble Porphyrius with a white-clad body of soldiers
were strong walls. Also those fifty orators who all,
standing manfully in faith and for the faith of Christ,
overcame death and the author of death through
her death.

Those watchmen of the walls robbed our virgin
of her cloak. [The narrative] followed: *I have passed
them by a very little [way], and thereupon I have found*
Song 3:4 *my spouse,** because, having been stripped of the
garment of the flesh that was more an impediment
than an ornament for her, she thereupon found her
beloved, whom she had sought through so many
and such dangers. And the king introduced her into
his chamber as had been promised to her by the angelic voice. Indeed the voice of heaven thundered
out, *Come, my beloved, into the bridal chamber of your
spouse*, whence she herself, with her wish already
fulfilled, having perceived the pay for her labors

in recompense for security, she broke forth saying, *I hold him and I will not let him go.** Truly, already joined to Christ, she held him, and, in partnership with her spouse, she will not let him go. In truth, by no condition whatever would she be separated from partnership with Christ, not she whom the sword could not separate from the love of Christ.*

*Song 3:4

*see Rom 8:37-39

Let us imitate this glorious virgin, O brothers, and if we cannot [travel] that admirable way through which the Lord God led her, let us at least, after her example, seek our beloved on our couch. This means, let us see God through a pure conscience, quiet contemplation, and a holy manner of life so that when the Lord comes, he will find us watching. And because we do not know the hour of his coming, we must always be *looking up* and always saying in our hearts, "Behold the way he will come, behold the way he will come." And thus let us always be on our guard and ready when, suddenly and unexpectedly in the middle of the night, the shout will be raised, *Behold the spouse comes.** Let us then run out to him on the way, with lamps burning, and let us go in with him to the eternal wedding-feast of joy, and let us live with Christ forever and ever, Amen.

*Matt 25:6

Appendix 4

Sermon for the Translation of the Relics of Edward the Confessor[1]

Translated by Tom Licence

*cf. 2 Cor
13:11 ("de
cetero fratres
gaudete"),
Phil 3:1
("de cetero
fratres mei
gaudete")

Brothers, rejoice* and give thanks to God, the
bountiful giver of all good things, for a holy day
has begun to dawn upon us,[2] a solemn day, the feast
day•[3] of Edward, glorious king of the English, your
patron,[4] your protector, your defender, the intercessor

•cf. Exod
12:16 ("dies
prima erit
sancta atque
sollemnis
et dies sep-
tima eadem
festiuitate
uenerabilis")

[1] This translation by Tom Licence is reprinted by permission
from CSQ, where it first appeared with Peter Jackson's article
(with critical edition) "*In translacione sancti Edwardi confessoris:*
The Lost Sermon by Ælred of Rievaulx Found?" CSQ 40, no. 1
(2005): 45–83. Biblical references appear in the margins, using the
standard CP abbreviations. Original footnotes of relevance only
to the edition of the sermon have been silently omitted. Notes 23,
34, and 40 refer to Paris sermons on Edward found in Paris, Bib.
Nat. MS nouv. acq. Lat. 294, discussed on pp. 50–54 of Jackson's
article. Complete references to works cited here are included in
the book's bibliography. Bracketed emendations are provided by
the author of this volume.

[2] Surely a reference to the time of day that the sermon was
delivered, at Vigils, just before dawn: see n. 40 below.

[3] The echo of the wording of God's instructions to Moses and
Aaron on the observance of the first Passover may only be a coin-
cidence, but it is interesting in view of the numerous references to
Moses and the book of Exodus found later in the sermon.

[4] *uestre* and *uestri* here and later in the sentence are completely
clear. The first letter of *uestris* (abbreviated to *uris*, with a sus-

for your sins, and the founder of your church. This is the day, I declare, of that most holy confessor of Christ, whose whole illustrious life from boyhood to old age shone brightly with virtues and miracles.* In particular it is told that although he was king he did not forsake humility, that in marriage he never violated the chastity he had always maintained, and since neither turtledove nor dove* was available for sacrifice he would offer in himself, a living and holy victim, the innocence of humility and the perseverance of chastity. He took a wife indeed of noble blood but nobler character,[5] likewise a virgin outstanding in beauty, greatly skilled in letters, in many arts,[6] and even in crafting precious things from gold and silver.[7] Yet virgin consecrated to God undertook to remain all the while in union with virgin so that each of them is believed to have obtained from God the dotal contract of virginity.[8]

*cf. Esth 3:13 ("a puero usque ad senem")

*Luke 2:24; cf. Gen 15:9; Lev 1:14; 5:11; etc.

---

pension mark and a dot above the *r*) could conceivably be an *n*, but by analogy with the rest of the sentence it is most likely to be a *u*. This is of course important evidence that the sermon was delivered (or intended for delivery) at Westminster by an outsider. See also n. 43 below.

[5] Cf. *Vita S. Edwardi*: "Erat praeterea pulchra facie, sed morum probitate pulchrior multo" (PL 195:747); *Relatio de standardo*: "Erat praeterea nobilis carne, sed christiana pietate longe nobilior" (Howlett [ed.] 3:183).

[6] Cf. the description of Lanfranc in the *Vita S. Edwardi*: "uir undecunque doctissimus, omnium etiam liberalium artium diuinarumque simul ac saecularium litterarum peritissimus" (PL 195:779).

[7] Probably a reference to Edith's skill in embroidering with gold ("sericis aurum intexere," *Vita S. Edwardi*, PL 195:747).

[8] "tabulae dotales" is the term used by Roman jurists for the "dotal contract." Containing "a statement of the contents of the dowry and agreements about what would happen to the dowry at the end of the marriage," this was "an important legal concomitant of marriage . . . often ratified at the wedding": Susan Treggiari, *Roman Marriage* (Oxford: Clarendon, 1991), 165. Cf.

Think, brethren, how great is this king of yours,[9] who in the midst of riches, luxuries,[10] and popular applause was neither wounded in his heart by pride nor polluted in his body by incontinence; no, indeed, he preserved the integrity of both unharmed, of his heart through humility, of his body through chastity. Consider therefore what virtue was in this king; how the charm of a noble and beautiful woman, among abundant riches and copious delights, was unable to overcome the constancy of his spirit,* violate his vow of virginity, or in any way draw this holy man into the embrace allowed by law, approved by the fathers, advantageous for the age,* and necessary for the succession to the throne. Indeed the king devoted to God elected to forsake his temporal heirs that an inheritance might be his in eternity.[11]

What can I say about his humility? Inasmuch as Scripture is my tutor and my own conscience my guide, his life, it seems, is seen truthfully depicted in those words of the gospels where one reads according to Luke that "a dispute arose among Jesus' disciples as to who among them was seen to be greater,"*[12] etc. For since this king was the greater and worthy

*cf. Jdt 9:14 ("da mihi in animo constantiam")

*Ps 144:15; 2 Macc 4:32; 14:5

*Luke 22:24

Peter of Celle, *In Ruth*, 1 (*ad* Ruth 1:1): "qui tabulas dotales, qui anulum et caeteros nuptialis apparatus, paranimphum" (CCCM 54:11; and see n. 42 below). The date of this work, however, is not certain (anywhere between 1145 and 1180), and there seems to have been no copy at Rievaulx.

[9] The initial *u* of *uester* is once more quite clear.

[10] Cf. Jerome, Ep 57, chap. 12: "inter Croesi opes et Sardanapalli delicias" (CSEL 54:526); and Aelred, *Vita S. Edwardi*: "Croesi opibus praetulissem" (PL 195:782).

[11] Cf. *Relatio de standardo*: "Nempe cum liberis careret haeredibus, licet ei nepotes strenui non deessent, de optimis tamen quibusque possessionibus suis Christum fecit haeredem" (Howlett 183).

[12] By the fourteenth century both this text and Luke 11:33 figured in the liturgy at Westminster for both of Edward's feasts:

of precedence he became as a subordinate and an attendant, and in the midst of his servants he was not the one who lies at ease, as it were, but the one who attends.* As a result he deserved, along with the rest of the elect, to hear the Lord say: "I assign to you my kingdom as my father has assigned it to me, that you may eat and drink at my table in my kingdom."* Read the books written about his life by our holy fathers,[13] and it will be found that this king was pious in spirit, often in silence, discreet in speech, thoughtful in council, prudent in judgment, of modest countenance, moderate in behavior, gentle in carriage, in gait regular,[14] abandoned always to all

*Luke 22:26-27

*Luke 22:29-30

Missale ad usum ecclesie Westmonasteriensis, Legg 2:737, 739, 975, 976 and 977.

[13] In addition to Aelred's, there were earlier Lives of Edward by Osbert of Clare and by an anonymous writer (*The Life of King Edward who Rests at Westminster*, ed. Barlow). The use of the plural here (*libros*) suggests that we are dealing with an early text; Aelred's *Vita* rapidly supplanted both the earlier ones.

[14] Inversion of this type is a notable characteristic of Aelred's style; see nn. 26 and 31 below. To the passage in general, cf. *Vita S. Edwardi*: "corpore castus, sermone rarus, simplex actu, purus affectu" (PL 195:742), "grauitas in incessu, simplicitas in affectu" (PL 195:745); *Vita S. Niniani*, chap. 2: "Interea dum castus corpore, animo prudens, in consiliis prouidus, in omni actu uerboque circumspectus" (Forbes 142); *De sanctis ecclesiae Haugustaldensis*, chap. 4: "Erat autem parcus in uerbo, in cibo sobrius, mediocris in habitu" (Raine 183). Several other late-twelfth-century texts ring the changes on this list of virtues; see, for example, a letter of 1173 from Odo, prior of Christ Church, Canterbury, to Alexander III, describing Richard, prior of Dover and later archbishop of Canterbury: "morum honestate et litterarum eruditione conspicuus, modestus in uerbo, prouidus in consiliis, discretus in opere" (*The Letters of John of Salisbury*, ed. W. J. Millor, H. E. Butler, and C. N. L. Brooke, 2 vols., Oxford Medieval Texts [Oxford: Clarendon, 1979–1986], 2:762 [Ep 311]); *Legenda sancti Ladislai regis* [c. 1200], chap. 4: "Erat itaque benignus in affectu, prouidus in consilio, uerax in sermone, constans in promissione, iustus in iudicio, serenus in corripiendo" (ed. Emma Bartoniek, *Scriptores rerum*

works of mercy, and, in short, well disposed with the entirety of his character to the mold of honest living.

It was proof of his great humility that when a poor cripple requested it out of reverence for Saint Peter the lofty king lowered his neck to him and offered himself as a beast of burden to bear the beggar whom he heard had been sent away from him. While he was carried this man was healed,[15] and the more the ulcerous pus flowed over the royal purple the more his returning health straightened the long-crippled sinews and strengthened the members lengthy illness had oppressed. Behold another Elisha![16] The one revived a dead man thrown onto him by the touch of his holy bones,* while the other healed a cripple set upon his back by the medicine of carrying him and the touch of his holy body alone. Nor is any man advised to say that it is better to restore the dead to life than to heal a cripple, for each, inasmuch as each is great, is wonderful. And as long as God can appear magnificent and wondrous in each it is not ours to inquire which of the two should take precedence, for the same Holy Spirit works all things in all,*[17] giving to each as he determines.•[18] He who worked this miracle in the dead prophet (to show how great in life was he who deserved to obtain so much through God's works after departing his body)

*see 2 Kgs 13:21 Vulg

*1 Cor 12:6 ("idem uero Deus qui operatur omnia in omnibus")

•1 Cor 12:11 ("haec autem omnia operatur unus atque idem Spiritus, diuidens singulis prout uult")

Hungaricarum, ed. Imre Szentpétery, 2 vols. [Budapest: Academia litter. hungarica, 1937–1938] 2:518).

[15] Cf. "dum ferit perit, dum impingitur frangitur" (*Relatio de standardo*, Howlett 186).

[16] Edward is compared to Elisha in a very different context in the *Vita S. Edwardi*: after his death, the saint punishes an impious girl, just as Elisha cursed the little boys who jeered at him (PL 195:783).

[17] Cf. *Vita S. Edwardi*: "qui omnia operaris in omnibus" (PL 195:742).

[18] See n. 38 below for another example of the conflation of two biblical quotations.

also performed a sign in the living king to reveal his great eternal inheritance, who in this miserable life and still oppressed by the monstrous flesh could bring this thing and others like it to pass.

A comparable marvel in this blessed king was that he exerted a spirit of prophecy, a gift through which unhesitating testimonies attest he saw many things and foresaw many future things in the spirit and in absence. Many things could detain us, but I will say a few words about the drowning of the king of the Danes in Denmark and how the Seven Sleepers in Greece turned over from one side to the other.

Now the traditions of our holy fathers[19] (of those who played a part in the stories of the aforesaid king and with revelations attested his honesty by the proven truth of the events) assert that when the king was resting in Westminster palace on the holy day of Easter with his nobles and bishops, he spied the Seven Sleepers on Mount Celion turning over onto the opposite side. It came to light[20] that the strangeness of such a miracle signaled a dire omen,

---

[19] The story of Edward's vision of the Seven Sleepers is first found in William of Malmesbury, *Gesta regum*, complete by c. 1125: William of Malmesbury, *Gesta regum Anglorum*, ed. and trans. R. A. B. Mynors, R. M. Thomson, and M. Winterbottom, 2 vols., Oxford Medieval Texts (Oxford: Clarendon Press, 1998–1999), 1:410–12 (2.225). It also occurs in an interpolation made between 1133 and 1143 in the Bury St. Edmunds copy of John of Worcester's *Chronicon ex chronicis*, and in Osbert's *Vita*, finished in 1138: *The Chronicle of John of Worcester. Vol. 2: The Annals from 450 to 1066*, ed. R. R. Darlington and P. McGurk, trans. Jennifer Bray and P. McGurk, Oxford Medieval Texts (Oxford: Clarendon Press, 1995), 648–50; Bloch, *La Vie de S. Édouard le Confesseur* 98–103 (chap. 18). The version in Aelred's *Vita* (PL 195:767–69) is adapted from Osbert's. See Barlow's comments in *The Life of King Edward* xli and 102 n. 255.

[20] Cf. the account of this episode in the *Vita S. Edwardi*: "dirum mortalibus omen hac laterum mutatione suorum signarunt" (PL 195:768).

attesting it most truthfully, as the outcome of events later proved beyond doubt.[21]

On the holy day of Pentecost moreover, while he stood by the altar of the Holy Trinity in Westminster to hear the solemn service of the Mass, he saw Sven, king of the Danes, his armies prepared and his ships drawn up, hurrying to ransack England.[22] Preparing to climb into his ship from a little boat his foot slipped, he toppled between the two and drowned, and by his death he freed both peoples, that is the Danes and the English, at once from sin and danger.[23] For that nation led their ships back to shore and returned home in peace, while our people, as if Pharaoh had been conquered and our enemies put to flight, passed easy days and an age full of peace from then thereafter in great tranquility under this new Moses.[24]

[21] This version of the story is heavily abbreviated. Aelred's *Vita* has the king predict seventy years of warfare and unrest until the Sleepers turn over again.

[22] Sven's name is given in Osbert of Clare's *Vita* (Bloch, *La Vie de S. Édouard le Confesseur* 76 [chap. 5]), but was omitted by Aelred when composing his own Life. Some confusion seems to have arisen in the course of transmission over which king of Denmark was the subject of this vision. Adam of Bremen, writing in 1072–1075/6, reported that Magnus the Good had died on board ship (not that he had drowned) in October 1047: *Magistri Adam Bremensis Gesta Hammaburgensis ecclesiae pontificum*, 3rd ed., by Bernhard Schmeidler, MGH: scriptores rerum germanicarum (Hanover and Leipzig: Hahn, 1917), 151–52 (3:12). His successor Sven Estridsen sent a fleet to England only in 1069, three years after Edward's death, and died uneventfully in 1074 or 1076: F. M. Stenton, *Anglo-Saxon England*, 3rd ed. (Oxford: Clarendon-Press, 1971) 602; Niels Lund, "Sven (II) Estridsen," *Dansk Biografisk Leksikon*, 3rd ed., ed. Sv. Cedergreen Bech, 16 vols. (Copenhagen: Glydendal, 1979–1984) 14:242–43, at 243.

[23] Cf. Paris sermon 1, f. 162v: "a clero pariter et populo." [This passage is similar to one in] an unprinted version of the *Vita S. Edwardi*.

[24] A similar story is told of Edward the Elder (d. 924) in the *Genealogia regum Anglorum*; there, the king has a vision of a drunken

To whom indeed, O great king, O sweetest lord
and most cherished father, to whom, I say, will I
more truthfully liken you[25] than to that greatest legislator and prince of the Hebrews who, as Scripture
says, "was the meekest of all the men who tarried on
earth"?* Who assuredly protected God's people by   *Num 12:3
law, armed them with faith, served them with good
counsel, fortified them with prudence, with wisdom
ruled them,[26] defended them with arms, raised them
up with prayers and, as much in times of peace as
in times of war, devoted to God, undertook with pa-
ternal affection to nurture and love them, or more
fiercely to convict and with harsher punishments to
chastise the proud and the rebels? Let us observe that
all these things, whether the life, the behavior, or indeed the actions and total excellence of Moses most
fittingly converge upon this Moses of ours, upon this
our legislator. For this man appeared as the meekest
among his people,* filled with wisdom and the grace   *Num 12:3
of God, and established a law and dictated justice for
his nation (which he found as uneducated as she was
untamed), according to which matters are settled and
verdicts determined unto this day in the kingdom of
the English.[27]

That which he taught with words, moreover, he
fulfilled with actions, and those same things he advised to be done he demonstrated in his own ac-

---

brawl in the Danish army preventing its intended invasion of
England (PL 195:723–24).

[25] Cf. *Eulogium Dauidis*, chap. 2: "Quis similis tui in regibus
terrae, O rex optime!" (Metcalfe 270).

[26] For the inversion of the verb/noun order here, see n. 14 above.

[27] On this well-known claim, see Barlow, *Edward the Confessor*,
178: "The *laga Eadwardi*, the laws of King Edward of Henry I's coronation charter, were the laws of England as they had stood before
1066. There is nothing to show that Edward was a law-giver and
little evidence that he was particularly interested in justice." See
also Wormald, *The Making of English Law* 1:128, 409–11.

*see
Exod 3–4

tions beforehand. The Lord summoned Moses out of Midian to rule his people,* and this our Moses, recalled from Neustria, was put in charge of the English people, as had been foreseen by wonders and revealed by oracles.[28] One was pursued by Egyptians, the other by Danes. One freed his people from Pharaoh's tyrannical oppression by divine virtue; the other, armed with God's grace, shook off from the necks of his people the fetter of servitude and the yoke of captivity that the Danes had imposed.[29] One, after the wicked king had drowned, sang praises to the Lord with hymns and timbrels for the victory obtained.* The other announced that perpetual peace had been delivered unto every border of the English now that King Sven had been overwhelmed by the waves, and in order that they should thereafter exert themselves more earnestly with divine praises now the enemy had been conquered, he roused them with a wholesome exhortation.[30] Thus all England rejoices and exults, over whose whole realm this man presided, acting at that time more like a father than a judge, offering mercy instead of censure and, as much as was permissible without jeopardizing the peace, leniency rather than punishment.

*see Exod
15:1-21

[28] A reference to the vision of Brihtwald, bishop of Wiltshire, that Edward would succeed to the throne and remain a virgin. For Aelred's treatment of the episode in the *Vita S. Edwardi*, see PL 195:742–43.

[29] Cf. *Vita S. Edwardi*: "Angli Danico iugo quasi ab Aegyptia seruitute liberati" (PL 195:744).

[30] This sentence and the sentences preceding are remarkably similar to a passage in one of Aelred's sermons on Saint Benedict (*sermo* 6): "Illos per ministerium Moysi eduxit Dominus de Aegypto, nos per ministerium sancti Benedicti eduxit de saeculo. Illi erant sub Pharaone rege pessimo, nos sub diabolo. Illi in seruitute Aegyptiorum, nos in dominio uitiorum" (CCCM 2A:54).

In the remotest confines of the realm he made peace, rebuking the unruly,* pronouncing justice and straightening the crooked, doing good and chastising the errant until tyrannical presumption had no opportunity to contrive evil, presumptuous injustice lacked the power to harm, and servile discord found no capacity to torment. All England rejoices, I say, which this holy king endowed with laws, with customs adorned, tamed at his command,[31] educated by his sagacity, strengthened by his faith, molded by his example, raised up by his authority, ornamented with his sanctity, and, leveling superiors and inferiors to a certain equality, ordered throughout its realm with judgment and justice (for justice and judgment prepared his throne).* As a result, in all his works mercy and truth preceded the king's face;* with these he calmly tempered the entire business of his realm so that the profligate would not evade their due punishment of condemnation and devout minds would find with him rewards befitting their integrity. This learned and prudent man elected to hold forth in his own personality that which was appropriate to whomsoever he met: to the good he displayed in himself that which they would love, to the perverse that which they would fear. He preferred to mend the tears in our morals[32] than to pile up riches, and to invest in souls, a more demanding sacrifice, than

*see
1 Thess 5:14
("corripite
inquietos")

*Ps 88:15
*Ps 88:15

[31] Another example of inversion; see n. 14 above.

[32] Cf. *De institutione inclusarum*, chap. 32: "mihi maximus labor incumbit ut fracta redintegrem, amissa recuperem, scissa resarciam" (CCCM 1:675–76). The verb is frequently used by Bernard of Clairvaux: see, for example, Ep 219, chap. 2: "Si qua in uobis sunt uiscera pietatis, tantis uos opponite malis, ne in illa praecipue terra scissura fiat, in qua solent, sicut optime nostis, scissurae aliae resarciri" (SBOp 8:81).

to spend money on material things.³³ Truly it is as the Lord says: "Everyone who has will be given more and will have it in abundance,"* and likewise "Seek first the kingdom of God, and all good things will be yours as well."* For since this holy king established divine charity and love in his heart the supernal grace bestowed upon him made him abound in all good things, and since his first concern was to seek and preach the kingdom of God,* worrying not after his own affairs but after those of Jesus Christ, all things better than could be wished for in this life were added to his lot and added in abundance.

Almighty God, rich to all who call upon him,* in whom all the treasures of wisdom and knowledge are hidden,* filled the mind of his saint with such wisdom and glorified his whole realm with such works that it can be truly said of him (as is read of Solomon) that "the glorious king exceeded all the kings of the earth in riches and wisdom, and the whole world desired to see his face that it might hear the wisdom God put into his heart."* ³⁴ For indeed the emperors of the Franks and the Germans and as many kings and princes³⁵ in the surrounding area³⁶

*Matt 25:29

*Matt 6:33

*Matt 6:33

*Rom 10:12

*Col 2:3

*1 Kgs
10:23-24
Vulg; cf.
2 Chr 9:22-23

---

³³ Augustine, *Enarrationes in Psalmos*, Ps 63, chap. 18: "siue secundum dispendium rei familiaris" (CCSL 39:820); cf. *Eulogium Dauidis*, chap. 4: "rerum dispendio fluctuantibus" (Metcalfe 272).

³⁴ Cf. *Vita S. Edwardi*: "Cuncti reges terrae desiderabant uidere faciem eius, et audire sapientiam illius" (PL 195:745); Paris sermon 1, f. 162v: "Magnificatus est rex gloriosus in diebus suis diuitiis et sapientia super uniuersos reges terre sue antecessores suos. Non fuit rex ante illum in Anglia qui posset ei comparari in diuitiis et gloria," etc.; Paris sermon 2, f. 164v: "Regibus et principibus terre proponitur rex iste gloriosus, docens misericordiam et iudicium, populum suum regens in mansuetudine et equitate," etc.

³⁵ "Reges et principes" is of course an extremely common expression. Cf., however, *Vita S. Edwardi*: "reges et principes pro tanta rerum mutatione admiratione procelluntur" (PL 19:745).

³⁶ Cf. 1 Macc 12:13 ("reges qui sunt in circuitu nostro"), Josh 11:12 ("omnes per circuitum ciuitates regesque earum"), 1 Kgs

as were close enough to hear of this great man, sending messengers and many gifts, humbly beseeched
him for his friendship and fraternity,[37] and submit-
ted themselves, their kindred, and their men to him
as though to a father and lord, to the extent that
he ordained that his will and command be obeyed
in all these realms as in his own. Anyone who had
acquired any agreement of friendship with King
Edward they called blessed, for God was with him,
and through him this man prospered in all things
he did, and he guided all his works.[38] The opulence
consequently acquired throughout the whole of England under the peace that had been obtained and
the sanctity of the king was such as one reads of in
the age of the aforementioned Solomon: "silver was
like stones,[39] and they abounded with much gold."*
Rarely would a poor man be seen unless, perchance,
if his own wickedness or innate stupidity had driven
him into want.

*see
generally,
1 Kgs 10:14-
22 Vulg;
2 Chr 9:13-21

And so England rejoices and with all devotion
honors the fame of this day which God, for the
glorification of his saint, illuminated with the sol-

4:24 Vulg ("et cunctos reges illarum regionum et habebat pacem
ex omni parte in circuitu").

[37] An expression used very often in the books of Maccabees
(but nowhere else in the Bible), in the context of diplomatic negotiations between Israel and other nations: 1 Macc 8:17; 12:3;
12:8; 12:16; 14:18; 15:17; 2 Macc 4:11; and cf. 1 Macc 8:20; 8:31;
10:16; 12:14; 14:40.

[38] A conflation of Gen 39:23 ("Dominus enim erat cum illo et
omnia eius opera dirigebat") and Gen 39:2 ("fuitque Dominus
cum eo et erat uir in cunctis prospere agens"). These quotations
are often used by Aelred, sometimes run together as they are here
[. . .]. They are particularly appropriate here, as they are taken
from the chapter in Genesis describing the attempted seduction
by Potiphar's wife of another male virgin (Joseph).

[39] 1 Kgs 10:27 Vulg ("fecitque ut tanta esset abundantia argenti
in Hierusalem quanta lapidum"); see 2 Chr 9:27; 1:15.

itary celestial stars[40] and lit up with the glories of everlasting renown. The whole world rejoices but especially, brothers, we[41] whom this holy king's esteem elects to be the elite servants of his innermost bedchamber[42]* and deems capable of preserving his holy body, venerating his trophies like so many bridegrooms. Others have his generosity; we have him. He enriched not only English churches but also many French ones with gold and silver along with estates and diverse possessions. To us,[43] however, he

paranimphos

[40] Perhaps a reference to the time the sermon was delivered, just before dawn; see n. 2 above. Cf., however, the quotation from Wisdom 50:6, "quasi stella matutina in medio nebulae, et quasi luna plena in diebus suis luxit," applied to King Edgar in the *Genealogia regum Anglorum* (PL 195:726) and to Edward in the Prologue to the *Vita S. Edwardi* (PL 195:738); also the description of King David of Scotland: "cum sol iste noctis tenebras emergens radiis suae lucis abigeret" (*Eulogium Dauidis*, chap. 12, Metcalfe 284). Cf. Paris sermon 2, f. 164v (immediately after the passage quoted above): "Hic est lucerna que a domino accensa peruersitatum tenebras fugauit, uitiorum nebulam dissoluit, et multis uirtutum radiis mundum illuminauit." Aelred discusses the role of the earthly king as the "lesser light," i.e., the moon, where the night signifies the secular world as opposed to the church, in *Sermones de oneribus* 11 (PL 195:402–3).

[41] See n. 43 below.

[42] Apparently used only once elsewhere by Aelred, in a sermon *In annuntiatione Dominica* printed from Paris, Bibliothèque Nationale de France, lat. 15157, fos. 116r–118v, by Gaetano Raciti, "Une allocution familière de S. Aelred conservée dans les mélanges de Matthieu de Rievaulx," *Coll[ectanea Cisterciensia]* 47 (1985): 267–80, at p. 277 (chap. 2): "quasi minister ad dominam, quasi inferior ad superiorem, quasi paranimphus ad sponsam." The term is also found in Peter of Celle's commentary on Ruth, *In Ruth*, 1; see n. 8 above.

[43] The initial letter is an unusually formed upper-case *N*, unlike any similar letter elsewhere in the manuscript. It is possible that the scribe misread or altered an upper-case *V* in his exemplar. The initial letter of *nos* and *nobis* in the surrounding passage could just as easily be *u*, but has been transcribed here as *n* in conformity with *Nobis*.

bequeathed something of greater worth than all, of a price beyond the value of every other precious thing: that is to say, he committed the priceless treasure of his incorrupt body to our sole keeping. For in this monastery that he himself had constructed in honor of the chief of the holy apostles Peter he chose his burial place, where signs and miracles ceaselessly illuminate the goodness of almighty God, and the magnitude of the virtue of his most holy confessor King Edward is manifested with a clearer light, as he reveals himself who lives and reigns for ever, world without end, amen. On the text: "No one lights a candle . . . ,"* etc. The light is the Word.•

*Luke 11:33

Translated by Tom Licence, Magdalene College, Cambridge cb3 0ag, England

•cf. Ps 118:105 ("Lucerna pedibus meis uerbum tuum")

Appendix 5

A Letter from Rievaulx to Archbishop Thomas Becket[1]

Translated by Jean Truax

Most beloved Lord and Father T., reverend archbishop of Canterbury, your poor and insignificant
brother M., the poorest and most insignificant of all
Christ's men at Rievaulx, but one who knows he is
able in the Lord.

What am I to you at this moment when you are
made father of the country, lord of the kingdom,
second to the king, and prince of the English church?
Amid the private councils of the kingdom, the
prince's public business, diverse ecclesiastical affairs, the innumerable demands of a variety of matters, the applause of the multitude, the clamor of
the poor, the needs of the religious community, and
other such importunities, you are mindful even of
those such as me who are insignificant. Even when
they are absent from your side, you do not allow
yourself to forget them. I cannot help but blush and
be amazed, for I view your condescension to me as
something of a miracle. Because of this evidence of

---

[1] Translated from the Latin text published by Frederick M.
Powicke, "Maurice of Rievaulx," *English Historical Review* 36,
no. 141 (1921): 17–29.

your esteem, how much sweetness burns in my heart for you! For the humility of your letter shows—and Lord H. de Morville diligently conveys—the presence of your devotion. With utmost dedication to his mission, he went more than twenty mileposts out of his way in order to discharge his duties faithfully and represented you in such an exemplary manner that his words could only assure me of your faith and hope. Therefore, with your permission, I will speak truthfully, my father.

I do not wish to deceive myself about the true purpose of your election. I pray you understand that your opinion is important to me. Examining the evidence from every angle, as if through a magnifying glass, I came to realize in my heart what conscience would not permit me to express. What the evidence fails to prove is excessive severity.

It is therefore too great a thing that you do. I am not what you think I am. You seek another under my title and give me an importance that I do not have. You attribute great virtue to me because of my religious title, but although I am esteemed worthy, I am truly insignificant and worthless. I speak, however, not only truthfully but from the heart as well when I say that in my judgment the matter is neither black nor white.

Nevertheless, however lowly my status, I believe in my heart and confess with my lips that I am bound to you by both affection and my vows and wish only the best for you. In any way that I can, I will further your interests and impress upon those who faithfully serve Christ with simplicity of heart to keep you in their prayers with great devotion and affection. I will do my utmost to ensure that your name and memory are openly blessed in the midst of their pious efforts so that the grace of divine mercy is yours in fullest measure. I will see to it, since I am the least virtuous, that those who have a greater abundance of virtue add their efforts to mine. And you, father, lifted up by their great numbers of hands and hearts, it is only fitting that you should reject fear and seize the pledge of hope, accepting and observing the just judgment of God. Supported in your undertaking by those gathered around you, you will not find yourself lacking in good fortune.

For who can resist the glance of one who chooses to be defined by kindness instead of fear, and whose mercy they hope to gain? So it is fitting that by this grace he came to you, enriched you, and lifted you up with the crown of glory. Yet he can as easily grant your honor to others and fill up the ranks of your followers with strangers, giving you reason to lament anew when your enemy becomes strong and prevails against you. Then your spirit dies the death of the just. But even if they turn against you, always remember that ingratitude is a deadly thing: the enemy of virtue and the foe of well-being. Nothing in humankind is abhorred more fiercely by the spirit of God. Therefore, beware lest friendship turn into anger. As the blessed holy one says, it is often thought that anger is greater because of former affection and affection greater because of former anger.

Nothing is more important than security, but even those who are secure can rest uneasy. Ever watchful in the actions of grace, you use your rank to uphold your reputation forcefully and spare no one in order to save your own soul. You hold an exalted position, and the honor of your office is great, but the weight of such honor is heavy, and the higher the station in life the harder the fall. For he will pronounce the most serious judgments on the rulers, and they will endure the most severe torments.

We live in dangerous times, and it has fallen to you to rule this difficult and unruly diocese in these evil days. There are certainly many things in the English church that need to be corrected, but you must exercise great caution. The most important facet of this endeavor is the management of the sovereign. The highest orders in society are accustomed to taking shameful advantage of sacred things and rationalizing their action as justified. Certainly the greatest love resides in taking up, or rather accepting, the care of souls, but the powerful do not view such care as important, and the well-being of souls is not their main concern. Their arrogance and despicable ambition pollutes the countenance of the bride of Christ with grave sin. I might even add that it injects a lethal poison. No wonder! As a wise man pointed out, ambition is a subtle evil, a secret poison, a hidden pest, the master of deceit, the teacher of hypocrisy, the author of malice, the origin of vice, the source of crime, destroyer of virtue, a wound to security, and a scar on the heart that creates sickness without remedy and engenders a disease beyond the reach of medicine. So it is that Adam has become a figure of shame.

Yet men of proven virtue, with a sense of culture and discipline, are disregarded and neglected, while students, boys, and beardless adolescents are promoted to ecclesiastical dignities and endowed with a crozier because of family connections. As someone else pointed out, they are granted the rule of churches, and that is sometimes even more destructive because they have seized the primacy rather than earning it through merit. And sometimes they have done it not so much because they want to rule, but to show that they have the power to take it. Who can resist them better than you? Who can confront them but you, the leader of the tribe of Israel? Such are the cares that are about to flood down upon you. If only God would pass your burden to me, in a hidden breath and quiet whisper!

In you everything that is most highly valued is combined, so that now all such evil can be eliminated. The power of the prince, with which you have the special grace of familiarity, has as its duty of office the use of the power of the state to promote abundant good fortune—that is to say, wisdom and knowledge. Who knows what human intention was in your promotion? Perhaps God granted you the first seat on this island so that the measure of your zeal for the house of Israel would be evident and your diligence no longer hidden. Secular duties may not be pleasing or trouble-free for you, but the position should not be lightly dismissed. The honors of this world may be an illusion and of no account, but they are important, and you should not deceive yourself.

Perhaps it is because the desire to rule is paramount, rather than the desire to serve. Such folly ensnares the human mind as it delights base human instincts. In open spaces we are easily blinded by the light, and now as the hour of catastrophe approaches we fail to realize how fickle and uncertain our fate and situation has become. If someone has everything under the sun, nothing is truly pleasurable to him, so he jumps from one thing to another, and only in change can he find relief. So he leaps out of the water into the fire, then back into the water, because neither can be endured for long. Thus, commencing a new endeavor becomes the cure for every trouble.

But there is nothing in this world that is solid and stable, nothing that is not uncertain and fleeting, nothing that is not a slave to chance and remains as it is. Daily we are changed, daily we are driven forward, daily precipitated into a whirlpool of misery as we fall headlong into the current.

I wish we could live the way we lived in the past, but life is different today. Character is lacking, and it is considered easier to flee than to stand firm. Certainly flight was always the refuge of the defeated, but then, in the end, life becomes a mist, subject to the slightest breeze, a passing shadow, a languorous sleep, a daily response to the death that continually threatens. A person's state becomes transient, a flight, a station, a journey, a presence, a failure, a certainty, a ruin. Years will go by, days will pass, hours will fly away, moments will slip past. The smallest bits of time will perish, vanishing beneath the stinging knowledge. If this is not so, where now are the rich and powerful men who were famous in their time, desirous of the honor of their ancestors, fixated upon pleasure, and rooted in all manner of vanities on earth? What clouds have fallen upon such names? Yes indeed, they have passed on unexpectedly. They were carried off, and in the blink of an eye they descended into the netherworld. They took nothing with them that they loved but in the end left everything behind. Now, now they wish for that happiness that might have been theirs! Be forewarned against that future unhappiness that is eternal and certain, which cannot fail to come to pass.

So what is there in all this that you should take measures against if, like the faithful and prudent servant, you wish to remove scandal from the kingdom of the Lord, your God? For without a doubt one who can correct a wrong but stands by and does nothing is guilty of wrongdoing. And to whom do you owe faith, to whom the duty of faith, if not to him who created you, raised you from the dust, advanced you, and placed you on the throne of glory? A short time after you were granted favor by your faithful benefactor, he demanded a return on his investment. After that, where is the breath of popular favor? Where then the crowd of followers? Where is the din of flattery, the murmur of acclamation all day long? Well done, well done, the one *who to his own hurt calls good evil and evil good,** thinking that light is a cloud and that a cloud is light, that sweetness is bitterness and bitterness is sweetness. In the end they stand at a distance like friends and kinsmen, their leaders shaking their heads over you and saying, "O how negligible is man! All the profit of the flesh and all his glory is like the bloom of a flower; it dries into hay, and the flower perishes."* And *O, what does it profit a person if he gains the whole world, but loses his own soul?** Everyone will flee from you and leave you alone with the burden of your conscience, that which knows wisdom and cannot conquer virtue or corrupt mercy.

So *let not the oil of sinners anoint* your *head.** The lord justly placed you in authority, not to dominate the clergy but so you might become an example for your colleagues. Moreover you should have disproved the invader of the alien law. You are appointed the shepherd of the flock of Christ not arrogantly to dominate them, but anxiously to watch over them. I ask you, if one is absent, did you seek another,* and did you try to remember what might happen to the one who was asked, *How do you enter here without the nuptial garment?* He was gagged, his hands and feet bound, and he was cast into the darkness outside.*

Therefore, as long as it is permitted, I will take the opportunity to point out the meaning of your title, keeping in mind your well-being and the success of your undertaking. The duty of the bishop is to

*Isa 5:20

*see Matt 6:30; Luke 12:28
*Mark 8:36

*Ps 140:5

*see Matt 18:12; Luke 15:4

*Matt 22:11-13

provide necessities for the poor, not to brood over his own wealth. The minister is ordained a steward and a servant, not to watch out for his own profit and gain but to give of himself. The treasure of the church is the affairs of the poor, the price of blood, and the inheritance of the crucified. And surely, just as a certain holy man says, it is a matter of sacrilege not to give to the poor what is theirs. As the scribes and Pharisees bear witness, truly it is not permitted to hurl the price of blood into the offering box,* and whoever might want to inherit the patrimony of the crucified is positioned as if on a wheel, which rises and falls. Above all, do not resist the will of the Lord, knowing to what he has appointed you, but, mindful of his commandments, be content when you bring it to a conclusion, just as your fathers were, who are clearly praised in the church of the saints. You imitate the example of such honorable endeavors, and, assisted by the favor of friends, you will earn even more favor, for favor is not given up for nothing but, even better, will be returned to you abundantly in a miraculous exchange.

*see Matt 27:6

With how much verbosity and with how many faults do I detain your eyes upon the overly long page? It causes me to neglect my intention of solicitude, affection, devotion, and genuine love. But now I make an end, begging Christ that it is finished to the justice of all believers that through him you may be able to live well now and, after this life, to reign with him in blessed eternity.

Bibliography

Works by Aelred of Rievaulx

Collected Works

Aelredi Rievallensis Opera Omnia. Vol. 1: *Opera Ascetica.* Edited by Anselm Hoste and Charles H. Talbot. Vols. 2ABC: *Sermones.* Edited by Gaetano Raciti. Vol. 2D: *Homeliae de oneribus propheticis Isaiae.* Edited by Gaetano Raciti. Vol. 3: *Opera historica et hagiographica.* Edited by Domenico Pezzini. Vol. 3A: *Vita S. Edwardi.* Edited by Francesco Marzella. Corpus Christianorum, Continuatio Mediaevalis 1–3 (CCCM). Turnhout: Brepols, 1971–2017.

Beati Aelredi Rievallis Abbatis. Edited by J.-P. Migne. Patrologia Latina. Paris, 1855. 195:209–796.

The Historical Works. Translated by Jane Patricia Freeland. Edited by Marsha L. Dutton. CF 56. Kalamazoo, MI: Cistercian Publications, 2005.

The Lives of the Northern Saints. Translated by Jane Patricia Freeland. Edited by Marsha L. Dutton. CF 71. Kalamazoo, MI: Cistercian Publications, 2006.

Treatises and Pastoral Prayer. Translated by Theodore Berkeley, Mary Paul Macpherson, and R. Penelope Lawson. CF 2. Kalamazoo, MI: Cistercian Publications, 1971.

Selected Individual Works

De anima (CCCM 1:683–754)
    Dialogue on the Soul. Translated by C. H. Talbot. CF 22. Kalamazoo, MI: Cistercian Publications, 1981.
Relatio de Standardo (CCCM 3:57–73)
    "The Battle of the Standard." In *Historical Works*, 47–69.
    "De bello standardii tempore Stephani regis." PL 195:701–96.

"Relatio venerabilis Aelredi, Abbatis Rievallensis, de standardo." In *Chronicles of the Reigns of Stephen, Henry II., and Richard I.* Edited by Richard Howlett. 4 vols. RS 82. London: Longmans, 1884–1890. 3:81–99.

De institutione inclusarum (CCCM 1:637–82)

"De vita eremetica ad sororem liber." In Augustine, *Opera*. PL 32:1451–74.

"Meditatio XV." In Anselm, *Liber Meditationum et Orationum*. PL 158:785–94.

"A Rule of Life for a Recluse." Translated by Mary Paul Macpherson. In *Treatises and Pastoral Prayer*, 43–102.

De Quodam Miraculo Mirabili (CCCM 3:135–46)

"A Certain Wonderful Miracle." In *Northern Saints*, 109–22.

"De sanctimoniali de Wattun." PL 195:789–96.

De sanctis ecclesiae Haugustaldensis et eorum Miraculis (CCCM 3:75–110)

"De sanctis ecclesiae Haugustaldensis." In *The Priory of Hexham: Its Chroniclers, Endowments, and Annals*, edited by James Raine. 2 vols. Surtees Society 44. Durham: Andrews and Co. 1864. 1:173–203.

"The Saints of the Church of Hexham." In *Northern Saints*, 65–107.

De speculo caritatis (CCCM 1:3–161)

The Mirror of Charity. Translated by Elizabeth Connor. Introduction and Notes by Charles Dumont. CF 17. Kalamazoo, MI: Cistercian Publications, 1990.

Speculum caritatis. PL 195:501–620.

De spirituali amicitia (CCCM 1:287–350)

De spirituali amicitia. PL 195:659–702.

Spiritual Friendship. Translated by Mary Eugenia Laker. CF 5. Kalamazoo, MI: Cistercian Publications, 1977.

Spiritual Friendship. Translated by Lawrence C. Braceland. Edited by Marsha L. Dutton. CF 5. Collegeville, MN: Cistercian Publications, 2010.

Epistola Aelredi Abbatis Rievallis ad Gilbertvm Venerabilem Episcopvm Lvndoniensem (CCCM 2D:3–5).

"Abbot Aelred of Rievaulx's Letter to Gilbert, Venerable Bishop of London." CSQ 45, no. 2 (2010): 119–24.

Genealogia regum Anglorum (CCCM 3:1–56)

Genealogia regum Anglorum. PL 195:711–58.

"The Genealogy of the Kings of the English." In *Historical Works*, 71–122.

Liber de Vita Religiosi David Regis Scotie (CCCM 3:5–21)

"De sancto rege Scotorum David." PL 195:713–16.

"Eulogium Dauidis Regis Scotorum." In *Pinkerton's Lives of the Scottish Saints*. Edited by W. M. Metcalfe. 2 vols. Paisley: Alexander Gardner, 1989. 2:269–85.

"Lament for David, King of the Scots." In *Historical Works*, 45–70.

Sermones

Homiliae de Oneribus Propheticis Isaiae (CCCM 2D).

"In translacione sancti Edwardi confessoris." Translated by Tom Licence. In Peter Jackson, "'*In translacione sancti Edwardi confessoris*': The Lost Sermon by Aelred of Rievaulx Found?" CSQ 40, no. 1 (2005): 45–83.

The Liturgical Sermons: The First Clairvaux Collection, Sermons 1–28: Advent-All Saints. Translated by Theodore Berkeley and M. Basil Pennington. CF 58. Kalamazoo, MI: Cistercian Publications, 2001.

The Liturgical Sermons: The Second Clairvaux Collection, Sermons 29–46: Christmas–All Saints. Translated by Marie Anne Mayeski. Introduction by Domenico Pezzini. CF 77. Collegeville, MN: Cistercian Publications, 2016.

Sermones de Oneribus. PL 195:361–500.

"Une allocution familière de S. Aelred conservée dans les mélanges de Matthieu de Rievaulx." Edited by Gaetano Raciti. *Collectanea Cisterciensia* 47 (1985): 267–80.

Vita sancti Edwardi (CCCM 3A)

"The Life of Saint Edward, King and Confessor." In *Historical Works*, 125–243.

Vita S. Edwardi regis et confessoris. PL 195:739–90.

Vita sancti Niniani (CCCM 3:111–34)

"The Life of Ninian." In *Northern Saints*, 35–63.

Lives of S. Ninian and S. Kentigern. Edited by Alexander Penrose Forbes. The Historians of Scotland 5. Edinburgh: Edmonston and Douglas, 1874.

"Vita Niniani." In *Pinkerton's Lives of the Scottish Saints*, edited by W. M. Metcalfe. 2 vols. Paisley: Alexander Gardner, 1889. 1:9–47.

Works by Bernard of Clairvaux

De consideratione (SBOp 3:393–493)

Five Books on Consideration: Advice to a Pope. Translated by John D. Anderson and Elizabeth T. Kennan. CF 37. Kalamazoo, MI: Cistercian Publications, 1976.

Epistolae (SBOp 7–8)
  The Letters of Saint Bernard of Clairvaux. Translated by Bruno Scott
  James. London: Burns & Oates, 1953. Reprinted Kalamazoo, MI:
  Cistercian Publications, 1998.
Liber ad milites templi (de laude novae militia) (SBOp 3:213–39)
  *In Praise of the New Knighthood: A Treatise on the Knights Templar and
  the Holy Places of Jerusalem.* Translated by M. Conrad Greenia. In-
  troduction by Malcolm Barber. CF 19B. Kalamazoo, MI: Cistercian
  Publications, 2000.
Sermones super Cantica canticorum (SBOp 1–2)
  On the Song of Songs I–IV. Translated by Killian Walsh and Irene M.
  Edmonds. CF 4, 7, 31, 40. Kalamazoo, MI: Cistercian Publications,
  1979–1983.
Vita sancti Malachiae (SBOp 3:307–78)
  The Life and Death of Saint Malachy the Irishman. Edited and translated
  by Robert T. Meyer. CF 10. Kalamazoo, MI: Cistercian Publications,
  1978.

Other Primary Sources

Abelard, Peter. *Epistolae.* PL 178:113–379.
Alan of Tewkesbury. *Vita Sancti Thomae, Cantuariensis Archiepiscopi et
  Martyris.* In MTB 2:323–52.
Ambrose. *De virginibus.* PL 16:187–232.
The Anglo-Saxon Chronicle. Edited and translated by Michael Swanton.
  New York: Routledge, 1998.
Annales Sanctae Colombae Senonensis. In MGH *Scriptores, Scriptores (in
  folio),* vol. 1. 102–9.
Anselm. *Epistolae.* In *Sancti Anselmi Cantuariensis Archiepiscopi Opera
  Omnia,* edited by F. S. Schmitt. 6 vols. Stuttgart-Bad Canstatt: Friedrich
  Frommann Verlag, 1963–1968. Vols. 2, 3.
Arnulf of Lisieux. *The Letter Collections of Arnulf of Lisieux.* Translated by
  Carolyn Poling Schriber. Lewiston, Queenston, and Lampeter: Edwin
  Mellen Press, 1997.
———. *The Letters of Arnulf of Lisieux.* Edited by Frank Barlow. Camden,
  3rd ser. 61. London: Royal Historical Society, 1939.
Bales, John. *Index Britanniae Scriptorum.* Edited by R. L. Poole and M.
  Bateson. Oxford: Clarendon Press, 1902.

Becket, Thomas. *The Correspondence of Thomas Becket, Archbishop of Canterbury 1162–1170.* Edited and translated by Anne J. Duggan. 2 vols. Oxford: Clarendon Press, 2000. [CTB]

Bede. *The Ecclesiastical History of the English People.* Edited and translated by Bertram Colgrave and R. A. B. Mynors. Oxford: Clarendon Press, 1969.

Benedict of Peterborough. *Gestis Regis Henrici Secundi Benedicti Abbas.* Edited by William Stubbs. 2 vols. RS 49. London: Longmans, 1867.

―――. *Passio Sancti Thomae Cantuariensis.* In MTB 2:1–19.

Bloch, Marc. "La vie de s. Édouard le Confesseur par Osbert de Clare." *Analecta Bollandiana* 41 (1923): 5–131.

The Book of St Gilbert. Edited and translated by Raymonde Foreville and Gillian Keir. Oxford: Clarendon Press, 1987.

Brut y Tywysogion or The Chronicle of the Princes, Red Book of Hergest Version. Edited and translated by Thomas Jones. Cardiff: University of Wales Press, 1955.

Calendar of Documents Preserved in France Illustrative of the History of Great Britain and Ireland, Vol. 1, A.D. 918–1206. Edited by John Horace Round. London: Eyre and Spottiswoode, 1899.

Cartulaire général de l'ordre du Temple 1119?–1150, Recueil des chartes et des bulles relatives à l'ordre du Temple. Edited by the Marquis d'Albon. Paris: Librairie Ancienne, 1913.

Cartularium Abbathiae de Rievalle ordinis Cisterciensis fundatae anno MCXXXII. Edited by J. C. Atkinson. Surtees Society 83. Durham: Andrews and Co., 1889.

Charters of the Honour of Mowbray, 1107–1191. Edited by Diana E. Greenway. Oxford: Oxford University Press for the British Academy, 1972.

The Charters of King David I: The Written Acts of David I King of Scots, 1124–53 and of his son Henry Earl of Northumberland, 1139–52. Edited by G. W. S. Barrow. Woodbridge: Boydell Press, 1999.

Chronica de Mailros, e Codice Unico. Edited by Joseph Stevenson. Edinburgh: Bannatyne Club, 1835.

Chronica Pontificum Ecclesiae Eboracensis. In *Historians of the Church of York and its Archbishops,* edited by James Raine. 3 vols. RS 71. London: Longmans, 1879–1894. 2:312–445.

Chronicle of Holyrood. In *The Church Historians of England,* edited and translated by Joseph Stevenson. 4 vols. London: Seeleys, 1856. 4, pt. 1:61–75.

Chronicon Angliae Petriburgense. Edited by John Allen Giles. London: D. Nutt, 1845.

Councils and Ecclesiastical Documents Relating to Great Britain and Ireland. Edited by Arthur West Haddan and William Stubbs. 3 vols. Oxford: Clarendon Press, 1869–1878.

Councils and Synods with Other Documents Relating to the English Church. Edited by D. Whitelock, M. Brett, and C. N. L. Brooke. 2 vols. Oxford: Clarendon Press, 1981.

Daniel, Walter. *The Life of Aelred of Rievaulx and the Letter to Maurice.* Translated by Frederick M. Powicke. Introduction by Marsha L. Dutton. CF 57. Kalamazoo, MI: Cistercian Publications, 1994.

———. *The Life of Ailred of Rievaulx by Walter Daniel.* Edited and translated by Frederick M. Powicke. Oxford: Oxford University Press, 1978.

Dugdale, William. *Monasticon Anglicanum.* Edited by the Rev. John Caley, Henry Ellis, and Bandinel Bulkeley. 6 vols. London: Harding and Longmans, 1830. Reprinted Westmead, England: Gregg International, 1970.

Eadmer. *Historia Novorum in Anglia.* Edited by Martin Rule. RS 81. London: Longmans, 1884.

———. *Lives and Miracles of Saints Oda, Dunstan, and Oswald.* Edited and translated by Andrew J. Turner and Bernard J. Muir. Oxford: Clarendon Press, 2006.

Early Yorkshire Charters. Edited by William Farrer. 12 vols. Edinburgh: Ballantyne, 1916.

Edgar, Robert. *An Introduction to the History of Dumfries.* Edited by R. C. Reid. Dumfries: J. Maxwell and Sons, 1915.

English Episcopal Acta 1: Lincoln 1067–1185. Edited by David M. Smith. Oxford: Oxford University Press for the British Academy, 1980.

English Episcopal Acta 2: Canterbury 1162–1190. Edited by C. R. Cheney and Bridgett E. A. Jones. Oxford: Oxford University Press for The British Academy, 1986.

English Episcopal Acta 5: York 1070–1154. Edited by Janet E. Burton. Oxford: Oxford University Press for the British Academy, 1988.

English Episcopal Acta 20: York 1154–1181. Edited by Marie Lovatt. Oxford: Oxford University Press for the British Academy, 2000.

English Episcopal Acta 24: Durham 1153–1195. Edited by M. G. Snape. Oxford: Oxford University Press for the British Academy, 2002.

English Lawsuits from William I to Richard I. Edited by R. C. Van Caenegem. 2 vols. London: Selden Society, 1990–1991.

Eyton, R. E. *Court, Household, and Itinerary of King Henry II, Instancing also the Chief Agents and Adversaries of the King in his Government, Diplomacy, and Strategy.* London: Taylor and Co., 1878.

Feodarium Prioratus Dunelmensis. Edited by William Greenwell. Durham: Andrews and Co. for the Surtees Society, 1872.

fitz Stephen, William. *Vita Sancti Thomae, Cantuariensis archiepiscopi et martyris.* In MTB 3:1–154.

Foliot, Gilbert. *The Letters and Charters of Gilbert Foliot, Abbot of Gloucester (1139–48), Bishop of Hereford (1148–63) and London (1163–87), an edition projected by the late Zachary N. Brooke and completed by Dom Adrian Morey and C. N. L. Brooke.* Edited by Zachary N. Brooke, Adrian Morey, and Christopher N. L. Brooke. Cambridge: Cambridge University Press, 1967.

The Foundation History of the Abbeys of Byland and Jervaulx. Edited by Janet Burton. Borthwick Texts and Studies 35. York: Borthwick Institute for Archives, University of York, 2006.

Garnier de Pont-Sainte-Maxence. *La vie de saint Thomas le martyr, archévêque de Canterbury.* Edited by Célestin Hippeau. Geneva: Slatkine Reprints, 1969.

Geoffrey of Coldingham. *Historiae Dunelmensis Scriptores Tres, Gaufridus de Coldingham, Robertus de Graystanes, et Willielmus de Chambre.* Edited by James Raine. Surtees Society 9. London: J. B. Nichols & Son, 1839.

Gervase of Canterbury. *Chronica.* In *Chronicles of the Reigns of Stephen, Henry II., and Richard I.,* edited by William Stubbs. 2 vols. RS 73. London: Longmans, 1879–1880. Vol. 1.

Gesta Abbatum Monasterii Sancti Albani. In *Chronica Monasterii S. Albani,* edited by Henry T. Riley. 12 vols. RS 28. London: Longmans, 1863–1878. Vol. 4.

Gesta in Concilio Trecensi Anni MCXXVIII. In *Recueil des historiens des Gaules et de la France,* edited by Léopold Delisle. 24 vols. Paris: Victor Palmé, 1869–1967. 14:231–33.

Gesta Stephani. Edited and translated by K. R. Potter. Revised by R. H. C. Davis. Oxford: Clarendon Press, 1976.

Gilbert of Hoyland. *Sermones in canticum canticorum.* PL 184:11–252C.

———. *Sermons on the Song of Songs, I–III.* Translated by Lawrence C. Braceland. CF 14, 20, 26. Kalamazoo, MI: Cistercian Publications, 1978–1979.

———. *The Works of Gilbert of Hoyland IV: Treatises, Epistles, and Sermons with a Letter of Roger of Byland, The Milk of Babes.* Translated by Lawrence C. Braceland. CF 34. Kalamazoo, MI: Cistercian Publications, 1981.

Grim, Edward. *Vita Sancti Thomae, Cantuariensis Archiepiscopi et Martyris.* In MTB 2:353–458.

Henry of Huntingdon. *Historia Anglorum: The History of the English People.* Edited and translated by Diana Greenway. Oxford: Clarendon Press, 1996.

Herbert of Bosham. *Vita Sancti Thomae, Archiepiscopi et Martyris.* In MTB 3:155–534.

Herman of Tournai. *Narratio restaurationis Abbatiae Sancti Martini Tornacensis.* PL 180:37–130C.

Historians of the Church of York and Its Archbishops. Edited by James Raine. 3 vols. RS 71. London: Longmans, 1879–1894.

Hugh the Chanter. *The History of the Church of York 1066–1127.* Edited and translated by Charles Johnson. Oxford: Clarendon Press, 1990.

Hugh of Kirkstall. *Narratio de fundatione Fontanis Monasterii in comitatu Eboracensis.* In *Memorials of the Abbey of St. Mary of Fountains,* edited by John Richard Walbran. London & Edinburgh: Andrews and Co. for the Surtees Society, 1863. 1–129.

Institutes of the Gilbertine Order. In William Dugdale, *Monasticon Anglicanum,* edited by John Caley, Henry Eales, and Bulkeley Bandinel. 6 vols. London, 1846. Vol. 6, pt. 2, insert after p. 945, xix–lviii.

Jocelin of Furness. *Vita S. Waltheni Abbatis.* In *Acta Sanctorum,* August 3, 248–77.

John of Fordun. *Johannis de Fordun chronica gentis Scotorum.* Edited by William F. Skene. Edinburgh: Edmonston and Douglas, 1871.

———. *John of Fordun's Chronicle of the Scottish Nation.* Translated by William F. Skene. Edinburgh: Edmonston and Douglas, 1872.

John of Hexham. *Historia.* In *Symeonis Monachi opera omnia,* edited by Thomas Arnold. 2 vols. RS 75. London: Longmans, 1882–1885. 2:284–332.

John of Salisbury. *Anselm and Becket: Two Canterbury Saints' Lives by John of Salisbury.* Translated by Ronald E. Pepin. Toronto: Pontifical Institute of Medieval Studies, 2009.

———. *Historia Pontificalis.* Edited and translated by Marjorie Chibnall. Oxford: Clarendon Press, 1986.

———. *John of Salisbury's Entheticus maior and minor.* Edited by Jan van Laaroven. 3 vols. Leiden: Brill, 1987.

———. *The Letters of John of Salisbury, Volume One, The Early Letters (1153–1161).* Edited and translated by W. J. Millor, S. J. Butler, and H. E. Butler. Revised by C. N. L. Brooke. Oxford: Clarendon Press, 1986.

————. *The Letters of John of Salisbury, Volume Two, The Later Letters (1163–1180)*. Edited and translated by W. J. Millor and C. N. L. Brooke. Oxford: Clarendon Press, 1979.

————. *Vita Sancti Thomae, Cantuariensis archiepiscopi et martyris*. In MTB 2:299–322.

John of Worcester. *The Chronicle of John of Worcester*. Edited by R. R. Darlington and P. McGurk. Translated by Jennifer Bray and P. McGurk. 3 vols. Oxford: Clarendon Press, 1995–1998.

La Chronique de Morigny (1095–1152). Edited by Léon Mirot. Paris: Picard, 1912.

Lambeth Anonymous. *Vita Sancti Thomae, Cantuariensis archiepiscopi et martyris*. In MTB 4:80–144.

Lancashire Pipe Rolls and Early Lancashire Charters. Edited by W. Farrer. Liverpool: Henry Young and Sons, 1902.

Lanfranc. *The Letters of Lanfranc, Archbishop of Canterbury*. Edited and translated by Helen Clover and Margaret Gibson. Oxford: Clarendon Press, 1979.

Lansdowne Anonymous. *"Excerpta e Codice MS*to *Lansdowniano 398,"* in MTB 4:145–85.

Lawrence of Durham. *Dialogi Laurentii Dunelmensis monachi ac prioris*. Surtees Society 70. Durham: Andrews and Co., 1880.

Lawrie, Sir Archibald Campbell. *Annals of the Reigns of Malcolm and William, Kings of Scotland A.D. 1153–1214*. Glasgow: Robert Maclehose & Co., 1910. Reprinted Oswald Press, 2008.

Leges Henrici Primi. Edited and translated by L. J. Downer. Oxford: Clarendon Press, 1972.

Liber Cartarum Sancte Crucis: Munimenta ecclesie Sancte Crucis de Edwinesburg. Edinburgh: Bannatyne Club, 1840.

Liber Eliensis. Edited by E. O. Blake. Camden 3rd ser. 92. London: Royal Historical Society, 1962.

Liber Monasterii de Hyda. Edited by Edward Edwards. RS 45. London: Longmans, 1866.

Liber S. Maria de Calchou: Registrum cartarum abbacie Tironensis de Kelso 1113–1567. 2 vols. Edinburgh: Bannatyne Club, 1846.

The Life of Christina of Markyate, A Twelfth Century Recluse. Edited and translated by C. H. Talbot. Oxford: Clarendon Press, 1959.

The Life of King Edward Who Rests at Westminster. Edited and translated by Frank Barlow. 2nd ed. Oxford: Clarendon Press, 1992.

MacQueen, John. *St Nynia*, with a translation of the *Miracula Nynie Epis-copi* and the *Vita Niniani* by Winifred MacQueen. Edinburgh: Birlinn Ltd., 2005.

Materials for the History of Thomas Becket, Archbishop of Canterbury. Edited by James Craigie Robertson. 7 vols. RS 67. London: Longmans, 1875–1885. [MTB]

A Mediaeval Chronicle of Scotland: The Chronicle of Melrose. Translated by Joseph Stevenson. London: Seeleys, 1853. Reprinted Lampeter, Scotland: Llanerch Press, 1991.

Miracula Nynie Episcopi. Edited by Karl Strecker. In MGH *Poetae Latini Aevi Carolini*. 6 vols. Weidmannsche: Berlin, 1978. Vol. 4, pt. 3:944–62.

Missale ad usum ecclesie Westmonasteriensis. 3 vols. Henry Bradshaw Society 1, 5, 12. London, 1891–1896. Vol. 2.

Narrative and Legislative Texts from Early Cîteaux. Edited and translated by Chrysogonus Waddell. Cîteaux: Commentarii Cistercienses, 1999.

Odo of Deuil. *De profectione Ludovici VII in Orientem*. Edited and translated by Virginia G. Berry. New York: Columbia University Press, 1948.

Orderic Vitalis. *The Ecclesiastical History*. Edited and translated by Marjorie Chibnall. 6 vols. Oxford: Clarendon Press, 1969–1980.

Otto of Freising. *The Deeds of Frederick Barbarossa*. Translated by Charles Christopher Mierow and Richard Emery. New York: Columbia University Press, 2004.

———. *Gesta Friderici I Imperatoris*. MGH *Scriptores, Scriptores rerum Germanicarum in usum scholarum separatim editi*. Vol. 46. Hannover: Hahnsche Buchhandlung, 1978.

Päpsturkunden in England. Edited by Walther Holtzmann. 3 vols. Berlin: Weidmannsche Buchhandlung, 1930–1952.

Peter of Celle. *Commentaria in Ruth*. Turnhout: Brepols Publishers, 1983.

Peter the Venerable. *The Letters of Peter the Venerable*. Edited by Giles Constable. 2 vols. Cambridge, MA: Harvard University Press, 1967.

Pipe Roll 31 Henry I. Edited by Joseph Hunter. London: Record Society, 1833.

Ralph of Diceto. *Radulphi de Diceto Decani Londoniensis Opera Historica: The Historical Works of Master Ralph de Diceto, Dean of London (to 1202)*. Edited by William Stubbs. 2 vols. RS 68. London: Longmans, 1876.

Recueil des Historiens des Gaules et de la France. Edited by Léopold Delisle. 24 vols. Paris: Victor Palmé, 1869–1967.

Regesta Pontificum Romanorum ad annum post Christum natum 1198. Edited by P. Jaffé. Revised by W. Wattenbach, S. Loewenfeld, F. Kaltenbrunner, and P. Ewald. 2 vols. Leipzig: Veit, 1885–1888.

Regesta Regum Anglo-Normannorum: The Acta of William I (1066–1087). Edited by David Bates. Oxford: Clarendon Press, 1998.

Regesta Regum Anglo-Normannorum 1066–1154, Vol. II, Regesta Henrici Primi 1100–1135. Edited by Charles Johnson and H. A. Cronne. Oxford: Clarendon Press, 1956.

Regesta Regum Anglo-Normannorum 1066–1154, Vol. III, Regesta Regis Stephani ac Mathildis Imperatricis ac Gaufridi et Henrici Ducum Normannorum 1135–1154. Edited by H. A. Cronne and R. H. C. Davis. Oxford: Clarendon Press, 1968.

Regesta Regum Scottorum: Vol. 1: The Acts of Malcolm IV, King of Scots 1153–1165 together with Scottish Royal Acts prior to 1153 not included in Sir Archibald Lawrie's Early Scottish Charters. Edited by G. W. S. Barrow. Edinburgh: Edinburgh University Press, 1960.

Regesta Regum Scottorum: Vol. 2: The Acts of William I King of Scots 1165–1214. Edited by G. W. S. Barrow. Edinburgh: Edinburgh University Press, 1971.

Reginald of Durham. *Libellus de admirandis beati Cuthberti virtutibus.* Surtees Society 1. London: J. B. Nichols and Sons, 1835.

———. *Libellus de vita et miraculis S. Godrici heremitae de Finchale.* Surtees Society 20. London: J. B. Nichols and Sons, 1847.

Register and Records of Holm Cultram. Edited by F. Grainger and W. G. Collingwood. Kendal: Titus Wilson and Son for the Cumberland and Westmorland Antiquarian and Archaeological Society, 1929.

The Registrum Antiquissimum of the Cathedral Church of Lincoln. Edited by C. W. Foster. 3 vols. Hereford: Hereford Times for the Lincoln Record Society, 1931–1935. Reprinted Woodbridge: Boydell, 2008.

Richard of Cirencester. *Speculum historiale de gestis regum Angliae.* Edited by E. B. Mayor. 2 vols. RS 30. London: Longmans, 1863–1869.

Richard of Hexham. *De gestis Regis Stephani et de Bello Standardo.* In *Chronicles of the Reigns of Stephen, Henry II., and Richard I.*, edited by Richard Howlett. 4 vols. RS 82. London: Longmans, 1884–1890. 3:139–78.

———. *History of the Church of Hexham.* In *The Priory of Hexham: Its Chroniclers, Endowments, and Annals*, edited by James Raine. 2 vols. Surtees Society 44 and 46. Durham: Andrews and Co., 1864. 1:1–62.

Robert of Torigny. *Chronica.* In *Chronicles of the Reigns of Stephen, Henry II., and Richard I.,* edited by Richard Howlett. 4 vols. RS 82. London: Longmans, 1884–1890. Vol. 4.

Roger of Hoveden. *Chronica Magistri Rogeri de Houedene.* Edited by William Stubbs. 4 vols. RS 51. London: Longmans, 1868–1871.

Roger of Pontigny. *Vita Sancti Thomae, Cantuariensis archiepiscopi et martyris.* In MTB 4:1–79.

The Rule of St. Benedict in English. Edited by Timothy Fry. Collegeville, MN: Liturgical Press, 1982.

Schmeidler, Bernhard, ed. *Magistri Adam Bremensis Gesta Hammaburgensis ecclesiae pontificum.* 3rd ed. MGH: Scriptores rerum germanicarum. Hannover and Leipzig: Hahnsche Buchhandlang, 1917.

Sigebert of Gembloux. *Chronica, Auctarium Corbeiense, Continuatio Praemonstratensis.* MGH *Scriptores. Scriptores (in folio).* 39 vols. 6:417–56.

Simeon of Durham. *Libellus de Exordio atque Procursu istius hoc est Dunhelmensis Ecclesie: Tract on the Origins and Progress of this the Church of Durham.* Edited and translated by David Rollason. Oxford: Clarendon Press, 2000.

———. *Opera Omnia.* Edited by Thomas Arnold. 2 vols. RS 75. London: Longmans, 1882–1885.

Staunton, Michael. *The Lives of Thomas Becket.* Manchester: Manchester University Press, 2001.

Suger. *L'histoire du roi Louis VII.* In *Vie de Louis le Gros par Suger suivie de l'histoire du roi Louis VII. Publiées d'après les manuscrits,* edited by Auguste Molinier. Paris: Picard, 1887. 148–78.

———. *Vie de Louis VI Le Gros.* Edited and translated by Henri Waquet. Paris: Société d'Édition Les Belles Lettres, 1964.

Summa causae inter regem et Thomam. In MTB 4:201–12.

The Templars: Select Sources Translated and Annotated. Translated by Malcolm Barber and Keith Bate. Manchester: Manchester University Press, 2002.

Thomas Saga Erkibyskups: A Life of Archbishop Thomas Becket, in Icelandic, with English Translation, Notes and Glossary. Edited by M. Eirikr Magnusson. 2 vols. RS 65. London: Longmans, 1875–1883.

Vita Sancti Willelmi. In *Historians of the Church of York and its Archbishops,* edited by James Raine. 3 vols. RS 71. London: Longmans, 1879–1894. 2:270–91.

Wigtownshire Charters. Edited by R. C. Reid. Scottish Historical Society, ser. 3, no. 51. Edinburgh: T. and A. Constable, 1960.

William of Canterbury. *Vita, passio et miracula S. Thomae Cantuariensis Archiepiscopi*. In MTB, vol. 1.

William of Malmesbury. *Gesta Pontificum Anglorum: The History of the English Bishops*. Edited and translated by M. Winterbottom and R. M. Thomson. 2 vols. Oxford: Clarendon Press, 2007. Vol. 1.

———. *Gesta Regum Anglorum: The History of the English Kings*. Edited and translated by R. A. B. Mynors, R. M. Thomson, and M. Winterbottom. 2 vols. Oxford: Clarendon Press, 1998. Vol. 1.

———. *Historia Novella: The Contemporary History*. Edited by Edmund King. Translated by K. R. Potter. Oxford: Clarendon Press, 1998.

William of Newburgh. *Historia Rerum Anglicarum*. In *Chronicles of the Reigns of Stephen, Henry II., and Richard I.*, edited by Richard Howlett. 4 vols. RS 82. London: Longmans, 1884–1890. Vol. 1.

William of Saint-Thierry, Arnold of Bonneval, and Geoffrey of Auxerre. *The First Life of Bernard of Clairvaux*. Translated with an introduction and notes by Hilary Costello. CF 76. Collegeville, MN: Cistercian Publications, 2015.

———. *Vita Prima Sancti Bernardi Claravallis Abbatis, Liber Primus*. Edited by Paul Verdeyen. CCCM 89B. Turnhout: Brepols, 2011.

Secondary Sources

Amélineau, E. "Saint Bernard et le schisme d'Anaclet II (1130–1138)." *Revue des questions historiques* 30 (1881): 47–112.

Amt, Emily. *The Accession of Henry II in England: Royal Government Restored, 1149–1159*. Woodbridge: Boydell Press, 1993.

Astell, Ann W. "To Build the Church: Saint Aelred of Rievaulx's Hexaemeral Miracles in the *Life of Ninian*." CSQ 49, no. 4 (2014): 455–81.

Atkinson, J. C. "Existing Traces of Mediaeval Iron-working in Cleveland." *The Yorkshire Archaeological and Topographical Journal* 8 (1884): 30–48.

Baker, Derek. "Patronage in the Early Twelfth-Century Church: Walter Espec, Kirkham and Rievaulx." In *Traditio, Krisis, Renovatio aus theologischer Sicht: Festschrift Winfried Zeller zum 65. Geburtstag*, edited by Bernd Jaspert and Rudolf Mohr. Marburg: Elwert, 1976. 92–100.

———. "*Viri Religiosi* and the York Election Dispute." In *Councils and Assemblies*, edited by G. J. Cuming and Derek Baker. Cambridge: Cambridge University Press, 1971. 87–100.

Barker, Lynn. "Ivo of Chartres and Anselm of Canterbury." *Anselm Studies* 2, no. 2 (1988): 13–33.

Barlow, Frank. *Edward the Confessor*. Berkeley and Los Angeles: University of California Press, 1970.

———. *The English Church: 1066–1154*. London: Longmans, 1979.

———. "The English, Norman, and French Councils Called to Deal with the Papal Schism of 1159." *English Historical Review* 51, no. 202 (1936): 264–68.

———. "Pont L'Évêque, Roger de (c. 1115–1181)." *DNB* 23961.

———. *Thomas Becket*. Berkeley and Los Angeles: University of California Press, 1986.

Bartoniek, Emma, ed. "Legenda sancti Ladislai regis." In *Scriptores rerum Hungaricarum*, edited by Imre Szentpétery. 2 vols. Budapest: Academia litter. Hungarica, 1937–1938.

Beeler, John. *Warfare in England, 1066–1189*. Ithaca, NY: Cornell University Press, 1966.

Bell, David N., ed. "Rievaulx, Yorkshire N.R. *Cist. Abbey of B.V.M.*" In *The Libraries of the Cistercians, Gilbertines and Premonstratensians*, edited by David N. Bell. Corpus of British Medieval Library Catalogues 2. London: The British Library in association with the British Academy, 1992. 87–140.

Bequette, John P. "Aelred of Rievaulx's *Life of Saint Edward, King and Confessor*: A Saintly King and the Salvation of the English People." *CSQ* 43, no. 1 (2008): 17–40.

Berger, David. "The Attitude of St. Bernard of Clairvaux toward the Jews." *Proceedings of the American Academy for Jewish Research* 40 (1973): 89–108.

Berman, Constance H. *The Cistercian Evolution: The Invention of a Religious Order in Twelfth-Century Europe*. Philadelphia: University of Pennsylvania Press, 2000.

———. "Men's Houses, Women's Houses: The Relationship between the Sexes in Twelfth-Century Monasticism." In *The Medieval Monastery*, edited by Andrew MacLeish. Medieval Studies at Minnesota 2. St. Cloud, MN: North Star Press of St. Cloud, 1988. 43–52.

———. "Were There Twelfth-Century Cistercian Nuns?" *Church History* 68, no. 4 (1999): 824–64.

———. *Women and Monasticism in Medieval Europe: Sisters and Patrons of the Cistercian Reform*. Kalamazoo, MI: Medieval Institute Publications, 2002.

Bethel, Denis. "English Black Monks and Episcopal Elections in the 1120s." *English Historical Review* 84, no. 333 (1969): 673–98.

Bliese, John R. E. "Aelred of Rievaulx's Rhetoric and Morale at the Battle of the Standard, 1138." *Albion* 20, no. 4 (1988): 543–56.

Bloch, Herbert. "The Schism of Anacletus II and the Glanfeuil Forgeries of Peter the Deacon of Monte Casino." *Traditio* 8 (1958): 159–264.

Bolton, Brenda. "St. Alban's Loyal Son." In *Adrian IV, The English Pope (1154–1159)*, edited by Brenda Bolton and Anne J. Duggan. Aldershot: Ashgate, 2003. 75–103.

Boswell, John. *Christianity, Social Tolerance, and Homosexuality: Gay People in Western Europe from the Beginning of the Christian Era to the Fourteenth Century*. Chicago: University of Chicago Press, 1981.

Bouchard, Constance Brittain. *Holy Entrepreneurs: Cistercians, Knights, and Economic Exchange in Twelfth-Century Burgundy*. Ithaca: Cornell University Press, 1991.

Boutiot, T. *Histoire de la ville de Troyes et de la Champagne méridionale*. 2 vols. Troyes: Duffey-Robert, 1870.

Bredero, Adriaan. "The Canonization of Bernard of Clairvaux." In *Saint Bernard of Clairvaux: Studies Commemorating the Eighth Centenary of His Canonization*, edited by M. Basil Pennington. CS 28. Kalamazoo, MI: Cistercian Publications, 1977. 63–100.

Brett, Martin. *The English Church Under Henry I*. Oxford: Oxford University Press, 1975.

Brooke, C. N. L. "Foliot, Gilbert (c. 1110–1187)," DNB 9792.

Brooke, Daphne. *Fergus the King*. Whithorn, Scotland: Friends of the Whithorn Trust, 1991.

———. *Wild Men and Holy Places: St. Ninian, Whithorn and the Medieval Realm of Galloway*. Edinburgh: Canongate Press, 1994.

Brooke, Z. N., and C. N. L. Brooke. "Henry II, Duke of Normandy and Aquitaine." *English Historical Review* 61, no. 239 (1946): 81–89.

Bulst-Thiele, Marie Luise. "The Influence of St. Bernard of Clairvaux on the Formation of the Order of the Knights Templar." In *The Second Crusade and the Cistercians*, edited by Michael Gervers. New York: St. Martin's Press, 1992. 57–65.

Burton, Janet. "The Abbeys of Byland and Jervaulx, and the Problems of the English Savigniacs, 1134–1156." In *Monastic Studies* 2, edited by Judith Loades. Bangor: Headstart History, 1991. 119–31.

————. "English Monasteries and the Continent in the Reign of King Stephen." In *King Stephen's Reign, 1135–1154*, edited by Paul Dalton and Graeme J. White. Woodbridge: Boydell Press, 2008. 98–114.

————. "The Estates and Economy of Rievaulx Abbey in Yorkshire." *Cîteaux; Commentarii Cistercienses* 49 (1998): 29–93.

————. "*Fundator Noster:* Roger de Mowbray as Founder and Patron of Monasteries." In *Religious and Laity in Western Europe 1000–1400: Interaction, Negotiation, and Power*, edited by Emilia Jamroziak and Janet Burton. Turnhout: Brepols, 2006. 23–39.

————. *The Monastic Order in Yorkshire, 1069–1215*. Cambridge: Cambridge University Press, 1999.

————. "Rievaulx Abbey: The Early Years." In *Perspectives for an Architecture of Solitude*, edited by Terryl N. Kinder. Turnhout: Brepols, 2004. 47–53.

Burton, Janet, and Julia Kerr. *The Cistercians in the Middle Ages*. Woodbridge: Boydell Press, 2011.

Burton, Pierre-André. *Aelred de Rievaulx 1110–1167: De l'homme éclaté a l'être unifié: Essai de biographie existentielle et spirituelle*. Paris: Les Éditions du Cerf, 2010.

————. "Aelred face à l'histoire et à ses historiens: Autour de l'actualité aelrédienne." *Collectanea Cisterciensia* 58 (1996): 161–93.

————. "Aux origines de l'expansion anglaise de Cîteaux: La fondation de Rievaulx et la conversion d'Aelred." *Collectanea Cisterciensia* 61 (1999): 186–214, 248–90.

————. "The Beginnings of Cistercian Expansion in England: The Socio-Historical Context of the Foundation of Rievaulx (1132)." *CSQ* 42, no. 2 (2007): 151–82.

————. "Le récit de la *Bataille de l'Étendard* par Aelred de Rievaulx: Présentation et traduction." *Cîteaux: Commentarii Cistercienses* 58 (2007): 7–41.

Cantor, Norman F. *Church, Kingship, and Lay Investiture in England 1089–1135*. Princeton, NJ: Princeton University Press, 1958.

Cheney, C. R. "Papal Privileges for Gilbertine Houses." In C. R. Cheney, *Medieval Texts and Studies*. Oxford: Clarendon Press, 1973. 39–65.

Cheney, Mary. "The Recognition of Pope Alexander III: Some Neglected Evidence." *English Historical Review* 84, no. 332 (1969): 474–97.

Cheyette, Frederic. "Suum cuique tribuere." *French Historical Studies* 6 (1970): 287–99.

Chibnall, Marjorie. *The Empress Matilda: Queen Consort, Queen Mother and Lady of the English*. Oxford: Blackwell, 1991.

Chodorow, Stanley A. "Ecclesiastical Politics and the Ending of the Investiture Contest: The Papal Election of 1119 and the Negotiations of Mouzon." *Speculum* 46, no. 4 (1971): 613–40.

Clanchy, Michael T. *From Memory to Written Record: England 1066–1307.* London: Edward Arnold, 1979.

Clay, C. T. "Notes on the Early Archdeacons in the Church of York." *Yorkshire Archaeological Journal* 36 (1946–47): 269–87, 409–34.

Constable, Giles. "Aelred of Rievaulx and the Nun of Watton: An Episode in the Early History of the Gilbertine Order." In *Medieval Women*, edited by Derek Baker. Oxford: Blackwell Press, 1978. 205–26.

———. "Diplomats and Dictators in the Eleventh and Twelfth Centuries: Medieval Epistolography and the Birth of Modern Bureaucracy." *Dumbarton Oaks Papers* 46 (1992): 37–46.

———. "The Disputed Election at Langres in 1138." *Traditio* 13 (1957): 119–52.

———. *Monastic Tithes from Their Origins to the Twelfth Century.* Cambridge: Cambridge University Press, 1964.

———. "On Editing the Letters of Peter the Venerable." *Quellen und Falschungen aus italienischen Archiven und Bibliotheken* 54 (1974): 483–508.

———. *The Reformation of the Twelfth Century.* Cambridge: Cambridge University Press, 1996.

Cowdrey, H. E. J. "Lanfranc, the Papacy, and the See of Canterbury." In *Lanfranco di Pavia e l'Europa del secolo XI: nel IX centenario della morte (1089–1989): atti del convegno internazionale di studi (Pavia, Almo Collegio Borromeo, 21–24 settembre 1989),* edited by G. D'Onofrio. Rome: Herder Editrice e Libreria, 1993. 439–500.

Cronne, H. A. "Ranulf de Gernons, Earl of Chester, 1129–53." *Transactions of the Royal Historical Society,* 4th ser. 20 (1937): 103–34.

Crouch, David. *The Beaumont Twins: The Roots and Branches of Power.* Cambridge: Cambridge University Press, 1986.

———. *The Reign of King Stephen, 1135–1154.* Harlow, UK: Pearson Education Ltd., 2000.

———. "Robert, Second Earl of Leicester (1104–1168)." DNB 1882.

Crumplin, Sally. "Modernizing St. Cuthbert: Reginald of Durham's Miracle Collection." *Studies in Church History* 41 (2005): 179–91.

Dalton, Paul. "Churchmen and the Promotion of Peace in King Stephen's Reign." *Viator* 31 (2000): 79–119.

Davies, Wendy, and Paul Fouracre. *The Settlement of Disputes in Early Medieval Europe.* Cambridge: Cambridge University Press, 1986.

Davis, R. H. C. *King Stephen, 1135–1154*. 3rd ed. London: Longmans, 1990.

Degler-Spengler, Brigitte. "The Incorporation of Cistercian Nuns into the Order in the Twelfth and Thirteenth Century." In *Hidden Springs: Cistercian Monastic Women*, edited by John A. Nichols and Lillian Thomas Shank. 3 vols. Medieval Religious Women. CS 113A. Kalamazoo, MI: Cistercian Publications, 1995. Vol. 3, bk. 1:85–134.

Delisle, Léopold. "Documents Relative to the Abbey of Furness, Extracted from the Archives of Savigny." *Journal of the British Archaeological Association* 6 (1851): 419–24.

DeVailly, Guy. *Le Diocèse de Bourges*. Paris: Letourzey et Ané, 1973.

Dickinson, J. C. *The Origins of the Austin Canons and Their Introduction into England*. London: SPCK, 1950.

Dietz, Elias. "Ambivalence Well Considered: An Interpretive Key to the Whole of Aelred's Works." CSQ 47, no. 1 (2012): 71–85.

Dimier, Marie-Anselme. "Henri II, Thomas Becket et les Cisterciens." In *Thomas Becket: Actes du colloque international de Sédières, 19–24 août 1973*, edited by Raymonde Foreville. Paris: Beauchesne, 1975. 49–53.

Donaldson, Gordon. "The Bishops and Priors of Whithorn." *Transactions of the Dumfriesshire and Galloway Natural History and Antiquarian Society*, series 3, 27 (1948–49): 127–54.

———. "Scottish Bishops' Sees Before the Reign of David I." *Proceedings of the Society of Antiquaries of Scotland* 87 (1952–1953): 106–17.

DuFour-Malbezin, Annie. *Actes des Évêques de Laon des origines à 1151*. Paris: CNRS Editions, 2001.

Duggan, Anne. "Henry II, the English Church and the Papacy, 1154–76." In *Henry II: New Interpretations*, edited by Christopher Harper-Bill and Nicholas Vincent. Woodbridge: Boydell Press, 2007. 154–83.

———. *Thomas Becket*. London: Arnold Publishing, 2004.

Duggan, Charles. "Bishop John and Archdeacon Richard of Poitiers: Their Roles in the Becket Dispute." In *Thomas Becket: Actes du colloque international de Sédières, 19–24 août 1973*, edited by Raymonde Foreville. Paris: Beauchesne, 1975. 72–83.

Dumont, Charles. "Autour des sermons *De Oneribus* d'Aelred de Rievaulx." *Collectanea Ordinis Cisterciensium Reformatorum* 19 (1957): 114–21.

———. Review of Gilbert of Hoyland, *Sermons on the Song of Songs*, vol. 1, CF 14. *Bulletin de Spiritualité* n. 749. *Collectanea Cisterciensia* 41 (1979): 469–71.

Dunbabin, Jean. "Canterbury, John of (c. 1120–1204?)." DNB 2062.

Dutton, Marsha L. "Aelred of Rievaulx on Friendship, Chastity, and Sex: The Sources." CSQ 29, no. 2 (1994): 121–96.

———. "The Conversion and Vocation of Aelred of Rievaulx: A Historical Hypothesis." In *England in the Twelfth Century: Proceedings of the 1988 Harlaxton Symposium,* edited by Daniel Williams. Woodbridge: Boydell Press, 1990. 31–49.

———. "Getting Things the Wrong Way Round: Composition and Transposition in Aelred of Rievaulx' *De institutione inclusarum.*" In *Heaven on Earth, Studies in Medieval Cistercian History IX,* edited by E. Rozanne Elder. CS 68. Kalamazoo, MI: Cistercian Publications, 1983. 90–101.

———. "A Historian's Historian: The Place of Bede in Aelred's Contributions to the New History of His Age." In *Truth As Gift: Studies in Honor of John R. Sommerfeldt,* edited by Marsha Dutton, Daniel M. La Corte, and Paul Lockey. CS 204. Kalamazoo, MI: Cistercian Publications, 2004. 407–48.

———. "Saints Refusing to Leave: Aelred of Rievaulx's *The Saints of Hexham* as an Inverted *Translatio.*" *The Medieval Translator, vol. 15, In Principio Fuit Interpres,* edited by Alessandra Petrina. Turnhout: Brepols, 2013. 187–200.

———. "*Sancto Dunstano Cooperante*: Collaboration between King and Ecclesiastical Advisor in Aelred of Rievaulx's *Genealogy of the Kings of the English.*" In *Religious and Laity in Western Europe 1000–1400: Interaction, Negotiation, and Power,* edited by Emilia Jamroziak and Janet Burton. Turnhout: Brepols, 2006. 183–95.

———. "This Ministry of Letters: Aelred of Rievaulx's Attempt to Anglicize England's King Henry II." In *Monasticism between Culture and Cultures: Acts of the Third International Symposium, Rome, June 8–11, 2011,* edited by Philippe Nouzille and Michaela Pfeifer. *Analecta Monastica* 14. Turnhout: Brepols, 2013. 169–93.

———. "Were Aelred of Rievaulx and Gilbert of Sempringham Friends? Evidence from Aelred's *A Certain Wonderful Miracle* and the Gilbertine Lay Brothers' Revolt," forthcoming in *American Benedictine Review,* 2017.

Dutton-Stuckey, Marsha. "A Prodigal Writes Home: Aelred of Rievaulx's *De institutione inclusarum.*" In *Heaven on Earth: Studies in Medieval Cistercian History IX,* edited by E. Rozanne Elder. CS 68. Kalamazoo, MI: Cistercian Publications, 1983. 35–42.

Elkins, Sharon K. "All Ages, Every Condition, and Both Sexes: The Emergence of a Gilbertine Identity." In *Distant Echoes,* edited by John A.

Nichols and Lillian Thomas Shank. *Medieval Religious Women*. 3 vols. CS 71. Kalamazoo, MI: Cistercian Publications, 1984. 1:62–82.

———. *Holy Women of Twelfth-Century England*. Chapel Hill, NC: University of North Carolina Press, 1988.

Fergusson, Peter. "Aelred's Abbatial Residence at Rievaulx Abbey." In *Studies in Cistercian Art and Architecture*, vol. 5, edited by Meredith P. Lillich. CS 167. Kalamazoo, MI: Cistercian Publications, 1998. 41–58.

Fergusson, Peter, and Stuart Harrison. "The Rievaulx Abbey Chapter-House." *Antiquaries Journal* 74 (1994): 216–53.

———. *Rievaulx Abbey: Community, Architecture, Memory*. New Haven, CT: Yale University Press, 1999.

Flanagan, Marie Therese. *The Transformation of the Irish Church in the Twelfth and Thirteenth Centuries*. Woodbridge: Boydell Press, 2010.

Foreville, Raymonde. "La crise de l'ordre de Sempringham au XIIᵉ siècle: Nouvelle approche du dossier des frères lais." *Anglo-Norman Studies* 7 (1983): 39–57.

———. *L'Église et la royauté en Angleterre sous Henri II Plantagenet (1154–1189)*. Paris: Bloud and Gay, 1943.

Fossier, Robert. "La vie économique de Clairvaux des origines à la fin de la guerre de Cent Ans: 1115–1471." Thèse, École des Chartes, 1949.

Freeman, Elizabeth A. "Aelred of Rievaulx's *De Bello Standardii*: Cistercian Hagiography and the Creation of Community Memories." *Cîteaux: Commentarii Cistercienses* 49 (1998): 5–28.

———. "Aelred of Rievaulx's Pastoral Care of Religious Women, with Special Reference to the *De institutione inclusarum*." CSQ 46, no. 1 (2011): 13–26.

———. "Gilbert of Hoyland's Sermons for Nuns: A Cistercian Abbot and the *cura monialium* in Twelfth-Century Lincolnshire." CSQ 50, no. 3 (2015): 267–91.

———. *Narratives of a New Order: Cistercian Historical Writing in England, 1150–1220*. Medieval Church Studies 2. Turnhout: Brepols, 2002.

———. "Nuns." *The Cambridge Companion to the Cistercian Order*. Edited by Mette Birkedal Bruun. Cambridge, UK: Cambridge University Press, 2013.

———. "Nuns in the Public Sphere: Aelred of Rievaulx's *De sanctimoniali de Wattun* and the Gendering of Authority." *Comitatus* 26 (1996): 55–80.

Garrity, Mariann. "'Hidden Honey': The Many Meanings of Saint Aelred of Rievaulx's *De bello standardii*." CSQ 44, no. 1 (2009): 57–64.

Geary, Patrick J. "Living with Conflicts in Stateless France: A Typology of Conflict Management Mechanisms 1050–1200." In Patrick J. Geary, *Living with the Dead in the Middle Ages*. Ithaca: Cornell University Press, 1994. 125–60.

———. "Moral Obligations and Peer Pressure: Conflict Resolution in the Medieval Aristocracy." In *Georges Duby: L'écriture de l'histoire*, edited by Claudie Duhamel-Amado and Guy Lobrichon. Brussels: DeBoeck Université, 1996. 217–22.

Gibbons, Joseph. Introduction to *Geoffrey of Auxerre: On the Apocalypse*. CF 42. Kalamazoo, MI: Cistercian Publications, 2000. 7–13.

Glidden, Aelred. "Aelred the Historian: The Account of the Battle of the Standard." In *Erudition at God's Service: Studies in Medieval Cistercian History XI*, edited by John R. Sommerfeldt. CS 98. Kalamazoo, MI: Cistercian Publications, 1987. 175–84.

Golding, Brian. *Gilbert of Sempringham and the Gilbertine Order, c. 1130– c.1300*. Oxford: Clarendon Press, 1995.

———. "Hermits, Monks and Women in Twelfth-Century France and England: The Experience of Obazine and Sempringham." In *Monastic Studies: The Continuity of Tradition*, edited by Judith Loades. Bangor: Headstart History, 1990. 125–45.

———. "St. Bernard and St. Gilbert." In *The Influence of St. Bernard*, edited by Benedicta Ward. Oxford: SLG Press, 1976. 41–52.

Grabois, Aryeh. "Le schisme de 1130 et la France." *Revue d'histoire ecclésiastique* 76 (1981): 593–612.

Graves, Coburn V. "The Economic Activities of the Cistercians in Medieval England." *Analecta Sacri Ordinis Cisterciensis* 13 (1957): 3–60.

Green, Judith A. *The Government of England Under Henry I*. Cambridge: Cambridge University Press, 1986.

———. *Henry I: King of England and Duke of Normandy*. Cambridge: Cambridge University Press, 2006.

———. "The Last Century of Danegeld." *English Historical Review* 95, no. 379 (1981): 241–58.

Guy, John. *Thomas Becket: Warrior, Priest, Rebel*. New York: Random House, 2012.

Gwynn, Aubrey. "St. Malachy of Armagh." *The Irish Ecclesiastical Record* 70 (1948): 961–78.

Harper-Bill, Christopher. "Bishop William Turbe and the Diocese of Norwich, 1146–1174." *Anglo-Norman Studies* 7 (1984): 142–60.

Haseldine, Julian. "Friendship and Rivalry: The Role of *amicitia* in Twelfth-Century Monastic Relations." *Journal of Ecclesiastical History* 44, no. 3 (1993): 390–414.

Heffernan, Thomas J. *Sacred Biography: Saints and Their Biographers in the Middle Ages.* Oxford: Oxford University Press, 1988.

Hill, Bennett D. "Archbishop Thomas Becket and the Cistercian Order." *Analecta Sacri Ordinis Cisterciensis* 27 (1971): 64–80.

———. *English Cistercian Monasteries and Their Patrons in the Twelfth Century.* Urbana: University of Illinois Press, 1968.

Holdsworth, Christopher. "The Affiliation of Savigny," In *Truth as Gift: Studies in Honor of John R. Sommerfeldt,* edited by Marsha L. Dutton, Daniel M. La Corte, and Paul Lockey. CS 204. Kalamazoo, MI: Cistercian Publications, 2004. 43–88.

———. "The Church." In *The Anarchy of King Stephen's Reign,* edited by Edmund King. Oxford: Clarendon Press, 1994. 207–29.

———. "Hermits and the Power of the Frontier." *Reading Medieval Studies* 16 (1990): 55–76.

———. "St. Bernard and England." *Anglo-Norman Studies* 8 (1986): 138–53.

Hollister, C. Warren. *Henry I.* Edited and completed by Amanda Clark Frost. New Haven, CT: Yale University Press, 2001.

Hollister, C. Warren, and Thomas K. Keefe. "The Making of the Angevin Empire." In *Monarchy, Magnates and Institutions in the Anglo-Norman World.* Hambledon Press History Series vol. 43. London: Hambledon Press, 1986. 247–71.

Holt, J. C. "1153: The Treaty of Winchester." In *The Anarchy of King Stephen's Reign,* edited by Edmund King. Oxford: Clarendon Press, 1994. 291–316.

Hoste, Anselm. *Bibliotheca Aelrediana, A Survey of the Manuscripts, Old Catalogues, Editions and Studies Concerning St. Aelred of Rievaulx.* Instrumenta Patristica 2. Steenbrugis: Abbey of St. Peter, 1962.

———. "A Survey of the Unedited Work of Laurence of Durham, with an Edition of His Letter to Aelred of Rievaulx." *Sacris Erudiri* 11 (1960): 249–65.

Hugenholz, Deira, and Henk Teunis. "Suger's Advice." *Journal of Medieval History* 12, no. 3 (1986): 191–206.

Huneycutt, Lois L. *Matilda of Scotland: A Study in Medieval Queenship.* Woodbridge: Boydell Press, 2003.

James, Bruno Scott. *St. Bernard of Clairvaux: An Essay in Biography.* London: Hodder and Stoughton, 1957.

Jamroziak, Emilia. "Considerate Brothers or Predatory Neighbours? Riev-aulx Abbey and Other Monastic Houses in the Twelfth and Thirteenth Centuries." *Yorkshire Archaeological Journal* 73 (2000): 29–40.

———. "Holm Cultram Abbey: A Story of Success." *Northern History* 45, no. 1 (2008): 27–36.

———. "Rievaulx Abbey and Its Patrons: Between Cooperation and Conflict." *Cîteaux: Commentarii Cistercienses* 53 (2002): 51–71.

———. *Rievaulx Abbey and its Social Context, 1132–1300*. Medieval Church Studies 8. Turnhout: Brepols, 2005.

Jobin, Jean-Baptiste. *Histoire du prieuré de Jully-les-nonnains avec pièces justificatives*. Paris: Bray et Retaux, 1881.

Jordan, William Chester. "The English Holy Men of Pontigny." CSQ 43, no. 1 (2008): 63–75.

Kelly, J. N. D. *Golden Mouth: The Story of John Chrysostom—Ascetic, Preacher, Bishop*. Ithaca, NY: Cornell University Press, 1995.

Ker, N. R., and A. J. Piper. *Medieval Manuscripts in British Libraries 4: Paisley-York*. Oxford: Clarendon Press, 1992.

King, Edmund. "A Week in Politics: Oxford, Late July 1141." In *King Stephen's Reign, 1135–1154*, edited by Paul Dalton and Graeme J. White. Woodbridge: Boydell Press, 2008. 58–79.

King, Peter. *Western Monasticism: A History of the Monastic Movement in the Latin Church*. CS 185. Kalamazoo, MI: Cistercian Publications, 1999.

Knowles, David. "The Case of Saint William of York." *Cambridge Historical Journal* 5, no. 2 (1936): 162–77, 212–14.

———. *The Episcopal Colleagues of Thomas Becket: Being the Ford Lectures Delivered in the University of Oxford in Hilary Term 1949*. Cambridge: Cambridge University Press, 1970.

———. "The Growth of Exemption." *Downside Review* 50 (1932): 201–31, 396–436.

———. *The Monastic Order in England: A History of Its Development from the Times of St. Dunstan to the Fourth Lateran Council*. 2nd ed. Cambridge: Cambridge University Press, 1963.

———. "The Revolt of the Lay Brothers of Sempringham." *English Historical Review* 50, no. 199 (1935): 465–87.

Knowles, David, and R. Neville Haddock. *Medieval Religious Houses, England and Wales*. London: Longmans Green, 1953.

Koziol, Geoffrey, "Baldwin VII of Flanders and the Toll of Saint-Vast (1111): Judgment as Ritual." In *Conflict in Medieval Europe*, edited by Warren C. Brown and Piotr Górecki. Aldershot: Ashgate, 2001. 151–61.

Lange, Marjorie E. "Walter Daniel: The Eyes Through Which We First See Aelred." Unpublished paper presented at the Cistercian Studies Conference held within the 45th International Congress on Medieval Studies, Kalamazoo, MI. May 13–16, 2010.

Lawrence, C. H. *Medieval Monasticism: Forms of Religious Life in Western Europe in the Middle Ages*. 3rd ed. Harlow, Essex, UK: Longman, 2001.

Leclercq, Jean. "L'Encyclique de Saint Bernard en faveur de la croisade." *Revue Bénédictine* 81 (1971): 282–308.

———. "Les lettres de Guillaume de Saint-Thierry à saint Bernard." *Revue Bénédictine* 79 (1969): 375–91.

———. "Solitude and Solidarity: Medieval Women Recluses." In *Peace Weavers*, edited by John A. Nichols and Lillian Thomas Shank. Medieval Religious Women. 3 vols. CS 72. Kalamazoo, MI: Cistercian Publications, 1987. 2:67–83.

———. *Women and St. Bernard of Clairvaux*. Kalamazoo, MI: Cistercian Publications, 1989.

Lenssen, Séraphin. "À propos de Cîteaux et de S. Thomas de Cantorbéry: L'abdication du bienheureux Geoffroy d'Auxerre comme abbé de Clairvaux." *Collectanea Cisterciensia* 17 (1955): 98–110.

Licence, Tom. *Hermits and Recluses in English Society, 950–1200*. Oxford: Oxford University Press, 2011.

Lund, Niels. "Sven (II) Estridsen." In *Dansk Biografisk Leksikon*, edited by Svend Cedergreen Bech. 3rd ed. 16 vols. Copenhagen: Glydendal, 1979–1984.

Lützelschwab, Ralf. "*Vox de coelis originem ducitis*: Aelred of Rievaulx as Preacher at Synods." Unpublished paper presented at the Cistercian Studies Conference, held within the 49th International Congress on Medieval Studies at Kalamazoo, MI, May 8–11, 2014.

MacQueen, John. "The Literary Sources for the Life of St. Ninian." In *Galloway: Land and Lordship*, edited by Richard D. Oram and Geoffrey P. Stell. Edinburgh: Scottish Society for Northern Studies, 1991. 17–25.

Mason, J. F. A. "Ranulf Flambard (c. 1060–1128)." DNB 9667.

Mathers, Ann Lawrence. *Manuscripts in Northumbria in the Eleventh and Twelfth Centuries*. Woodbridge: D. S. Brewer, 2003.

Matthew, Donald. *King Stephen*. London: Hambledon Press, 2002.

Mayeski, Marie Anne. "'The Right Occasion for the Words': Situating Aelred's Homily on St. Katherine." CSQ 33, no. 1 (1998): 45–60.

———. "*Secundum Naturam:* The Inheritance of Virtue in Aelred's *Genealogy of the English Kings*." CSQ 37, no. 3 (2002): 221–28.

Mayr-Harting, Henry. "Functions of a Twelfth-Century Recluse." *History* 60, no. 200 (1975): 337–52.

———. "Hilary, Bishop of Chichester (1147–1169), and Henry II." *English Historical Review* 78, no. 397 (1963): 209–24.

———. *Religion, Politics and Society in Britain, 1066–1272*. London: Longmans, 2011.

———. "Two Abbots in Politics: Wala of Corbei and Bernard of Clairvaux." *Transactions of the Royal Historical Society*, 5th ser. 40 (1980): 217–37.

McDonald, R. Andrew. "Scoto-Norse Kings and the Reformed Religious Orders: Patterns of Monastic Patronage in Twelfth-Century Galloway and Argyll." *Albion* 27, no. 2 (1995): 187–219.

McDonald, R. Andrew, and Scott A. McLean. "Somerled of Argyll: A New Look at Old Problems." *The Scottish Historical Review* 71, nos. 191 and 192, pts. 1 and 2 (1992): 3–22.

McGuire, Brian Patrick. *Brother and Lover: Aelred of Rievaulx*. New York: Crossroad Publishing Co., 1994.

———. "The Cistercians and Friendship: An Opening to Women." In *Hidden Springs: Cistercian Monastic Women*, edited by John A. Nichols and Lillian Thomas Shank. Medieval Religious Women. 3 vols. CS 113A. Kalamazoo, MI: Cistercian Publications, 1995. Vol. 3, bk. 1:171–200.

———. "Sexual Awareness and Identity in Aelred of Rievaulx (1111–1167)." *The American Benedictine Review* 45 (1994): 184–226.

———. "Taking Responsibility: Medieval Cistercian Abbots as Their Brothers' Keepers." *Cîteaux: Commentarii Cistercienses* 39 (1988): 249–68.

Melville, Gert. *The World of Medieval Monasticism: Its History and Forms of Life*. Translated by James D. Mixson. Foreword by Giles Constable. CS 263. Collegeville, MN: Cistercian Publications, 2016.

Merton, Thomas. "St. Aelred of Rievaulx and the Cistercians." Pt. 1, CSQ 20, no. 3 (1985): 212–23; pt. 2, CSQ 21, no. 1 (1986): 30–42; pt. 3, CSQ 22, no. 1 (1987): 55–75; pt. 4, CSQ 23, no. 1 (1988): 45–62; pt. 5, CSQ 24, no. 1 (1989): 50–68.

Morey, Adrian. "Canonist Evidence in the Case of St. William of York." *Cambridge Historical Journal* 10, no. 3 (1952): 352–53.

Morey, Adrian, and C. N. L. Brooke. *Gilbert Foliot and His Letters*. Cambridge: Cambridge University Press, 1965.

Münster-Swendsen, Mia. "Irony and the Author: The Case of the *Dialogues* of Lawrence of Durham." In *Modes of Authorship in the Middle Ages*, edited by S. Rankovic, E. Mundal, A. Conti, I. Budahl, and L. Melve. Toronto: Pontifical Institute of Medieval Studies, 2005. 151–71.

————. "Setting Things Straight: Law, Justice and Ethics in the *Orationes* of Lawrence of Durham." *Anglo-Norman Studies* 27 (2012): 151–68.

Murray, Thomas. *The Literary History of Galloway From the Earliest Period to the Present Time*. Edinburgh: Waugh and Inness, 1822.

Nederman, Cary J., and Karen Bollerman. "'The Extravagance of the Senses': Epicureanism, Priestly Tyranny, and the Becket Problem in John of Salisbury's *Policraticus*." *Studies in Medieval and Renaissance History*, series 3, (2011): 1–26.

Newman, Martha G. *The Boundaries of Charity: Cistercian Culture and Ecclesiastical Reform, 1098–1180*. Stanford, CA: Stanford University Press, 1996.

Nicaise, Auguste. *Épernay et l'Abbaye Saint-Martin de cette ville*. 2 vols. Châlons-sur-Marne: J. L. Le Roy, 1869.

Nicholl, Donald. *Thurstan, Archbishop of York (1114–1140)*. York: Stonegate Press, 1964.

Norton, Christopher. *St. William of York*. York: York Medieval Press in association with the Boydell Press, 2006.

Oram, Richard D. *David I: The King Who Made Scotland*. Stroud, Gloucestershire, UK: History Press Ltd., 2004.

————. "A Family Business? Colonisation and Settlement in Twelfth- and Thirteenth-Century Galloway." *The Scottish Historical Review* 72, no. 194, pt. 2 (1993): 111–45.

————. "Fergus, Galloway and the Scots." In *Galloway: Land and Lordship*, edited by Richard D. Oram and Geoffrey P. Stell. Edinburgh: Scottish Society for Northern Studies, 1991. 117–30.

————. "In Obedience and Reverence: Whithorn and York c. 1128–c.1250." *Innes Review* 42, no. 2 (1991): 83–99.

————. *The Lordship of Galloway*. Edinburgh: John Donald, 2000.

Pacaut, Marcel. *Louis VII et les Élections Épiscopales dans le Royaume de France*. Paris: J. Vrin, 1957.

————. *Louis VII et son Royaume*. Paris: S.E.V.P.E.N., 1964.

Peers, C. R. "Rievaulx Abbey: The Shrine in the Chapter House." *The Archaeological Journal* 86 (1929): 20–28.

————. "Two Relic-holders from Altars in the Nave of Rievaulx Abbey, Yorkshire." *Antiquaries Journal* 1, no. 4 (1921): 271–82.

Petit, François. *Norbert et l'origine des Prémontrés*. Paris: Éditions du Cerf, 1981.

Phillips, Jonathan. *The Second Crusade: Extending the Frontiers of Christendom*. New Haven, CT: Yale University Press, 2007.

Ponsoye, Pierre. "Saint Bernard et la Règle du Temple." *Études Traditionelles* 364 (1961): 81–88.

Poole, A. L. "The Appointment and Deprivation of St. William, Archbishop of York." *English Historical Review* 45, no. 178 (1930): 273–81.

——. *From Domesday Book to Magna Carta, 1087–1216.* 2nd ed. Oxford: Clarendon Press, 1955.

Poulle, Béatrice. "Savigny and England." In *England and Normandy in the Middle Ages*, edited by David Bates and Anne Curry. London: Hambledon Press, 1994. 159–68.

Powicke, Frederick M. *Ailred of Rievaulx and His Biographer Walter Daniel.* Manchester: Longmans, Green and Co., 1922.

——. "The Dispensator of King David I." *The Scottish Historical Review* 23, no. 89 (1925): 34–40.

——. Introduction to *The Life of Ailred of Rievaulx by Walter Daniel.* Edited and translated by Frederick M. Powicke. Oxford: Oxford University Press, 1978. ix–lxxxix.

——. "Maurice of Rievaulx." *English Historical Review* 36, no. 141 (1921): 17–29.

——. *Ways of Medieval Life and Thought: Essays and Addresses.* London: Odhams Press, 1950.

Quéguiner, Jean. "Jouarre au XIIᵉ et au XIIIᵉ siècles." In Yves Chaussy, *L'abbaye royale Notre-Dame de Jouarre.* 2 vols. Paris: G. Victor, 1961. 1:89–107.

Radford, Lewis B. *Thomas of London Before His Consecration.* Cambridge: Cambridge University Press, 1894.

Ransford, Rosalind. "A Kind of Noah's Ark: Aelred of Rievaulx and National Identity." In *Religion and National Identity: Papers Read at the Nineteenth Summer Meeting and the Twentieth Winter Meeting of the Ecclesiastical History Society*, edited by Stuart Mews. Oxford: Basil Blackwell, 1982. 137–46.

Reuter, Timothy. "Zur Anerkennung Papst Innocenz II: Eine neue Quelle." *Deutsches Archiv für Erforschung des Mittelalters* 39, no. 2 (1983): 395–416.

Ridyard, Susan J. "Functions of a Twelfth-Century Recluse Revisited: The Case of Godric of Finchale." In *Belief and Culture in the Middle Ages: Studies Presented to Henry Mayr-Harting*, edited by Richard Gameson and Henrietta Leyser. Oxford: Oxford University Press, 2001. 236–50.

Ritchie, R. L. Graeme. *The Normans in Scotland.* Edinburgh: Edinburgh University Press, 1954.

Roby, Douglas. "Chimera of the North: The Active Life of Aelred of Rievaulx." In *Cistercian Ideals and Reality: Studies in Medieval Cister-*

cian History III, edited by John Sommerfeldt. CS 60. Kalamazoo, MI: Cistercian Publications, 1978. 152–69.

Rosof, Patricia J. F. "The Anchoress in the Twelfth and Thirteeth Centuries." In *Peace Weavers*, edited by John A. Nichols and Lillian Thomas Shank. 3 vols. Medieval Religious Women. CS 72. Kalamazoo, MI: Cistercian Publications, 1987. 2:123–44.

Russell, J. Stephen. "The Dialogic of Aelred's *Spiritual Friendship.*" CSQ 47, no. 1 (2012): 47–69.

———. "Vision and Skepticism in Aelred's *De Oneribus.*" CSQ 49, no. 4 (2014): 483–97.

St. John Hope, W. H. "The Gilbertine Priory of Watton, in the East Riding of Yorkshire." *The Archaeological Journal* 58 (1901): 1–34.

Salter, H. E. "Two Lincoln Documents of 1147." *English Historical Review* 35, no. 138 (1920): 212–14.

Saltman, Avrom. *Theobald, Archbishop of Canterbury.* New York: Greenwood Press, 1969.

Scammell, Geoffrey V. *Hugh du Puiset, Bishop of Durham.* Cambridge: Cambridge University Press, 1956.

Schmale, Franz-Josef. *Studien zum Schisma des Jahres 1130.* Cologne: Böhlau, 1961.

Scholz, B. W. "The Canonization of Edward the Confessor." *Speculum* 36, no. 1 (1961): 49–60.

Schriber, Carolyn Poling. *The Dilemma of Arnulf of Lisieux: New Ideas Versus Old Ideals.* Bloomington, IN: University of Indiana Press, 1990.

Scott, J. G. "The Origins of Dundrennan and Soulseat Abbeys." *Transactions of the Dumfriesshire and Galloway Natural History and Antiquarian Society*, series 3, 62 (1988): 35–44.

Simpson, W. Douglas. *St. Ninian and the Origins of the Christian Church in Scotland.* Edinburgh: Oliver and Boyd, 1940.

Somerville, Robert. *Pope Alexander III and the Council of Tours.* Berkeley: University of California Press, 1977.

Sommerfeldt, John R. *Aelred of Rievaulx on Love and Order in the World and the Church.* New York: Newman Press, 2006.

Southern, R. W. *Saint Anselm and His Biographer: A Study in Monastic Life and Thought, 1059–c. 1130.* Cambridge: Cambridge University Press, 1963.

Squire, Aelred. "Aelred and King David." *Collectanea Ordinis Cisterciensium Reformatorum* 22 (1960): 356–77.

———. *Aelred of Rievaulx: A Study.* CS 50. Kalamazoo, MI: Cistercian Publications, 1981.

Stacpoole, Dom Alberic. "The Public Face of Aelred, 1167–1967." *Down-side Review* 85 (1967): 183–99.

Stalley, Roger. *The Cistercian Monasteries of Ireland: An Account of the History, Art, and Architecture of the White Monks in Ireland from 1142–1540.* New Haven, CT: Yale University Press, 1987.

Staunton, Michael. "Exile in the *Lives* of Anselm and Thomas Becket." In *Exile in the Middle Ages: Selected Proceedings from the International Medieval Congress, University of Leeds, 8–11 July 2002,* edited by Laura Napran and Elisabet van Houts. Turnhout: Brepols, 2004. 159–80.

Stenton, F. M. *Anglo-Saxon England.* 3rd ed. Oxford: Clarendon Press, 1971.

Stiegman, Emero. "'Woods and Stones' and 'The Shade of Trees' in the Mysticism of Saint Bernard," in *Truth as Gift: Studies in Honor of John R. Sommerfeldt,* edited by Marsha L. Dutton, Daniel M. La Corte, and Paul Lockey. CS 204. Kalamazoo, MI: Cistercian Publications, 2004. 321–54.

Stringer, Keith. "Galloway and the Abbeys of Rievaulx and Dundrennan." *Transactions of the Dumfriesshire and Galloway Natural History and Antiquarian Society,* series 3, 55 (1980): 174–77.

———. *The Reign of Stephen: Kingship, Warfare and Government in Twelfth-Century England.* New York: Routledge, 1993.

———. "State-building in Twelfth-Century Britain: David I, King of Scots and Northern England." In *Government, Religion, and Society in Northern England, 1000–1700,* edited by John C. Appleby and Paul Dalton. Stroud: Sutton Publishing, 1997. 40–62.

Stroll, Mary. *Calixtus II (1119–1123): A Pope Born to Rule.* Leiden: Brill, 2004.

———. *The Jewish Pope: Ideology and Politics in the Papal Schism of 1130.* Leiden: Brill, 1987.

Swietek, Francis R. "The Role of Bernard of Clairvaux in the Union of Savigny with Cîteaux: A Reconsideration." *Cîteaux: Commentarii Cistercienses* 42 (1991): 289–302.

Sykes, Katharine. *Inventing Sempringham: Gilbert of Sempringham and the Origins of the Role of the Master.* Zurich and Berlin: LIT Verlag, 2011.

Tabuteau, Emily Zack, "Punishments in Eleventh-century Normandy." In *Conflict in Medieval Europe,* edited by Warren C. Brown and Piotr Górecki. Aldershot: Ashgate, 2001. 131–49.

Tait, James. *Mediaeval Manchester and the Beginnings of Lancashire.* Manchester, UK: Manchester University Press, 1904.

Talbot, C. H. "New Documents in the Case of St. William of York." *Cambridge Historical Journal* 10, no. 1 (1950): 1–5.

Thomas, Hugh M. "Mowbray, Sir Roger (I) de (d. 1188)." DNB 19458.

Thompson, Sally. "The Problem of the Cistercian Nuns in the Twelfth and Early Thirteenth Centuries." In *Medieval Women*, edited by Derek Baker. Oxford: Blackwell, 1978. 227–52.

———. *Women Religious: The Founding of English Nunneries after the English Conquest.* Oxford: Clarendon Press, 1991.

Treggiari, Susan. *Roman Marriage.* Oxford: Clarendon Press, 1991.

Truax, Jean. *Archbishops Ralph d'Escures, William of Corbeil and Theobald of Bec: Heirs of Anselm and Ancestors of Becket.* Aldershot: Ashgate, 2012.

———. "*Miles Christi*: Count Theobald IV of Blois and Saint Bernard of Clairvaux." CSQ 44, no. 3 (2009): 299–320.

———. "Winning over the Londoners: King Stephen, the Empress Matilda and the Politics of Personality." *Anglo-Norman Studies* 8 (1996): 43–61.

Tudor, Victoria. "The Cult of St. Cuthbert in the Twelfth Century: The Evidence of Reginald of Durham." In *St. Cuthbert: His Cult and His Community to A.D. 1200*, edited by Gerald Bonner, David Rollason, and Clare Stancliffe. Woodbridge, UK: Boydell Press, 1989. 447–67.

Vacandard, Elphège. "Saint Bernard et le schisme d'Anaclet II en France." *Revue des questions historiques* 43 (1888): 61–123.

Vaughn, Sally N. *Anselm of Bec and Robert of Meulan: The Innocence of the Dove and the Wisdom of the Serpent.* Berkeley and Los Angeles: University of California Press, 1987.

———. *Handmaidens of God: A Study of Anselm's Correspondence with Women.* Turnhout: Brepols, 2002.

Veissière, Michel. *Un communauté canoniale au Moyen Age: Saint-Quiriace de Provins (XIᵉ–XIIIᵉ siècles).* Provins, France: CNRS Editions, 1961.

Vernon, R. W., G. McDonnell, and A. Schmidt. "The Geophysical Evaluation of an Ironworking Complex: Rievaulx and Environs." *North Yorkshire Archaeological Prospection* 5 (1998): 181–201.

Voaden, Rosalynn. *God's Words, Women's Voices: The Discernment of Spirits in the Writing of Late-Medieval Women Visionaries.* York: York Medieval Press, 1999.

Waddell, Chrysogonus. "St. Bernard and the Cistercian Office at the Abbey of the Paraclete." In *The Chimaera of His Age: Studies on Bernard of Clairvaux, Studies in Medieval Cistercian History V.* Edited by E. Rozanne Elder and John R. Sommerfeldt. CS 63. Kalamazoo, MI: Cistercian Publications, 1980. 76–121.

Wardrop, Joan. *Fountains Abbey and Its Benefactors, 1132–1300.* CS 91. Kalamazoo, MI: Cistercian Publications, 1987.

Warren, Ann K. *Anchorites and Their Patrons in Medieval England.* Berkeley and Los Angeles: University of California Press, 1985.

Warren, W. L. *Henry II.* Berkeley and Los Angeles: University of California Press, 1973.

Watt, D. E. R. *Series Episcoporum Ecclesiae Catholicae Occidentalis ab Initio Usque ad Annum MCXCVIII, Series VI, Britannia, Scotia et Hibernia, Scandinavia, Tomus I, Ecclesia Scoticana.* Stuttgart: Anton Hiersemann, 1991.

Watt, J. A. *The Church and the Two Nations in Medieval Ireland.* Cambridge: Cambridge University Press, 1970.

Werner, Karl Ferdinand. "Kingdom and Principality in Twelfth-Century France." In *The Medieval Nobility: Studies on the Ruling Classes of France and Germany from the Sixth to the Twelfth Century,* edited and translated by Timothy Reuter. Amsterdam: North Holland Publishing Co., 1979. 243–90.

White, Graeme J. "The End of Stephen's Reign." *History* 75, no. 1 (1990): 3–22.

———. *Restoration and Reform 1152–1165: Recovery from Civil War in England.* Cambridge: Cambridge University Press, 2000.

White, Hayden V. "The Gregorian Ideal and St. Bernard." *Journal of the History of Ideas* 21, no. 3 (1960): 321–48.

White, Stephen D. "'Pactum . . . legem vincit et amor iudicium': The Settlement of Disputes by Compromise in Eleventh-century Western France." *American Journal of Legal History* 22 (1978): 281–308.

Wieruszowski, Helene. "Roger II of Sicily, Rex-Tyrannus, in Twelfth-century Political Thought." *Speculum* 38, no. 1 (1963): 46–78.

Wilmart, André. "Un court traité d'Aelred sur l'étendue et le but de la profession monastique." *Revue d'ascètique et de mystique* 23 (1947): 259–73.

Wilson, James. "The Passages of St. Malachy through Scotland." *The Scottish Historical Review* 18, no. 70 (1921): 69–82.

Wormald, Patrick. *The Making of English Law: King Alfred to the Twelfth Century.* 1: *Legislation and its Limits.* Oxford: Blackwell Press, 1999.

Yohe, Kathleen. "Aelred's Recrafting of the Life of Edward the Confessor." *CSQ* 38, no. 2 (2003): 177–89.

Young, Alan. "The Bishopric of Durham in Stephen's Reign." In *Anglo-Norman Durham 1093–1193,* edited by David Rollason, Margaret Harvey, and Michael Prestwich. Woodbridge: Boydell Press, 1994. 353–68.

———. *William Cumin: Border Politics and the Bishopric of Durham 1141–1144.* Borthwick Papers 54. York: York University Press, 1978.

Index

Items are indexed by page numbers.